Alien Constructions

ALIEN CONSTRUCTIONS

Science Fiction and Feminist Thought

PATRICIA MELZER

University of Texas Press ⌄⌄ Austin

*Requests for permission to reproduce material
from this work should be sent to:*
    Permissions
    UNIVERSITY OF TEXAS PRESS
    P.O. Box 7819
    Austin, TX 78713-7819
    www.utexas.edu/utpress/about/bpermission.html

⊛ The paper used in this book meets the minimum requirements
of ANSI/NISO Z39.48-1992 (R1997) (Permanence of Paper).

Library of Congress Cataloging-in-Publication Data

Melzer, Patricia
Alien constructions : science fiction and feminist thought /
Patricia Melzer . — 1st ed.
    p.   cm.
Includes bibliographical references and index.
ISBN-13: 978-0-292-71306-2 ((cl.) : alk. paper)
ISBN-10: 0-292-71306-1
ISBN-13: 978-0-292-71307-9 ((pbk.) : alk. paper)
ISBN-10: 0-292-71307-X
1. Science fiction, American—History and criticism. 2. Science fiction,
English—History and criticism. 3. Feminism in literature. 4. Alien resurrection
(Motion picture). 5. Matrix (Motion picture). I. Title.
PS374.S35A79 2006
813'.08762099287—dc22
2005033703

For my parents, Anna Maria and Dr. Klaus-Jürgen Melzer

CONTENTS

ACKNOWLEDGMENTS

WRITING A BOOK on feminist science fiction can be an outer-worldly experience. Thankfully, I had a supportive intellectual community and a
tight network of friends who kept me grounded during the process.

For their support in the early stages of the project, I owe gratitude
to my advisors at Clark University—Eric Gordy, Maria Acosta-Cruz,
and Dianne Rocheleau—who consistently supported me in my rather
unusual research. I could not have had a more supportive group to
work with. A very special thank you also goes to Claudia Springer,
who, in her gracious generosity with her time and her inspiring conversations, has enabled me to feel part of a debate and not isolated
in my writing. I also want to thank those who provided the necessary support in the initial stages of my research at Clark University,
in particular Vijaya Joshi, Insook Kwon, Joanne Ljungberg, and Claire
Cummings.

In the crucial time of re-envisioning my project as a book, I was surrounded by a group of senior faculty at Temple University who showed
real interest in my progress and who encouraged me in my work:
Rebecca Alpert, Laura Levitt, Rickie Sanders, and Miriam Solomon.
They mentored and advised me during the various stages of the book
project, and I learned how to navigate the many hoops of academic
publishing with their encouragement and humor. These women kept
me going with their insistence that there really is light at the end of the
tunnel. Cynthia Enloe's unwavering support of my feminist academic
career from afar has been wonderful, and Eric Gordy's consistent en-
thusiasm for my work has been inspirational. A warm thank you also
to Carmella Watson, who has supported me with her generous spirit
and unfailing competence.

The students in my class "Gender and Technology in Popular Culture" at Temple University in Spring 2004 creatively influenced this
project. Their critical and insightful readings of the texts and our spir-
ited class discussions kept reminding me of the relevance of my in-

quiries. In particular my conversations with Katie Bashore, "minion extraordinaire," were inspirational.

Thank you also to the editors at the University of Texas Press, Alex Barron and Jim Burr, who patiently answered my numerous questions and expressed confidence in my project. Thanks also to Liz Gold, who carefully copyedited this manuscript. Leslie Tingle greatly accommodated my work schedule by shipping the manuscript overseas when I was doing research in Germany and overall did a wonderful job ensuring the timely completion of the book. I received invaluable technical support from Pete Hanley at Temple University's Instructional Support Center, who with endless patience and a stroke of genius helped me master the complicated world of digital imagery.

This book truly would not exist in its present form without the friendship and intellectual support of a group of very special friends and colleagues. Michelle Renee Matisons from across the country kept reminding me "that there is no spoon" and unfailingly read those final versions, when it counted the most. Soraya Alamdari, in endless working days spent together, has been a proverbial rock. Thanks also to the F3ers in Philadelphia, the best writing group one can ask for: Shelley Wilcox, Lee Talley, and Soraya Alamdari. Their consistent friendship and intellectual feedback kick-started this project and kept me sane.

As with everything else I have accomplished in my life, I could not have done this without my family, the Melzer Clan. Thanks to my sisters, Kathrin, Nanette, and Temesgen, and my parents, Annemie and Klaus, and the "extended" family, Marina Walter and Natali Schirm. A very special thank you goes to Natali, whose support and calm presence (as well as impeccable eye for just the right photo) in the last two weeks of the project ensured its completion. Finally, my endless gratitude and love (and a dozen sushi dinners) go to Karl, personal editor, sounding board, lover, and best friend: I would not have wanted to do this without you.

Introduction

Science Fiction's Alien Constructions

Upon their release at the turn of the twenty-first century, the *Matrix* films had an immediate impact on popular imagination in the United States. The Hollywood-produced science fiction trilogy triggered questions about reality, self-determination, and resistance while setting new standards for film technology. With its clever plotline and breathtaking special effects, the trilogy became both a blockbuster hit surrounded by the usual media hype and an inspiration for academic debates. *The Matrix* also introduced a new female character to our cultural imagination: the movie-going public fell hard for Trinity, a strong, smart, action-driven resistance fighter and the hero's romantic interest. Trinity joins the ranks of a number of extraordinary female science fiction heroes, such as Ripley from the *Alien* film series and Sarah Connor from the *Terminator* movies. These female characters share an unusual display of technological know-how, empowerment, and the habit of saving the world. They also have "unnatural" female bodies (often technologically enhanced or genetically engineered) and do "unfeminine" things. Significantly, it is within science fiction—film and literature—a genre usually understood to be predominantly male, that we seem to reimagine gender relations most radically. Here the controversial female cyborg challenges conventional ideas of gender, race, and nation, often at the same time as she reinforces them. Through figures like the female cyborg, *Alien Constructions* explores the relationship between science fiction and a feminist discourse that is attempting to conceptualize issues of difference, globalization, and technoscience.[1]

Science fiction is valuable to feminists because of its particular narrative mode. Two textual aspects that define science fiction are the *structures and/or narrative devices* that constitute its mode, on one hand, and *themes and approaches* on the other. Several structures and narrative devices of science fiction have been identified in classical science fiction criticism, such as the element of estrangement, or the confrontation of normative systems/perspectives, and the implication of new sets of norms that result in the factual reporting of fiction. Spatial and temporal displacement as well as absent paradigms that structure the reading process are typical for science fiction. Also characteristic for science fiction are "worlds," or systems of representation that create the freedom to voice assumptions otherwise restricted by a realist narrative frame, and the geographic displacement of identity formations.

All of these elements shape the reading process, which in turn defines the genre. In addition to structural and narrative devices, there are recurrent themes and approaches in science fiction: the exploration of socioeconomic relations, the conflicting elements of modernity and postmodernity played out in urban science fiction, the construction of nature and culture, and the implications of technology—one of the most recognizable heuristic markers of science fiction—on human relations and life in general. Science fiction writer and critic Joanna Russ defines science fiction as "a mode rather than a form (a form would be something like the sonnet, the short story, etc.). It is, basically, anything that is about conditions of life or existence different from either what typically is, or what typically was, or whatever was or is. . . . Science fiction is about the possible-but-not-real" ("Reflections on Science Fiction" 243).[2]

Science fiction stories can create "blueprints" of social theories. Only within genres of the fantastic is it possible to imagine completely new social orders and ways of being that differ radically from human existence as we know it. *Alien Constructions* is a recent intervention in the ongoing debate that examines the relationship of theory to science fiction. It explores how some science fiction engages with feminist thought in a way that enables us to understand oppression and to envision resistance beyond the limits set by much of feminist discourse. *Alien Constructions* is aimed at readers interested in feminist discourses as well as genre readers. While either audience at times might encounter familiar intellectual and narrative territories, some of the connections between science fiction and feminist thought made in the textual analyses within these pages will be new and hopefully will inspire further explorations.

Science Fiction as Cultural Text

The success of *The Matrix* and its status as one of the primary cultural points of reference in the United States at the turn of the twenty-first century stands in the long tradition of science fiction texts that have provided blueprints for our imagination.[3] Since the late 1970s, the success of films such as the *Alien* series, the *Terminator* trilogy, and, of course, the *Star Wars* saga, whose narrative continues to span several decades, is mirrored in the success of prime-time television shows. Shows like the *Star Trek* series and its spin-offs *Next Generation, Deep Space Nine, Voyager,* and *Enterprise,* as well as *Roswell, The X-Files,* and, more recently, *Battlestar Galactica,* have reached millions of viewers every week. Although the public's fascination with popular genres extends to mystery and romance novels, TV sitcoms, and horror movies, there is something persistent and unique in our use of science fiction imagery, not only to speculate about the future, but to explain the present. The obsession of United States culture with futuristic explorations and alien life-forms also manifests itself in the popularity of science fiction literature, which is still one of the most pervasively read genres. Science fiction is a stage on which we imagine humanity's fate, and it is in its fantastic extrapolations that we develop the terminology to describe our future.[4] To recognize the magnitude of the genre in the cultural imagination of United States society is to treat it as a space where the exchange between the text and the reader/viewer engages with political as well as social concepts.

What exactly makes us turn to a fantastic genre to imagine not only social and political change but new understandings of who we are in the present and what our future will look like? Popular culture's fascination with science fiction is rooted in the combination of strangeness and familiarity that make up the particularities of the genre. This tension between the "known" and the "unknown" is at the heart of science fiction. It creates a reading process based on estrangement, which places familiar issues into strange territory: even when we are not familiar with a new planet and its corresponding new technology being described, the social and personal issues within the narrative speak to our experiences. This estrangement also creates spaces of abstraction for theorizing. In his classic essay on science fiction literature, "On the Poetics of the Science Fiction Genre," published in 1972, Darko Suvin refers to the genre as a "literature of cognitive estrangement" (372).[5] At the same time, science fiction creates personal narratives of identification: we grow to know the protagonists and their world intimately. Science fiction's concept of theorizing grows from both the strategy of estrangement and the power of storytelling. Different forms of storytelling—such as myths, legends, and spiritual and creation narratives, all of which are found in popular culture—are crucial tools for shaping cultural identities. As in other types of fiction, the "realness" of science fiction narratives enables individuals (and groups) to relate to and recognize the debates as relevant to their own lives.

As a genre defined by its relationship to technology as well as by its futuristic framework, science fiction is understood as a cultural arena that explores the anxieties of what Frederic Jameson termed the "postmodern condition."[6] Moreover, in the past three decades it has received considerable attention for its potentially subversive depictions of alternative worlds. While science fiction criticism still inhabits a marginalized position within academic discourse—which mainly treats it as a pulp or popular genre outside of "serious" theoretical frameworks—in the past 20 years, works by critics such as Darko Suvin and Carl Freedman have placed the genre in relation to critical theory and literary theory. In *Critical Theory and Science Fiction* (2000), Freedman, instead of simply applying critical theory to science fiction, emphasizes "*structural* affinities between the two modes of discourse" (xix, emphasis his), such as their dialectical thinking.

Feminists in particular recognize the political implications of the genre and increasingly employ science fiction narratives to explore social relations. Donna Haraway was one of the first critics to emphasize feminist science fiction as a form of feminist theorizing (not simply as a reflection of feminist politics). In *Terminal Identity* (1993), Scott Bukatman observes the attraction the genre holds for feminist writers, readers, and viewers: "Given a thematics profoundly engaged with social structures and sexual difference and potentially heterotopic discursive practices, the relevance of SF to a feminist politics should not be mysterious" (21). *Alien Constructions* points to the dialogic relationship between science fiction and contemporary feminist thought. Both science fiction texts and feminist theories conceptualize issues of difference, globalization, and technoscience that increasingly affect women's lives, and both are concerned with contested boundaries and definitions of bodies and cultural/social territories. Thus feminist writings (and readings) of science fiction can be understood as part of a feminist criticism of existing power relations.[7] In order to establish a shared context for genre readers as well as readers familiar with feminist thought, what follows is a brief summary of science fiction since the "New Wave," which introduced radically new literary elements to the genre, and a review of relevant concepts within science fiction and feminist thought.

Science Fiction since the New Wave

Science fiction's alien settings on distant planets, revolutionary technology, and futuristic time frame potentially allow the genre to explore power relations in ways different from realistic fiction—here we can credibly create completely novel societies and cultures. Yet the genre also has a tradition of conceptualizing themes of colonialism and social orders in conservative, and at times reactionary, ways. Beginning with the New Wave in the 1960s, Western science fiction texts and criticism have developed from a mainly white, male, heterosexual genre into a more diverse body of texts with the potential to radically reconceptualize power relations. This development coincided with radical feminist interventions into male-defined liberation movements and theories. Authors such as Samuel Delany, Brian Aldiss, Thomas Disch, Ursula Le Guin, and Philip Dick transformed science fiction by dramatically improving literary quality through narrative experimentation and the crossing of genre lines inspired by a growing postmodern influence in mainstream literature.[8]

In 1972, science fiction writer and critic Joanna Russ criticized the conservative content of mainstream science fiction in the United States and Great Britain, which she referred to as "Intergalactic Suburbia." The term criticizes not only gender but also class and race structures that Russ saw as perpetuated within the science fiction genre, which described "white, middle-class suburbia. Mummy and Daddy may live inside a huge amoeba and Daddy's job may be to test psychedelic drugs or cultivate yeast-vats, but the world inside their heads is the world of [suburban] Westport and Rahway *and that world is never questioned*" ("Image of Women" 81, emphasis hers). Science fiction—both literature and film[9]—produced since Russ's criticism that reflects the influence of New Wave literary inventions is of the greatest interest to this study.

The new literary styles in science fiction were accompanied by shifts in narrative content as well. For example, the extrapolation of the classical space opera, with its formulaic focus on human outer space expansion and technology, was countered by the psychological dimension of "inner" space and cultural identities as well as complex character formations. The introduction of formerly taboo subjects, such as depictions of sexuality, violence, and race relations, accompanied a growing appreciation of the "soft" sciences (social sciences such as anthropology and linguistics), formerly positioned as either irrelevant, ineffective, or dangerous in contrast to the traditional "hard" sciences (chemistry, physics, and biology). Both literary innovations and narrative explorations beyond the traditional science fiction adventure story, which had dominated popular science fiction, added a complexity to science fiction that transformed the boundaries of the genre. These changes were also reflected in technological, stylistic, and narrative innovations in science fiction films, such as Stanley Kubrick's *2001: A Space Odyssey* (1968), while technological special effects in films such as *Star Wars* (1977) revolutionized the genre on the silver screen.

The growing literary quality and narrative complexity of New Wave science fiction literature resulted in an expansion in readership from mainly young, white, technologically inclined men to include readers interested in mainstream literature. Although changes in the genre were mainly stylistic, there was also increasingly more emphasis on sex and violence, as reflected in publications such as Harlan Ellison's *Dangerous Visions* (1967) and *Again, Dangerous Visions* (1972), collections of short stories formerly rejected by mainstream science fiction magazines because of their new, controversial focus. Yet it was the influence of writers of color and female authors that expanded the New Wave's innovations. Social criticism, including criticism of racism and class exploitation in a neocolonial framework, enriched the narratives and became one of the central features of contemporary science fiction. Thomas Moylan observed the connections between the growing number of women and authors of color who were writing science fiction and the increased literary and intellectual quality of the genre when he stated in 1980 that "the most aesthetically interesting and socially significant contemporary science fiction is being produced by women and non-white writers, as well as by a few alienated and critical white males" ("Beyond Negation," 237–38). Even though science fiction since the 1960s has increasingly engaged with issues of race and class, many narratives insist on employing non-Western cultures as representing the ultimate "other." This practice perpetuates existing racist ideologies at the same time as it makes them visible.[10]

In the late 1980s, science fiction experienced further fundamental innovations through the influence of cyberpunk fiction, with its focus on communication technology and consumer culture. In *Neuromancer* (1984), William Gibson set the stylistic markers of cyberpunk's narrative conventions, which are dominated by the interface of computers and humans. Gibson's exploration of technology's influence on subjectivity and its potential for alienation is also seen in Ridley Scott's film *Blade Runner* (1982), where it manifests in a *film noir* quality, and culminates in the special effects of the *Matrix* film trilogy twenty years later. In much of cyberpunk literature, the narrow focus on the angstridden subjectivity of the technologically savvy antihero grew from a synthesis of cross-media influences of punk music, street anarchy, and hacker culture. This aspect has been further developed by women and writers of color who have (again) complicated the stylistic novelties with more substantial social and political elements.

Feminist Science Fiction

Even though science fiction has the reputation of being a male-dominated genre, it has always included women writers, and as a narrative style it is open to feminist appropriation. In *In the Chinks of the World Machine: Feminism and Science Fiction* (1988), Sarah Lefanu writes: "[Science fiction literature] makes possible, and encourages (despite its colonisation by male writers), the inscription of women as subjects free from the constraints of mundane fiction; and it also offers the possibility of interrogating that very inscription, questioning the basis of gendered subjectivity" (Lefanu 9).[11] In early science fiction, women often wrote under gender-neutral pseudonyms (such as C.L. Moore, who wrote pulp science fiction in the 1940s), and in general the number of women writers was considerably lower than that of their male counterparts. Since the early 1970s, the number of women who write science fiction has increased dramatically, with popular authors such as Octavia E. Butler, C.J. Cherryh, Kathleen Goonan, Suzette Haden Elgin, Anne McCaffrey, Suzy McKee Charnas, Vonda McIntyre, Marge Piercy, Joanna Russ, James Tiptree Jr. (Alice Sheldon), Joan Vinge, Kate Wilhelm, Marion Zimmer Bradley, and, in a new generation of writers, Nicola Griffith, Nalo Hopkinson, Severna Park, and Melissa Scott.[12] Feminist science fiction irreversibly shaped the genre, first in the 1970s with its criticism of gender roles, racism, and class exploitation, and later in the 1980s with a growing use of postmodern elements such as the exploration of linguistics and disrupted narrative structures.[13] The presence and influence of women writers were made visible in the 1970s with publications like Pamela Sargent's edited *Women of Wonder* series, which were collections of stories by women science fiction writers. While feminist science fiction in the 1960s and 1970s explored feminist resistance to women's oppression mainly through separatist societies (e.g., lesbian utopias) and/or reversal of gender roles (e.g., matriarchal societies), later feminist science fiction understands a disruption of gendered power less as a question of a simple role reversal (even though some narratives explore the ramifications of this) than of undermining and subverting that power (e.g., through the use of technology) and linking it to material relations.

One central narrative theme is the effect of science and technology on our future, the fictitious manifestations of which have become the major metaphors in science fiction. Feminist science fiction, especially in the early 1970s, undermined the ideological separation of "soft" and "hard" sciences within traditional science fiction, which portrayed technology as good and the sciences as progressive, rational, and predictable (i.e. masculine), pitched against alien "sciences" such as telepathy and telekinesis that were considered witchcraft, evil, manipulative, obscure, and subjective (i.e. feminine). Feminist science fiction has instead emphasized cultural and social ("soft") sciences, such as anthropology, linguistics, and social theories. At the same time, authors have explored the ambiguous relationship of women and technology. On one hand, feminist writers reclaim the figures of witch and healer within a science fiction setting and develop alternative sciences.[14] On the other, feminist science fiction writers explore the liberating potential of the hard sciences (in particular, reproductive technologies) that promise elimination of traditional gender roles that link women to maternity. The growing identification with the alien/other in many texts is accompanied by a shift in narrative perspective as more and more texts relate the experiences of those colonized by traditional science fiction heroes.

Postmodern science fiction mirrors ideas of fragmented cultural experiences and new linguistic forms of expression as they question the ontological basis for realities and offer subversive point of views. This trend especially resonates in feminist appropriations of cyberpunk, in which texts explore implications of new media and biotechnologies. The metaphor of the cyborg, a concept that becomes central to both feminist fiction and feminist criticism, emerges from explorations of the interface of technology and humans and the boundary dissolutions that accompany biotechnologies and global capitalism's consumerism.

Unlike the growing body of literary texts classified as feminist science fiction, there is not (yet) a genre of feminist science fiction *film*. One example of a feminist science fiction film is *Born in Flames* (1983), which explores possible future political developments of fractions of the feminist movement. In "Feminist Futures: A Generic Study" (1990), Anne Cranny-Francis suggests that a hypothetical contemporary feminist science fiction cinema would be based in an intertextual relationship between "science fiction writing and its generic conventions; feminist cultural practice; and cinema itself—particularly science fiction film and feminist film—as a set of discursive and signifying practices" (219).

Science Fiction and Feminist Theory

In the past thirty-five years, feminist science fiction and feminist *readings* of science fiction have challenged existing gender relations and have explored theoretical and political debates of the time. Critics such as Marleen Barr in *Alien to Femininity* (1987), Sarah Lefanu in *In the Chinks of the World Machine* (1988), and Jenny Wolmark in *Aliens and Others* (1994) discuss feminist science fiction in the context of feminist theories. Women's increased involvement in science fiction has proven to be crucial both for the development of the subgenre of feminist science fiction and for feminist theorizing *outside* the science fiction community. If we view the contemporary author as sharing a cultural climate with feminist political and theoretical debates, it becomes necessary to read science fiction texts as contributions to feminist debates as well as reflections of them.

Even though direct connections exist between feminist writing and feminist politics,[15] the question of who produces theoretical models within these texts is less framed in terms of the "intentionality" of the author (especially when considering science fiction films) than in relation to systems of representation that are created in an active exchange process between reader/viewer, context, and text, thereby producing connections and links between groups of texts and political moments. One context for a reading of these science fiction narratives, for example, is feminist discourse; another is postcolonial studies. So theories and texts do not necessarily inform each other directly but are based in a shared "climate of opinion" (Hayles, *Cosmic Web* 22) that makes certain ideas worth pursuing in different disciplines.[16] Production of meaning does not take place in a dualistic relationship of either reader and text (interpretation), or text and social context (social construction). Instead, meaning is produced in complex constellations where texts and theories are situated, in the treatment of the text as *both* a semiotic and a material structure:

> The text must be . . . understood as a term in a process, that is to say a chain reaction encompassing a web of power relations. What is at stake in the textual practice, therefore, is less the activity of inter-pretation than of decoding the network of connections and effects that link the text to an entire sociosymbolic system. In other words, we are faced here with a new materialist theory of the text and of textual practice. (Braidotti, *Nomadic Subjects* 154)

The reader, therefore, becomes just as important as the author or di-rector in the production of feminist theory within/through a given text. In addition, the meaning of the symbolic manifestations in the text changes with each new theoretical context of analysis brought to the text. A crucial part of this process is that this production of theory is closely related to the identity of the theorist (writer? reader? viewer?). Since subjectivity here is understood to be a discursive, con-stantly changing process, cultural texts and their systems of represen-tations are as significant as interactions with the social world and its institutions: "The acquisition of subjectivity is therefore a process of material (institutional) and discursive (symbolic) practices, the aim of which is both positive—because the process allows for forms of em-powerment—and regulative—because the forms of empowerment are the site of limitations and disciplining" (Braidotti, *Nomadic Subjects* 157).

Thus creative explorations of cultural anxieties in science fiction often involve theoretical *investigations* as well as theory *production* through complex interactions of reader, writer, and text. As feminist biologist and theorist Donna Haraway observes in *How Like a Leaf,* "science fiction is political theory" (120). The intersections of theory, politics, and pleasures of imagination enable creative and complex the-orizing. *Alien Constructions* is informed by Haraway's idea that some science fiction texts not only incorporate feminist theory but actually produce it. Locating feminist theory in cultural texts contests the sepa-rations of cognitive realms, such as creativity and abstract thought, on which the Western-defined concept of theorizing rests. It shifts dis-courses away from a hierarchical structure of theory building toward

a more open, multileveled production of theory and toward interdisciplinary approaches within feminist inquiry.

Alien Constructions

Science fiction's fantastic aliens and distant planets can thus become
the imaginative testing grounds for feminist critical thought. These
texts create a link between cultural imagination and political positions:
they function as "case studies" of how feminist theories "work." For
many readers, consuming feminist science fiction serves as an introduction to feminist politics and theories and offers concrete manifestations of the complex theories at hand. Within the narratives, these
readers encounter "alien constructions"—metaphors and concepts specific to the genre, such as the cyborg, human/alien hybrids, and aliens
—that provide unfamiliar images for familiar identities and concepts
and explore the implications of theories within a (pleasurable) narrative framework. These alien constructions, embedded within a narrative context that enables identifications, can provide us with empowering metaphors that allow critical evaluations of the theories we rely
on to explain our social realities. To read science fiction in conjunction with feminist theories can therefore foster a new and more intimate understanding of the theories, their limits, and their co-optation
by dominant culture.

To this end, *Alien Constructions* examines a selection of popular science fiction texts from a feminist perspective and points to connections between these cultural texts and feminist debates in academic
and political arenas. The texts discussed here are all post–New Wave,
and their literary and cinematic explorations offer theoretical interventions that stand in complicated relationship to postmodern feminist
thought. In my critical readings, I take an interdisciplinary approach
to political and theoretical concepts by combining analyses of science
fiction literature and film. While science fiction film and literature
share a preoccupation with futuristic technology and alien/fantastic
bodies, their respective media create different forms of representation.
As Annette Kuhn points out in the introduction to *Alien Zone,* there is
a significant difference between science fiction *literature* and science
fiction *film:* "[T]he most obvious difference . . . lies in the latter's mobi-
lization of the visible, the spectacle. If cinema is one among a number
of narrative media, it also has its own language, its own codes, through

which it makes meaning and tells stories" (6). Thus mainstream science fiction film caters to identification mechanisms very much based on the pleasure of the visual and acoustic spectacle (special effects therefore are the backbone of successful science fiction cinema), while feminist science fiction literature often creates characters that embody complex intersections of political and social ideas and uses stylistic devices to create gripping narratives. The female cyborgs, aliens, and species-hybrids that populate mainstream science fiction film are further complicated in feminist science fiction literature, which offers potentially more progressive and subversive feminist characters and settings. Both media offer representations of displaced cultural anxieties and hopes around the relationship of the gendered body to technology and the identities that grow out of this relationship. Much of the literature explored in this book has been created and is consumed within an explicitly feminist context; other works, especially the Hollywood films discussed here, are not, and demand a different interpretative approach.

The science fiction texts I discuss include literature by Octavia E. Butler, Richard Calder, and Melissa Scott and the mainstream movies of the *Matrix* and *Alien* series. The alien constructions of these texts— of the deviant bodies and subjectivities that populate their worlds— envision utopian as well as dystopian ways of being. The readings in *Alien Constructions* do not focus on just *one* aspect of the narratives (such as technology or alternative sciences). Instead, they examine how the texts engage with important concepts within feminist thought (such as identity versus difference, racism, economic relations, sexuality, and gender identities) and with theories rarely placed in connection with science fiction (especially feminist postcolonial and critical race theory).

Alien Constructions examines how contemporary science fiction literature and films explore multinational corporations' reordering of world relations in the aftermath of colonialism, and how these works represent implications of new technologies such as genetic engineering, virtual reality, and nanotechnology. Science fiction addresses issues of subjectivity (the interface of individual and technology) as well as of social organization (discourses of groups and technology). Reconfigurations of gender roles and gender identities, as well as sexual desires, are central to the challenging of existing social orders—and the body becomes the main contested territory.

Alien Constructions explores how the science fiction texts in question represent debates and concepts in three areas of feminist thought: identity and difference; feminist critiques of science and technology; and the relationship between gender identity, body, and desire. Key political elements that shape these debates are global capitalism and exploitative class relations within a growing international system (relationship between First and Third Worlds, postcolonial relations); the impact of technologies on women's lives (Internet, global industries, medical establishment, reproductive technologies); and posthuman embodiment (biotechnologies, body/machine interface, the commodification of desire). From the intersections of feminist discourses exploring these issues emerge science fiction's alien constructions and their posthuman bodies, such as cyborgs, clones, androids, aliens, and hybrids. They reflect the crisis the human/machine interface induces within the Western concept of subjectivity, thereby destabilizing cultural and ideological boundaries of nature/culture (or race or ethnicity) and human/machine.

The decentered bodies that grow from new technologies and populate postmodern science fiction are both troubling and potentially empowering. The appropriation of these constructed bodies as signs of resistance and the reconstruction of their designated subject positions as those signifying agency are the theoretical aims of feminist theories of representation. As semiotic tools, these bodies foreground issues of representation and the constructions of cultural meaning, drawing science, economic theories, and their representation in cultural texts into the analysis of power relations. They become symbols of technology's ambivalent relationship to the body and function in at least two conflicting ways: first, they constitute elements of political empowerment and resistance; and second, they embody the contradictions and potentials of feminist and queer theory and point to the limits of some of these theories.

Science fiction narratives relate to feminist concerns as unique cultural texts; the issues of meaning production and construction of reality in the reading/viewing process are related to inscriptions of identity and subjectivity that are envisioned in the strange alien constructions found within the texts. It is in the creative synthesis of these two topics—questions of subjectivity, and technology as a social force—that the contemporary science fiction texts in *Alien Constructions* engage the reader in theoretical exchanges.

Identity and Difference in Feminist Thought
SELF/OTHER

The relationship of self/other is one foundation of political subjectivity in Western philosophy.[17] The traditional self is constituted through the notion of otherness. The inherent structure of this relationship is dependent on a clear line between I and not-I; it is dependent on the duality of the terms. Western feminist thought emphasizes the critique of the masculine/feminine dualism that establishes a self/other relationship based on sexual difference. This critique is most famously expressed by the French feminist Simone de Beauvoir in her classic text *The Second Sex:* "She is defined and differentiated with reference to man and not he with reference to her; she is the incidental, the inessential as opposed to the essential. He is the Subject, he is the Absolute—she is the Other" (xxii). In *Nomadic Subjects,* Rosi Braidotti explains the emphasis European (especially French) feminist theories place on sexual difference in relation to language in the Western tradition: "In my understanding, there can be no subjectivity outside sexuality or language; that is to say, the subject is always gendered: it is a 'she-I' or a 'he-I'" (199). This binary is not always as unambiguous as feminist discourse (re)presents it: transgender identities further complicate notions of the gendered subject. The analytical aspect of transgender subjectivity, which finds itself invisible in feminist discourse on binary sexual difference, often is not considered in debates on how to conceptualize a feminist subjectivity. Incorporating transgender subjectivities into a criticism of the "eternal feminine" and the "generic masculine" of Western philosophy makes the construction of gender categories visible. Also, the construction of gendered subjects in terms of language and desire does not account for homosexual desire. Homosexuality does not correspond with the dichotomous psychological and economic relations between "man" and "woman." As Monique Wittig argues in "One Is Not Born a Woman," a lesbian is not a "woman," since she stands outside the heterosexual economy that defines the identity of "woman." The identity "lesbian" thus is understood to be liberating from (heterosexual) gender oppression. The notion of sexual orientation as identity is problematized further by Judith Butler in "Imitation and Gender Subordination," in which she calls the subversive function of identity labels into question, arguing that they keep the subject locked in relation to the dominant heterosexual matrix.

The issue of sexual difference as it manifests itself in Western philosophy and other related discourses is complicated by critical race and postcolonial theorists who define race and ethnicity as a variable of female subjectivity. Feminist theories of women of color have informed United States feminist discourse in terms of a multifaceted concept of difference that is as much defined by race (and class) as it is by gender.[18] Thus it becomes impossible to speak of the construction of gender identity without including race. Evelyn Brooks Higginbotham raises the point that white feminists have failed to conceptualize "white" as a racial identity and instead base their analysis of gender on a "neutral" (white) gender identity. They construct black women as individuals possessing two identities—one shaped by gender, one by race—and gender identity generally is perceived to be the same for all women.[19] As a location of structural advantage and race privilege, and as a standpoint as well as a set of cultural practices that usually are unmarked and unnamed, whiteness shapes women's lives as much as any other racial identity. Thus the concept of self/other, which feminist philosophy has criticized as gendered and rooted in patriarchal power, needs to be understood in relation to other systematically assigned categories such as sexuality, race, class, and nation. "Woman" cannot be a generic identity; instead, it is inevitably linked to various (and at times very different) sets of experiences and discursive practices.

FEMINIST POSTMODERN SUBJECTS

Considering that race and gender are inseparable categories of identity formation, attempts to assert a female subjectivity denied by traditional Western philosophy need to integrate the theoretical deconstruction of "woman" as a stable gender identity. To quote Braidotti, "One of the points of tension . . . is how to reconcile the feminist critiques of the priority traditionally granted to the variable *sexuality* in the Western discourse about the subject with the feminist proposition of redefining the embodied subject in a network of interrelated variables of which sexuality is but one" (*Nomadic Subjects* 199).[20] One of the most productive sites where this tension is worked through is within postmodern feminist thought. Feminist discourse develops and grows in an (at times dialectical) exchange with other discourses. Postmodern feminist discourse is especially connected to poststructuralism and postcolonial theories; this connection, and the controversies it brings, is part of feminist discourse at large. Both poststructuralism and postmodern feminism reconceptualize power and agency as decentralized, and the subject not as an autonomous entity but rather as the product of discourses and their institutions. Some feminists criticize postmodern theory for being unpolitical due to its constant denial of any political "truth" and because it destabilizes women as agents and forgers of their own histories. Other feminists appreciate the decentering of center/margin, self/other as a potential strategy for undermining power relations and for asserting agency.

One main point of discord between the two very large and internally diverse discourses of poststructuralism and postmodern feminist theories is the conceptualization of the postmodern subject. While many feminists agree with the notion of a fragmented and dislocated subject, they do not accept postmodernism's often implicit depoliticization of debates. In reference to the "death of the subject," feminists point out that the subject afflicted with "postmodern conditions" always has been white and male. Consequently, they appropriate the theoretical space of fragmentation as a potential for resistance and political empowerment, not despair. Using what Carole Boyce Davies, throughout *Black Women, Writing, and Identity*, traces as "transgressive speech"— a tool for the political appropriation of the now empty subject-position after the demise of the modern subject—feminists are politicizing new concepts of selfhood.

Instead of fragmentation, these feminists see *multiplicity,* and instead of the notion of a scattered and incoherent *self,* they favor the image of flexibility and fluid *selves,* each one representing situated knowledges of locations. Mostly committed to a materialist conception of these identities, feminist theories consistently return to questions of oppression through capitalism and its systematic exploitation of labor that is structured by race and gender.[21]

EMBRACING DIFFERENCE

Western feminist debates around identity until the mid-1980s were trying to theorize a "preconceived, pregiven 'women's identity,' . . . an identity common to all women, woman's 'identity' as 'the other'" (Crosby 130–31). Twenty years later, the discourse is dominated by "difference"—the notion that "woman" consists of many diverse components that are positioned in very different relations to power. The danger of this approach is that the concept of difference becomes a simplified prefix of diversity, without being further problematized as the moment when something is defined as "other": that " 'differences' work now more or less as 'identity' did before" (Crosby 130). Difference, therefore, remains in the theoretical position of being not-I, a nonidentity, whereas the identity of the I is still the defining element. Neither the notion of identity, nor what Trinh Minh-ha terms the "politics of differentiation" (*Woman, Native, Other* 82)—that is, the historical motivations behind the constructions of difference—are themselves questioned. Just as identity is not stable and its claim of stability is a self-perpetuating myth, difference is a shifting constituent. As Trinh points out, we need to find ways to conceptualize identity so that it "refers no more to a consistent 'pattern of sameness' than to an inconsequential pattern of otherness" (*Woman, Native, Other* 95). Otherwise, one critique of the construction of otherness (gender) leaves another intact (race). In *Nomadic Subjects*, Braidotti advocates an approach to feminist subjectivity that is equally opposed to binary analyses. Her "feminist nomadism" (*Nomadic Subjects* 158) includes feminist theory on three complex, interwoven, and coexisting levels: " 'difference between men and women,' 'differences among women,' and 'differences within each woman' " (*Nomadic Subjects* 158).[22] This approach to subjectivity connects with Mae Gwendolyn Henderson's notion of a simultaneity of discourses (147) in which black women write; it addresses the position of "speaking both to and from the position of the other(s)" (146).

None of these theories account for identities and differences that are located *between* the binary concept of female/male. Queer theory conceptualizes desire in ways that destabilize the naturalized correlation between sex, gender, and sexuality and make room for shifting identities *within* the categories of gender and sexuality.[23] An analysis of the ways in which sexualities contribute to the construction of identity is necessary in order to understand the subversive potential of women writers' voices.

Feminist debates on difference thus address the complex ways in which women are positioned in relation to power based on race, class, nationality, and sexual difference.[24] The significance of various categories of identity becomes apparent within postcolonial and anticolonial theories that explore the effects of cultural hybridity and diaspora on subjectivity. They inform feminist theories on resisting postcolonial subjectivity, such as Gayatri Chakravorty Spivak's *subaltern consciousness* and Chela Sandoval's *oppositional consciousness*.

Two approaches to difference are present in feminist and postcolonial theoretical debates. One treats difference as a given that precedes power structures (*difference* as a descriptive word, a noun), and the other views difference as actively created, as a process (*difference* as an active and changing word, a verb). The latter position demands accountability within the "politics of differentiation" (Trinh, *Woman, Native, Other* 82), which produce not only power relations but categories that these inequalities are based upon. Science fiction engages with both feminist and postcolonial theories in its narrative explorations of subjectivity, and it further troubles notions of identity (that which needs to be "uncovered," that is "real," that is "I") and difference (that which "separates," which is the "other," "not-I"). Much of *feminist* science fiction critically explores the dimensions and implications of the two concepts of difference and contributes to the deconstruction of difference as "other" to a stable identity by challenging boundaries between categories on which the separation of "self" and "other" rely. Here difference is not the opposite component of identity but becomes a part of the self.

Science fiction also fleshes out ideas of boundary dissolutions and border identities in terms of nationality, race, and ethnicity, as well as gender and sexuality. The texts analyzed in *Alien Constructions* are in dialogue with feminist theories about subjectivities of women of color that view identity as a continuous negotiation of conflicting experiences more than as a final product. This view embraces differences as persistent components of subjectivity and integrates them into the model of the *inappropriate other* (Trinh Min-ha) and into the concept of *impurity* as resisting subjectivity (Maria Lugones). Theories of *borderline identities* (Gloria Anzaldúa), *nomadic subjects* (Rosi Braidotti), and *migratory subjects* (Carole Boyce Davies) speak to issues of geographical (and social/political) displacements, and their effect on identity formation. Models of *cyborg identities* (Donna Haraway) address the effects of specific systems of technology on our cultural and political identities. Feminist theories of subjectivity are challenged and enhanced by queer theory's emphasis on transgressive sexualities and by the emerging discourse on *transgender* and *genderqueer* identities. In all of these theories, the question of the construction of social categories such as gender, class, nationality, sexuality, and race are central. The negotiations of categories of sameness and difference play a crucial role in issues of global power relations, identity politics, and agency. These negotiations find complex representations in contemporary science fiction texts and their unfamiliar bodies and subjects, which challenge and reinvent the terms on which discourse relies.

Feminist Science and Technology Critiques

Globalization is driven by technology, and late capitalism is defined by the commodification of biotechnologies such as genetic engineering. The interrelations of capitalism, science, and technology, which Haraway defines as "technoscience," affect women globally. Feminist criticism of science and technology defines science and technology as either inherently patriarchal, and thus disempowering to women, or as a tool that, if used strategically, can be liberating to women and other oppressed social groups. Science fiction explores this tension that characterizes feminists' relationship to technoscience and its institutions.

In general, feminist science and technology critiques in Western discourse problematize the gendered, classed, and raced relations women inhabit in economic, social, and cultural terms. They are concerned with women's position regarding structures of scientific inquiry and the impact of new technologies. Feminist theorists of science and knowledge criticize the Cartesian approach in Western science that positions the scientist as a neutral observer opposing an inert natural world. Instead, they argue, scientific knowledge entails power and holds social and political authority. Feminist science critics view scientific knowledge as patriarchal knowledge, based on the "god trick" perspective that defines the scientist as the knower and that values knowledge that is *disconnected* from the social world. Some feminist science critics delineate science's development as a (cultural) narrative and lay out its history in respect to its impact on gender and race politics, noting for example that in Western scientific discourse woman has been traditionally aligned with nature, based on her reproductive function. Others analyze science and knowledge as interdependent constituents and document the ways they contribute to the construction of both culture and nature.[25]

Closely connected to feminist debates on science are feminist critiques of technology. Feminist positions conflict over whether technology is liberating or destructive to women. As Judith Wajcman puts it in *Feminism Confronts Technology,* "Throughout these debates there has been a tension between the view that technology would liberate women—from unwanted pregnancy, from housework, and from routine paid work—and the obverse view that most new technologies are destructive and oppressive to women" (13). The debate revolves around the question of whether technology is *controlled* by a male-dominated establishment or is *inherently* misogynist and patriarchal.

Feminist science fiction has a tradition of exploring these aspects of science and technology.[26] The most powerful narrative strategy has been the creation of alternative sciences, utopian technologies that do not dominate or exploit, but enrich and empower. As Jane Donawerth explains in *Frankenstein's Daughters,* alternative sciences created by feminist writers are based on a utopian paradigm in that they promote

> women's participation in science as subjects not objects, revised definitions and discourse of science, inclusion in science of women's issues, treatment of science as an origin story that has been feminized, a conception of humans' relation to nature as partnership not domination, and an ideal of science as subjective, relational, holistic, and complex. (2)[27]

These issues are reconceptualized in science fiction when its writers use technology as a means to deal with issues of resistance and agency. Feminist concerns with exploitative labor relations and invaded bodies are mirrored in science fiction, where these bodies represent the complicated impact of neocolonial relations. Technology again becomes science fiction's defining theme because it transforms the traditional Western basis of identity—the body. Feminist theories and science fiction both are concerned with the body and its construction through what Foucault (in *The History of Sexuality*) calls "bio-power": scientific discourse and technology's systems, institutions, and representations. New technologies redefine the terms of power by simultaneously creating and transgressing established boundaries of nature and culture. Here, it is technology, together with the discourse of biology, that challenges conceptions of what defines a gendered human subject. While patriarchal technoscience is invasive and problematic, its undermining of the very power structures and categories it relies on creates potential moments of resistance, which are explored in science fiction's unique creatures.

Feminist science fiction produces representations of the female body within technoscience and speculates on subversive political identities that might develop from exploitative power relations. Many science fiction texts redefine women's relationship to technology: the appropriation of technology developed within a patriarchal context becomes an act of resistance, and the female cyborg becomes a metaphor for a feminist identity with agency. Women hackers, women warriors with surgically enhanced technobodies, genetically gender-variant figures, and women with complex relationships to machines/artificial intelligence negotiate hostile social environments. The conflicting representations within science fiction—cyborgs, technologically enhanced bodies, aliens—point to the contradictory social effects of technology and remind us of the relevance of acknowledging and examining different feminist positions within this debate. One of the major metaphors for these positions is the cyborg figure.

CYBORG FEMINISM

The effects of science and technology on people's lives have inspired debates since the scientific revolution in the sixteenth century, and have increasingly influenced Western social theory since the industrial revolution (Marxism is one of the more prominent examples). In *Electronic Eros*, Claudia Springer points out that an association between technology and violence is not new, and she reminds us that aggressive industrial technology impacts cultural imaginations (99). But it is the technology since World War II that defines the discourse around cyborgs: the increasing importance of cybernetics[28] in scientific theory shaped the development of high technology and biotechnology, and computer and other communication technologies that function on an invisible level created new anxieties and fears.[29] These developments, in conjunction with the rapid commercialization of science and technology, have changed the implications of machines and their relationship to human subjectivity in fundamental ways.

In relation to the effects of information technologies on women's lives, two related but distinct discourses have developed within feminist theories: *cyborg feminism* (usually associated with Donna Haraway's work) and *cyberfeminism* (often related to the philosophy of Sadie Plant). Sadie Plant's *Zeros and Ones* engages with Western philosophy's reliance on binary sexual difference—which renders the "eternal feminine" as either inscrutable or invisible—and the erasure of women's activities in history. She views the multiple, layered, and relational "nature" of computer technology as complementary to women's contributions to the sciences, which developed from complex and often hidden/erased positions. She declares that cyberculture has liberating potential for women's subversive subjectivities. While Plant's theoretical approach is in direct relation to philosophical discourse (such as the writings of Luce Irigaray), it has been criticized (by at times antitheoretical readers) as abstract and removed from material realities women face, just as cyberspace is criticized as a social arena that privileges disembodied subjectivities. In *Reload*, a recent collection of fiction and criticism on women and technology, editors Mary Flanagan and Austin Booth refer to cyberfeminism as follows:

> Cyberfeminism is concerned with the ways in which cybertechnologies affect women's lives in particular. Women software developers, hackers, online chat enthusiasts, performance artists, cyberpunk writers, technosex participants, game designers, and digital artists create narratives that explore both the pleasures and pitfalls of digital culture for women, creating complex positions for themselves in a digital world that potentially allows for new types of relations among women, men, and machines. (11)

The emphasis on "digital" or "cyber" culture, however, is often understood to be in danger of neglecting exploitative global class (and race/national) relations and questions of embodiment in relation to capitalist technoscience.

Cyborg feminism is a field within Western feminist theory that focuses on identity formation, embodiment, and political resistance in relation to high technology and science. Unlike cyberfeminism, whose theoretical interventions are mainly focused on digital culture, cyborg feminism is concerned with the ways in which corporate capitalism, technoscience, and cyberspace, as social, economic, and political factors, affect women's lives and reshape subjectivities. While digital culture is a central part of postmodern technoscience, it represents only one of several areas structured by new technologies. (Others include biotechnology and medical, military, and surveillance technology.) The central metaphor in cyborg feminism is the cyborg, a creature both human and machine, whose existence simultaneously relies on and redefines the relationship between humans and technology. While it is important to recognize overlaps between cyberfeminism and cyborg feminism, the theoretical framework that informs *Alien Constructions* is committed to the material basis underlying cyborg feminism.

Donna Haraway's "A Manifesto for Cyborgs: Science, Technology, and Socialist Feminism in the 1980s," originally published in 1985,[30] offered a feminist rereading of cyborg myths and representation. Later republished as "A Cyborg Manifesto," Haraway's essay created a feminist metaphor through which the discourse on posthuman existence (defined through humans' relationship to technologies) could explore the anxiety-inducing questions of dissolving boundaries between culture and nature and the growing invasion of the body by postmodern technology.[31] Economic relations—shaped by an exploding global capitalism based on exploitative historical legacies of colonialism—are part of these changing relationships. As a semiotic tool—a metaphor—the cyborg foregrounds representation and the constructions of cultural meaning, drawing both science and economic theories and their representations into the analysis of power relations. And, finally, the cyborg addresses the pressing questions of agency and posthuman subjectivity.

In her theorizing, Haraway has been directly inspired by the writing of science fiction author Octavia E. Butler, and in general she approaches "science fiction [as] political theory" (Haraway, *How Like a Leaf* 120). This acknowledgment of theory within (science) fiction is one of the most valuable contributions of cyborg feminism. Haraway's cyborg especially addresses the boundary crossings that result from the implosion of "nature" and "culture" derived from a new system of domination that she calls "technoscience." She directly links the economic exploitation of women (especially of women of color) to high technology, while situating both resistance and pleasure in close proximity to technology. In "A Cyborg Manifesto" and *Modest Witness@Second Millennium,* she describes feminist (science) fiction as a form of cultural production that resists United States patriarchal structures. Forming the main focus of her complete body of work is her conceptualization of the economic, political, and social role of science and technology, or "technoscience," which is examined in detail in her book *Modest Witness.*

According to its "technological" definition, the cyborg is "a cybernetic organism, a hybrid of machine and organism"; understood as a metaphor, this figure is simultaneously "a creature of social reality as well as a creature of fiction" (Haraway, "Manifesto" 149). Its existence derives from three major boundary dissolutions that threaten dualisms (Western thought's primary system of social organizing): human versus animal, organisms versus machines, and physical versus non-physical (challenged, for example, by invisible technologies such as wireless technology). It is important to understand the cyborg figure metaphorically: its "technological" manifestation in science fiction is its origin, not its only form or signification. The cyborg symbolizes a state of consciousness that has developed from certain social-political circumstances and has manifested as a metaphor within science fiction literature. It is a deeply troubling figure, whose ironic nature grows from the contradictions of exploitation and agency that the particular historical moment produces.

The cyborg's origin thus is rooted both in real material and technological relations and in (science) fiction. The realms of imagination/representation and material relations are closely dependent and reproduce each other; the cyborg speaks about both social power and politics of representation.

> A cyborg is a cybernetic organism, a hybrid of machine and organism, a creature of social reality as well as a creature of fiction. . . . The cyborg is a matter of fiction and lived experience that changes what counts as women's experience in the late twentieth century. This is a struggle over life and death, but the boundary between science fiction and social reality is an optical illusion. (Haraway, "Manifesto" 149)

The cyborg is conceptualized in science fiction; especially in feminist science fiction, it critically revisits the ideological opposition of human/machine, claiming a kinship that undermines Western dualistic power relations. While theorists recognize that "the means of production of technology is rarely beneficial for women" (Flanagan and Booth 11), many view the cyborg as ultimately liberating in its subversion of existing dualistic categories of power. The most basic dualism of Western thought, reason/nature, which historically has paired women with nature *and* with machines, has been criticized in numerous feminist works. This seeming contradiction is derived from the claim that both machines and nature are unable to reason, an inability also ascribed to women. Many feminists reject technology as inherently oppressive, a position based on the observation that technology, together with ideologies of progress and capitalist expansion, exploit both women and nature and need to be resisted.[32] Cyborg feminism, on the other hand, while recognizing the destructive dimensions of patriarchal techno-science, argues that the implosion of binaries facilitated by technology will make it possible to think and act beyond Western dualistic reasoning—including binary gender categories.

The cyborg makes impossible clear categories that structure power relations based on gender, race, and class, including a feminist resistance based in a division of the world into static categories (such as men versus women, culture [technology] versus nature). Instead, contributors to the cyborg feminist debate opt for theoretical and practical models of ambivalence and ambiguity that undermine binary hierarchies and point to the complexity of relations. By embracing ambivalence and partiality instead of stability in terms of subjectivity, cyborg feminism insists on recognizing problematic tendencies within feminist thought that hold on to a notion of female subjectivity modeled after an enlightened modern subject. Cultural texts within this discussion are understood as tools of domination as well as of imagination and resistance; issues of representation and the production of meaning are central to cyborg feminism. Cultural texts are thus part of cyborg feminism's analyses of oppression, and science fiction is its main site of theory production.

One of cyborg feminism's main concerns is the *embodiment* of inter-relations of technoscience. The cyborg and related figures are understood to be material fictions within a system of domination, and their bodies simultaneously represent and create cultural meaning. The female body is always seen in an ambivalent relationship to technology and the power discourses involved—the feminist cyborg metaphor is fully aware of Foucault's bio-power, which shapes and marks bodies. Thus the cyborg as an empowering political identity is critically revisited by Anne Balsamo, who, in *Technologies of the Gendered Body* (1996), examines how the body is simultaneously material *and* produced by discursive technologies, and how a postmodern reconstruction of bodies often reproduces notions and structures of sexual difference. The cyborg thus can be both a patriarchal fantasy of dominating technologies and a feminist tool of resistance. N. Katherine Hayles, in *How We Became Posthuman* (1999), further explores the potentials and limitations of the body's relationship to technology. Hayles investigates the body's dual reality of material experience and disembodied existence in cyberspace. In her examination of the history of computer theory, she is critical of the celebration of disembodiment as the ultimately posthuman existence and insists on the importance of the body's material reality as well as its discursive quality. Posthuman embodiment, in cyborg feminism, is not about being bodiless but about an empowered boundary transgression that enables bodies to resist exploitative power relations.[33]

Described in "A Cyborg Manifesto" as "Informatics of Domination" (161), the relations between technoscience and its semiotic representations create ideological categories and their social manifestations (such as labor relations, cultural productions, and medical practices), redefining them in terms of high technology. The metaphor of the cyborg is thus defined by the historical moment of global capitalism that creates powerful structures of exploitation based on nationality, race, and class. The "Cyborg Manifesto" points to the radical insights and positions developed within United States Third World feminist thought, and it relies for its structure and methodologies on the "breakup of versions of Euro-American feminist humanism in their devastating assumptions of master narratives deeply indebted to racism and colonialism" (Haraway, Introduction to *Simians, Cyborgs, and Women* 1). Chela Sandoval, in "New Sciences: Cyborg Feminism and the Methodology of the Oppressed," emphasizes the alliances and intellectual legacies of theories by women of color that run through Haraway's work. Of some concern is the fact that, as Sandoval states in "New Sciences," "Haraway's metaphor . . . in its travels through the academy, has been utilized and appropriated in a fashion that ironically represses the very work that it also fundamentally relies upon, and this continuing repression then serves to reconstitute the apartheid of theoretical domains once again" (409).[34]

Thus we need to understand feminist cyborg subjectivity both in the context of a Westernized concept of postmodernity and posthumanism dominated by technologies and institutions (such as we find in the work of poststructuralist writers such as Foucault, Deleuze and Guattari, Lyotard, Baudrillard, Jameson, etc.), and of an increasingly global capitalism in which Western technologies are imposed onto a Third World. Joseba Gabilondo warns in "Postcolonial Cyborgs: Subjectivity in the Age of Cybernetic Reproduction": "When Foucault proclaimed the death of 'Man' in 1966, he did not realize that capitalism does not get rid of its old technologies and apparatuses; instead it exports them to the Third World" (424). A feminist cyborg consciousness can only be transgressive and oppositional when developed in a critique not only of sexual but also of racial and class difference.

The cyborg's relationship to technology is always *ambivalent:* histories of science and technology tell us that technology is *never* innocent and is most often developed in a patriarchal, militaristic, and imperial context. Instead of denying the use of patriarchal technology, the cyborg is about appropriating those aspects of technoscience that enable resistance and political participation, and it recognizes the pleasure inherent in some technology. In fact, it is the *conflicted* quality of the cyborg's position within technoscience that makes its subversions most promising. So the cyborg is never an innocent figure, since there are no relations devoid of patriarchal and imperialist histories. As a partial subject, the cyborg resists cultural feminism's anxieties around acknowledging difference (and power) between women, and instead points to the complex ways feminist subjectivities can develop. Cyborg feminism is at its most convincing when written in relation to feminist thought—and standpoint theory more specifically[35]—that manages to speak of the socially constructed experiences of women as grounded in their *material* and *historical* relations (not their biological nature as "women"). By emphasizing material experiences, not biological givens, cyborg feminism does not diminish the political impact of speaking of women as a social group.[36]

What makes cyborg feminism's approach so valuable for my analysis is its recognition of interrelated aspects of cultural/textual productions and social/economic structures, and the systems of representations in which they operate. Its analysis of the semiotic displacement of technoscience's power relations foregrounds the importance of metaphorical meanings in the process of situating women in their diverse range of social and political positions. It is in the rearrangement, what Haraway calls new "figurations," of the social actors involved—their representation in relation to the dominant center—that the potential for political resistance lies. "Figures must involve at least some kind of displacement that can trouble identifications and certainties. Figurations are performative images that can be inhabited" (Haraway, *Modest Witness* 11). The refigurations in cultural texts become part of a resistance that Sandoval defines as "meta-ideologizing," "the operation of appropriating dominant ideological forms and using them whole in order to trans-form their meanings into a new, imposed, and revolutionary concept" (Sandoval, "New Sciences" 410). Cultural texts provide the blueprints for the figurations, the reclaiming of metaphors and myths in their function of creating cultural semiotics, which can form the basis for naming progressive politics. The focus of this analysis is the issue of representation that makes up a large part of cyborg debates and much of which takes place in the discourses on science fiction literature and film, the seemingly most "natural" realm of the cyborg.

Queer Desires, Transgender Identities, and Intersexed Bodies

In commercialized technoscience, bodies form the main contested territories, and heterosexual male desire dominates intersections of global consumerism and perverse desire. It seems that female and non-normative (e.g., disabled or racialized) bodies are particularly vulnerable to constraints created by sexualized consumerism and class exploitation. Examples of this consumerism and exploitation include the global sex trade and its trafficking in women and children, and the growing international pornography industry, which, despite a diversity of sexual practices and genres, is still dominated by the heterosexual male consumer (and entrepreneur). In science fiction narratives, the correlation between sex, gender, and sexuality (i.e. body, identity, and desire)—which in our world is ideologically equivalent to a straight, normatively gendered and sexed body—is reconfigured in the female cyborg and other "unnatural" bodies.

A feminist debate on identity and bodies needs to include not only feminist queer theoretical concepts of *gender performativity* (Judith Butler), *new taxonomies* (Eve Sedgwick), and the erotic pairing of *pleasure and danger* (Carole Vance) but also the growing body of texts dealing with nonnormatively gendered and intersexed (when a person's sex is ambiguous) identities. The fluidity not only of gender expression (such as *female masculinities,* Judith Halberstam) but also of desire resonates in *genderqueer* identities and politics. Issues around invisibility and passing, body transformations, and gender performativity inform this discourse that challenges the sex/gender binary and the investment many feminist theories have in it.

The trans and intersexed movements' theories on gender add a new dimension to queer and feminist theories—what Judith Butler in *Undoing Gender* refers to as the "New Gender Politics" (4). These New

Gender Politics address issues of gender variance less in terms of play-fulness and deconstruction than as matters of survival and "livable lives." The performativity of gender is understood to take place within highly regulative sets of norms that both enable identity and deny it; these changing norms define what "does and does not count as rec-ognizably human" (J. Butler, *Undoing Gender* 31). Attempts at redefin-ing how gender operates—and how it is "undone"—are not aimed at creating new imperative categories of what a gender identity should or should not be. Instead, "[t]he normative aspiration at work here has to do with the ability to live and breathe and move and would no doubt belong somewhere in what is called a philosophy of freedom" (*Undoing Gender* 31). Theorizing transgender and intersexed experi-ences and identities therefore should not be understood as a linear de-velopment away from feminist criticisms of patriarchal social orders, or from queer interventions into heterosexist formulations, but instead as taking place in complicated relationships to them. As Judith Butler puts it, "There is no story to be told about how one moves from feminist to queer to trans. [T]hese stories are continuing to happen in simul-taneous and overlapping ways as we tell them. They happen, in part, through the complex ways they are taken up by each of these move-ments and theoretical practices" (*Undoing Gender* 4). Science fiction is one cultural location where these "theoretical practices" are repre-sented and negotiated.

While feminist science fiction has always explored the construc-tion of gender roles and identities through androgynous and gender-neutral figures, in more recent science fiction texts, transgender iden-tities have often been conceptualized as similar to online, Internet communities that create a "genderless" (i.e. bodiless) space. This opti-mistic vision of transcending gender in cyberspace often is in conflict with the material-based discourses around nonnormatively gendered *bodies* (transsexual and intersexed), where embodiment is not sepa-rate from a trans identity, as discussed by Allucquere Rosanne Stone in *The War of Desire and Technology* (1995) and Thomas Foster in *The Souls of Cyberfolk* (2005). The celebration of bodiless existence within cyberspace is also problematic in terms of racial passing, which often is neglected by the debate on virtual transgender identities, as Lisa Nakamura argues in *Cybertypes* (2002). Science fiction's nonnorma-tively gendered and sexed bodies explore not only how transgendered identities are technologically produced but how they rely on existing notions of how sex, gender, and sexuality are correlated, at the same time as they subvert the gender binary.

These three areas of feminist thought—identity and difference; feminist critiques of science and technology; and the relationship between gender identity, body, and desire—cannot be separated, and all recur in the three sets of readings of science fiction texts in this book. Reading cultural texts (literature and film) in relation to these theories enables us to understand and explore the ramifications and contradictions within feminist thought. My analysis of science fiction texts is structured into three parts, each of which contains two chapters. The parts address issues identified within the three areas of feminist discourse, and offer different critical approaches. Some theoretical concepts (and the texts/authors connected with them) run through the entire book, such as cyborg feminism and boundary crossing as an empowering political strategy. Even though the chapters are separate analyses of specific cultural texts, they are all connected through the general aim to critically examine science fiction's radical potential to illuminate issues within feminist theories.

Part I constitutes a close analysis of Octavia E. Butler's writing, in which notions of identity and difference are central. An extensive analysis of her work, which reaches a broad popular audience and inspires intense academic feminist debates, will illustrate how her narratives echo issues in feminist postmodern theories. The dissolutions of boundaries that dominate in Butler's narratives are always accompanied and/or overshadowed by narratives of enslavement and resistance. Chapter 1, "Cultural Chameleons: Anticolonial Identities and Resistance in Octavia E. Butler's *Survivor* and *Dawn*," explores how Butler's work addresses contemporary political issues linked to diaspora and anticolonial movements by staging accounts of colonization on foreign worlds. She offers concrete embodiments for subjectivities conceptualized within postcolonial theories in the forms of extraterrestrials and human-alien hybrids. By engaging in several anticolonial discourses, Butler conceptualizes political resistance in connection with the subject positions of black women.

Butler's conceptualization of new worlds and past experiences mirrors anticolonial theoretical concerns with geographical displacement and economic oppression justified by ideological constructions, such as slavery. Here the aspect of identity is one of resistance, of survival against the odds. It is from a marginalized, colonized perspective that the tales are being told. These are tales of constant negotiations with the environment, of survivors testing the limits of the endurable and in return setting limits for those in power. The multiple perspectives offered by Butler destabilize the notion of center and margin, and therefore correspond to a theory of cultural displacement that emphasizes the notion of various forms of displaced existence and explores the possibilities for new centers and new modes of existence.

Butler's characters act out Ashis Nandy's concept of the "uncolonized mind" that resists definition through a dominant other. In my critical reading of two of her novels, *Survivor* and *Dawn*, I lay out the multilayered discourses in Butler's science fiction and how they relate to feminist anticolonial thought. Butler develops two main strategies of resisting a colonized identity in her narratives: *survival* as resistance (an emphasis on adaptation rather than assimilation), and the *recreation of myths* (a rejection of Christian salvation myths that are part of Western ideology).

In Chapter 2, "The Alien in Us: Metaphors of Transgression in the Work of Octavia E. Butler," I place Butler's narratives in the context of the dissolution and transgression of boundaries discussed by feminist postmodern theories. I examine how the political reconceptualization of difference is mirrored in Butler's fiction, on a symbolic level, mainly in the interactions of her human characters with aliens and other unhumans, and how these interactions destabilize the opposition of difference and identity. My textual analysis of Butler's work (including her *Xenogenesis* trilogy, *Kindred,* and her *Patternist* series) highlights her main contribution to feminist discussions of difference and power relations: her principle of boundary crossing (culturally and bodily) as resistance to colonization and domination. This chapter establishes the major metaphors Butler employs in her exploration of difference and identity—extraterrestrials, human-alien hybrids, and human mutants—that challenge and destabilize familiar categories we generally take for granted (such as "human") and provide concrete alternative ways to imagine feminist subjects.

An analysis of Butler's creation of models of identities follows a closer look at the way in which Butler destabilizes existing constructions of race and gender. These models, in their promotion of multiple subjectivities, correspond with feminist notions of oppositional identities and queer sexualities. Theoretical models that inform my analyses in this chapter include Donna Haraway's cyborg identity; borderline identities and nomadic and multiple subjectivities developed by feminist theorists such as Trinh Minh-ha, Gloria Anzaldúa, Maria Lugones, and Rosi Braidotti; and Judith Butler's theories on desire and the performativity of gender.

While Octavia Butler's narratives are cultural reflections of these theories, her work also points to the theories' limitations, especially in their generalizations and their attempts to erase contradictions. Despite the deconstruction of categories that her narratives display, Butler remains critical of simplified approaches to difference. Her writing thus never offers one-dimensional solutions but is critical of the liberal approach that assumes a normative sameness (an approach also found in feminist discourse). Instead, Butler's narratives stress the *process* of creating difference and destabilize any notion of pre-given categories of self/other. And finally, she disrupts the often generalizing theoretical approach to social relations that romanticizes the position of difference; she creates complex and contradictory characters whose personal experiences are inseparable from their encounters with institutionalized power.

The focus of Part II is mainstream science fiction film and its representations of the body's ambiguous relationship to various technologies —in particular, of cyborg embodiment and posthuman subjectivities. While the different conceptual and representational origins of science fiction literature (as written text) and science fiction film (as visual/acoustic text) is recognized, the focus of the two analyses is on systems of representations in the movies, not their technological design or special effects as science fiction film.

At the heart of Jean-Pierre Jeunet's film *Alien Resurrection* are changing cyborg bodies and their gendered codes of representation, which I examine in Chapter 3, "Technoscience's Stepdaughter: The Feminist Cyborg in *Alien Resurrection*." In my analysis of *Alien Resurrection*'s heroine, Ripley, the emphasis is on the (technological) construction of woman as monstrous (m)other, and the protagonist's appropriation of this position into a resisting cyborg identity. The film works through some of cyborg feminism's most controversial claims about technology's effect on gender and agency, and it offers progressive models of cyborg subjectivities with its female cyborgs and other deviant bodies. Finally, I address how the image of the feminist cyborg is represented (or co-opted) by Hollywood cinema and whether it retains its radical potential in the process.

In Chapter 4, "Our Bodies as Our Selves: Body, Subjectivity, and (Virtual) Reality in *The Matrix*," my analysis of *The Matrix* focuses on the body's relationship to identity as it is conceptualized in feminist critiques of cyberpunk's disembodied subject. The discussion of the film taps postmodern theories of how computer technology changes our subjectivity and offers a feminist criticism of the fetishization of a terminal identity separate from the body. The figure of Trinity, the female love-interest of the hero, reflects the complex gender politics of the movie, in terms of both narrative and representation: her identity as resistance fighter (and latex-clad body) counters her identity as the hero's dedicated lover. *The Matrix*'s complex representations of the body's relationship to technology in the end ignores the progressive visions offered by feminist cyberpunk critics, where the body and technology are synthesized into a new subjectivity in which they do not annihilate each other, and therefore do not have to be rejected in favor of a humanist identity model that ultimately depends on the exclusion and containment of everything "other" for its existence.

One concern of this analysis is the tense relationship between feminist theories of representation and popular cultural texts. This tension develops when mainstream culture appropriates feminist theoretical interventions into systems of meaning: the female warrior becomes less threatening to patriarchy and instead is appropriated as a sex object. It is crucial to examine how feminist models of subjectivity/resistance are represented in mainstream cultural texts and the ways in which the strategic position of "other" is undermined by its representation by and for mainstream audiences. If the appropriation and re-creation of popular images is a subversive move, how does a *reappropriation* by mainstream culture of these images affect the process of resistance? In what ways can the text remain subversive, and does the reappropriated image actually undermine the radical potential of the counter-discourse it reflects? Thus an alternative subject position may result in the familiar exoticization and eroticization of the other. My analysis examines the tension between appropriation and resistance in the openly affirmative ways in which these two films deal with issues within cyborg feminism and feminist cyberpunk critique (such as through their female figures) and the questions that arise from their representations: In what way are feminist cyborg images coopted through mainstream appropriation? How is the cyborgian body, with its threatening boundary transgressions, assimilated into hegemonic representations, and does this assimilation render the subversive nature of feminist cyborg identity harmless to the system?

Finally, Part III deals with the question of nonnormative bodies, desire, and the limits of our binary sex/gender system. In Chapter 5, I analyze representations of female posthuman embodiment in Richard Calder's dystopia *Dead Girls*, and how his cyborg creations differ from feminist cyborg subjectivities. His narratives point to the importance of developing critical visions in regard to technology's impact on social orders. In Chapter 6, I return to Octavia Butler's work and discuss the ways she challenges notions of fixed gender identities with her characters' transgressive androgyny, on one hand, and queer sexualities, on the other. In the second part of the chapter, I examine Melissa Scott's *Shadow Man* and the implications of her depiction of a sex/gender system based on *five*, rather than two, sexes.

Discussing science fiction's relationship to feminist thought recognizes popular culture's role in creating meaning through representation, and it acknowledges the spaces of agency located within the process of consuming and producing cultural texts. Therefore, the main focus is on the intersections of technoscience and representations, which reinforce the power relations of global capitalism, neocolonialism, and a continuously patriarchal form of social organizing at the same time as they create moments of resistance. Reading in this way does not diminish the pleasure aspect of consuming (and producing) cultural texts; instead, it understands imagination, narrative, and desire as part of feminist theorizing.

As gendered and racial subjects, black women speak/write in multiple voices—not all simultaneously or with equal weight, but with various and changing degrees of intensity, privileging one *parole* and then another. One discovers in these writers a kind of internal dialogue reflecting an *intrasubjective* engagement with the *intersubjective* aspects of self, a dialectic neither repressing difference nor, for that matter, privileging identity, but rather expressing engagement with the social aspects of self ("the other[s] in ourselves").

—Mae Gwendolyn Henderson, "Speaking in Tongues"

Born in 1947, the science fiction author Octavia E. Butler was raised in Pasadena, California, by her mother and grandmother, as her father died when she was very young. The women in her life worked hard to support their families, and Butler learned early about the invisibility and economic vulnerability of working black women. She learned to love reading science fiction when she was a child, and she started writing when she was only ten years old.[1] In 1978, in *Contemporary Authors,* Butler recalled:

When I began to read science fiction, I was disappointed at how little . . . creativity and freedom was used to portray the many racial, ethnic, and class variations. Also, I could not help noticing how few significant woman characters there were in science fiction. Fortunately, all this has been changing over the past few years. I intend my writing to contribute to the change. (F. Foster, 38)

Twenty-five years later, Butler has published twelve books and is considered "the" major African American woman science fiction writer.[2] She depicts complex societies in which alien species force-breed with humans and humans mutate into alien forms, in which time travel and shapeshifters exist, and in which humans have telepathic abilities. Her style is engaging; her stories captivating. Butler's science fiction narratives are intriguing because of the complex and at times contradictory reading experience they offer; they juxtapose affirmation of difference with experiences of colonization and slavery. At the center of her narratives, which Ruth Salvaggio defines as "stories of power," are the struggles of strong female characters who negotiate contradictions of "enslavement and freedom, control and corruption, survival and adjustment" (Salvaggio, "Octavia Butler" 6). Butler's writing raises issues of how to resist racism, sexism, and exploitation in ways that elucidate many of the concepts we encounter in feminist thought.[3]

Two themes that run through Butler's literary narratives are the focus of Part I of *Alien Constructions.* The first is the theme of *colonial experiences,* which is discussed in Chapter 1. The second, which is closely connected to the first and examined in Chapter 2, is *difference,* through which the "other" is constituted, and its relation to *identities.* Central to Butler's narratives is the notion of *negotiated* as opposed to *given* identities; she challenges colonial discourses of the colonizer as superior "self," and the "native" as inferior "other." Butler's focus on both colonial experience and alternative ways of dealing with difference invites at times seemingly contradictory interpretations. This apparent contradiction is especially visible in the Oankali, the alien race in her *Xenogenesis* trilogy. An anticolonial context highlights their negative role as colonizers, while a critical examination of the relationship of identity and difference points out the alternative, anti-essentialist logic of identity they embody. These conflicting narrative constellations are typical for Butler, who rejects a one-dimensional understanding of complicated processes.

Butler's often troubling narrative contradictions derive from her engagement with several discourses: science fiction, black women's writing, and anticolonial and feminist debates. Through her characters' negotiations of power and her rewriting of cultural and religious myths, Butler addresses contemporary political issues linked to diaspora and anticolonial movements that are problematized in feminist debates. In accordance with the critical position of analyzing how popular texts reflect and produce cultural and political identities,[4] I believe it is necessary to place Butler's science fiction within the wider framework of black women's imagination as well as that of science fiction and cultural identity.⁵ Science fiction's exploration of colonial experiences through metaphors of aliens and space travel reaches a diverse audience often not included in theoretical debates on anticolonial identities. The objective of the critical readings offered here is not to give a close textual analysis of individual narratives, but instead to clarify feminist concepts by tracing them in thematic patterns in Butler's writing.

Octavia E. Butler and Black Women's Writing—"Speaking in Tongues"

Viewing Butler only in relation to science fiction limits the understanding of her work in terms of black women's imagination and cultural production, as Teri Ann Doerksen remarks in a footnote in "Octavia E. Butler: Parables of Race and Difference":

> It is unfortunate that because [Butler's] work is marketed under the rubric of science or speculative fiction, it has been considered apart from other genres, including the body of mainstream African American fiction, and that as a result it is only rarely that she is discussed in a context that includes other African American female writers. (33)

Doerksen's observation points to the artificial distinction between popular culture texts and "literature." As a result, those texts consumed by readers outside the "mainstream"⁶ are often not considered in debates about how differences shape identities.

How is the identity of the author (either her or his own or that prescribed by critics and readers) relevant to the meaning of the text? What perspectives on power do concepts of identity and difference provide? In order to explain her fascination with power, Butler has said, "I began writing about power because I had so little" (quoted in Govan, "Connections" 82). In *Black Women, Writing, and Identity,* Carole Boyce Davies examines the construction of female subjectivity through literary and cultural texts. The focus of her study is how black women writers "re-negotiate questions of identity" (3) and develop new concepts of community. This renegotiating of identities, Davies states, is fundamental to both migration in general, and black women's writing in particular, because it reflects on the different demands of the changing surroundings in which black women often find themselves. Black women's literature mirrors the "migratory subjectivity" that displaced women develop; black women writers use this concept as a narrative device to make sense of displaced lives. Davies views black women's *writing* as crucial for understanding how women negotiate identities in the context of migration and colonial displacement: "It is the convergence of multiple places and cultures that renegotiates the terms of Black women's experience that in turn negotiates and re-negotiates their identities" (3). Davies argues that, while it is imperative to recognize a shared experience of geographical and/or cultural dislocation, the cultural identity of black women should be regarded as an instance of "migratory subjectivity" that resists the establishing and exclusion of the other:[7]

> Black women's writing . . . should be read as a series of boundary crossings and not as a fixed, geographical, ethnically or nationally bound category of writing. In cross-cultural, transnational, translocal, diasporic perspectives, this reworking of the grounds of "Black Women's Writing" redefines identity away from exclusion and marginality. (*Black Women* 4)[8]

In placing Butler not only within the context of other science fiction texts but also in relation to the cross-cultural context of black women's writing, we can attempt to understand how her narratives fit into debates on cultural imagination and subjectivity: they deconstruct categories of difference that dominate academic and political discourses at the same time as they problematize the romanticizations and generalizations of many postmodern theories of identity. Because they are based in science fiction stories, these configurations are able to project creative and innovative ways of approaching gender and race relations that move beyond debates that involve only "mainstream" literature.

It is best to approach Butler's work from an intellectual position that acknowledges the interdependent constitution of categories like gender, race, and class.[9] Her stories reflect intersections of feminist theories, anticolonial discourses, science fiction, and black women's writing, and correlate with what Mae Gwendolyn Henderson calls "simultaneity of discourses." The embeddedness of Butler's work within multiple discourses reflects the notion of "speaking in tongues" as "the ability to speak in diverse known languages" (Henderson 149). In accordance with Davies's argument that black women are constantly negotiating changing geographies, Henderson sees black women's writing as inherently transgressive because of the marginalized subject position they inhabit. Subjectivity, then, not only is established in opposition to the other but also includes aspects of "otherness" *within* the self. As a result, black women writers speak not only *to* the other but from the position *as* other, "privileging (rather than repressing) . . . 'the other in ourselves' " (147). Butler reminds us in "The Monophobic Response" how vulnerable the position of other can be in a context of xenophobia: "No wonder we so often project alienness onto one another. This . . . has been the worst of our problems—the human alien from another culture, country, gender, race, ethnicity. This is the tangible alien who can be hurt or killed" (415).

The voice of the other is a primary point of reference in Butler's depiction of human relationships with un-human[10] beings (aliens, hybrids, and mutants), and this voice also decenters the conventional science fiction story line that prioritizes the human perspective. Butler creates scenarios that demand that her characters (and her readers) enter (simultaneous) discourses alien to them and construct a sense of self from them. She evokes disruptions that in turn offer points of interference into the construction of "others." Without glorifying dislocation as the only space where agency develops, Butler's narratives insist that displacement is not always paralyzing and instead offer models of agency and resistance.

The Worlds of Octavia E. Butler

Butler's work is mostly categorized as science fiction; she has several times won the science fiction community's two most prestigious awards in the United States: the Hugo Achievement Award (for the short stories "Speech Sounds" and "Bloodchild") and the Nebula Award (for "Bloodchild" and her latest novel, *Parable of the Talents*).[11] Even though she is mainly viewed as a science fiction writer, one of the most remarkable features of her books is a strong interweaving of elements from different genres. *Wild Seed* and *Kindred* contain structures found in both the historical novel and the slave narrative,[12] and stylistic elements of fantasy are present in *Wild Seed, Patternmaster,* and *Mind of My Mind. Parable of the Sower* and *Parable of the Talents* work with a "realist" symbolism that is grounded in the style of journal entries, and *Parable of the Sower,* in particular, resembles a coming-of-age novel. *Survivor, Clay's Ark,* and the *Xenogenesis* trilogy work within an unambiguous science fiction framework of space flight and extraterrestrials. The many overlapping genre elements in Butler's writing are mirrored in the composition of her audience. She has gained readers outside the science fiction milieu and has achieved cult status simultaneously with feminist, black, and science fiction readers alike (see Williams 72, and Kenan 495). It is especially surprising that her work is rarely discussed in the context of other black women writers in the United States.

Butler's writing is interesting not so much for its style as for its content (plot), characterization, and metaphors that create new forms of representation. In these aspects, Butler's work conveys its postmodern significance, located primarily in her depiction of difference and boundary crossing and their relation to power. As Frances Bonner puts it in "Difference and Desire," Butler's style is "traditional" (387)—her narratives stand in the typical science fiction tradition of the adventure tale. She does not engage in postmodern fragmentation per se. Only in her latest novel, *Parable of the Talents,* is her narrative strategy explicitly disruptive, employing journal entries that tell the story from different perspectives. In some of her earlier work, most noticeably in *Survivor,* Butler does use a technique of changing narrative perspective that leaves parts of the tale fragmented, but in a subtler, less obvious way.

Five of Butler's novels with loose narrative connections form the *Patternist* series: *Wild Seed, Mind of My Mind, Clay's Ark, Patternmaster,* and *Survivor.* In this series, Butler describes the evolution of humankind into three warring groups: the Patternists, who develop psychic and telepathic powers and are connected through a mental net, the "pattern"; the Missionaries, a Christian-based religious group of "mutes" (humans who stand outside of the pattern), who understand their mission to be the preservation of the human form as the image of God; and the Clayarks, human mutants who come into existence through an infection with an alien virus that was accidentally brought to Earth from a space expedition.

While the novels *Wild Seed, Mind of My Mind, Patternmaster,* and *Survivor* contain few references to each other, all deal to some extent with the descendents of a 4000-year-old Nubian, Doro. His apparently immortal existence is as a parasitical, mental-energetic form of being without an inherent shape. Doro relies on the appropriation of the bodies of humans he kills for bodily representation, and he feeds on the life energy, the "soul," of the victim during the kill. His ambition to create a unique human race (which turns out to be the Patternists) runs through the *Patternist* series but is dealt with most directly in *Mind of My Mind* and *Wild Seed.* He searches for potential breeders and produces his descendents on two continents over the course of hundreds of years.

In the *Xenogenesis* series (*Dawn, Adulthood Rites,* and *Imago*), Butler introduces another variation of human evolution: fusion with an alien species. In *Clay's Ark,* Butler had already taken up issues that dominate the later trilogy, such as alterations of genetic material and the effects of these alterations on our understanding of humanity. The Oankali, alien "gene traders," save the human race from self-destruction in a nuclear war started on a polluted Earth. The goal of the Oankali is to carry out a gene exchange through reproduction with humans; execution of this plan, and human resistance to it, make up the narrative framework of the trilogy. One of the central points of discussion in the series is that the Oankali define humans as genetically flawed because they are simultaneously intelligent and hierarchical; therefore, as a species, they are prone to self-destruction—a point apparently proven by the nuclear war. In the center of the *Xenogenesis* series stands the question Butler introduced in her earlier work: "Who or what has 'fully human status'" (Haraway, *Primate Visions* 376)? This question is closely linked to feminist debates surrounding power structures based on race and gender. In her award-winning short story "Bloodchild," Butler further explores questions of reproduction, power, and social categories of gender and race in a metaphorical framework of cross-species reproduction.

Kindred is not written in a science fiction context—the element of time travel in the novel is based on inexplicable psychically-induced phenomena, rather than on a scientific paradigm developed by the narrative. Time travel gives the story a fantastic framework not unlike those of magical realism. As in parts of *Wild Seed,* Butler fuses elements of the historical novel and the slave narrative to examine critically the historical development of contemporary racist structures. This, as Govan notes, deviates from the genre appropriation usually found in science fiction: "She has chosen to link science fiction not only to anthropology and history, via the historical novel, but directly to the Black American slavery experience via the slave narrative" (Govan, "Homage" 79). With her *Parable* novels, *Parable of the Sower* and *Parable of the Talents,* the author creates an even more familiar framework than the historical context of slavery. Set in mid–twenty-first-century California, these narratives explore utopian alternatives to racist, sexist, and capitalist systems.[13]

Much of the recent critical work on Butler has been inspired by the connections Donna Haraway drew between feminist science fiction and feminist social theory in "A Cyborg Manifesto," and by her analysis of the *Xenogenesis* trilogy in the final chapter of her *Primate Visions.* Haraway's writing places these science fiction narratives within feminist theoretical speculations on transgressive subjectivities. I want to return to the theories that initially inspired Haraway's contemplations of the actual science fiction texts[14] and trace how their concepts are echoed in Butler's writing. Thus I will draw on critical race and anticolonial theory when discussing the models of subjectivity we encounter in Butler's narratives.

There are, of course, other writers who share with Octavia Butler an alternative vision of human relations within a science fiction and/or fantasy setting. Many of them are contributors to the anthology *Dark Matter: A Century of Speculative Fiction from the African Diaspora,* edited by Sheree R. Thomas, such as contemporary writers Samuel Delany, Nisi Shawl, Charles Saunders, Steven Barnes, and Nalo Hopkinson. Butler's novels are thus not the only place where explorations of the "human" take place in terms of gender, race, and nationality. What sets her work apart from that of most other writers is her engagement with simultaneous discourses, which creates such challenging reading experiences, and the critical resonance her work has ignited. Her influence on feminist thought and the reading of her novels outside the science fiction context have inspired my analysis of her work in relation to contemporary feminist thought. Perhaps most importantly, Butler's work refuses to claim *one* position based on a sexual, racial, and/or gender identity (an aspect her writing shares with that of Delany, as Jeffrey Allen Tucker discusses in *A Sense of Wonder: Samuel R. Delany, Race, Identity, and Difference*).[15] Instead of creating safe, unambivalent social identities for her characters, Butler resists any tokenism within the white-dominated genre of science fiction by consistently troubling its paradigms; thus she contributes to a general debate on oppression and liberation.

1. Cultural Chameleons

Anticolonial Identities and Resistance in Octavia E. Butler's Survivor *and* Dawn

It is in the process of the creation of selfhood that self-cognition occurs, identity is taken on, and a politics is initiated.

— Rajeswari Sunder Rajan, *Real and Imagined Women*

Octavia Butler's work foregrounds the experiences of *female* characters and therefore can be understood as part of a feminist tradition in science fiction literature. However, her representations of *black* heroines differentiate her writing from much of feminist science fiction. In 1984, Ruth Salvaggio noted in her article "Octavia Butler and the Black Science-Fiction Heroine":

> In a sense, Octavia Butler's science fiction is a part of the new scenario [created by feminist science fiction], featuring strong female protagonists who shape the course of social events. Yet in another sense, what Butler has to offer is something very different. Her heroines are black women who inhabit racially mixed societies. Inevitably, the situations these women confront involve the dynamic interplay of race and sex in futuristic worlds. (Salvaggio, "Black Science-Fiction Heroine" 78)

Butler is one of the few black science fiction writers publishing in English (others include Samuel Delany, Steven Barnes, Charles Saunders, and Nalo Hopkinson), and her work needs to be understood within the context of the traditions of the genre. Her work reflects a concern with the invisibility of the black experience in popular imagination, particularly in science fiction[1] — a concern shared by Sheree R. Thomas, editor of *Dark Matter: A Century of Speculative Fiction from the African Dias-*

pora: "Like dark matter, the contributions of black writers to the SF genre have not been directly observed or fully explored" (Thomas xi).

The invisibility of blacks in science fiction refers not only to authors but also to readers, as seen in the persistent claim that black people do not read or write science fiction. Adele S. Newson dispels this claim as a "widespread myth" that is "fed by the notion that [blacks] cannot afford to indulge in fantasy" (390). And Samuel R. Delany, in "Racism and Science Fiction," recalls Harlan Ellison's point that the pulp writers of early popular magazines were known only by name, and there was no way to tell the ethnic origin of the contributors or their gender: "[W]e simply have no way of knowing if one, three, or seven of [these writers]—or even many more—were blacks, Hispanics, women, Native Americans, Asians, or whatever. Writing is like that" (Delany, "Racism and Science Fiction" 384).

It is important to destabilize claims of silence, for they themselves often have the effect of silencing. But it is also necessary to recognize the racism of the genre—in its texts as well as in its communal boundaries (such as conventions, conferences, awards, etc.). Delany's account of a painful encounter during an award ceremony in 1968 reflects how racial identities are ascribed to us by racist United States society. A well-intended joke reminded Delany during the award ceremonies,

> No one here will ever look at you, read a word you write, or consider you in any situation, no matter whether the roof is falling in or the money is pouring in, without saying to him- or herself (whether in an attempt to count it or to discount it), "Negro . . ." The racial situation, permeable as it might sometimes seem (and it is, yes, highly permeable), is nevertheless your total surround. (Delany, "Racism and Science Fiction" 391)

In an interview a little less than twenty years later, Octavia Butler recalled that an editor of a science fiction magazine voiced his belief that black characters should not be included in science fiction stories since their presence would distract the reader from the story. "He stated that if you were going to write about some sort of racial problem, that would be absolutely the only reason he could see for including a black" (Beal 18).

Next to the racial politics of the science fiction community, the texts themselves often either propagate a typical liberal color blindness or are racist—openly as well as implicitly.[2] One extreme is the refusal to deal with "actual" racism, which results in an abstraction of the issue into metaphors and avoidance of any treatment of existing power structures. Frances Bonner observes this phenomenon in "Difference and Desire, Slavery and Seduction: Octavia Butler's Xenogenesis," in which she discusses the complex constellations Butler creates that differ from traditional treatment of otherness in much science fiction:

> [T]here has been the belief that aliens can substitute as all-purpose others. One big blue extra-terrestrial whose humanity is revealed and accepted can be metaphorically substituted for an examination of any number of actual social divisions, as witness many past discussions on the absence of women/non-Caucasians/homosexuals/disabled people from SF. (Bonner 52)

Perhaps more obvious is the employment of openly racist themes within contemporary science fiction. Charles Saunders, in his discussion of the "Africa theme" in the imagination of nonblack science fiction writers, notes that there have always been some writers who deal in complex ways with issues of race (see Saunders 401–2). But recent publications that deal with Africa as inspiration also include works like those by Mike Resnick, whose depiction of Africa as an alien and mystifying place aligns its position with the "dark continent" that inspired the fascination of white colonialism and shaped much of white literary imagination. Insofar as Africans were (and are) seen as people to be dominated, they also inspire fear in the white imagination, which never attempts to *know* the other since that knowledge would destabilize the dichotomy of self/other, master/slave. Thus the fascination with darkness as other/alien is also infused with a threat of the unknown: "People have always been frightened by what they cannot see—and the specter of blackness looms large in the white imagination" (Thomas xiii).

As "products of a particular cultural moment" (Leonard 4), science fiction texts reveal cultural imaginations pertaining to race relations. Beyond that, however, they also function as "imagined alternatives" that can both "reenact and alter racial codes and representations" (Leonard 4) by reinventing human relations. Other writers who explore these issues include the Canadian-Caribbean writer Nalo Hopkinson, the Canadian fantasy writer Charles Saunders, and the short-fiction writer Nisi Shawl, as well as Samuel Delany, who often is viewed as a "trailblazer for black sf writers" (Tucker 1). The following analysis of Butler's writing situates her work within anticolonial debates and understands her writing in the tradition of these writers' interjections into the (at times problematic) representations of colonial relations within science fiction.

Colonial Displacements and Legacies

Since the Zapatista rebellion in Mexico in 1994, followed five years later by the World Trade Organization protests in Seattle in the United States, the industrial world has become increasingly aware of a rapidly growing anti-globalization movement within the "new world order." Based in local, grassroots groups organizing around economic issues worldwide, this movement resonates with larger, often national groups' attempts to shape economic relations. From workers' rights and ecological concerns to pro-democracy movements, the anti-globalization movement is international yet decentralized, and its diverse and multiple organizations bring a wide range of criticisms to the debate. The anti-globalization movement counters industrialized countries' market-driven celebration of a growing consumption of Western commodities in the Third World and the establishment of free trade zones as economically progressive. Instead of viewing these developments as the cross-cultural effects of a globalization that minimizes differences, anti-globalization activists point to the resulting cultural and economic exploitation. As Ania Loomba states, "often globalisation [sic] is celebrated as the producer of a new and 'liberating' hybridity or multiculturalism, terms that now circulate to ratify the mish-mash of cultures generated by the near unipolar domination of the Western, particular United States, media machine" (Loomba 257).

Many activists and theorists understand the economic imbalance between First and Third World to be a result of centuries of European colonialism and base their work on an anticolonial critique.[3] One major effect of contemporary neocolonialism's economic system is migration and the forced displacement of people it brings.

Contemporary global capitalism relies on the migration of countless people who, in search of economic and political stability, follow the shifting labor market. From diverse cultural, class, and educational backgrounds, migrants form complex and multilayered communities with shifting cultural identities and economic positions. Women's living conditions are thus influenced by global capitalism, and these issues find their ways into women's narratives. Women writers consider the formation of new cultural identities and fragmented subjectivities, which are also conceptualized in postcolonial and diaspora studies. Beyond theoretical and political discourses, however, cultural productions of black women worldwide give insight into the fears and desires underlying the diasporic experiences that inform "dislocated" group and individual identities. They enable a sharing of experiences outside social and cultural boundaries and create spaces where visions become concrete. Concepts of colonial and postcolonial subjectivities—as they relate to diaspora and local identities as well as social, political, and economic relations—are extensively treated in postcolonial and anticolonial discourses, including feminist ones. As one of science fiction's major themes, stories of colonization and migration of groups revisit (and/or often confirm) the complex power relations of European colonialism. In these narratives, scenarios of subjectivity and resistance are played out, echoing and commenting on anticolonial discourses.

What sense of cultural identity can develop from global (capitalist) relations? Smadar Lavie and Ted Swedenburg place the anticolonial debate into the context of the conventional Western idea that cultures, peoples, identities, and specific places are immutably linked, creating cultural identities inseparable from a particular geographical place. This concept has served to ground modern ideas of nations and cultures by ideologically constructing a center (the West) as the norm, and an *other* who is situated in the colonized world, which has to be contained and defined within its own space.

Underpinning [the construction of the *other* in the discipline of anthropology] was the assumption of a homology between the modernist space of the nation-state Here and linear time that progresses toward enlightenment. It was also assumed that if one is positioned in the modernist linear time-space, one is then able to compare and contrast homogeneities of timeless Out There cultures. This relativist notion of culture, based on the inseparability of identity from place, was not peculiar to anthropology, but reigned throughout the humanities and the social science as well as in the political institutions of the nation-state that shape public discourse. (Lavie and Swedenburg 2)

Several phenomena have challenged this construction, calling the framework of center and margin into question.[4] One is the massive migration of nonwhite people into Western countries in Europe and North America, which transports the constructed other into the center. Notions of cultural identities "on the move" emphasize the shifting and changing constitution of the margins, and the power relations that accompany and shape them. This aspect of heterogeneously shifting positions can be found within postcolonial theories at the same time as it is neglected in postmodern writing about the notion of a fragmented multiculturalism. "Displacement . . . is not experienced in precisely the same way across time and space, and does not unfold in a uniform fashion. Rather, there is a range of positionings of others in relation to the forces of domination and vis-à-vis other Others" (Lavie and Swedenburg 4). Not all migrants are subversive or progressive in their displaced identities and politics; hence it is the *colonized* identity that is of interest, the subject position that is forced to redefine itself under colonialism and that subverts hegemonic structures. The problem with defining colonial and postcolonial subjectivity partly lies in the fact that colonial experiences are not homogeneous but vary, both by the economically determined intention of the colonizer, and by the precolonial society of the colonized, as well as by historical specificities. An attempt to understand "the" colonial experience is thus impossible, and it

> also makes it very difficult to 'theorise' colonialism—some particular instance is bound to negate any generalisation we may make about the nature of colonialism or of resistances to it. There is always a certain amount of reduction in any attempt to simplify, schematise and summarise complex debates and histories, and the study of colonialism is especially vulnerable to such problems on account of colonialism's heterogeneous practices and impact over the last four centuries. (Loomba xiii)

In order to neither romanticize nor trivialize colonial identities, the variety of experiences of "dislocation" and local colonization needs to be recognized. For example, experiences vary depending on different motifs for migration—such as exploration, eviction, or flight—as well as on cultural alienation of local communities and the socioeconomic context the colonized subject finds herself in. So the situation of a Third World academic coming to a United States university is different from that of a United States academic going to a Mexican university, and both are very different from the experience of an illegal Mexican immigrant crossing the border, just as an Indian computer specialist working in Europe negotiates different conditions than does a Filipino domestic worker.

Acknowledging the heterogeneity and local specificity of a colonial encounter does not undermine a criticism of colonialism; instead, it creates a more comprehensive picture of the ramifications: "The point, however, is not that we need to know the entire historical and geographic diversity of colonialism in order to theorise [sic], but rather that we must build our theories with an awareness that such diversity exists, and not expand the local to the status of the universal" (Loomba xvi). At the same time, theories analyzing the effects of colonial experiences, as well as *texts* about that process, are crucial for exploring the development and implementation of colonial ideology.

Colonial Experience in Octavia E. Butler's Science Fiction

Science fiction has a long tradition of conceptualizing themes of colonialism "as the protagonists (usually human) encounter new and extraordinary races across the vast reaches of time and space" (Flodstrom 159). Even though adventure literature in Anglo-Europe and the United States after the nineteenth century started to develop towards a more critical stand regarding colonialism (see Flodstrom 159–60), it was only in the 1960s that the genre of adventure literature (and science fiction) was evaluated for its imperialism, inspired by the "publication of works like Frantz Fanon's *Black Skin, White Masks* and Edward Said's *Orientalism*" (Flodstrom 160). These works point to the process of colonialism as a *construction* of the colonized as other. In *Orientalism,* Edward Said states that the concept of oriental "helped to define Europe (or the West) as its contrasting image, idea, personality, experience" (Said 2). Said argues that colonized cultures as they are represented today, and the resulting cultural hegemonies, are a discourse produced by the West: "European culture was able to manage—and even produce—the Orient politically, sociologically, militarily, ideologically, scientifically, and imaginatively during the post-Enlightenment period" (3). In accordance with this analysis, the science fiction genre has a tradition of conceptualizing themes of colonialism in conservative, and at times reactionary, ways. A general shift in science fiction literature since the

1960s towards an increasing engagement with race and gender issues notwithstanding, racist tendencies that treat non-Western cultures as metaphorical stand-ins for "otherness" persist. These narratives continue to confirm colonial relations at the same time as they provide moments where power becomes visible in our cultural narratives.

Octavia Butler's narratives consistently deviate from prevailing stereotypes in science fiction as well as from anticolonial stories that fail to move beyond existing notions of the "noble savage."[5] Critics mostly relate her themes of diasporic identity and slavery to the Black Diaspora and African American identity or place them into a wider feminist context.[6] As Hanchard observes, the notion of diaspora creates a "transnational dimension to black identity."[7] Along similar lines, in *The Black Atlantic*, Paul Gilroy argues that this concept of a "rhizomorphic, fractual structure of the transcultural, international formation I call the black Atlantic" (4) undermines ethnocentric and nationalistic approaches in racial discourse, and is based on a "desire to transcend both the structures of the nation state and the constraints of ethnicity and national particularity" (19). Butler evokes this desire in her tales of geographical displacement. Her accounts of diaspora include direct comments on the historical moment of slavery in the United States (such as in *Wild Seed* and *Kindred*); as well as analogous experiences (such as in the oppression of the Patternists and Missionaries in the *Patternist* series and of the humans in the *Xenogenesis* trilogy).

Yet, in addition to developing themes of the African Diaspora and engaging with issues of pan-nationalism, her narratives contribute to the discourse that concentrates on the question of colonized identity constructed, not by geographical displacement, but by colonial intrusion and resistance to the process, such as through nationalism. With her complex representations of black subjectivity, Butler thus places black experience into the wider context of anticolonial debates, engaging with the question, What if the intruder stays?[8]

The multilayered discourses of black women's subjectivities and anticolonial[9] identities in Butler's science fiction are embodied in her protagonists' experiences. Two examples can be found in Alanna, the protagonist in *Survivor* (1978), and Lilith, the central character in *Dawn* (1987)—the first book of the popular and widely discussed *Xenogenesis* trilogy (with *Adulthood Rites*, 1988; *Imago*, 1989). Both Alanna and Lilith are displaced geographically (they are both migrants) and at the same time find themselves confronted with colonial powers that control their environment. The two major effects of colonialism—migration/displacement and the local colonial encounter—are thus reconfigured and examined. As a young orphan, Alanna is adopted by Missionaries, a Christian group marginalized on Earth because they lack telepathic abilities—a skill that characterizes the ruling class, the Patternists. Alanna never adopts their limited worldview but adapts enough to be accepted. Her cultural flexibility is further tested when the Missionaries set out to colonize an alien planet, and a resisting tribe captures her. Again she needs to adapt enough to survive. Similarly, Lilith's interactions with colonizing aliens are defined by their power over her. Earth has been destroyed by a nuclear war, and aliens have made it habitable again. The price for the survival of humans is a "gene exchange" with the Oankali—cross-species breeding that would change the definition of "human" irreversibly. Lilith is chosen by the aliens to prepare other humans for this exchange.

Both protagonists find themselves in tense relationships with those who claim them and subsequently demand their loyalty. In *Survivor,* Alanna is caught between the humans' attempt to colonize the foreign planet and the resisting "natives," comprised of two warring tribes, the Garkohns and the Tehkohns. Her cultural alliance with the aliens culminates in the child she has with her Tehkohn mate, a child who later dies in the armed conflict between the Garkohns and the humans. Her transgression represents colonial imagination's worst nightmare: a colonizer "gone native" (see Loomba 136–39). In the *Xenogenesis* series, other humans reject Lilith's role in negotiating the colonization of the human species by the Oankali. Despite her efforts to ensure the survival of human elements within the forced cross-reproduction with the aliens, she is declared a traitor to the human race for even negotiating at all with the aliens. In both characters, the conflicts and contradictions of colonialism are played out. Their hybrid identities and ambiguous positions in their struggles with systems of power point to the limits of political organizing without engaging with the intersections of various discourses that inform the colonial experience.

Strategies of Resistance: Survival and the Recreation of Myths

The need for the colonized to define an identity separate from colonial powers underlies many anticolonial debates. Economic and political goals are accompanied by the desire to attain an "uncolonized mind," which would enable colonized peoples to define their identities not as victims/slaves but as agents. As Ashis Nandy reminds us in *The Intimate Enemy*, "we are concerned with a colonialism which survives the demise of empires," (Nandy xi) which does not simply "disappear" once the colonizers have "left." Instead, in addition to leaving lasting economic distributions, it bequeaths a "state of mind" (Nandy 1) that continues to exist in the consciousness of those colonized and the colonizers, and in remaining power structures cemented in economic and political domination. As Rajeswari Sunder Rajan states in *Real and Imagined Women*, "Thus, although colonialism may have been only a portion of the histories of postcolonial nations, its impingement upon their present social, political, economic and cultural situation is not simply a matter of 'legacies' . . . but of active, immediate and constitutive determinations" (Rajan 6–7). Creative resistance against hegemonic cultural and political practices, which has grown from these colonial relations, is explored within feminist and postcolonial discourse.[10] Resistance to colonial power, and the subjectivities that grow from it, are conceptualized in relation to representation (in literature) in various forms. Gayatri Chakravorty Spivak's now famous question "Can the Subaltern Speak?" which she raised in an article of the same name in 1988, examines the possible resistance of the oppressed. There is a need to uncover the absent text that can " 'answer one back' after the planned epistemic violence of the imperialist project" (Parry 36). Spivak demands a reading strategy that will uncover the silenced subject—the non-elite, subaltern woman, muted by both colonial ideologies and local patriarchal rule. The "subaltern consciousness" that, in the process of analyzing postcolonial identities, should be retrieved is less a positive, complete, self-defined identity, than a "subject-effect," a product of an "immense discontinuous network . . . of strands that may be termed politics, ideology, economics, history, sexuality, language, and so on" (Spivak, "Subaltern Studies" 213). She finds "pockets of non-co-operation in the dubious place of the free will of the (female) sexed subject" (Parry 41).

Spivak develops a "strategic essentialism," a situationally constructed, exclusive mechanism (the insistence of belonging to a colonized group and of speaking from that position) that enables the articulation of political interests. Spivak's approach to an anticolonial identity is anti-essential, yet committed to the recognition that subjectivity is shaped by specific historical experiences. Essentialism becomes a political strategy. "It is hard for the dogmatic philosopher to grasp that a strategist is a trickster, since there is no free play. In his view therefore, a strategic essentialism becomes a 'pessimistic essentialism'" (Spivak, "More on Power/Knowledge" 159).

Spivak's claim that the subaltern *cannot* speak, that it is not represented in any of the colonial exchanges, draws attention to the gendered and classed nature of colonial relations—it is the native *woman* and non-elite native man who are silenced in particular. This is not in the foreground of Homi Bhabha's uncovering of resisting native voices in his readings of colonial texts. He views the "mimicry" of the colonizer's discourse by the colonized as disruptive to colonial hegemony. By rearticulating the colonizer's texts (language, novels, speeches, plays, etc.), the colonial subject produces a "hybrid" text that ultimately undermines colonial discourse. Bhabha believes the subaltern *can* speak; he locates resistance in the voice that emerges "when the scenario written by colonialism is given a performance by the native that estranges and undermines the colonialist script" (Parry 36). As compelling as Bhabha's notion of resisting hybridity is, it does not account for those who are unable to participate in the colonial discourse.[11] Butler's characters face epistemic violence when their knowledge is discounted, but they nevertheless find ways to rearticulate their colonizers' discourse, thereby ensuring their voice is heard in colonial negotiations.

In Butler's work, her characters' confrontations with colonial powers (dominant entities trying to define the protagonists) take place through two basic experiences: diaspora and being colonized "at home." The process in which an invader colonizes the geographical and cultural space of the "native" is problematized especially in *Survivor*, where the Missionaries are typical colonizers, and in the *Xenogenesis* series, where the alien Oankali colonize Earth. Butler's short story "Bloodchild" deals with geographical dislocation and the experience of being colonized as well, yet complicates the diasporic theme by instilling a colonizing desire in the humans who have fled their home world. Butler makes it difficult to work with existing binary categories like oppressed/oppressor because of her subtle undermining of expectations. Her slightly ironic comments regarding the narrative set-up in

her award-winning short story "Bloodchild" reveal her acute awareness of colonial histories as they are reflected in most of traditional science fiction:[12]

> In earlier science fiction there tended to be a lot of conquest: you
> land on another planet and you set up a colony and the natives have
> their quarters some place and they come in and work for you. There
> was a lot of that, and it was, you know, let's do Europe and Africa
> and South America all over again. And I thought, no, no, if we do get
> to another world inhabited by intelligent beings, in the first place
> we're going to be at the end of a very, very, very, long transport
> line. . . . So you are going to have to make some kind of deal with the
> locals: in effect, you're going to have to pay the rent. (Interview with
> Kenan 498)

Accordingly, in her narratives, oscillating slave-master-slave relationships dominate. In *Survivor,* even though the Missionaries have themselves fled persecution by the telepathic Patternists, their mission includes the oppression of others. Ultimately, their colonizing aspirations
fail when the colonized "natives" end up controlling them.

At the same time as Butler's narratives display painful experiences
of colonization, they also offer strategies of resistance. The two main
strategies are *survival* as resistance, with an emphasis on adaptation rather than assimilation, and the *recreation of myths,* the rejection of Christian salvation myths that are part of Western ideology.
While the first strategy is part of the narrative content (it is expressed
in her figures' actions and motives), the latter takes place through
the narrations themselves—their structures, names, and figures. From
these interventions into colonial consciousness, Butler creates complex
models of agency.

Survival as Resistance

Butler's narratives of survival pay close attention to the process of
negotiating identities with a powerful opponent, exploring what Sara
Suleri calls the "peculiar intimacy" (111–13) of colonizer and colonized. Moments of selfhood and independence are always tested within
frameworks of oppression; thus, the Western ideal of an autonomous
individual self is demystified. We can understand colonialism to be a
"shared culture," imposed by the political separation of ruler and ruled,

which creates a "psychological state" of colonialism (Nandy 2) that reaches beyond the mere physical presence of an occupying force. As in Antonio Gramsci's concept of hegemony, the colonial system relies on a "cultural consensus" that concurrently represents a latent threat to the rulers, since it can be undermined by the ruled through an "alternative frame of reference" (Nandy 11). Therefore, while this "cultural consensus" ensures cultural subjugation through hegemony, it simultaneously enables moments of resistance.

A "counter-hegemony" can develop from resistance to the coercing of consent of the oppressed through ideological measures, as examined by Chela Sandoval in "U.S. Third World Feminism: The Theory and Method of Oppositional Consciousness" and *Methodology of the Oppressed*. Sandoval introduces the concept of a "differential consciousness" instead of an identity imposed by the colonizer. It has at its center the notion of creative alternatives developed from an alliance between various positions that are all defined as "different" from dominant culture: "[A theory of oppositional consciousness] focuses on identifying forms of consciousness in opposition, which can be generated and coordinated by those classes self-consciously seeking affective oppositional stances in relations to the dominant social order" ("U.S. Third World Feminism" 2). The process of identifying the ideological basis for social positions, and the ability to articulate positions counter to that basis, is what enables diverse groups to form alliances against a shared hegemonic culture.

Oppositional consciousness is crucial when reading Butler because, in their often traumatic experiences, her protagonists are never passive; they always undermine hegemonic colonial mechanisms. Consequently, their resistance is strategically aimed at survival first, seemingly at any cost. As Nandy explains, one effective form of resistance is not to engage in battle with the oppressor on his terms because doing so would keep the sense of self and conditions of living within the parameters of the colonizer's worldview. This resistance is reflected in Butler's female protagonists. They refuse to accept the terms we conventionally associate with heroic resistance: armored fight, honored death valued over dishonored capture, self-sacrifice, or resistance until death. Instead, they survive—and often force their opponents to meet them halfway. They mirror what Nandy describes as the "savage outsider," an agent of resistance "who is neither willing to be a player nor a counterplayer" (Nandy xiii), and who rejects the colonizer's construction of "her-self." It is significant, therefore, that Butler's protagonist in *Dawn* is Lilith, rather than one of the human "resisters" who fight the Oankali "the good old way." The resisters either die in the long run or lead isolated, sterile lives due to the infertility that the aliens inflict on any human who refuses to partake in the "genetic exchange."

Lilith's struggle with her colonizers is complicated by the fact that the Oankali save humanity from self-destruction by nuclear annihilation,[13] an action motivated by their continuous drive for xenogenesis, a process that will eradicate humanity's familiar selfhood as "human." The aliens do not kill or enslave humans they save from death by radiation—they value human life as much as their own. Their goal is not domination or exploitation but "trade," which involves change for *both* aliens and humans. The colonial process in *Dawn* thus is different from that in *Survivor,* where the Missionaries impose a racist and anthropocentric worldview onto their encounter with the native aliens. Nonetheless, the Oankali completely control the humans' every movement, their social interactions, and their reproduction (humans who refuse to take part in the crossbreeding are rendered infertile), and they "punish" violent resistance by putting rebellious humans into hypersleep. Throughout the trilogy, aided first by Lilith and later by two of her *construct* children (half-Oankali, half-human), the "resisters" insist on their right to self-determination. They negotiate for a separate human colony on Mars, which would enable them to procreate as purely "humans," and succeed in the end.

In Butler's development of Lilith as a complex protagonist, her narrative creates a conflicted reading experience. The antagonism the reader feels toward the Oankali is partly redeemed by the alien culture's values, which include the appreciation of diversity and the preservation of life at all costs; humans at times seem childish and violent in comparison.[14] The "resisters," who counter the colonization process with violence and single-mindedness, enact futile attempts to prevent the inevitable fusion with the oppressor, and their resistance results in disempowerment. In contrast, Lilith's negotiations represent the conflicting and painful relationship that exists between oppressor and oppressed: they deny the binary of black and white. The conflict of self-determination versus survival (often presented as the only options for the colonized) results in forced hybridity. Lilith and the others are given only one choice if they want to survive: to merge with the aliens as a species (those who refuse to have children with alien genes are rendered infertile by the Oankali) and as a culture (they are denied fundamental human practices, such as writing and the arts). With this predicament, which recalls practices during slavery in which the colonizers had access to and control over black women's bodies and reproduction, Butler emphasizes gendered aspects of colonial experience. When Lilith recognizes that any access to a precolonized subjectivity is impossible, and she engages in negotiations with the aliens, the reader is confronted with the reality of irrevocable change that colonialism brings.

Instead of an invincible and extremely clever science fiction hero who never surrenders and uses ingenuity to get out of any dangerous situation, Butler presents characters who are given a simple choice: survival by adaptation—that is, the ability to see change and to use it to one's advantage—or literal death of the self. In presenting her characters with the ability to survive, Butler defines agency for them; they learn to use any opportunity to act—to recognize and understand this opportunity. This survival-as-resistance mentality is reflected in Lilith's strategic thinking once she realizes that she cannot protect her fellow humans from occupation by the Oankali. Resisting a sense of guilt for cooperating with the colonizers, she reasons: "[She would wait] until she had some idea how to help them, how not to betray them, how to get them to accept their captivity, accept the Oankali, accept anything until they were sent to Earth. Then to run like hell at the first opportunity. . . . 'Learn and run!'" (*Dawn* 117–18).

In her constant negotiations, Lilith refuses to comply with the Oankali's colonizing of her body and her mind/soul. Although she compromises on certain issues, she sets limits as well, resisting their hegemony. Recognizing the inevitability of her colonization by the aliens, she does not go into the "combat mode" the reader might like her to take on; instead, her resistance lies in negotiating the limits of her colonization in order to retain a sense of self. For example, she must accept body modifications that heighten her senses and strength, but she sets the terms under which they take place. She represents what Nandy calls the archetypical survivor: "Seemingly [the archetypical survivor] makes all-round compromises, but he [sic] refuses to be psychologically swamped, co-opted or penetrated. Defeat, his [sic] response seems to say, is a disaster and so are the imposed ways of the victor" (Nandy 111).

In order to survive, both Lilith in the *Xenogenesis* series and Alanna in *Survivor* push boundaries and adapt to situations their imaginations could not have accepted before. Neither of them is ever a passive victim, patiently enduring abuse and oppression. As much as they compromise, they also set limits on the power of others over them—they resist, if necessary, with violence. In *Survivor*, when Alanna is in a conflict with Diut, a Tehkohn who later becomes her husband, survival as resistance takes a backseat to her violent refusal to comply: " 'And I have your bow and arrows.' She looked at me for a long time, her face already bruised and swollen, her eyes narrowed, the knife steady in her hand. 'Then use them to kill me,' she said. 'I will not be beaten again' " (*Survivor* 113).

While in the *Xenogenesis* trilogy the Oankali colonize others in order to advance their species through genetic exchanges, in *Survivor* Butler creates a colonizing people, the Missionaries, who leave their homeland's restrictive social order in search of freedom. Oppressed by the Patternists on Earth, they head out to claim a distant planet as their home. Their search for the "promised land" and their religious framework are reminiscent of people who came to colonize North America—to find a place where they could live unpersecuted by the dominant culture, while simultaneously colonizing the "primitives" they encountered. The Missionaries classify the alien native species, the Kohns, as subhuman and inferior. Kohns are divided into two tribes: Garkohns and Tehkohns. The Missionaries attempt to colonize the Garkohns whereas the Tehkohns live outside the territory claimed by the Missionaries. Although Butler initially introduces the Missionaries in terms of the conventional science fiction narrative of humans going out and colonizing planets and peoples, she undermines this reading by complicating the Missionaries' relationship to those they would colonize. The Kohns refuse the typical representation of colonized people who either die in heroic battle against the intruders or are assimilated into the rulers' culture. Instead, the Garkohns undermine the Missionaries' position as colonizers by doing a pretty good job of colonizing *them* in return, and the Tehkohns resist any contact with the humans.[15]

Alanna, the protagonist of *Survivor*, is "in-between" conflicting cultures, a boundary creature. Seemingly part of the colonizing culture, she rejects the Hegelian "master" identity and refuses to objectify the aliens the way the self-righteous humans do. Adopted by a Missionary couple as a child on Earth after struggling to survive in a chaotic environment dominated by violence and death, she never identified with their rigid worldview, yet she adapted to survive. Reflected in the title of the novel, Alanna's ability to conform externally to the realities of her environment without losing a sense of self is at the center of the narrative. Evoking Carole Boyce Davies's concept of migratory subjectivity (in *Black Women, Writing, and Identity*), Alanna develops into a "mental chameleon" (*Survivor* 117); she refuses to be assimilated and adapts only as much as is necessary. She is not subject to the prescriptions inherent in her environment; instead, she resists their definitions and creates her own identity. Thus, when Tehkohns kidnap her, her strategy is spelled out: "It would only be the Missionary experience again then. In exchange for food, shelter, and safety I would learn to say the right words and observe the right customs—change my cultural 'coloring' again and fade into Tehkohn society as much as I could" (*Survivor* 49). Alanna's strength lies in her acceptance of ambiguities, her rejection of an ideological model that would lock her within a particular cultural context and lead to assimilation. Instead, she assesses the conditions based on their situational specifications, not on an ultimate set of values. This ethos of flexibility and transgressing of boundaries is a particular form of hybridity that enables her to maintain a sense of self not separate from, but independent of, her colonizers.

At the same time, Butler does not romanticize survival as resistance; instead, she makes clear that the process of colonization always entails a price. Lilith, despite her decision to embrace the moment of change the Oankali bring to humankind and to accept her new hybrid identity, cannot forget the fact that it was only partly her choice:

> . . . Lilith had these flares of bitterness sometimes. They never seemed to affect her behavior, though often they frightened people. . . . "It's as though there's something in her trying to get out. Something terrible." Whenever the something seemed on the verge of surfacing, Lilith went alone into the forest and stayed away for days. [T]hey used to worry that she would leave and not come back. (*Adulthood Rites* 25)

Hybridity in colonial and postcolonial discourse is a contested term whose complex facets Butler explores in her narratives.[16] Alanna's strategy of developing a hybrid cultural knowledge, which allows her to retain a sense of self independent from the cultural environment in which she is forced to live, gives her agency. Also, her child with an alien "native" threatens racial purity for both the Missionaries and the Kohns, making hybridity a strategy of resisting ideologies of purity. The experiences of Butler's characters call into question the insistence on returning to a pure, precolonial identity as the only strategy of combating colonization of the mind, as advocated in some anticolonial discourses (especially those of nationalism).[17] This insistence locks the self into a binary power relationship with the colonizer since the self can only be defined as that which the colonizer is not, and it denies existing identities grown from complex relations with the oppressor. At the same time, forced reproduction results in a hybridity that the colonized has little control of, and contradicts the notion of self-determination. Since there is no future without the colonizer, Butler's characters often opt for hybridity.

Instead of defining separation from the colonial process as the only form of resistance, Butler raises complex questions about agency with her strategy of survival. These questions are reflected in the hybrid nature of her protagonists' offspring. Both Alanna's and Lilith's children are products of the colonial process and defy the notion of "pure" identity (the second and third book of the *Xenogenesis* trilogy are each narrated by one of Lilith's construct children). This hybridity makes Alanna and Lilith mothers of new peoples—and reflects the contradictory, heavily gendered (subject) position women hold in anticolonial debates and movements. As reproducer of the new colonized subject, the colonized woman's significance for both the colonizer and the colonized man is pivotal in deciding the colonized people's fate. In nationalism's rhetoric and in community politics that resist colonial rule, she is constructed as the mother of a precolonial people, which defines her in terms of the nationalism of the oppressed. Therefore, her political subjectivity often is reduced to a symbol in the nationalist discourse that "repeatedly invoke[s] a glorious pre-colonial past or traditions (symbolised by 'culture', the family, language, religion and women) trampled upon by the invader" (Loomba 196). Her role in the anticolonial struggle is defined as mother or wife of the colonized revolutionary; she is "called upon to literally and figuratively reproduce the nation" (Loomba 216). At the same time, she is utilized by the colonizer as an object of oppression (by her own patriarchal culture) who then needs to be rescued by the "civilized" colonizer.[18] The colonized woman is thus both "cultural *essence* and cultural *differences*" (Loomba 218, emphasis hers). Both Lilith and Alanna resist the reductive definition as mother by either colonizers or colonized and instead develop identities in relation to, but not dependent on, those who are trying to control their social status.

Survival as resistance here is clearly manifested in adaptation, not assimilation. Assimilation ideologically emphasizes change determined by a dominant culture that is redeemed by the promise of acceptance. In contrast, adaptation denies this whitewashing of colonized identities and acknowledges the violence that forces change, while retaining a sense of separateness. Butler leaves the reader with provocative questions about her strategy of survival: Where are the boundaries of surrender after which the self is lost? What are the limits of negotiation? How can forced change, in cultural and social traditions, be accepted without losing identity? And how can one resist colonization of home and culture without risking violent subjugation by the oppressor?

Narratives of Resistance: Rewriting Religious and Cultural Myths
The theme of survival through adaptation as a means of retaining an "uncolonized mind" is accompanied by the reinscription of Christian salvation myths in the *Xenogenesis* series and in *Survivor,* at times in ironic ways. Most colonial processes are driven and justified by religious conflicts, such as when religious minorities flee the home country to settle new territory and colonize the people they encounter, or when religious "superiority" lends an ideological justification for the economic exploitation of colonized countries and cultures. Historically, the colonization of the South/East by the North/West was dominated by a Christian value system, which was employed to rationalize the domination of non-Christian societies (see Loomba 105–6). Thus, rewriting Christian myths is an important narrative strategy in anticolonial writings.[19] Especially through her female figures and her hybrid creatures, who defy any ideological link to Genesis, Butler reinscribes Christian myths and destabilizes the legitimacy of the West's religious narratives of domination. In Lilith, whose name already represents a challenge to Christian doctrine[20]—as Adam's first wife, she "was unsatisfactory because she would not obey him" (Butler in McCaffery, "Interview with Octavia E. Butler" 68)—Butler creates a mother of a new race whose children defy categorization as "human," while insisting on their right to their humanity. As Donna Haraway observes: "At the end of *Dawn,* Butler has Lilith . . . pregnant with the child of five progenitors, who

come from two species, at least three genders, two sexes, and an indeterminate number of races. Adam's rib would be poor starting material to mold this new mother of humanity or her offspring" (Haraway, *Primate Visions* 378). While Butler's descriptions of Lilith are reminiscent of conventional iconography of the holy Mother of God, they also represent an appropriation of the patriarchal image: "The woman was not beautiful. Her broad, smooth face was usually set in an expression of solemnity, even sadness. . . . It made her look saintly. A mother. Very much a mother. And something else" (*Adulthood Rites* 37).[21]

The Oankali choose Lilith, a woman of color, as a mediator between humans and aliens. Her position in human society does not retain structural power; thus her perspective on human interactions is necessarily flexible. In her position as other she is "privileging (rather than repressing) . . . 'the other in ourselves' " (Henderson 147). Lilith is confronted with her lover's realization of how her social experiences awarded her with her role as mediator: "Do you understand why they chose you—someone who desperately doesn't want the responsibility, who doesn't want to lead, who is a woman?" (*Dawn* 157).[22] As Michelle Green observes, Lilith, "after years of oppression by other humans . . . has less prejudice toward the aliens and a stronger appreciation of the need for change. While she resents the unequal power relationships between Oankali and humans, she resents as well the unequal relationships among the humans she supervises" (Green 187). Lilith shares this position at the margin with Alanna in *Survivor.* Alanna's refusal to adopt the mentality of the colonizer might be rooted in her experience of living in the boundary territories before the Missionaries adopted her. She has resisted oppression by the Patternists, not by turning to the religious culture of salvation myths, as the Missionaries do, but through constant negotiations and adaptations to things and situations previously unknown. Having experienced further discrimination by the Missionaries, and having dealt with their expectations in return for shelter, her understanding of power relations enables her to adapt to the alien Tehkohn culture.

In *Survivor,* the Western salvation narrative of a Paradise for the Good (which echoes United States society's ideological origin as the "City upon the Hill" valorized by John Winthrop in 1630, which marks the God-designated position of Puritan society as chosen and unique) is exposed as a colonial framework for racism, hypocrisy, and dishonesty, and as a justification of oppressive social practices. The Missionaries name the planet they colonize "Canaan" (*Survivor* 37), the Promised Land in the Bible.[23] Instead of merely searching for a safe place to settle, removed from the oppression they endured from the Patternists, the Missionaries seek to spread the holy image of their God through the continuation of their race. Faithful to their belief—which prescribes the worship of the One, including the duty of representing the "sacred image" (Haraway, *Primate Visions* 379)—the Missionaries separate themselves from the aliens. They arrogantly categorize the aliens as subhuman because they do not correspond to the "sacred image." The Missionaries understand the aliens as a caricature of themselves, echoing familiar patterns of European Christians who colonized the "heathens": "[Their religion] had helped them justify their belief that the Kohn were lower creatures—higher than apes, but lower than true humans who have been made in the image of God" (*Survivor* 5). Their religious mission gives the Missionaries' domination "cultural meaning" (their belief that they are superior to the natives), and therefore "colonialism proper can be said to have begun" (Nandy 6).

The "master" identity of the Missionaries makes it impossible for them to consider the Garkohns as anything but passive victims, whom they believe to be in awe of the superior race. Yet the beautiful and fertile valley in which they settle is treacherous; the delicious fruit *meklah* that the Garkohns offer the settlers when they arrive—part of their own daily diet—leads to physical addiction. Withdrawal attempts are usually fatal, but humans are unaware of this danger until it is too late: "People were not even conscious of being addicted unless they left the valley—went into the mountains where the tree did not grow. Or unless they simply chose not to eat" (*Survivor* 27). The Missionaries refuse to entertain the notion that these "primitives," the Garkohns, might have some (physical/cultural/political) power over them, as this possibility is inconceivable to their worldview. They deny their basic fear that

the colonized will reject the [cultural] consensus [of the Missionaries' superiority] and, instead of . . . becoming the counterplayers of the rulers according to the established rules, will discover an alternative frame of reference within which the oppressed do not seem weak, degraded and distorted men [sic] . . . [and that] the subjects might begin to see their rulers as morally and culturally inferior, and feed this information back to the rulers. (Nandy 11)

The counter-domination—counter-hegemony—by the Garkohns explicitly lays out the inherent structures of colonialism, demonstrating that the effects of colonization are not limited to the oppressed culture but also change the culture of the colonizer. Butler makes clear that encounters in what Mary Louise Pratt calls the "contact zone" (Pratt 6) affect *both* colonizer and colonized. Pratt defines the "contact zone" as "the space of colonial encounters, the space in which peoples geographically and historically separated come into contact with each other and establish ongoing relations, usually involving conditions of coercion, radical inequality, and intractable conflict" (6). The Missionaries' attempt at dominating that "contact zone" with their hegemonic belief system backfires. Butler undermines the binary of colonizer-colonized and its inherent power relations by creating a complex web of power structures in her narratives: the dominated one sets out to dominate, and in turn ends up being dominated.[24]

Canaan turns into a parody of the Garden of Eden; its promise to the settlers is a lie. The scene of temptation that precedes the Fall in Genesis is ironically reenacted when the leader of the Garkohns uses the "forbidden" fruit temptation against Alanna, who resists the false paradise. He tells her: "Do exactly as I say, and you will live. Do anything else, and you will die. Now. Pick the fruit" (*Survivor* 11). Alanna finds allies in the Tehkohn people, whose eventual acceptance of difference stands in contrast to the Missionaries' bigoted ignorance and the Garkohns' desire not only to resist but to dominate the colonizers. Butler again utilizes the perspective of the other to undermine the dominant culture's norm when Diut, a Tehkohn, tries to get used to Alanna's appearance: "There was a strange beauty to her when one did not try to fit her into the Kohn image—when one did not see her as a twisted Kohn" (*Survivor* 150).

Butler's figures refuse to become part of the patriarchal structures around them and often create kinship relations that transcend Western society's struggle for power. This "other order of difference" is also symbolized in the "resistance to the imperative to recreate the sacred image of the same" (Haraway 378–379). The other, in all its diversity, becomes the standard for subjectivity—broken, irregular, and fragmented, not unified and whole. Alanna sets her child against the "image of the same" and dares to modify the sacred image, the self-definition of the Missionaries as "humans": "You know Diut is a man, as you are a man. Otherwise, how could I have born his child?" (*Sur-*

vivor 185). Alanna evokes the ultimate fear of the colonizer: hybridity. As a racial and cultural (ideological) boundary transgression, hybridity undermines difference and thus makes it hard for the colonizer (and colonized) to separate from it (Loomba 119). In a similar fashion, Lilith's offspring, the construct children in the *Xenogenesis* series, whose genes are half-alien, redefine what it means to be human. Their existence undermines the naturalization of the category, thus challenging those categories our own order is based on, such as gender (her children have three sexes). Unlike in *Survivor,* here it is the colonized who fear an eradication of their identity through the Oankali's hegemony—for the colonizing aliens, "hybridization" is the goal of their colonizing project. In either case, hybridity poses a threat to purity and the ability to reject difference. The complex resistance of Butler's protagonists to a "colonized mind" represents a form of agency that defies victimization without trivializing the extent of exploitation involved in colonization. By placing these strategies of boundary crossing within the imaginative context of science fiction, Butler takes part in the reconstruction of our future that is firmly rooted in histories of past and present:

> Being in the 'beyond', then, is to inhabit an intervening space, as any dictionary will tell you. But to dwell 'in the beyond' is also . . . to be part of a revisionary time, a return to the present to redescribe our cultural contemporaneity; to reinscribe our human, historic commonality; *to touch the future on its hither side.* In that sense, then, the intervening space 'beyond', becomes a space of intervention in the here and now. (Bhabha 7, emphasis his)

Butler's main contribution to the feminist discourse on difference and power relations is her principle of boundary crossing as resistance to colonization and domination. The familiar order of power relationships based on dualisms is not sustainable in Butler's imaginative social interactions. Instead, the other becomes inseparable from the self, thereby threatening clear distinctions and ideological territories. The other, the alien, takes up the position of normative existence while the self suddenly becomes other. By destabilizing boundaries and shifting narrative perspectives, Butler challenges the legitimacy of positions of power, and in so doing, her narratives intersect with postmodern notions of shifting subjectivities and changing cultural identities.

Without conflating diverse experiences of colonization, Butler's science fiction challenges aspects of anticolonial debates dominated by political stakes based in historical realities, enabling us to reimagine established boundaries of identities. Butler's fiction engages in several discourses on anticolonial resistance and subjectivities. This strategy of "simultaneity of discourses" in Butler's writing enables her to conceptualize political resistance in connection with black women's subject positions. In her work, we can see how the experience of having to "change [one's] cultural 'coloring' again" is a source of agency as much as of oppression, and her work argues for the importance of considering black women's imaginative writing as a source for refiguring postcolonial relations.

2. The Alien in Us

Metaphors of Transgression in the Work of Octavia E. Butler

If you deny any affinity with another person or kind of person, if you declare it to be wholly different from yourself . . . you may hate it, or deify it; but in either case you have denied its spiritual equality, and its human reality. You have made it into a thing, to which the only possible relationship is a power relationship. And thus you have fatally impoverished your own reality. You have, in fact, alienated yourself.

—Ursula Le Guin, "American SF and the Other"

Octavia Butler's fiction acknowledges the complex construction of gender in relation to factors such as race and class, and the desire to find representations that correspond to one's own experiences, not those of a "master identity" that constructs them as other.[1] Butler's writing shares with feminist theories examined here the insistence on multiple subject positions grounded in particular historical moments, the idea of "identity as a site of differences" (Braidotti, *Nomadic Subjects* 157), not sameness. In accordance with these theories, Butler conceptualizes multiple subjectivity as an element that has grown from fragmentation, displacement, and loss. In its contradictory makeup and often painful experiences, this multiple subjectivity creates spaces of disjunction that carry the potential for resistance.

The focus of this analysis of Butler's representations of difference will be on her dismantling of the Western construction of dualisms of self and other, based on categories of sameness (normative) and difference (deviant), which form a relationship of power that is naturalized and not open to change (see Plumwood 47–48). Butler counters the construction of dualisms by assuming multiple, contradictory notions of self that undermine the binary and by creating an alternative way to view difference—as an essential part of the self, not something to create boundaries against. These approaches result in the strategy of embracing difference: neither upholding nor denying it, but accepting it as a part of identity. Her writings respond to Audre Lorde's call for "new patterns of relating across difference" (Lorde, "Age, Race, Class, and Sex" 123): "Now we must recognize differences among women who are our equals, neither inferior nor superior, and devise ways to use each other's difference to enrich our visions and our joint struggles" (122).

In Butler's work, difference is used as a tool of creativity to question multiple forms of repression and dominance: she destabilizes categories of gender as well as race and exposes the process of differentiation. In doing so, she distances herself from feminist writings (theoretical and fictional) that celebrate the general category of "woman," as well as from those who, in a simplified fashion, romanticize ethnic and cultural heritages. Butler writes against mainstream perception, in which the subjectivity of women of color, instead of being conceptualized within its own framework, is understood as sentimental and personal. She always remains critical of unambiguous and seemingly unproblematic approaches to dealing with difference and power. Instead of creating fictional relations based on one-dimensional theoretical models, Butler's narratives are infused with contradictions and dilemmas that mirror unresolved conflicts within feminist discourse. They explore how generalized theoretical implications clash with the specificity of situations in which characters find themselves, and with desires and drives that interfere with simple solutions.

Butler's narratives interweave two main contradictory themes: colonial experiences and resistance (as discussed in Chapter 1), and affirmative encounters with difference—the focus of this chapter. So while the context often is that of a colonial encounter, Butler is interested in exploring the ways in which difference is conceptualized not as oppositional but as complementary to identity.[2] Difference is solidified through *markers* that identify it as nonnormative. These markers in turn are defined by *boundaries* that enclose the subject. Butler's writing is filled with symbolic boundaries that represent the attempt to define the self, to negotiate identity in relation to difference. These boundaries and their markers constantly shift, making it impossible to establish a subject position based on a stable identity.

Thus, boundary crossing is the main characteristic of Butler's representations of difference, the main "ingredient" of her fluid subjectivity, which emphasizes a denaturalization of categories—it means refusing the limits set by those in power, as well as those derived from one's own prior experiences. Boundaries that are subject to negotiations in Butler's fiction manifest themselves externally as well as internally, and they are symbolically represented on various levels: from physical differences between species, which in turn are converted into social structures (in *Patternmaster, Wild Seed, Mind of My Mind,* and the *Xenogenesis* series), to mental networks (such as that of the Patternists), sensory fusion (in *Parable of the Sower*), and permeability of temporal dimensions (in *Kindred*). Butler undermines the establishment of these boundaries in two ways: through transgression and transformation of divisions of difference, and through integration and acceptance of the other. The *embracing of difference,* in which these two mechanisms (deconstruction of existing structures and acceptance of that which is not-I) are combined, makes a clear demarcation of "I" and "not-I" (the dualism of "us" versus "them") impossible. It destabilizes the discursive opposition of identity and difference (the basis for dualisms in Western thought) and constitutes the main hopeful element in Butler's writing.

Butler creates various figures that transgress boundaries in her narratives. Aliens occupy a special position: they signify boundary crossing per se—as a metaphor, they *are* difference. They are the focus of the first part of this chapter. The second part examines Butler's deconstruction of categories such as race, gender, and sexuality through her alien figures and through the relationships between humans, and between humans and aliens. Like her aliens, female figures in Butler's narratives engage in boundary crossing, often triggered by "states of emergency" (Zaki 242) that place them outside conventional social formations and force them to cross boundaries to prevent the destruction of themselves and others. Her female characters are the focus of the last part of this chapter. Butler emphasizes contradictions her heroines have to negotiate—there are no simple choices or stable positions in the character's interactions. This rejection of any one-dimensional theoretical approach is one of Butler's most powerful contributions to feminist debates, and her "alien constructions"—aliens, hybrids, and other denaturalized subjectivities—which grow from her theoretically heterogeneous stand, serve as metaphors of transgression.

Representations of Difference: Deconstructing the Alien as the Other

One of the main symbolic representations of difference in science fiction is the "un-human being" (Scholes and Rabkin 179). "Un-human beings in science fiction take either of two forms. Either they are constructs, artificial creations such as androids, robots, or golems, or they are the products of some unearthly evolution—aliens" (Scholes and Rabkin 179). These un-humans take many shapes: cyborgs, constructed from both organic and inorganic materials; artificial intelligence; independently thinking computers, which often appear in the form of androids; and the phenomenon of the doppelgänger, often a nonmaterial apparition that is physically explicable. Traditionally, aliens and other un-human beings have signified the other in a dualistic relation to the human hero. In *Aliens and Others,* Jenny Wolmark observes that the alien is therefore one of the most commonly employed metaphors: "it enables difference to be constructed in terms of binary oppositions which reinforce relations of dominance and subordination" (Wolmark 2). Feminist science fiction, together with other postmodern science fiction, moves beyond the dualistic construction of self/other in the representations of aliens and uses the science fiction metaphor of the alien to "explore the way in which the deeply divisive dichotomies of race and gender [and class] are embedded in the repressive structures and relations of dominance and subordination" (Wolmark 27).

Destabilizing Human Identity

Butler's un-human figures supersede conventional definitions: she incorporates elements of fantasy and mythology, thereby transforming otherwise familiar science fiction mechanisms to utilize them for new definitions and approaches. Consequently, it is not only the moral and ethical component of human-machine constructions and relationships that she addresses.[3] Butler's constructions take place on a biological level that mediates human experiences through the body. She confronts the reader not just with creatures, either man-made or alien, but also with hybrids between aliens and humans, with human mutants, and with humans with apparently supernatural abilities such as telepathy and shape-shifting. Her constellations question the (seemingly) most notable element of our identity: our humanness. Instead of accepting humanist assumptions, she asks: What is *human?* How is this category constituted, and how is it symbolically estranged/complicated?[4]

As earlier studies of feminist science fiction demonstrate,[5] feminist science fiction since the 1970s enhances the understanding of *man-made* through portrayal of *woman-made* technology (and ideology); in these texts, in a much more radical fashion, universal "humanness" itself is disclosed as a patriarchal concept—and as a white-supremacist one. Butler uses science fiction to create new categories based on biological pre-givens and thus destabilizes essentialist notions of "humanness." Butler's strange, intelligent species who are agents of change, such as the Oankali, challenge our ideas of what constitutes a (human) subject. These new forms of "humanness" are presented, not necessarily as "better" (what is *better?*), but as *different,* as revealed in an exchange between an Oankali and Lilith: " 'And you think destroying what was left of our cultures will make us better?' 'No. Only different' " (*Dawn* 32). By questioning the category "human," especially through mutation in *Clay's Ark* and through the fusion of alien and human genes in the *Xenogenesis* trilogy and *Survivor,* Butler problematizes any pre-given notion we have about our identity and anything about it that we might take for granted. "The *real,* nothing else than a *code of representation,* does not (cannot) coincide with the lived or the performed" (Trinh, *Woman, Native, Other* 94; emphasis hers). Representations, then, become tools of redefinition.

In her destabilizing of boundaries, Butler crosses the physical boundary between un-human and human creatures, and thus undermines the privileged position of humans. The constructs in the *Xenogenesis* series, who are born from the union of humans and Oankali ("true" aliens), and the Clayarks—human mutants that develop from an alien virus—are examples of this type of boundary crossing. Butler also approaches the definition of humanness through internal and often psychic boundary transgressions. She thus problematizes human characteristics that go beyond visual (i.e. physical) markers. Patternists, with their mental network, and Anyanwu, the shape-shifter in *Wild Seed,* are examples of these inner "un-humanizations." The biological metaphor that describes the "process by which humanity becomes other to itself" (Wolmark, *Aliens and Others* 40) is complicated by Butler's depiction of human violence based on familiar categories of sexual and racial difference, such as rape and racial murder, which she juxtaposes with her alien constructions.[6] Existing categories, insufficient for defining various life-forms, are exposed to be nothing but mechanisms for delimitation. Both inner and outer boundary transgressions become apparent in the elusiveness of Doro's figure in the *Patternist* series: "A mutation. A kind of parasite. A god. A devil. You'd be surprised at some of the things people have decided I was" (*Mind* 88). Butler writes against the liberal "general call for diversity, pluralism" (Crosby 131), which keeps power relations intact, by refusing to accept the boundaries of categorized differences.[7]

Otherworldly Creatures

Many descriptions of aliens in traditional science fiction narratives are limited to representing either warring opponents, who resist colonization of their planet by the heroes or terrorize a sector of the universe; or gentle, often dumb creatures, who, as "sympathetic aliens" (Le Guin, "American SF and the Other" 209), shyly shake the hero's hand in farewell.[8] There is no identity confirmation through acts of demarcation and exclusion, such as colonization or wars against other species, in Butler's work.[9] She does not offer clear distinctions between "us" and "them"; she presents an other that is, or will become, a part of the "we." Often without a choice to act, forced into passivity, her characters are subject to those at whom the (metaphorical) laser gun is usually pointed (see Butler in Kenan 498). By constantly shifting narrative positions, Butler tries to break from a tendency toward separate identifications that is based on viewing difference as an inherent division.

Both extraterrestrials and mutants in Butler's texts take on diverse forms: the humanoid Kohns have fur whose changing colors express emotions, and whose base color determines their status within the society. The Clayarks' form resembles a Sphinx; the massive T'lics in "Bloodchild" are worm- or insect-like. Sensory organs that are reminiscent of tentacles cover the humanoid torsos of the Oankali in the *Xenogenesis* series. Clayarks are mutated humans whose species is especially characterized by their drives and animal-like sensory organs —making them the antipode to the "civilized" human. Patternists are human but have "un-human" abilities that enable them to enslave others and to program them like robots.

The Oankali are classic aliens: they are intelligent, and despite some humanoid elements (they have both arms and legs and walk upright), they possess plenty of attributes from the realm of the abject (tentacles being the most prominent). They are unique mainly because of their

goal to blend genetically with humans, to create a diffusion of boundaries. The Kohns, aliens in *Survivor*, accept a human into their society
and integrate the offspring of this "miscegenation" into their community. The offspring of the T'lics, "bug-monsters" typical for science fiction, are carried to term by human bodies. Here, the differences of the
dominated other become part of the self—"they" become part of "us,"
and the self becomes a carrier of difference. This blurring of boundaries, the growing inability to draw clear distinctions between self and
other, is what constitutes the most threatening and fascinating aspect
of Butler's alien constructions.

In her dealings with difference, Butler does not resort to liberal fantasies of mutual acceptance based on enlightened and rational minds.
Instead of creating either a pleasant and romantic first encounter or
a (at times regrettable) conquest of the noble savage/alien, she begins
her *Xenogenesis* narrative by acknowledging the threatening aspect
of inviting the other "in." After a long period of imprisonment by her
anonymous captors, Lilith, the protagonist in *Dawn*, is confronted visually with what she thinks are her human opponents. Her first contact
with an alien describes an emotional turmoil of familiar fears and unfamiliar facts: the realization that the one looked at is not human, combined with the negative associations that this realization generates,
turns her meeting with the Oankali into the "ultimate confrontation
with the Other" (McCaffery, "An Interview with Octavia E. Butler" 56).
The woman's reaction to the alien recalls fears of what Julia Kristeva
terms "the abject": creatures most alien to human self-perception remind us of the fundamental psychic fear of that which threatens our
illusion of a whole self, the primal fear of the (m)other.

"Oh god," she whispered. And the hair—the whatever-it-was—
moved. Some of it seemed to blow towards her as though in a wind
—though there was no stirring of air in the room. She frowned,
strained to see, to understand. Then, abruptly, she did understand.
She backed away, scrambled around the bed and to the far wall.
When she could go no farther, she stood against the wall, staring at
him. Medusa. Some of the "hair" writhed independently, a nest of
snakes startled, driven in all directions. . . . The tentacles were elas-
tic. At her shout, some of them lengthened, stretching toward her.
She imagined big, slowly writhing, dying night crawlers stretched
along the sidewalk after the rain. She imagined small, tentacled sea

slugs—nudibranchs—grown impossibly to human size and shape, and obscenely, sounding more like a human being than some humans. (*Dawn* 11-12)[10]

By foregrounding the fears that accompany a confrontation with difference, Butler critically addresses the "philosophy of 'differentiation'" (Trinh, *Woman, Native, Other* 82) that contains "diversity" within the ideology of domination. Different reactions of humans to aliens' otherness include fear, contempt, depreciation, and ignorance. Humans' definition of what constitutes humanness, therefore, is always the standard of measure. Human reactions to difference differ from those of the aliens due to a fundamental fear of the other, a fear to become what is marginalized from socially accepted experiences. Thus Rane in *Clay's Ark* justifies her rejection of the Clayark community: "'I can't stand them,' she said. 'They're not human. Their children don't even look human . . .'" (*Ark* 145).

Difference and Power Structures: The "Politics of Differentiation"
In Butler's narratives, manifestation of this human/un-human demarcation does not take place in typical science fiction pattern, and it disrupts the familiar narrative of the successful (or tragically unsuccessful) erection of boundaries. Positions of power are switched; the other becomes the norm, becomes the position from which decisions are made and from which control over others is exerted. By placing "us" *into* the other, Butler undermines the ideology of separatism. Instead, the reader is forced into Henderson's concept of a dialogue with the aspects of "otherness" within the self, "the other[s] in ourselves" (161).

The inevitable attempts of humans to dominate an other are placed within an uncomfortably *biological* framework by Butler. In the *Xenogenesis* series, the Oankali detect a deadly combination of intelligence and hierarchical tendency in humans, which causes the fatal nuclear war on earth. It is a genetic condition that predestines human self-destruction. Butler presents the destruction of human habitat and humanity's own species, not as a process embedded in a historical context (such as the Cold War), but as an inevitable given. So an Oankali evaluates the possibility of a Mars colony, where humans could procreate without the aliens, as follows: "'[Y]ou will give them the tools to create a civilization that will destroy itself as certainly as the pull of gravity will keep their new world in orbit around its sun.' . . . Its certainty was an Oankali certainty. A certainty of the flesh. They had read Human genes and reviewed Human behavior. They knew what they knew" (*Rites* 233–34). Butler seems to assess human nature as inherently violent: the "Human Contradiction," developed through evolution, privileges *hierarchical* behavior (which contains difference) over *intelligence* and results in an inability to tolerate (especially physical) differences. Butler elaborates on this violent propensity in *Dawn* when Lilith has to confront hostilities from the people whom she awakes from suspended animation to prepare them for life with the aliens. Increasingly, she needs to defend herself against the growing animosity of members of her own species, once they realize that she has had contact with the Oankali, the other, and as a result has changed physically.[11] The conflict seems a foregone conclusion. Even before everybody in the group is awakened, Lilith has to consider possible violent acts, fend off rape attempts, and cope with fights (*Dawn* 115–96, 199–241). Intolerance, magnified through loss of control and fear at the realization that difference cannot be contained, suppresses any rationality: "We're nervous. We don't know what's going to happen. We're scared. You shouldn't have to take the brunt of our feelings, but . . . but you're the different one. Nobody knows how different" (*Dawn* 214).

Based on their frameworks of genetic dispositions, both the *Patternist* and the *Xenogenesis* series paint desolate, dystopian outlooks for the future, especially in their depiction of human relations. Thus the mental ability of the Patternists is hereditary, even inbred, as are the colors of the Kohns' fur in *Survivor*, which decide the social status of members. Diut, a Tehkohn, reflects in *Survivor:* "Respect for the blue was inborn with us. No one questioned it. It seemed impossible not to value it" (*Survivor* 109). These genetic markers produce categories that define not only human relationships but also social orders. Like the hierarchies of gender and race in Western cultures, these markers indicate the differences on which hierarchical structures are based. Discrimination and slavery are present in these worlds as much as in ours; since differences are connected to values and functions, racism and sexism seem to be transferred onto different contents without being truly transformed. By constructing these alien worlds, Butler posits that it is not differences themselves that are foundational, but *categories*. She destabilizes the naturalization process that defines difference as a given and instead points out that how we *deal* with difference is what creates the binary of self and other.

FEAR VERSUS EMBRACING OF DIFFERENCE

Unlike humans, many of Butler's un-human beings react positively to difference and consequently do not attempt to shut out humans; instead, they try to achieve unification and/or mix with humans—*their* Unknown. In "Bloodchild," the T'lic, T'Gatoi, points out to the human boy the fundamentally different reactions of the two species when encountering each other: the humans' attempt to colonize the aliens fails, and instead they find themselves forced into a symbiotic relationship with the alien species. In *Survivor,* the Missionaries accept the help of the Garkohns yet view them as inferior and avoid any rapprochement of their cultures. In contrast, Alanna's integration into Tehkohn society, coupled with the love her Tehkohn-mate Diut feels for her, demonstrates an acceptance of her otherness. Unlike the people of his tribe, Diut does not judge Alanna based on her otherness; instead, he is attracted to her because of her difference: "My difference repelled her. Her differences interested me. She was ugly almost beyond description, and yet her appearance was as natural to her as mine was to me" (*Survivor* 72). It is through Alanna's and Diut's acceptance of their differences that the Missionaries' and Kohns' racist separatism is transgressed. This starting point of each encounter between her creatures is crucial for Butler—a basic acceptance that other forms of being exist, outside one's own realm of experience.

The main narrative developments in the *Xenogenesis* series also reflect the conflicting approaches to dealing with difference that Butler explores: while humans categorically reject any transformation of their form and immediately translate difference into categories and delimitation, the Oankali view difference as elementary to the existence of their species. The aliens understand the active element in establishing difference; they recognize it as a *practice* that ensures the destabilization of identity. By welcoming and appreciating connections with the other and simultaneously deconstructing familiar categories, the Oankali embrace difference. Lilith explains the contrasting standpoints of aliens and humans to her construct son, Akin.

"Human beings fear difference," Lilith had told him once. "Oankali crave difference. Humans persecute their different ones, yet they need them to give themselves definition and status. Oankali seek difference and collect it. They need it to keep themselves from stagnation and overspecialization. If you don't understand this, you will.

You'll probably find both tendencies surfacing in your own behavior. . . . When you feel a conflict, try to go the Oankali way. Embrace difference." (*Rites* 80)

The contrasting concepts of difference that Butler describes engage with women of color's criticism of difference as pre-given or natural. Constructed difference is defined by those in power in ways that do not threaten their own positions but instead confirm their identity; it is "a difference or an otherness that will not go so far as to question the foundation of their beings and makings" (Trinh, *Woman, Native, Other* 88). Instead of denying difference, Trinh contends, those in power control it, place it into a framework of stasis: "We no longer wish to erase your difference, We demand, on the contrary, that you remember and assert it. At least, to a certain extent" (89). Here, difference is treated simply as a counterpoint to identity and ends up controlled by sameness, as we see in the liberal discourse on "multiculturalism" that "celebrates" difference by creating spaces where it can be contained (e.g., on "special days" and in "special events" where "authentic" multicultural practices are displayed). As Trinh sees it, the view of differences as "pre-givens" grew out of dualistic Western thought, which locks the notion of difference into relations of power: "The differences made *between* entities comprehended as absolute presences—hence the notions of *pure origin* and *true* self—are an outgrowth of a dualistic system of thought" (90, emphasis hers). These "politics of differentiation" that Trinh Minh-ha theorizes create hierarchies by presenting difference as a static opposition to sameness/self.

Difference can be reconceptualized in a way that perceives identities, not as stable and autonomous, but as multiple and changing. This concept of difference constitutes a fundamental threat to the "illusion of continuity" (94) and wholeness that our craving for sameness instills in us, and it is reflected in Butler's boundary crossing, which renders distinctions between "I" and "i" impossible.

Thus the binary of self/other, identity/difference, is undermined by the notions of multiplicity, layers, and flexibility that are part of Butler's narratives.[12] Agency and political resistance become possible when the sense of fragmentation and separation is overcome by accepting difference as *part* of the self. Most interesting for this analysis is how the notion of multiple selves undermines binary constructions of self/other, in that the self has no sense of stability beyond context. It is the situation that forms the self, and not vice versa—difference then becomes less a threat than an orientation for the self. Since the formation of subjectivity is a fluid process, with no coherent closure, difference becomes relative as well. Boundaries become negotiable instead of forming demarcations for rejection.

DIFFERENCE AS IDENTITY — BECOMING THE OTHER

The concept of layers of multiple identity components is reflected in the Oankali. They live for constant transformation of their species through "gene trading" (*Dawn* 39), that is, reproduction with other life forms. As Eric White points out in "The Erotics of Becoming," the Oankali possess a "genetically-encoded instruction to become other" (403)—their inevitable change as a species represents their embrace of the other per se. Motivation for gene trading grows, not from a desire for power over others, but from the search for permanent diversity and adoption of new genetically induced abilities that will facilitate the next gene trade. "The Oankali thus become other in order to . . . become other" (White 404).[13]

The Oankali define themselves, not through their form, but through the genetic exchange—therefore they *are* difference. The constitution of identity through physical appearances does not exist, and therefore there is also no exclusion of an other: the "not-I" has no physical markers. The alien species does not choose one form, a sacred image, to define themselves; instead, the very *tool* that enables change is their defining trait. So the only consistent make-up of the species is a specific cell: the "organelle" that carries the potential for gene manipulation, which is transferred with every gene trade. The group in each generation that does not partake in the latest gene exchange and therefore differs in form from the other Oankali, are still considered Oankali: "It was as Oankali as any intelligent being constructed by an ooloi to incorporate the Oankali organelle within its cells" (*Rites* 209). Identification through and with the possibility of gene trade is mirrored in the name of the alien species: "One of the meanings of Oankali is gene trader. Another is that organelle—the essence of ourselves, the origin of ourselves. Because of that organelle, the ooloi can perceive DNA and manipulate it precisely" (*Dawn* 39).[14] The Oankali have no choice but to give in to the drive for constant development: "We do it naturally. We *must* do it. It renews us, enables us to survive as an evolving species instead of specializing ourselves into extinction or stagnation" (*Dawn* 39).

The Oankali's reason for existence comes to its full completion at the end of the trilogy: the ooloi children who grow from the human-Oankali connection, so-called constructs, become able to change form individually through the control of fast-growing (human) cancer cells. (Previously, transformation was possible only from one generation to another; characteristics of the new genetic material were given to the offspring, who kept a constant form during their life span.) In addition, as shape-shifters, constructs become able to adapt physically to the next gene trade partner, preventing the formation of boundaries and categories of "us" and "them" from the beginning. With constructs, acceptance of the other is complete; instead of having to await the offspring of a genetic exchange, constructs as individual members of the species can embody, and thus mirror, the other whenever it is encountered.

The shift of narrative perspective in the *Xenogenesis* trilogy from Lilith to her children signifies the development of subject positions that are increasingly removed from familiar oppositions that define difference (see Wolmark, *Aliens and Others* 36), which enables Butler to speculate on alternative ways of relating to difference. The voice of the ooloi-construct Jodahs—the narrator in *Imago,* the third novel—reflects Trinh's point that difference is not an identity, and that to declare a tolerance of difference (as identity) is to perpetuate the dual character of self/other. Instead, "[d]ifference . . . is *that which undermines the very idea of identity*" (Trinh 96, emphasis hers). Thus Jodahs's voice is generated, not by a core self (that is different from *my* core self) that speaks from a place conventionally referred to as "elsewhere" and that we agree to listen to, but by the "infinity [of] layers whose totality forms 'I' " (Trinh 96).[15] Because the Oankali crave difference, their differences are perceived as threatening by humans, who operate from the delusion of a stable identity, from their insistence that "human" (i.e. "white" or "male") is a pre-given, normal state, instead of a process.

The negotiations that a rethinking of difference demands are painful and disconcerting—at times, even disempowering. Wolmark identifies this painful process as a "tension between sameness and difference" (*Aliens and Others* 39) that Butler places at the center of her tales. Human fears of difference are at times too much to bear and result in tragedies. Butler does not paint the picture of a tolerant pluralism that preaches "acceptance of difference"; instead, she points to the difficulties that negotiations of power relations bring. Her constellations of hybrid offspring and xenogenesis, of humans "going native" in alien societies and the sensual pleasure this change evokes in the reader, serve as metaphors for what Robert Stam in "Multiculturalism and the Neoconservatives" defines as "polycentric multiculturalism." According to Stam, polycentric multiculturalism does not ignore the "political realities of injustice and inequality and the consequent existential realities of pain, anger, and resentment." Instead, it "calls for a kind of diasporization of desire, the multiplication, the cross-fertilization, and the mutual relativization of social energies" (200).

Constructions of Difference: Race, Gender, and Sexuality

Butler's narratives problematize issues of difference mainly through two of their major structural manifestations: gender (based on "sexual difference") and race (based on "racial difference").[16] To address these issues, she uses both metaphors (aliens) and concrete references—relationships between humans, especially her black female protagonists' relationships to (often nonblack) men. With both narrative devices, Butler is able to disclose the construction of demarcations based on difference and the power structures legitimized by them.

Racism and sexism are always linked to power relations that are legitimized by social hierarchies and by relationships that are declared "personal," such as between husband and wife (see Salvaggio, "Black SF Heroine" 79). Both are constructed and enacted within particular historical communities. Accordingly, Butler's discussions of gender always imply the construction of race and vice versa.

Alien Others: Denaturalization of Racial Difference
Xenophobia and racism in science fiction are usually transferred onto representations of aliens. These symbolic representations often replace any direct discussion of racism and fail to really address the problem, as Butler states:

> Science Fiction has long treated people who might or might not exist—extraterrestrials. Unfortunately, however, many of the same

science fiction writers who started us thinking about the possibility of extraterrestrial life did nothing to make us think about here-at-home human variations. (quoted in Govan, "Connections" 87)

At the same time, science fiction metaphors do constitute powerful tools to transgress boundaries through analogies, and Butler uses these tools in a critical way.[17]

Butler does not simply turn strange creatures into objects of xeno-phobia (fear of the unknown); her critical representations of racism are much more complex. She places racism within relationships of humans with the other—both human and un-human. By problematiz-ing racism, not only in terms of existing categories of difference but also in terms of new ones, she discloses their inherent absurdity and randomness. Whether due to a genetic illness that isolates ill people from others ("The Evening and the Morning and the Night"), a myste-rious infection that robs humans of their capability to speak and read and produces chaos and jealousy ("Speech Sounds"), or a phenome-non that turns humans into mutants (*Clay's Ark*), in Butler's worlds, humans differ from each other in ways beyond their control. The clas-sification that differences bring is therefore horrifyingly familiar: "Pat-ternists and Clayarks stared at each other across a gulf of disease and physical difference and comfortably told themselves the same lie about each other . . . : 'Not people' " (*Patternmaster* 122).

While Butler points to the ways in which existing categories are constructed, she also makes clear that although race is an ideology, it has real consequences for people. Without trivializing the power that discourse produces, Butler resists naturalizations of categories in our thought; she reflects on the Foucaultian fact that biology is not the body itself, but a discourse that constructs the body and our knowledge about it. Butler confronts the reader with new "biological" facts (i.e. forms of difference) that find their place within a discourse whose mecha-nism of separation might change in content, but not in consequence.[18] Therefore, it is not the "fact" of racial differences that is significant for social order, but the positions assigned to those differences within the social hierarchy.

In her discussion of race, Butler employs various forms of repre-sentation. In *Survivor*, she places her heroine, Alanna, between two highly hierarchical societies: the Missionaries' community, which is grounded in a belief in their own spiritual superiority; and the Kohn tribes, whose social stratification is based in the color of their fur. Just as Missionaries are exclusive in their definition of "human," Kohns rely on a social order reminiscent of human racism, in which color determines one's status in society—as leader, judge, artisan, and so on. Alanna is the only one who refuses the respective categories, thus forcing those close to her to change the ways they deal with difference. In *Kindred, Wild Seed,* and the *Parable* novels, the emphasis lies on the historical construction of race in the United States. The close connection between race relations and power structures becomes apparent in the *Patternist* series. Here, new markers of difference create stratifications that result in control mechanisms reminiscent of those during slavery. The Patternist society consists of telepaths and humans without telepathic abilities—*mutes*—who are controlled by the telepaths and at times even held as their slaves.[19] In this hierarchy, Butler reconstructs the historical construction of racial difference in the United States, through which power structures such as slavery are legitimized. The *stigma* of being a "Negro" is what makes a human a slave or not; it is the power of the sign, not the skin color itself. In *Mind of My Mind,* at the birth of the pattern, Emma/Anyanwu confronts Doro with the parallel:

> "Mutes!"
> ... "It's a convenient term. People without telepathic voices. Ordinary people."
> "I know what it means, Doro. .... It means niggers! ... And if you don't think they look down on us non-telepaths, us niggers, the whole rest of humanity, you're not paying attention." (*Mind* 155)

Familiar categories of difference brand the undirected Patternists (the inbred offspring of Doro's attempts to create a "super race") as mad and insane until their power is channeled through the pattern. It seems as if Doro's ambitions undermine existing categories. His utopian legacy, passed down to his descendents, lies in the possible transcendence of differences—through his un-human, bodiless existence he transgresses external markers, such as race. Yet Doro's transcendent element ultimately fails to come through: from his breeding attempts, he creates a "super race" that produces new mechanisms of separation and power.

The problematic category of "human" in Butler is frequently symbolic of the signifying power of racial markers: to be "human" is to be racially "pure"—that is, "white." Humans' reproduction with the Oankali in the *Xenogenesis* series points to the dissolution of external attributes that define a race. In *Survivor,* Alanna's relationship with the alien Diut evokes negative reactions in Missionaries that are similar to those that racial miscegenation triggered in the past, and still does today (*Survivor* 156–57). However, once visual demarcations of "pure humanness" are blurred, power relations reliant on markers of sexual and racial differences are challenged and need to be redefined.

Conceptualizing Gender and Sexuality

Just as she decenters the point of reference by recounting the events from the perspective of the racialized other, Butler breaks with the homogeneous male "us" as it is constituted in traditional science fiction and in its reception.[20] A woman, in her narratives, is never merely the object of or reason for the actions of a masculine hero. She acts and reacts in direct relation to the events around her. Violence is part of her resistance to power, both in self-defense and in defense of others, echoing black women's centuries-long resistance. By concentrating on the relationships of her heroines with often powerful men or aliens (with the latter, like the women, representing an other), Butler shifts the debate on race and gender away from traditional discourse, toward the perspective of the other. The relationships of her women characters with powerful men mirror relations to power that are defined by both gender and race, relations that Butler's protagonists consistently challenge. Butler destabilizes the model of center-margin by placing her characters into more complex relationships of power. While the primary relationships between humans that Butler creates are usually heterosexual, her cross-species sexual encounters take place outside heterosexual norms.[21] A queer reading of Butler's narratives makes visible her deconstruction of normative heterosexuality and desire.[22]

According to Foucault's theory of discursive power, gender roles and functions that supposedly are based on sexual differences in reproduction and in desire do not develop from "biological facts" but are produced through discourse. Bodies themselves (and the desire that supposedly comes with them, based on their "natural" sex) do not determine relations between the genders, but their interpretation does. Paralleling Foucault's insistence on the "de-naturalization" of categories relating to sex, Butler undermines Western dualistic think-ing, which assigns social value to sexual difference and is extremely inflexible.

Butler continually reminds the reader of this dualistic thinking within power relations and the extent to which it defines their control over our lives. Consonant with the experiences of women (especially those of women of color), loss of control over the body connotes female attributes, as a human explains to Lilith about a man's reaction to his sexual possession by an ooloi:

> He's not in control even of what his own body does and feels. *He's taken like a woman.* . . . He knows the ooloi aren't male. He knows all the sex that goes on is in his head. It doesn't matter. It doesn't fucking matter! Someone else is pushing all his buttons. He can't let them get away with that. (*Dawn* 203, emphasis mine)

Butler makes clear that power in Western societies is not associated with women. Their powerlessness is comparable to the helplessness experienced by a whole species controlled by aliens. Thus a man tells a construct ooloi, "You treat all mankind as your woman" (*Imago* 77).[23] In *Dawn,* when a skeptical ooloi, who has studied human cultures and thought, questions Lilith's ability to lead her people, Butler leaves no doubt that gender/sexual difference is linked to ascribed functions: "I didn't want to accept you, Lilith. Not for [the partnership with the ooloi] Nikanj or for the work you'll do. I believed that because of the way human genetics were expressed in culture, a human male should be chosen to parent the first group. I think now that I was wrong" (*Dawn* 110).[24]

Butler challenges the seemingly inevitable social order built on sex-ual difference with her female protagonists who demand new struc-tures. One example is Amber in *Patternmaster,* who rejects marriage, the legitimized form of being together in Patternist society. Considering the price she would have to pay, her independence is more important to her than the relationship with the hero.

> "Stay with me, Amber. Be my wife—lead wife, once I have my House." . . .
> "No." The word was a stone. "I want what I want. I could have given my life for you [. . .]. But I could never give my life *to* you." (*Patternmaster* 134)[25]

Butler discusses gender relations and sexual difference also in terms of reproduction. In this way she evokes historical violations, especially of women of *color*'s bodies, sexualities, and reproductive choices. In all of her fiction, children play a central role—they are the future, and they define affiliations. Especially in the *Xenogenesis* series and in "Bloodchild," Butler "reflects on the extent to which patriarchal cultures find it necessary to use ideology, violence, and oppression to force women to participate in 'natural' reproduction" (Green 171). In the *Xenogenesis* series, both women and men are made infertile by the Oankali unless they agree to have children with alien genes, and in *Dawn*, Lilith is made pregnant by her ooloi without her consent. In *Adulthood Rites* she speaks about that moment of exploitation:

> "They forced you to have kids?" the man asked.
> "One of them surprised me," she said. "It made me pregnant, then told me about it. Said it was giving me what I wanted but would never come out and ask for."
> "Was it?"
> . . . "Oh, yes. But if I had the strength not to ask, it should have had the strength to let me alone." (*Rites* 25)

Butler explores outcomes of power relations beyond one-dimensional concepts of winning and losing. By including unresolved contradictions and their consequences (which contribute to the at-times frustrating experience of reading Butler's narratives), Butler resists the temptation of basing fictional exploration on the simplified and generalized solutions that theoretical discourses offer.

In "Bloodchild," Butler reminds us that the reproductive function of women does not produce "natural" social structures, but that these structures are constructed by power. In the cross-species breeding between humans and T'lics, a young man is in the position of a person who gives birth under life-threatening circumstances. He ends up questioning the reduction of his existence to his reproductive function—creating a bizarre reversal of familiar sexual difference. The figures of the "pregnant man" and the "impregnating woman" (Helford 264) in "Bloodchild" destabilize the reproduction process as we know it, and therefore make the "natural" construction of categories impossible.[26] "When 'woman' emerges through the metaphor of an impregnated young boy, as it does in 'Bloodchild,' we are invited to examine and challenge our understanding of the construction of gender" (Helford 261).[27]

In addition to challenging the naturalization of gender roles and reproduction, Butler problematizes aspects of violent (hetero)sexuality and power. Especially in her depictions of alien sex with humans, we find decidedly queer elements where desire and physical stimulation are physically decentered. Homosexuality and heterosexuality become insufficient labels to categorize sexual encounters between five people of two species and three gender/sexes. Butler explores aspects of power and desire as they shape notions of female sexuality as a site of victimization as well as agency.

Oankali sexuality is physically decentralized: sexual activities are not concentrated on sexual organs. Ooloi-produced stimulation includes the whole body surface. As Eric White notes, "Undoing the privileging of genital over other erogenous zones, alien sex is polymorphously perverse" (404). Thus the prescribed, determined functions of sexual organs are diffused; concepts such as the Oedipus complex, fear of castration, and penis envy become obsolete. During sexual contact there is no separation between self and other(s); pain as well as pleasure is felt by everyone. "[S]he discovered that if she touched me now with her hand, she felt the touch as though on her own skin, felt pleasure or discomfort just as she made me feel" (*Imago* 111).

Even though Oankali society seems to disrupt conventional gender definitions through their reproductive unit of five, Butler paints a picture of compulsory heterosexuality based in the Oankali's drive for reproduction (just as arguments based on reproduction are brought against human homosexuality). There do not seem to be sexual relationships between alien partners beyond either a "monogamous" household or an act of reproduction, and there are no cases of homosexuality described in alien and/or human constellations anywhere in the trilogy.[28] Nevertheless, the family structure of the human/alien families seems to entail implicit homosexual patterns: the act of reproduction takes place with five people—one ooloi, a human heterosexual pair, and an Oankali heterosexual pair. Oankali do not have problems with this arrangement, but Butler portrays homophobia, especially between men, manifested in male paranoia about intimacy with same-sexed people: the human male in Lilith's family cannot meet his male Oankali partner without feeling inhibited after a sexual act but is comfortable interacting with his female Oankali partner (*Rites* 179). So even though homosexuality is not conceptualized outside the reproductive unit, it is an integral and necessary part of the process. In addition, Oankali are constantly physically and emotionally close, especially when they belong to a kinship group, which includes same-sexed relations.[29]

In her depiction of the human/Oankali relationships, Butler portrays "sexual relationships between beings of unequal power" (Bonner 58). Queer theories have extensively explored relationships between power and pleasure (most noticeably in pornography and s/M debates). At first glance, sexual violence, especially rape, seems impossible considering the nature of the Oankali's sexual contact, which transports any sensations, including pain, to everyone involved. The horror and pain of the victim would assault the rapist simultaneously.[30] However, people who are resistant to sexual contact are "seduced" through biochemical stimulation by the ooloi, and as Bonner points out, this stimulation produces a *physical* consent, but the act remains a rape through forced change of mind (see *Dawn* 158–62). The aliens' assurance that they know what humans "really want" is reminiscent of men's disregard of women's "no" in rape cases.[31] This "pleasure within oppression" is the object of queer theorists like Carole Vance, who, in her introduction to *Pleasure and Danger*, demands an exploration of the link between patriarchal interference with female desire and women's experiences of their own passion as dangerous. Butler complicates matters further by placing *men* into the subject position usually inhabited by women: women's sexuality is culturally coded as passive (i.e. feminine), while men are associated with an active (i.e. masculine) sexuality (see Vance 6). Her ambivalent depiction of human sexuality in an Oankali context concurs with Vance's position that "to ignore the potential for variation [in what might constitute women's sexual pleasure] is to inadvertently place women outside of culture except as passive recipients of official symbolic systems" (Vance 15).

Reading Butler's representations of sexuality as queer also discloses the links between race, power, and sexuality. As Eve Kosofsky Sedgwick demands in *Between Men: English Literature and Male Homosocial Desire*, feminists need to develop a theoretical framework to explore sexual and power relationships that goes beyond gender violence. Literary texts, she argues, offer insights into the inconsistencies in how the sexual relates to the social. Sexual meaning is always produced from a particular standpoint, shaped by race as well as by gender: representations of a violent sexual encounter between a white man and a white woman have different implications than depictions of an encounter between a white man and a black woman.[32] The act of sexual violence (rape) is informed by power and domination based on race as well as gender relations, complicating definitions and analyses of representations of sexual violence: "the white male alienation of a Black woman's sexuality is shaped differently from the alienation of the white woman's, to the degree that rape ceases to be a meaningful term at all" (Segdwick 10).

Butler problematizes the link between sexual violence and power in the relationships her female protagonists have with men—both human and alien. Alanna "consents" to intercourse with Diut because a sexual relationship with him will secure her freedom—yet he factually rapes her. As a black female human, Alanna's status in the highly stratified Kohn society is close to nothing, while Diut's blue fur reflects his high social position. Only acceptance by the Tehkohn leader can secure her a minimum social status. Thus race, sexuality, and domination intersect, echoing colonial historical realities (*Survivor* 99–100).

Butler's narratives destabilize familiar categories of race, gender, and sexuality and disclose them as both ideologically constructed and real in their social consequences. Her characters' resistance to and negotiations of these categories challenge normative social roles. At the same time, Butler engages with questions around desire, pleasure, and violence that trouble feminists' explorations of female sexuality, and she depicts sexuality as inextricably linked to power.

Feminist Subjectivities: Metaphors of Subversive Transgressions

To be different, or alien, is a significant if familiar cultural metaphor which marks the boundaries and limits of social identity. It allows difference to be marginalised and any dissonance to be smoothed away, thus confirming the dominance of the centre over the margins. (Wolmark, *Aliens and Others* 27)

Butler uses aliens and mutants as symbols that destabilize markers of difference and redefine social relations. Another major strategy she employs to explore the relationship of identity and difference is creating feminist subjects based on notions of resisting identities (such as the feminist cyborg). These models for feminist subjectivities share a new approach to identity, portraying it not as an enclosed, stable entity but as one that is relational and shifting. By exploring elements of these alternative ways of envisioning identity in Butler's female characters, we are better able to understand transgressive metaphors and may find new ways of thinking about their (theoretical) implications.

Geographical displacement forms the metaphorical and actual foundation for many of these feminist subjectivities: in Carole Boyce Davies's migratory subjectivity as well as in Rosi Braidotti's nomadic subject, the notion of movement and flexibility of social location are central. Similarly, in the writings of Chicana feminism, the idea of the *mestiza*, a woman of Mexican/Indio descent, represents a new consciousness that emerges from collisions between cultures and their violent histories. One model of feminist subjectivity that grew from feminist science fiction texts, and in return shaped feminist theory, is the cyborg metaphor developed by Donna Haraway. The cyborg represents a political identity that emerges from contradictions produced by the historical moment of global capitalism and the consequent implosion of boundaries between nature and culture. What all of these models share, however, is the thought that identity is a fluid and transforming process that is never completed.

Boundary Crossing: Cyborgs, Nomadic and Migratory Subjects, and the Mestiza

Elements of feminist subjective theories run through Butler's narratives. Her main thematic and narrative device is the crossing of boundaries reflected in the conflicting and contradictory figure of Donna Haraway's cyborg, a metaphor for a feminist political identity whose main characteristic is its crossing of culturally defined boundaries. The cyborg shares this characteristic with other politicized feminist identities: the nomad's subversions of "conventional views and representations of . . . female subjectivity" (Braidotti, *Nomadic Subjects* 3); the *mestiza*'s borderland identity, which rejects the control of multiplicity by the "logic of purity" (Lugones 462); and the migratory subject, which undermines discourse by consistently changing positions and locations. In cyborg feminism, the figure of the cyborg emerges beyond its manifestation in science fiction; its meaning is developed from the context of the texts in relation to social conditions and power relations.

The cyborg is one of the "boundary creatures" (Haraway, "Actors Are Cyborgs" 21) that has been marginalized within the critical rationalist discourse and has developed a perspective from its unique position—a position that is inherently one of agency. It is in the fusion of differences, including those between women (not the liberal "celebration" of them), that the potential for new political strategies of change is situated. "So my cyborg myth is about transgressed boundaries, potent fusions, and dangerous possibilities which progressive people might explore as one part of needed political work" (Haraway, "Manifesto" 154). The innovative approach to the cyborg, a hybrid constructed through conflicting social factors, is not to reject but to embrace its contradictions: "There are several consequences to taking seriously the imagery of cyborgs as other than our enemies. Our bodies, ourselves—bodies are maps of power and identity. . . . We are responsible for boundaries; we are they" ("Manifesto" 180).

The notion of the cyborg as a political identity results from the changing relations between machines and organisms. The main factor in the development of a cyborg identity is therefore contesting ideologically constructed categories of difference: "The dichotomies between mind and body, animal and human, organism and machine, public and private, nature and culture, men and women, primitive and civilized are all in question ideologically" ("Manifesto" 163). This is where Butler's narratives are most closely related to the cyborg: they contest existing definitions of difference by undermining the very notion of sameness. The attempt to control the dissolution of boundaries is characterized by Haraway as a "border war." Battles of this border war take place in social spheres of production, reproduction, and imagination, and in the past decade have reached new dimensions through advanced technoscience, including genetic engineering. The battlegrounds of the border wars are often semiotically manifested, representing (often hidden) struggles to define and rearrange racialized and gendered interactions. Related to representations are economic interests, which are a major factor in the contestations of boundaries and affect the everyday lives of people in the (ideological as well as economic) margins.

Another site of these border wars are the borderlands Gloria Anzaldúa describes in "La consciencia de la mestiza: Towards a New Consciousness." They represent a terrain where exploitation of labor, racism, poverty, and denial of citizenship are terms the *mestiza* needs to resist. Anzaldúa proposes a concept of feminist subjectivity that is derived directly from the subject position of the *mestiza*,[33] "a product of the transfer of the cultural and spiritual values of one group to another" (377) that denies sameness as the basis for identity. Grown from the "cultural collision" (378) between Mexican, Indio, and American cultures, the *mestiza*'s homeland is the "borderlands" of the Southwest, the geographical site of economic, political, territorial, and sociological conflicts. A woman without a homeland that is not constantly culturally contested (she is neither Anglo nor Mexican nor Indio) is a "country-less woman," as Ana Castillo describes it in *Massacre of the Dreamers* (21). At the same time, she needs to meet the demands of each cultural space.

This multiple subject position, which grows from geographical and cultural "homelessness," results in a "schizophrenic-like existence" (Castillo 39) as the *mestiza* is confronted with representations and power structures that deny her reality. In order to transcend this traumatic state of being, she needs to reject what Maria Lugones calls the "logic of purity" (462), which denies the complexity and heterogeneity of social reality and of oppression. Instead, Lugones argues, *mestizaje* needs to be recognized as a metaphor for impurity and resistance, as "impure resistance to interlocked, intermeshed oppressions" (459). The mixed racial and cultural backgrounds that make up the origin of the *mestiza*, the "hybrid progeny" (Anzaldúa 377), should inspire a consciousness in her that opposes a fixed sense of self and is devoid of internalized oppression: "a new *mestiza* consciousness, *una consciencia de mujer*" (377). Thus impurity becomes an act of resistance. Confronted with constant demands to renegotiate terms of identity, the *mestiza* is characterized by a "tolerance for ambiguity," grown from the realization "that she can't hold concepts or ideas in rigid boundaries" (Anzaldúa 378). She therefore "operates in a pluralistic mode" (379), enabling the *mestiza* to redefine relations based on oppressive categories of difference. The becoming of this multilayered consciousness is at times painful: Anzaldúa argues that the struggle to become a self is inseparable from our surroundings—the *mestiza*'s psyche mirrors the geographical borderlands, their economic hardships and their strengths. In defining resistance against oppression, Anzaldúa insists, we need to start with ourselves and the representations we hold:

The struggle is inner: Chicano, *indio,* American Indian, *mojado,* *mexicano,* immigrant Latino, Anglo in power, working class Anglo, Black, Asian—our psyches resemble the bordertowns and are populated by the same people. The struggle has always been inner, and is played out in the outer terrains. Awareness of our situation must come before inner changes, which in turn come before changes in society. Nothing happens in the "real" world unless it first happens in the images in our heads. (385)

The *mestiza*'s agency, which grows from positions declared as marginal by mainstream discourse, is related to that of the nomadic subject and the migratory subject. These metaphors of identities transgress *national* as well as cultural boundaries, as well as the link of identity to one particular place. In *Black Women, Writing, and Identity,* Davies uses the metaphors of migration and exile to suggest that black women's writing cannot be located and framed in terms of one specific place but exists in myriad places and times. It constantly eludes terms of the discussion and creates a subjectivity that is flexible and in motion, never static. The main characteristic of this subjectivity is that it is defined by migration, by movement, and therefore constantly reclaims new forms. This migration of the subject, argues Davies, is the basis for agency and subverts discourse by evading its static definitions. "In the same way as diaspora assumes expansiveness and elsewhereness, migrations of the Black female subject pursue the path of movement outside the terms of dominant discourses" (37). The metaphor of migration as process is grounded in black women's experiences and history of diaspora.[34] "It is the convergence of multiple places and cultures that re-negotiates the terms of Black women's experience that in turn negotiates and re-negotiates their identities" (3).

The question of what constitutes home becomes central in black women's writing, as does the question of how to have community. As Braidotti states in *Nomadic Subjects,* the nomadic subject, with its shifting relationship to identity positions, calls for an alternative concept of community that does not rely on the shared notion of a "homeland," and offers an alternative to the subject constructed by the modern nation.[35] The nomadic subject is unlike some aspects of diaspora, which bind identity to a mythical homeland.[36] In contrast, the nomad does not have a homeland but "carries her/his essential belongings with her/him wherever s/he goes and can recreate a home base anywhere"

(Braidotti, *Nomadic Subjects* 16). The knowledge of home-making as a process is the strength of the nomadic subject; it constitutes the flexibility that comes with shifting subject positions, and it allows the transgression of boundaries without losing a sense of the necessity of location.

Postmodern theories that rely on non-Western social orders for metaphors and theoretical formulations have been criticized by feminists and race theorists alike for romanticizing and overgeneralizing these societies. It is just in these problematic aspects that Butler's narratives are so valuable; they caution against utopian generalizations and insist on the specificity of negotiated power relations. In her fiction the liberating implications as well as the limits of these theories are explored. In this context, metaphors need to be understood as *theoretical tools* (as well as comments on material realities), which have the power to transform not only systems of representation but concepts of identity as well. Thus, within the discussion of transgressive, nomadic identities, it is paramount to emphasize that a lack of any fascist or absolute elements is the only guarantee of a liberated society.

While the *mestiza*'s consciousness develops from the erosion of cultural, economic, and geographic boundaries, and nomadic and migratory subjects evolve from experiences of changing places, the figure of the cyborg, according to Haraway, has developed analogously to three main dissolutions of boundaries in our society. First, the boundary between human and animal is increasingly effaced. According to biotechnological research, the genetic material in humans and animals differs only minimally (e.g., 90 percent of the idioplasm of Homo Sapiens is identical to that of primates). Genetic science and biotechnology are the main areas in which these borders are being explored. The figure of the cyborg appears where the boundary between humans and animals is transgressed. The second dissolution of boundaries takes place between humans and animals as a group (organisms) and machines. Their realms and opportunities for action increasingly overlap—machines are becoming more intelligent and even assume cognitive processes. In science fiction, the cyborg therefore is usually the main figure in the discussion about the "human" status of a creature. Finally, the boundary between the physical and nonphysical is collapsing; our technologies are chiefly designed electronically, and their controlling processes are not visible. The figure of the cyborg similarly eludes every fixation and stands outside visible structures (see Haraway, "Manifesto" 151–55). These figures defy Christian-Western narratives of a pure, innocent beginning of the subject: "An origin story in the Western humanist sense depends on the myth of original unity, fullness, bliss, and terror, represented by the phallic mother from whom all humans must separate" ("Manifesto" 151).

The main feature of the metaphor of the cyborg is its evasion of culturally constructed categories and their ascribed social positions. This evasion entails radical implications for politics in its emphasis on agency developed from spaces that conventionally are defined as disempowered. The cyborg intersects with other models of feminist identity: by rejecting the notion of sameness and of a stable identity as a position of resistance, these models locate power between the fixed boundaries of those in dominant subject positions and represent the subjectivity of the disempowered from their perspective.

Transgressive Elements in Butler's Narratives

The two aspects of the cyborg within feminist discourse, the metaphorical and the literal, are also present in the science fiction produced by women in the United States. Some science fiction writers create cybernetic organisms, or states of consciousness shaped by cyberspace, as narrative devices to problematize the issue of technology.[37] Others, such as Octavia Butler, discuss cyborg identity through the creation of aliens, human hybrids, and genetic engineering; this kind of science fiction "translates" the idea of the technological cyborg into a feminist identity of boundary crossing and acceptance of differences.[38] Discussion of her work reveals the liberating potential of the cyborg metaphor and also discloses its limits.

How is technology's political power represented in Butler's work? She does not create high-tech science fiction narratives; instead, new senses and biological abilities dominate her futuristic worlds. Her stories are characterized by a diffusion of boundaries reminiscent of high technology's impact on our social interactions, yet it is symbolized more through the elaboration of relations between humans and un-humans, and less through relationships between humans and machines. In Butler's work, technology's effects, such as the implosion of cultural categories, are displaced as cross-species breeding. This crossbreeding evokes extreme anxieties in the characters (as well as in the reader!), thereby problematizing notions of authentic racial purity.

The fusion between animals and humans in the *Xenogenesis* trilogy is displaced onto the Oankali's gene exchange with other species: as genetic engineers, they consistently collect the genetic information of both plants and animals, integrating it into their gene pool, thereby renewing and transforming it. "[They] collect life, travel and collect and integrate new life into their ships, their already vast collection of living things, and themselves" (*Rites* 166). The "animalization" of the Clayarks conceptualizes the boundary between humans and animals in a more direct way than the relationship between aliens and humans. The Clayarks' attempt to separate their humanness from their beastness is disconnected from appearance; it dismisses biological makeup as a defining factor in boundary setting: " 'We've changed, but we have ethics. We aren't animals" (*Ark* 37).

Transgressions of boundaries between machines and organic life forms are also present in the Oankali: their technology is purely organic, ranging from building materials and transportation means to their spaceships. The Oankali's main technology is signified through its symbiotic relationship with other life forms: genetic engineering. It creates machines from organisms through reproduction, thus destabilizing boundaries between machine and organism.

Finally, the communication systems in the *Patternist* series, which are based in mental mechanisms, echo the growing invisibility of communication technology, such as cell phones and wireless Internet access. Strength and perseverance are measured, not in physical terms, but in terms of mental power—they are invisible and unpredictable (reminiscent of cyberpunk's celebration of mental capacities within cyberspace), creating new dimensions of strength and competence. In the *Xenogenesis* trilogy, sexual encounters between aliens as well as between aliens and humans are established through neurological stimulation that resembles an experience within virtual reality—caresses from the sexual partner are experienced without being executed (see *Dawn* 161–63, 169).

Within the context of science and technology, the boundary-defying connection between human (the self) and animal/alien (the other) symbolizes the reversal of subject and object positions, the reversal of the "field" with the familiar empirical reality. In *Dawn*, Lilith experiences this shift when the Oankali keep her under observation: " 'I was majoring in anthropology.' She laughed bitterly. 'I suppose I could think of this as fieldwork—but how the hell do I get out of the field?' " (*Dawn* 86). As an agent of boundary crossing, Lilith is recruited into territories whose boundaries are impossible to differentiate. Subject becomes object, and vice versa, as fields of study are reversed and mixed up, authorities are undermined. "The cyborgs populating feminist science fiction make very problematic the statuses of man or woman, human, artifact, member of a race, individual identity, or body" (Haraway, "Manifesto" 178). The semiotic structure of the meaning of her fictional characters regarding their genetic impurity, especially in her *Xenogenesis* series and *Wild Seed*, is akin to Haraway's analysis of the meaning of the genetically engineered OncoMouse™ in *Modest Witness*. All of Butler's hybrid creatures challenge the authority of normative systems of knowledge and their role in the socioeconomic system.

Boundary Transgression in Butler's Female Characters

In most of Butler's stories, female figures fulfill the function of the cyborg in their transgression of boundaries.[39] All of them take up special places in their society and often have experiences in which they are marginalized, and sometimes these experiences make them into powerful agents. All are what Audre Lorde termed "Sister Outsiders" (see also Haraway, "Manifesto" 174), located one step outside the norm and acting from this position. Most of them do not posses extraordinary abilities while others have almost magical powers. None are technologically enhanced like the classical cyborg figure although some are genetically altered. Alanna in *Survivor*, Lauren in *Parable of the Sower* and *Parable of the Talents*, Dana in *Kindred*, Keira in *Clay's Ark*, and Lilith in the *Xenogenesis* trilogy are women who do not possess extraordinary abilities. It is the epistemological standpoint that they acquire in their social position as black women or women of color that sets them apart from their environment and gives them specific ways of knowing and understanding situations of conflict and of power. All of them are survivors and have been geographically displaced, made into migratory subjects whose "journeys redefine space" (Davies, *Black Women* 1). They are characterized by their strong will and their ability to adapt to situations forced upon them. It is their perspective from the margins, disconnected from positions of power, which enables them to shift boundaries and which makes them so valuable to the creatures inhabiting these shadowy territories. These women exist in a constant state of negotiation with their environment; as survivors, they test limits and set limits for those in power. They are permanently confronted with the fact that "[y]ou think you can choose your own realities. You can't" (*Clay's Ark* 79).

Even though she is critical of generalizations, Butler embeds her female characters into migratory experiences: they become metaphors of displaced feminist subjects, whose diasporic experiences force them to reimagine and renegotiate their identity in relation to their environments. In *Survivor,* Alanna is forced to negotiate her identity first when Missionaries adopt her, and again when the aliens on the planet (whom the Missionaries are trying to colonize) kidnap her. In *Wild Seed,* the shape-shifter and healer Anyanwu possesses a subjectivity defined by "slipperiness, elsewhereness" (Davies, *Black Women* 36), which allows her to escape subjugation and finally to negotiate the terms of her existence. And in both *Parable of the Sower* and *Parable of the Talents,* migration becomes the metaphor not only of resistance but also of survival. It is inherent in the aspirations of the protagonist, Lauren, to fly her people to the stars in order to evade the destructiveness of people on Earth, and it is deeply engraved in the novels' narrative form (particularly in *Sower*) as the journal of a journey: "Black female subjectivity asserts agency as it crosses the borders, journeys, migrates and so reclaims as it re-asserts" (Davies, *Black Women* 37).

In addition to Butler's female figures, the nomadic Oankali, with their transgressive subjectivity that understands difference as part of identity, are a people without a homeland. Beyond that, they share with the cyborg a disconnection from any psychosocial Genesis narrative, which determines gendered subjectivity for humans and which strongly influences our conception of truth and moral purity; the cyborg has no dream and no goal of a higher unity of self. Butler's figures have no past to draw on, no creation myth of innocence to which to return. In the *Xenogenesis* series, Lilith asks about the Oankali's homeworld and whether they desire to return there: "No, Lilith, that's the one direction that's closed to us. This is our homeworld now" (*Dawn* 34). The Oankali correspond with the "nonoriginal" (Haraway in Penley and Ross 13) character of the cyborg. They are "space-going people" (*Imago* 11), whose origins take multiple forms and whose future is oriented, not to the past, but to the infinite diversity of the unknown. As such, the Oankali become metaphors for the nomadic subjects that Braidotti conceptualizes, who—like the cyborg—are not bound by a concrete or a mythical homeland. Because the promises of Western myths do not apply to them, these myths hold no authority over the cyborg: "The cyborg would not recognize the Garden of Eden; it is not made of mud and cannot dream of returning to dust" (Haraway, "Manifesto" 151).

Thus Butler's characters negotiate situations that are always linked to displacement and the boundary crossing we find in feminist nomadic theories. It is not the fact that they are displaced that turns Butler's characters into figures of resistance, but how they position their experience in relation to difference. Only in this combination (both displacement and the embracing of difference) do they develop their particular feminist elements.

In *Wild Seed,* the progenitrix of the Patternists, Anyanwu, who is an immortal shape-shifter and healer, is Butler's most explicit translation of the technological metaphor of the synthesized human into a consciousness, demonstrating a connection with the *mestiza.*[40] In Anyanwu, the principle of a new knowledge that defies the oppressive application of conventional science and technology finds its strongest expression. She comprehends the structure of other living things through her shape-shifting—her transgression of boundaries is complete. She *becomes* the other, lives their experience, and knows their being. Other female protagonists share the power to dissolve demarcations between themselves and those around them. Lauren, in *Parable of the Sower* and *Parable of the Talents,* experiences this form of boundary transgression through an affliction that affects her neurological transmitters: she "shares" the pain and pleasure of other living beings through visual and acoustic contact. Finally, in *Mind of My Mind,* the *pattern* that Mary controls becomes the center where all boundaries meet and dissolve.

These women's extraordinary ability to manipulate boundaries is the basis for Butler's explorations of political resistance. Their talents place these women in positions of influence, yet they refuse to misuse power on any level. The rejection of the use of power for personal goals is defined by Butler as an explicitly female trait, born out of a marginalized social location—a position shared with the cyborg inhabiting Haraway's texts. In her narratives, Butler associates the concepts male/masculine with the abuse of power, and female/feminine with life giving and the rejection of power. This polarization of gendered power engages both with cultural feminists' assumptions of the essentially benign nature of women and with radical constructionist feminists' claim that men and women learn approaches to power through an ideology that prescribes gendered relations to it.

The gendered use of power is inherently problematic and forms one of the contradictions that Butler consistently explores.[41] When viewed within the context of feminist standpoint theories, however, her constellations of female versus male power can be understood as metaphors for social location and resulting epistemological differences. These differences also entail conflicting ethical approaches, especially regarding power. Lilith, the heroine in *Dawn*—who is less a leader than a mother to the group of humans assigned to her care by the aliens who are planning to cross-breed with them—constitutes a doubly marginalized figure as a woman of African descent. In actions taken from a position of influence, she forms an antipode to the aggressively dominating figure of the white man. The Dankali chose her because of her standpoint and her relation to power as a (black) woman.

Feminist standpoint theories examine the development of particular knowledge systems that are based on shared social experiences. The concept of "epistemic privilege" is based on Marx's idea that the proletariat has revolutionary potential because of its relation to the means of production. This concept has been developed into notions of a feminist standpoint based on the sexual division of labor. Since early feminist standpoint theories, such as the work of Nancy Hartsock and Dorothy Smith, feminist standpoint theorists have developed increasingly sophisticated models of social consciousness. One example is Patricia Hill Collins's work on black feminist thought, which examines the relationship of gender to race/class standpoints. The most important innovation in standpoint theory is the differentiation between an essentialist and a materialist approach to epistemological patterns, that is, a "biological" versus an "achieved" standpoint, as Michelle Renee Matisons describes it in *Systems, Standpoints, and Subjects: Marxist Legacies in U.S. Feminist Theories*. Instead of basing analysis on the vague and imprecise category of "women" (who are somehow "different" from each other yet still form one analytic category), standpoint theorists believe that complex demographics, based on race and class as well as gender, shape knowledge.[42] The notion of epistemic particularities is also present in the *mestiza*. Here, economic and racial positioning are joined in their production of knowledge by psychosocial processes particular to the cultural borderlands the *mestiza* negotiates. Her transgressive consciousness is not a biological essence, but a product of the repressive conditions in which she finds herself. Accordingly, while Butler's female protagonists are always women of color, she is careful not to essentialize their standpoint. For Butler, standpoint is not rooted in biological factors, nor based in an exclusive, transcendental, racial and cultural memory, but developed from material and cultural experiences grown from social formations. Thus the opposition of female versus male power is a metaphor for differing epistemic positions, not an essential polarization.

Monstrous Bodies

Despite the displayed power of some of Butler's female figures, they are mostly positioned as others. The creatures in Butler's work, her symbolic cyborgs, have in common their "marked bodies" (Haraway, *Primate Visions* 378). In addition, they also *reproduce* marked bodies, deformed monsters who redefine embodied subjectivity. This state of being marked represents the boundary experience, which on one hand lies outside of any power position, but on the other is firmly grounded in the system of power that repudiates the existence of the other. "Monsters share more than the word's root with the verb 'to demonstrate'; monsters signify" (Haraway, *Primate Visions* 378). Butler discloses symbolic and sociological markers of bodies defined by power. Before Rufus, Dana's white ancestor in *Kindred,* begins whipping slaves himself, he is one of the oppressed. The welts that his father inflicts on him define him as heteronomous and turn him into an ally of the slaves: "Tom Weylin had probably marked his son more than he knew with that whip" (*Kindred* 39). This subject position changes the instant that Rufus finds his place within the system as a white male: "He's no good. He's all grown up now, and part of the system. He could feel for us a little when his father was running things—when he wasn't entirely free himself. But now, he's in charge" (*Kindred* 223). Butler thematizes this aspect of marked subject positions, especially through representations of women's bodies marked by experiences and stigma. Dana loses an arm when she returns from her time travel after killing Rufus. Her maimed condition represents the scars inflicted by the system onto her body: she is "not coming back whole" (Butler in Kenan 498). The experience took a part of her—literally.

Lilith fears the marking her children will suffer; these markings will marginalize them from central human experiences and will define them as other: " 'But it won't be human,' she whispered. 'It will be a thing. A monster' " (*Dawn* 246). In the end, it is the monster that promises a new beginning: with her alien-human hybrids—babies with tentacles—Butler creates what Haraway calls an "other order of difference" (Haraway, *Primate Visions* 379), which is not formulated in the context of the order governed by the white man's story of the Oedipus complex.[43] This order of difference is not situated in the realm of the father, where the narrative of traditional science fiction so often takes place.[44] Instead, these monster children, signifiers of both racial impurity and a lack of origin and history—and thus of a prescribed social order—redefine the basis of "human" subjectivity.[45]

In addition to rejecting patriarchal family narratives, Butler contrasts (human) stigma with the acceptance of difference, especially with her use of metaphors of shape-shifting and transformation. Alanna, as a "mental chameleon," and Anyanwu, as a shape-shifter, both have transformation at the center of their identities. Constructs, products of Oankali-human cross-breeding, gain transformational ability through the gene exchange: "You'll be able to change yourself. What we can do from one generation to the next—changing our form, reverting to earlier forms—you'll be able to do within yourself" (*Imago* 26). The hybridity of construct children also reflects the notion of the *mestiza* as a metaphor for impure resistance. Like the cyborg, she represents a consciousness that grows from more than one origin, which cannot be separated into fragmented parts.

All of Butler's female figures share a marginalized position, an origin that is somehow connected to African ancestors, and the ability to live between and cross boundaries and to negotiate power.[46] It is in these characteristics that their power lies. Similarly, the figure of the cyborg is utopian in a postmodern sense of boundary transgressions; it does not correspond to the traditional sociopolitical definition of the term "utopian." Recombination and transmutation are emphasized, rather than conquest and assimilation. Butler's female protagonists adapt to new situations, refuse power over others, have compassion, and accept and respect differences. Butler utilizes the typical science fiction metaphor, the cyborg, in innovative ways, especially in regard to its boundary-transgressing function. She does not create "real" cyborgs, creatures made from organic and inorganic material, but creates figures that can be understood as "cyborgian," especially on a mental level.[47] The confusion of boundaries that Haraway advocates is manifested in Butler's symbols of integration and appreciation of difference, which reveal the "politics of differentiation" at the same time as they suggest alternative forms of approaching difference. Like the cyborg, her figures are situated within the system, but outside its power structures. Only from that position can power be redistributed.

Butler's transgressive narratives, in their often painful negotiations of power and violent boundary crossings, never offer simple, one-dimensional solutions to feminist concerns. Yet, as complex tales of colonization, as well as of migration, they do create powerful moments of resistance, even if these are never without contradictions. Butler's most valuable contributions to feminist discourse lie in the concepts of feminist agency within her strange worlds and alien constellations—in her creation of places that the cyborg, nomad, *mestiza,* and migrant would recognize as their own.

If, as . . . feminist critics of science have argued, there is a relation among the desire for mastery, an objectivist account of science, and the imperialist project of subduing nature, then the posthuman offers resources for the construction of another kind of account. In this account, emergence replaces teleology; reflexive epistemology replaces objectivism; distributed cognition replaces autonomous will; embodiment replaces a body seen as a support system for the mind; and a dynamic partnership between humans and intelligent machines replaces the liberal humanist subject's manifest destiny to dominate and control nature. Of course, this is not necessarily what the posthuman *will* mean—only what it *can* mean if certain strands among its complex seriations are highlighted and combined to create a vision of the human that uses the posthuman as leverage to avoid reinscribing, and thus repeating, some of the mistakes of the past.

—N. Katherine Hayles, *How We Became Posthuman*

The alien (re)constructions we encounter in some feminist science fiction literature challenge conventional notions of female bodies as "different." While, historically, scientific discourse and popular belief have relied on biology to construct and create sexual difference,[1] in science fiction narratives *technologies* are central to this process of "othering" women's bodies. As Linda Janes puts it in *The Gendered Cyborg,* "In the case of the alien and android creatures that represent a defining trope of the science fiction genre it is, of course, actually technology, rather than biology, that reproduces gender and thereby challenges conceptions of what it is to be human, gendered, a stable subject" (93). When it comes to science fiction film, this aspect is further complicated by the technologies of the medium itself. While science fiction writers conceptualize technology and its impact on the human, science fiction films' representations of technology *are* themselves applications of technology: "In film this technological construction occurs at the level of both the material production of film itself and within the narrative" (Janes 93).

Science Fiction Film and Identifications

Science fiction film adds another aspect to the consideration of technology's relationship to the human: as a technological project in itself, the science fiction film's relationship to technology is different from that of the written science fiction text. In addition, mainstream science fiction films shape cultural meanings through their systems of representation to a much broader extent than does science fiction literature, which is consumed by a more selective audience than that of the mainstream Hollywood science fiction film. The following analyses of *Alien Resurrection* and *The Matrix* look at mainstream representations of technology and difference in which film's nature as a medium of spectacle is relevant, and they examine elements of a posthuman cyborg feminist subjectivity within these representations.

In *The Aesthetics of Ambivalence: Rethinking Science Fiction Film in the Age of Electronic (Re)Production,* Brooks Landon reexamines the relationship of science fiction literature and film and argues that different science fiction texts demand different critical discourses. Landon suggests that science fiction film "has its roots in spectacle rather than in narrative" (xiv) and thus moves the visual and acoustic sensation produced by special effects into the center of the text, dominating the narrative aspect. Or, as Annette Kuhn puts it in *Alien Zone: Cultural Theory and Contemporary Science Fiction Cinema,* "the technology of cinematic illusion displays the state of the art of its own art in science fiction films" (7).

In Part II of *Alien Constructions,* I examine the genre's obsession with not only the implications of science but also representations of technology. These representations play themselves out most dramatically in science fiction film, where visual and acoustic special effects place the narrative content within a sensual experience: technology becomes the medium (special effects spectacle) as well as the narrative drive (science fiction). The spectacle, as much as the narrative content, is the source of pleasure in the consumption of science fiction films. I explore representations of the interface of technology and the human in science fiction film and their implications for women's agency. These elements are discussed within the context of theories of cyborg feminism and cyberfeminism, where the feminist cyborg embodies the notion of an at times subversive, yet always problematic, identity within the exploitative conditions of global technoscience.

While feminist science fiction literature creatively deconstructs the white male subject position, the female embodiment of difference finds its most problematic representation in science fiction films. Both the cyborg narrative (characterized by cloned and enhanced technobodies) and cyberpunk (dominated by the computer-human interface) originally were defined as dominated by a white male subject position, but because of their ambivalent constructions have also been appropriated by feminists. Technology as a medium of representation (the science fiction film as spectacle) offers pleasurable as well as problematic identifications for the feminist viewer confronted with female cyborgs and virtual bodies.

Even though I recognize the specific representations of technology that science fiction film produces, my approach to *Alien Resurrection* and *The Matrix* is embedded within cultural theory's interest in what Kuhn calls the "cultural instrumentality" of texts: "perhaps more interesting, and probably more important, than what a film *is* is the question of what, in cultural terms, it *does*" (*Alien Zone* 1, emphasis hers). The cultural context to which I relate the films is cyborg feminism and its concern with the technological embodiment of difference. Therefore, the main focus here is not on the technological special effects of *Alien Resurrection* and *The Matrix,* but on the movie's relationship to cyborg feminism as a counter-discourse in the case of *Alien Resurrection,* and on the film's relationship to cyberpunk's representations of the body and subjectivity in the case of *The Matrix.* Both films produce conflicting images that simultaneously support and undermine tenets of cyborg feminism and its concepts of subjectivity.

The viewing of a movie involves processes of identification, based on the stylistic features of the film on one hand, and its narrative elements on the other. Both initiate certain interactive moments of recognition on the part of the audience and thereby create a relationship with the spectator. Identification in this context does not necessarily imply that the individual viewer wants to be (or thinks s/he is) a specific character on the screen, but rather that the viewing process allows moments of recognition and pleasure based on specific textual features, such as camera work, editing, visual effects, and narrative forms and content. Within the production and reception of movies, dichotomous criteria of identification are created for the self (dominant notions of ideal identities, economic and political power, the norm, the voice) and for the other, defined by difference (the abject, the horrifying, the rejected, the feared, the silenced). Identification criteria are established through practices of inclusion and exclusion, recognition and rejection, which are at work both in film techniques (framing, editing, etc.) and in cultural contexts and subject positions.[2] These practices simultaneously confirm and produce social structures of domination.[3] Familiarities like genre conventions serve as stabilizing effects on cultural positions; they "help to reinforce the cultural truths to which we subscribe and of which we may be unaware as the meanings of the text unfold" (Robertson 177). However, although movies are produced within an ideological framework, the viewer's interactions with the film can result at times in resistance to identifications—or subversive readings. These resistant reading processes create agency in the reception of films and of cultural texts in general.[4]

Therefore, in the consumption of popular cultural texts, the process of meaning production and identification is ambiguous and often unpredictable. At the same time, subversive or oppositional readings of texts are limited by the industrial and economic aspects of their production. Popular films are aimed to please as many people as possible—their (financial) success relies on it. Consequently, representations of radical and oppositional concepts are mostly translated into fashionable "others" who ultimately do not threaten dominant ideologies. Geoff King and Tanya Krzywinska caution in *Science Fiction Cinema* that it is important to consider the money factor in the production of popular culture:

> Social-cultural and industrial explanations can be mutually reinforcing, but not always. A specific focus on the industrial dimension can also provide some protection against the temptation to make too many generalised assumptions about the cultural 'meaning' of popular film. Neither science fiction films nor any others 'plug in', immediately, to social concerns. Such concerns, as far as they are manifested in the cinema, are mediated through commercial/industrial imperatives. (13)

What does this suggest for a potential subversive reading of any mainstream science fiction film? Dick Hebdige, in *Subculture: The Meaning of Style,* recognizes the co-optation and appropriation of subversive styles by dominant (consumer) culture, which depoliticizes them.[5] He points out "the dialectic between action and reaction which renders these objects meaningful" (2). When applied to the wider context, not merely of objects with applied meaning, but also of images and representations within popular culture (and the science fiction film in particular), this recognition of cultural meaning as a *dialectical process* that can be manipulated opens a window for a subversive reading of *Alien Resurrection* despite its blockbuster appeal, at the same time as it points to the weakness of *The Matrix*'s mainstream representations of cyberpunk.

3. Technoscience's Stepdaughter

The Feminist Cyborg in Alien Resurrection

Every story that begins with original innocence and privileges the return to wholeness imagines the drama of life to be individuation, separation, the birth of the self, the tragedy of autonomy, the fall into writing alienation; that is, war, tempered by imaginary respite in the bosom of the Other. These plots are ruled by a reproductive politics—rebirth without flaw, perfection, abstraction. In this plot women are imagined either better or worse off, but all agree they have less selfhood, weaker individuation, more fusion to the oral, to Mother, less at stake than masculine autonomy but there is another route to having less at stake in masculine autonomy. . . . It passes through women and present-tense, illegitimate cyborgs, not of Woman born, who refuse the ideological resources of victimization so as to have a real life.

—Donna Haraway, "A Cyborg Manifesto"

As of 2005, four films in the *Alien* series have been produced in the span of 18 years: *Alien* (1979), *Aliens* (1986), and *Alien³* (1992), referred to as the "trilogy," and *Alien Resurrection* (1997).[1] I agree with Stephen Scobies in "What's the Story, Mother? The Mourning of the Alien" that despite the differences in directors and production crews, the movies can be treated as "one extended work" (80), based on the unity provided by the protagonist, Ellen Ripley (played by Sigourney Weaver in all four movies), and the visual representation of the alien. In addition, the expectations of the audience make it one work: spectators treat the movies as a series. I thus discuss *Alien Resurrection* as part of the series.

The *Alien* series draws on elements of both the horror and science fiction genres[2] and creates narratives dominated by the fear of the alien—the other. The films display displacements of social and cultural fears and anxieties concerning otherness and the means to control it, as well as a resistance to this "marking" of the other. At the center of the *Alien* movies are questions about embodiment and the threat of a violation of the self's boundaries by the other. Accordingly, the most frightening element in the *Alien* series is the alien's invasion of the human body. The images and terrors connected to the alien's appropriation of the human form center around reproduction: "impregnation" followed by eruption from the body and the alien's mindless drive to reproduce. Throughout the trilogy, Ripley's mission is to protect the human self as the danger of invasion by that which is not-self (i.e. of becoming "pregnant" with an alien) steadily increases. This situation changes in *Alien Resurrection*, where the boundary crossing climaxes in the genetic recombination of Ripley and the alien queen, and Ripley's identity is defined by her merging with the other. Here the focus is on the development of Ripley's identity away from a rejection of the other and towards an acceptance of the other as *part* of the self. This process is filled with contradictions, since the other (the alien) remains fearful and strange, while simultaneously Ripley's growing connectedness with the alien enables a subversive reading of the movie. I read *Alien Resurrection* through a feminist cyborg lens, which emphasizes the appropriation of boundary crossing as central to a posthuman identity. Of interest is how the merging of the abject other and the self, facilitated by technoscience's tools, creates a posthuman identity that is empowering, not disempowering. This merging also results in the appropriation of an object position (as a scientific experiment and mother of an aberration) that is transformed into a subject position (as an agent of resistance).

Representations of the other that define the subject's relation to the center, and mechanisms that resist this process—such as the formation of counter-identities—are related to larger social institutions and structures. The appropriation of these representations as a means to resist construction as other, as emphasized in feminist cultural theories, constitutes a political potential within readings and productions of cultural texts.[5] Cyborg feminism argues that one of the main elements of cultural anxieties that shape representations is technology's relationship to the subject. Thus cyborg feminism examines the implications of dissolving boundaries between technology and humans, and between nature and culture, as they are being represented in science fiction narratives.

The female body finds itself in ambivalent and painful relationships to technology's offspring, machines. Both are understood to be separate from Man, the rational subject, in Western discourse; and both are seen, in seemingly paradoxical reasoning, as closer to nature than Man. Machines are viewed as identical to animals' mechanical functioning, which lacks a soul as well as rationality, and women's reproductive functions align them with nature's irrationality. When compared with the subject's (male) body, the female body is constructed as deviance, as Simone de Beauvoir (referring to sources such as Aristotle) points out in *The Second Sex:* "for it is understood that the fact of being a man is no peculiarity. . . . He thinks of his body as a direct and normal connection with the world, which he believes he apprehends objectively, whereas he regards the body of woman as a hindrance, a prison, weighed down by everything peculiar to it" (xxii).[4]

Both woman and machine undermine the white male subject position. Thus representations of women, together with technology's manifestations, incorporate displaced (patriarchal) cultural anxieties around issues of subjectivity, control, and self-determinism—they represent the ultimate "other," which simultaneously repulses and sparks desire of control. Female embodiment of difference finds its most complex representation in science fiction films: technology is part of both the medium (film as spectacle) and the narrative (science fiction), placing the body (both male and female) in relation to technology from the outset. As Linda Janes explains, feminist film theorists "develop the argument that the conceptual interrelationship between technoscience and gender is a defining representational characteristic of science fiction film texts" (92). Therefore technology is often understood to be inseparable from issues of *re*production, as Mary Ann Doane puts it in "Technophilia: Technology, Representation, and the Feminine," "And when technology intersects with the body in the realm of representation, the question of sexual difference is inevitably involved" (163). Furthermore, the Western binary of self/other, which defines sexual relations as well as human/un-human relations, also creates dualisms based on the racialized and classed other.

The *Alien* series disrupts the displacement of the other as an alien (or other un-human) that is conventional to many science fiction movies.[5] First, by juxtaposing the "classical" alien with another marginalized position, that of a woman, the films problematize conventional gendered mechanisms of identification:

> To add to the horror [of the alien], the viewer, in order to escape with a living model for emulation, must relate to and identify with a female character, whether the viewer is male or female. Women viewers have long been accustomed to the rather confusing situation of having to cross gender lines to identify with a heroic character or relate to the female victims . . . rescued by the masculine hero. (Bell-Metereau 10–11)

Secondly, constructions of the other in *Alien Resurrection* are manifested through the apparatus of technoscience, which is representative of patriarchal capitalism. Instead of controlling and destroying these aberrations, the system is challenged by its own creations: androids, clones, and alien monsters created in labs dominate the narrative and form the center of the spectacle the movie produces.

Alien Resurrection contains elements of contradiction between the displacement of the other as fearful and repulsive (the deviant) and the subversions of cultural paradigms (deconstruction of the norm) that its representations offer. Boundary transgressions that either create hybrids (in terms of species, i.e. human/alien, as well as in terms of technology, i.e. cyborgs) or consume the (human) individual are not uncommon in science fiction films; in fact, they constitute a major element. But conventionally they are depicted as terrifying, such as in *The Fly*, *The Invasion of the Body Snatchers*, and *The Thing*; more recently in *The Terminator* movies, *Species* and *Species II*, and *Star Trek Next Generation—First Contact*; and, of course, throughout the *Alien* trilogy. "Friendly" creatures of technology usually are purely mechanical with no human components (such as the robots C3PO and R2D2 in the *Star Wars* saga), with the notable exception of RoboCop, a human-based cyborg with a human consciousness who upholds the social status quo in his function as cop. In *Alien Resurrection*, these conventions are disrupted by Ripley's increased alignment with the alien as other. Thus there is no supporting character to either provide comic relief or disrupt normative representations through a (mostly racialized) hybridity—an element that Hollywood has always incorporated into its narratives (such as the "Indian half blood" in the Western). Instead, the protagonist is not only a construct, but a construct who claims a subject position.

A subversive reading of the film is complicated by the fact that, as a Hollywood production, the film is embedded within mainstream culture's tendencies to appropriate (and therefore depoliticize) subcultural elements, driven by a profit-oriented industry. Newman, in a review of the film, points out how *Alien Resurrection* is linked to merchandizing production. Since *Alien* was released, "there has been [a] proliferation of novel spin-offs and comic books . . . not to mention a line of successful action figures. [*Alien Resurrection*] is the first film to take back all the merchandising and incorporate it into the plot" (Newman 37). Not surprisingly, an expert in mass audiences wrote the screenplay: Joss Whedon, the creator of the television shows *Buffy the Vampire Slayer* and *Angel*. I am interested in exploring the film's liberating potential despite its commercialized status because the film seems to have much to offer feminists in its visualization of cyborg identities.

The *Alien* movies have attained cult status as a science fiction series,[6] and they fascinate with their rich and conflicting images. Central to this fascination is the figure of the protagonist, Ellen Ripley. Hailed as science fiction films' first female character who is both "hero" and survivor, she inspires feminists' interest in the constellation of woman and monster[7] at the same time as she serves as the male adolescent (or lesbian) viewer's wet dream. Her controversial role as the female "hero" dominates the violent encounters with the alien species in the trilogy and is at the center of the fourth movie, *Alien Resurrection*. Even though the series shares certain narrative elements (most consistently the figure of Ripley and the visual representation of the alien), each of the movies possesses a distinct quality that separates it from the others. This quality is based on the aesthetic choices of each movie's director and screenplay writers and is reflected in their representations of the characters.[8]

The constellation of figures whose identity and embodiment are created by the relations of technoscience links *Alien Resurrection* to cyborg imagery. Their identity formations imply an appropriation of their imposed existence and thus a claim of agency *within* the destructive constructions of power. A subversive "figuration" is reflected in *Alien Resurrection*, in which the boundary between other and self becomes blurred. This creates a text open to a subversive feminist interpretation of unstable identities, boundary crossing, and appropriation of positions of marginality as positions of empowerment. Here, Donna Haraway's argument about the importance of science and technology ("technoscience") in defining and controlling of contested boundaries finds new forms of representation.

In science fiction film, technology is often employed within the mise-en-scène to make visible how the system first constructs the other, only to then exclude it from its social structures.[9] In *Alien Resurrection,* we encounter a variety of these organic and mechanical cyborgian creatures who are designed to serve the interests of the system:[10] a human and an extraterrestrial clone who share genes (as well as numerous offspring of the latter), an android, and a human-alien hybrid. The lineup of technoscience's creations, which speaks to mind-bending technological achievements, is put into stunning contrast with "familiar" forms of marginalized existence, such as disabled people, reflected in Vriess (Dominique Pinon), one of the renegades, who is bound to a wheelchair. Jennifer Gonzalez reminds us that the cyborg is a creature that is not above or beyond existing power structures, but deeply embedded in them: "I do not see the cyborg body as primarily a surface or simulacrum which signifies only itself; rather the cyborg is like a symptom—it represents that which cannot otherwise be represented" (Gonzalez 268). Thus there are "subthemes" underlying the hunt for the alien in *Alien Resurrection,* including the relationships of Ripley (as a constructed female human) to un-human products of technology (androids) and to the alien itself, which supercede conventional representations of technology. Out of these "subthemes" of boundary crossing, a counter-identity or "cyborg consciousness" is developed (Gonzalez 268). At the core of this consciousness is the embodiment of difference, reflected in Ripley's embrace of her own identity as the "monster's mother."

The Construction of Ripley and the Alien as Others

Monsters have always defined the limits of community in Western imagination. (Haraway, "Manifesto" 180)

Alien Resurrection opens with the scanning of the "unrecognizables," what we later learn are genetically engineered mutants. The camera then rests on a figure asleep in a tank of water, a young girl visibly aging into the familiar form of Ripley.[11] Her adult voice, in a voice-over to the camera's movements, quotes Newt, the dead girl-child from *Aliens:* "My Mommy always said there were no monsters. No real ones. But there are." As if ironically commenting on the words that originally described the deadly aliens, the camera is now fixed on Ripley, a prod-

Figure 3.1. The scientists admire their creation, the cloned Ripley, in *Alien Resurrection.* Who is the monster now?

uct of human technoscience, while the accusing words are spoken. The scene is like a premonition of what Ripley is, and it introduces the central theme of the movie: Who is the monster now? (Fig. 3.1).

In science fiction movies, otherness is a structuring narrative element. Traditionally, aliens—extraterrestrials—represent the other, that which is feared most by the dominant voice and which needs to be conquered, destroyed, or mastered, reinforcing cultural narratives of (Western) domination.[12] In *Alien Resurrection,* the cultural narrative of the domination of the other is disrupted by violations of boundaries between self and other, between human and alien.

The Alien

From the outset, the most frightening aspect of the alien is its invasion of the human body as a host for its offspring. This characteristic is inevitably linked to notions of reproduction and the unconscious fear of the (m)other it entails, as displayed in the central (horrific) scene in *Alien,* where the creature erupts from a feminized male body. The threat to Ripley from that which is not-self becomes more pressing as the series unfolds and the aliens slaughter everyone around her.

The movies' increasing reliance on visual representation of the alien to induce horror, the spectacle that defines the viewer's relationship with the drama, foregrounds their insistence on the embodiment of difference. What in *Alien* starts out as mainly fear of the unknown (the crew—and the viewer—do not know what it is they have to confront) quickly becomes a fear of a thing that constantly transforms itself, and that is ultimately never revealed in its completeness until the end. In *Aliens*, the fear has grown into an oppressive fear of the uncontrollable known, as disgust and repulsion for the constitution and sheer number of the species increase.[13] The underlying main anxiety, the intrusion of the alien into one's own body, is fulfilled in *Alien³* when Ripley becomes host to precisely what she fears and hates most. In the laboratories of *Alien Resurrection*, the monster is finally seen close-up by the protagonist and the viewer alike. This development, the growing "intimacy" of Ripley (and the spectator) with the alien, climaxes with Ripley's actually becoming the "mother" of a new species in *Alien Resurrection*—her existence has made that of the hated other possible, and she loses some of her humanness in the process.

Throughout the series, the alien is placed within the realms of both the natural and the mechanical. This seemingly conflicting constellation echoes Descartes's definition of animals as machines, which forms the basis of a mechanical view of nature and which also places women and animals together into the category "different from man." The correlation of the alien's representation as both nature and technology discloses "the natural" as a cultural construction. In *Alien Resurrection*, the construction of "nature" becomes overt in the technological reproduction of not only the "animal," but also "woman."

The alien is *"mysteriously ungraspable* [in *Alien*], *viciously implacable, improbably beautiful"* (Greenberg 93, emphasis his), forming an opponent which produces immense anxieties within the viewer, reflecting simultaneous repulsion and fascination with/attraction to the other. Its transformation is one feature of the alien that reflects anxiety towards the foreign. The alien's existence seems determined by its reproductive cycle. Its eggs hatch creatures (the "face-huggers") that clamp onto humans' faces to inseminate them in order to carry aliens to term in their chests. After their deadly birth, the aliens shed skin as they grow into full size. The queen—female center of the horror—reaches a staggering size to produce the eggs. The explicitly sexual imagery of the visual representation of the alien speaks to the "sexual

Figure 3.2. The adult alien is terrifying in its deadly efficiency in *Aliens,* even as its techno-organic imagery is eerily beautiful.

nature of the creature's otherness" (Bell-Metereau 15) throughout the series.[14] In all its stages, the alien is animal-like in its features and movements. Starting with *Aliens,* its kind is increasingly compared to an insect-like society; the language of *hive, eggs, nest, queen,* and *drones,* used in this context, firmly places the alien within some ideological part of the animal kingdom. The face-hugger emerging from the organic egg is reminiscent of a starfish; the chest-burster looks like a deadly snake. The skeletal, mature alien crouches on all fours and has an immensely strong tail, a huge head with no visible eyes, a mouth full of long teeth, and a tongue with an additional small head with teeth, which hisses before it catapults into the enemy, destroying it. The mature alien is eerily beautiful; it has a "sumptuous elegance" (Greenberg 96) composed of techno-organic imagery (Fig. 3.2). Its frightening physique is combined with a cunning intelligence geared toward the survival of the species—at all costs.

This mindless striving associates the alien with nature—it is a perfect organism, designed to survive. Its bestiality makes it immune to cultural restrictions and obligations, setting it apart from the humans it encounters and anticipating Ripley's position in *Alien Resurrection.* Ash, the android in *Alien,* senses kinship with a being as separate from humanity as himself: "I admire its purity. A survivor. Unclouded by conscience, remorse, or delusions of morality." Our culture's fear of "Mother Nature," who resists control and domination, is met in the alien's fearsome physicality, as Robbie Robertson points out in "The Narrative Sources of Ridley Scott's *Alien*":

> The life cycle, its connotations, and the creature's savagery all become emblematic of the strangeness and ferocity to be found, barely-hidden, in nature. That power and ferocity, the otherness that our culture inscribes into 'nature', itself an invention subject to regular transformations, has the potential to disrupt not only narratives but also, most terrifying of all, our own lives. As the alien disrupts the order [the characters] are helpless before it, and their terror arouses a fearful recognition of our own vulnerability to the effects of nature's darkness. (Robertson 178)

While it is defined as part of mindless nature, the alien at times is reminiscent of the technology that dominates the world it so violently enters. Its ideological alignment with both nature and technology (as oppositional to the human) is visible in its bony body, which at times resembles mechanical structures. The alien's visual proximity to technology is reflected in the scene in *Alien* when it camouflages itself as part of the shuttle and is indistinguishable from the machinery surrounding it. And in *Alien³*, when Ripley searches for the alien in the basement, the spectator expects it to be hidden within the steel pipes and pillars, revealing a familiarity with the mise-en-scène: the lighting, the setting of industrial technology, the frightened, desperate human. The same scene places the alien overtly into lower regions of the sociocultural psyche of the viewer when Ripley answers the question of how she knows where it can be found: "I have a pretty good idea of where it is. It's just down there. In the basement. . . . (laughs) It's a metaphor."[15]

Lt. Ellen Ripley

Conflicting representations of the other are most dominant in Ripley and her relationship to the alien species. The main, obvious other—everything "we," the ideal audience, are not—is the alien, but it is joined in its rank as abject by Ripley, the protagonist. In *Alien,* she forms a "doubled other" because, as a *woman,* she fights what is evil to Man: "as human rather than alien, and feminine rather than masculine, she is both 'man' and not-man" (Belling 41). As a woman in the sphere of cultural production—a female on screen—her presence is both assuring (the alien does need an opponent) and disturbing, since a woman is conventionally perceived as the one to be saved. The eighteen years separating the production of *Alien,* which introduces Ripley as the female hero, and *Alien Resurrection* have brought changing cultural perceptions of gender roles in action on screen; the spectator is used to seeing women actively participating in the fight against evil, even though the division of labor in the battle is still clearly defined as requiring moral and ideological justifications for women's use of violence.[16] Yet, in *Alien Resurrection* Ripley is not only a woman but also a construct, a creature of un-human origin, which complicates the viewer's relationship to her as the female hero.

In "Time Travel, Primal Scene, and the Critical Dystopia," Penley argues that in science fiction films "the question of sexual difference—a question whose answer is no longer 'self-evident'—is displaced onto the more remarkable difference between the human and the other" (Penley 72). Penley observes that both *Alien* and *Aliens* create representations of (seeming) equality between men and women in terms of division of labor attire, and so on. As Penley states, *Aliens* includes "a mixed squad of marines, in which the women are shown to be as tough as the men, maybe tougher" (73). But the invisible sexual difference is reinstated in *Aliens* through the conservative marking of Ripley as feminine, based on her maternal feelings for the girl Newt.

Furthermore, in the course of the series, instead of being deferred only onto representations of un-humans, sexual difference is worked out on various levels. Representations of sexual difference change: in *Alien³*, sexual difference is presented as ideologically intact, as Ripley, the only female in the movie, is simultaneously stigmatized as the sinful sex by the religious convicts and becomes victim to their sexual assaults. It is also the first time Ripley is sexually active in the series. However, the visuals produce a pervasive sense of androgyny (the uniform of ragged, gray/khaki clothes and her shaved head assimilate Ripley into the lines of the all-male convicts) and lend the sensual encounter between Ripley and the doctor an almost homosexual or transgendered quality.

In *Alien Resurrection,* Ripley's otherness, generated by her genetic modifications, is significantly tied to a heightened sexuality as well as to more aggressive behavior. She is clad in tight leather and displays naked, lean, muscular arms (Fig. 3.3). Her spiky green nails link her

Figure 3.3. In *Alien Resurrection,* Ripley's un-human strength is paired with a heightened sexuality. She is a "sexed-up" female warrior with distinctly queer qualities.

with both the animalistic visuals of the aliens and the female/femme vamp. For the first time in the series, Ripley is represented like other sexualized warrior women on screen, such as *The Terminator*'s Sarah Connor and Trinity in the *Matrix* films. When the chronically horny Johner (Ron Perlman), in stereotypical masculine fashion, makes intimidating sexual advances on Ripley, she first toys with him and then knocks him down. Her otherness *enhances* her sexual difference, as it does for other female cyborgs whose relationship to technology or alien contact lets their dangerous female sexuality go rampant, such as Eve VIII in *Eve of Destruction* and the alien-infected breeder-woman in *Species I* and *II*. The differences between these figures and Ripley is that the other figures are cast in the "evil" role to begin with, while the latter is placed in an ambivalent relationship with dominant culture at the outset. In addition, Ripley's sexuality is distinctly "queered."[17]

Sexual Difference, Race, and Class

Missing from Penley's analysis is an examination of the displacement of sexual difference from "the more remarkable difference between the human and the other" onto differences based on class and race. While feminist theories on film emphasize the psychoanalytic dimension of sexual difference, other theories point to the limits of sexual difference as the only analytical variable, without racial and class difference. Many writers have established that science fiction literature and film often depict the (white) cultural fear of being "othered" by the racialized other.[18] The at times contradictory representations of anxieties regarding race, class, and gender lend *Alien Resurrection* its cyborgian feminist quality. For example, sexual difference finds some of its most conventional heterosexual representations, such as Johner's sexual advances toward anything that has breasts, and the scene of sexual intimacy between the pirate's chief, Elgyn (Michael Wincott), and his partner, Hillard (Kim Flower). The movie also embraces a (typically liberal) erasure of sexual difference through the absence of a visible division of labor: the science team as well as the renegade group include women with scalpels and big guns, respectively. However, the film's portrayal of sexual difference is also complicated by Ripley's relationship to the female android Call (Winona Ryder), which has lesbian undertones; by her rather aggressive sexuality, which is not available to men; and by Ripley's monstrous maternity, which is actually produced by a patriarchal system. Science fiction films *align* differences based on gender, race, class, and sexuality, creating hybrids and otherness that threaten the masculine, stable self, based on more than just sexual difference.

In "Born Again," Michael Eaton points to the class-oriented nature of *Alien*, in which a working-class crew is undermined by The Company's saboteur, an android. James Kavanaugh, in "Feminism, Humanism, and Science in *Alien*," critically examines the film's recurring humanism from a Marxist perspective. In *Aliens*, class differences are still intact but are complicated by the fact that this time The Company's disposable bodies are military. In contrast, in *Alien³*, Ripley's co-fighters are criminals, outcasts, and convicts. Throughout the trilogy, The Company, a capitalist institution, is Ripley's enemy in her fight against the alien. In *Alien Resurrection*, capitalist power is realigned with military power: The Company is now United Military Systems. (In *Aliens* the military is presented, in typical Hollywood fashion, as a group of good foot soldiers who are the innocent tool of corrupt politics.) Throughout the series, capitalism is omnipresent, at the heart of the narrative structure, and represents institutionalized power. Mark Schemanske points to Susan Jefford's observation that The Company's seeming invincibility is reminiscent of the alien: both are "omnivorous, insatiable, and deadly" (128). The Company's power is reflected in the visuals: the huge freight spacecraft *Nostromo* in *Aliens* and the gigantic industrial plant in *Alien³* speak to capitalism as we know it.

In the fourth movie, technoscience lends capitalism a new outfit: scientific laboratories dominate its representations. The film still reeks of disposable bodies, however: the pirates capture a group of miners to be used by the scientists as breeders for the project. Their unconscious bodies are kept in hypersleep in metal, coffin-like boxes—cryotubes. Once the alien face-huggers hatch from their eggs, scientists watch from behind a glass wall while the aliens latch onto the faces of the restrained miners, who, now conscious, scream in terror. The working-class body is expendable; it is nothing but a commodity within the capitalist system of exchange (the pirates get paid by the United Military Systems for the "cargo"). One of the miners is still carrying the alien inside him when the renegade group encounters him in a destroyed lab. At first he is unaware of the abuse his body has suffered at the hands of the scientists; he learns from Ripley of the monster inside him. As a mere object within a reproductive process directed by technological interference, his body is feminized in its pregnancy with the unwanted alien, and here class difference and sexual difference collapse. After the group decides to take him with them onto the *Betty* (the renegades' spacecraft) to "freeze" and later save him, he dies when the alien erupts from his chest. In a defiant last act of resistance, he pulls the scientist—who commodified and dehumanized his working-class body in the name of technoscience—in front of him, using the alien to kill him in the process of its birth. *Alien Resurrection* reflects the power of the labs, whose capitalist endeavor disposes of the bodies of laborers—and depicts Ripley and her group as resistant to that process.

Gonzalez points out that there "seems to be a general tendency to link the 'otherness' of machines with the otherness of racial and sexual difference" (275). This tendency is problematic in that it conflates racial and sexual difference, erasing historical constructions of racism. Racialized difference is, as Eaton argues, one of the key elements in *Aliens,* the most conservative of the four movies in its representations of difference: "The protean outsider was a threat to the stability of the family unit, space-alien consciously (if jokingly) equated with the 'illegal alien'. Paranoia from the Right" (8). The seemingly endless reproduction of aliens and literal consumption of the planet's colonists(!) reflect the white colonists' fear of invasion by the oppressed racial other. It is also in *Aliens* that Ripley's status as woman warrior (with its threatening violation of traditional gender roles) is balanced by her cultural whiteness. The only other woman in the film is the female marine, Vasquez. The Latina/Chicana Vasquez stands in a complex visual relationship to Ripley that is enhanced by race. As Ros Jennings points out in "Desire and Design," "Because the marines are made up of men and women doing the same job, ideas about gender are liberated from the constructs created by patriarchal division of labor. The effectiveness of the scene [in negotiating sexual difference], therefore, depends on the use of other visual codes to indicate difference" (199). In addition to the codes of military/civilian and butch/femme, racial codes emphasize the difference between Vasquez and Ripley. Earlier, *Alien* represents its only black figure as equal to his white coworkers, basically avoiding any real portrayal of race relations. *Alien³*'s treatment of race is more subversive: the powerful figure of the black priest, who historically has proven a threat to United States white supremacy, becomes Ripley's ally. The representation of the black male in *Alien Resurrection* is the most antiestablishment: Christie (Gary Dourdon) is a Rastafarian, whose looks and language align him with black counterculture; as a member of the renegade group, he is already positioned outside the (literally) white system (all of the scientists are white). It is interesting that the general in charge of the operation is Latino—here the film regressively feeds into the stereotype of the power-hungry Latin American dictator.

The main underlying racial themes of *Alien Resurrection* are miscegenation and "passing." Ripley's crossover to the other is complete with

Figure 3.4. In *Alien Resurrection,* after passing as human, Call is discovered to be an android. She immediately becomes an outsider to the humans and becomes aligned with Ripley's otherness.

her contamination with alien blood. She becomes stronger through the genetic exchange; it is impossible to control her. She is a true racial other in that her origin is impure. The female android Call, on the other hand, is a technological other. In addition to her technological (and sexual) otherness, her role offers an analogy to racial passing: apparently a weak, smallish woman, she is "outed" as a virtually invincible cyborg, confusing expectations and certainties. Consonant with racial passing, Call's personal safety is threatened by a discovery—her right to equal treatment by others is based on their belief in her humanity. After a scientist shoots her, she is discovered to be a robot. Immediately she is constructed as an outsider; she loses her position as part of the group and suddenly finds herself aligned with Ripley and her "racialized" otherness. This detachment of Call from the group is reinforced by the camera angle, which places Call's tear-streaked face in close-up in the foreground, while the others' distance to her is emphasized by their positioning in the background (Fig. 3.4). Once she is discovered to be a machine, the humans (some of whom thought of her as a friend) reject her as a "freak" and dehumanize her. Thus Johner makes jokes at her expense: "You got a socket wrench? Maybe she just needs an oil change."

Call's identity can also be read in terms of gender passing. She is definitely coded as a desirable woman: Jonah constantly lusts after her, and Elgyn refers to her as "extremely fuckable." Once her origin is disclosed (as nonfemale, i.e. gender-variant), that desirability is revoked—Jonah is repulsed and relieved to turn her rejection of him into his salvation:

"I can't believe I almost fucked a robot!" Just as racial and gender passing are threatening to the social order, technological passing undermines hierarchies and denaturalizes categories by disclosing them as
constructed: until she was "outed" as a machine, Call was perceived as
a rather overemotional, sexually attractive woman. Once she is known
to be an android, she is recategorized as un-human.[19]

Thus Ripley is threatening to the viewer as an actual construct—
not just as a woman. Her connection to the hated alien disrupts and
disturbs the spectator's pleasure, the sexy and hip images notwithstanding. In the course of the series, Ripley's status as an outsider, a
figure at the external bounds of structures of power, gradually inten-
sifies as her obsession to destroy the alien species makes her increasingly an opponent of The Company (representing social, economic,
and political power), and a "freak" to the people she works with (such
as the marines in *Aliens* and the all-male convicts in *Alien³*). In *Alien
Resurrection*, she is further isolated from other humans through her
physical kinship with the alien, as her strength and instinct set her
apart. (The scientist's comment about her mental capacities is "She's
freaked," whereas the ultimate challenge uttered towards her—ironically, by an android—is "She's not human!") As a product of technoscience, she becomes defined as the other, and shares this status with
the despised alien.

The growing connectedness between Ripley and the alien in *Alien
Resurrection* constitutes the most disturbing, but also the most promising, element in terms of theories of boundary transgression. The transformational makeup of the alien, its progression through various stages
to finally reach its mature form, echoes the relationship of Ripley with
it—a literal love-hate bond with uncertain identities and undefined
loyalties, subject to constant change and adaptation. The genetic kinship, engineered by science, forms the climax of Ripley's equation with
the monster as other and removes her completely from the realm of the
norm into a social space as yet undefined and unmapped by dominant
discourse.

"She's a Toaster Oven": Subversion of
Technology's Constructions

In *Terminal Identity*, Scott Bukatman points out that science fiction repeatedly explores the overlap of human/machine that has its epistemo-

logical and analytical origin in cybernetics' definition of the human as an information-processing system, especially since technological developments are redefining the human shape. Bukatman writes: "The overlap of technology and biology ceases to be a categorical question and becomes instead a fundamental, existent, cyborg fact" (322). Science fiction thereby explores the implications of changing definitions of the human in both directions: either it depicts technology as problematic in its impact on our understanding of what is human, or it points to the limits of a purely biological category. "In both cases the human is presented as one part of a broader technological matrix; a science fiction in a much broader sense" (Bukatman 322).

In its representations of technoscience's products, *Alien Resurrection* takes up these two directions in dealing with technology's relationship to the human. Ripley's cloned existence (and the way she is treated/viewed by others because of it) makes her inseparable from technology; it reduces her to a functionalist entity that can be reproduced at will. Although she is of human origin (she did exist, at one point, as a human), without technology she would not be, which places her onto shaky ontological grounds. This aspect is, of course, further complicated by her mixed genetic makeup, which would not have been possible without technoscientific interference—after all, the "original" alien is not out to crossbreed with humans. The female android Call, in contrast, is not biologically human; yet, like the replicants in *Blade Runner* and Data in *Star Trek—Next Generation,* she displays human sentiments, challenging the biological definition of human. Ripley and Call both implode the separation of human and machine, and insist that humanity is more than its biology:

> The offspring of these technocientific wombs are cyborgs—imploded germinal identities, densely packed condensations of worlds, shocked into being from the force of the implosion of the natural and the artificial, nature and culture, subject and object, machine and organic body, money and lives, narrative and reality. (Haraway, *Modest Witness* 14)

In science fiction, as in social relations, technology is a means to control the other since access to technology and know-how is closely connected to social power. Thus relationships to technology are gendered (and racialized) in their symbolism.[20] The industrial, mechanical technology, controlled by communication technology in the trilogy, is enhanced by *bio*technology in *Alien Resurrection*. Technoscience here is represented in its most familiar and graspable form, with scientists performing experiments in the service of an organization that profits commercially from these operations and gains political power.

The spaceships' board computers in *Alien* and *Alien Resurrection*[21] both connect communication technology directly to a gendered position: "Mother," the computer in *Alien*, is the "representative of the will of the appropriately absent Father (the Company)." She is nurturing at the same time as she is destructive: "the alien's life support, is the ship itself, the computer Mother" (Kavanaugh 76–77).

In *Alien Resurrection*, the patriarchal will is very much present—the board computer "Father" makes the mediation of the mother unnecessary: the "children" on the ship are not born by her; they are constructed through patriarchal technoscience, rendering the maternal presence obsolete. Doane quotes the postmodern cultural critic Andreas Huyssen, who states that "the ultimate technological fantasy is creation without the mother" (Doane, "Technophilia" 168). Braidotti points out the age-long dream in Western thought of creating children without mothers—the "Fantasy of Male-Born Children" (Braidotti, *Nomadic Subjects* 87). Thus these "unnatural" offspring represent patriarchal desire to control the maternal—the monstrous. Ripley, the alien, and Call are aligned in a perverse kinship in their motherless existence, as well as in their resistance to it—even though this resistance admittedly takes very different forms.

On a narrative level, technology in the *Alien* movies is often employed to counter the alien, creating a dualism of technology versus alien. Ironically (and significantly!), high technology usually fails to control the alien, and Ripley and those around her resort to primitive weapons—usually fire. This irony reaches its climax when the seemingly all-powerful technoscientific apparatus in *Alien Resurrection* is overpowered by a savage creature with no other technology than its body. In one scene, a scientist approaches one of the cells holding an alien in order to taunt it. Separated from the alien by a glass wall, the scientist mimics the alien's hiss and menacing lip curling, ridiculing its threat and reveling in its powerlessness. The mirror effect of the scene echoes the concept of self/other, where the self identifies through *not* being the other, and where identity and power relations are produced in one's containing the movements and freedom of the other. The scien-

Figure 3.5. In the science lab, the cloned Ripley meets herself in Mutants 1–7. Sharing the same alien/human genes with these "unrecognizables," her impure existence is built on their silence and sufferings.

tist punishes the growing aggression of the alien by hitting a red button, which releases a painful ice-mist. This scenario and power structure later are almost comically reversed by the alien's act of mimicry when the aliens escape and a soldier is killed by human technology: when the soldier investigates the cell, the alien—now on the other side of the glass wall—hits the red button, freezing the man to death.

Biotechnology, as the central manifestation of high technology in *Alien Resurrection,* reflects concrete fears in contemporary Western societies, in which the cloning of animals (and humans) and genetic engineering of plants dominate technological discourses. Ripley has the number 8 tattooed onto her forearm, and in the course of the movie she finds the chamber where cloning experiments Numbers 1 through 7 are preserved—kept alive for scientific purposes (Fig. 3.5). After she realizes what she is seeing, and finds one of the mutants alive and able to communicate with her—the mutant tells her to "kill me"—Ripley destroys them. The viewer realizes at this point that the scenes at the start of the movie were camera close-ups tracing the outlines and features of these mutants, not revealing their shapes as a whole, but presenting them as fragmented. These "unrecognizables" are the creatures inhabiting laboratories' unpublished reports: deranged mutants who are hurting, incomplete, and suffering, with no voice to articulate their identity—the precursors to Ripley's impure, but perfected, existence. They are the origins of the creatures born from technoscience; there is no mythical and miraculous delivery from an innocent vantage point, only the commercialized and remorseless experiments in the name of science.[22] The scene has no real narrative purpose (there are, after all, no aliens to kill in that chamber) and finds closure with its end, never to be referred to again in the film. Yet, as Eaton observes, "this sequence of narrative stasis seems somehow the omphalic centre of the picture, suddenly making physical the film's themes of scientific experimentation, monstrous birth and genetic hybridisation" (8).

Gendered Cyborgs

Ripley's relation to the mutants removes her from the cultural family of the masculine cyborgs that dominate popular culture. Even though there are many forms of cyborgs represented in our culture, hypermasculine figures such as the Terminator and RoboCop represent the prototypical cyborg to many people. As Springer explains, "While television, science-fiction literature, and comic books have explored diverse and imaginative ways to depict the fusion of humans and technological artifacts, mainstream films have privileged the violently masculinist figure" (96). Representations of technology are thus linked to metaphors of gender: hard, muscular, armed masculine bodies oppose fluid, morphing, unstable feminine forms. The body as armor, with technology as a shield to prevent invasion and dissolution of the ego, as it is examined by Klaus Theweleit in *Male Fantasies,* is discussed by Mark Dery in "Body Politic" and by Claudia Springer in *Electronic Eros.* Springer and Dery point to the explicitly masculine and feminine representations of technology, which relate to the threat feminine elements pose to the protofascist ego, described by Theweleit in his analysis of German *Freikorps* soldiers. "Many mainstream commercial films remain firmly entrenched in a tradition that upholds conventional sex roles and maintains a stable masculine subject position by constructing a gaze assumed to be male" (Springer 97). This is visible in the contrasting forms of the two terminators in the second *Terminator* movie, *Judgment Day,* in which the masculinist hard bodies of both Connor and the old Terminator are threatened by the feminine morphing of the new Terminator, which ultimately finds concrete form in the female Terminator in *Terminator 3.*

Springer's and Dery's observations of cyborg representations emphasize that "technophallicism remains at odds with technofeminism" (Dery 105). Springer's detailed analysis of gendered representations of technology in science fiction film and comic books reveals how female resistance to patriarchal technology (the masculine cyborg), as well as to the threat of the all-consuming feminine other (the alien), often resorts to masculine bodies and weapons. The figure of Sarah Connor in the *Terminator* movies is the most prominent example of the "warrior woman" in science fiction film, and of course Ripley, especially in *Aliens,* and more recently Trinity in the *Matrix* films also fit this model. While Dery dismisses these representations as male fantasies ("Hollywood's exploitation of the Freudian subtext of a sweaty woman squirting hot lead from a throbbing rod could hardly be called empowering" [105]), Springer points to the ambivalence of these images, which do invoke satisfaction as feminist revenge fables in female viewers, even as they are recognized as problematic. They create a troublesome "clash of protofascist masculine imagery with feminist ideals, often in the same films" (Springer 113).

A crucial difference in terms of representations lies between *human* female resistance (the woman warrior) and female *technology* as a threat to patriarchy (the female cyborg). While it can be argued that female viewers can appropriate both Connor and Ripley in the trilogy as moments of resistance (they do win the battles they fight), representations of female cyborgs are more problematic. Some of the most violent and disturbing hybrids represented in contemporary science fiction films are female, such as Eve VIII in *Eve of Destruction,* the alien-hybrid in *Species I* and *II,* the Borg Queen in *First Contact,* and the Terminator in *Terminator 3.* While male cyborg figures like the Terminator and RoboCop are violent, armored bodies, female cyborgs are most threatening based on their aggressive sexuality, such as that of Eve VIII,[23] and on their reproductive drives, such as those of the sex-obsessed woman in *Species.* These women sport excessive sexual traits and feminine attire, so that often their dangerous makeup lies hidden inside their reproductive system. Eve VIII looks harmless (like a sexy blond woman), yet hides a nuclear device in her womb(!), and the genetically infected woman in *Species* is an attractive, promiscuous young woman. While the most obvious threat of the Borg Queen lies in her relationship to technology, her main strategy to win Data is sexual seduction. All are a threat to the patriarchal system that defeats their (decidedly feminine-coded) aspirations of boundary transgression and their drives. Unlike these rather unpleasant (and disempowering, since they usually die) cyborg women, both Ripley and Call represent more ambivalent existences that are born from the problematic liaison between the human and technology.[24]

Both Ripley and Call are cyborgs in that they only exist as the direct result of technoscientific processes, but they differ from their male counterparts in their relationship to technology. Both the Terminator's and RoboCop's relationships to technology are troublesome: in the first movie, the Terminator *is* pure technology—void of any emotions, he is completely inhuman. RoboCop, on the other hand, never stops being human—his figure is always connected to his (lost) identity as a man. In both figures, the relationship between man and machine is quite clearly laid out: machines are inhuman and therefore evil *(The Terminator)*, or the human is superceded by technology, and therefore the human touch is precious and always superior to pure technology *(RoboCop)*. In contrast, *Alien Resurrection* complicates our relationship to technology: as in the movie *Blade Runner,* the biological category "human" is challenged in the figures of both Ripley and Call, and similar strategies are employed in both films, such as having these characters engage in passing and bringing in the unreliable concept of memory as a human trait. The origins of these female cyborgs lie in postindustrial communication technology and genetic engineering, and the metaphors that come with them. And their origins correspond more to cyberpunk's lean, tech-savvy bodies than to the protofascist body as armor. Here, technology is not represented as body (as) armor, a comforting, clunking industrial machine that, as Springer tells us, reassures patriarchal fears of boundary transgression: typical male cyborgs "perpetuate and even exaggerate the anachronistic industrial-age metaphor of externally forceful masculine machinery, expressing nostalgia for a time when masculine superiority was taken for granted and an insecure man needed only to look at technology to find a metaphor for the power of phallic strength" (111).[25] Instead, technology suddenly is part of what we define as human, so Call is much more "humane" than the humans around her. And Ripley's eightfold existence raises the question of *when* her humanity begins—she is declared "perfect," "done," when her form resembles the human form, yet her genetic makeup is the same through all eight attempts.

Thus the main representational function of Ripley and Call is boundary transgression, the implosion of the dualisms that keep patriarchal power structures intact. *Alien Resurrection* seems to celebrate the implosion of categories: Ripley, instead of dying or (the major threat of her genetic crossover) changing over to the side of the aliens, remains the competent protagonist and hero. This outcome, of course, also embodies the danger of appropriation of the cyborg by a mainstream film: by opting to save humankind, not the aliens, Ripley ideologically positions herself with humanism, despite the unease she instills in the viewer.

At the same time as Ripley and the alien represent biotechnology's highest triumph, they are also its defeat: the merging of two species, the exchange of genes, produces knowledges and strengths which get out of control and develop their own rules and dynamics. The United Systems Military's attempt to achieve the "natural" perfection of the monster through technoscience fails dramatically. Instead of passively breeding, the aliens decide to destroy their re-creators, and instead of meekly playing along with their rules, Ripley refuses to be "tamed."

"I Am the Monster's Mother": Cyborg Identity and the Acceptance of Difference

[The mother] is there in the text's scenarios of the primal scene of birth and death; she is there in her many guises as the treacherous mother, the oral sadistic mother, the mother as the primordial abyss; and she is there in the film's images of blood, of the all-devouring vagina, the toothed vagina, the vagina of Pandora's box; and finally she is there in the chameleon figure of the alien, the monster as fetish-object of and for the mother. But it is the archaic mother, the reproductive/generative mother, who haunts the *mise-en-scène*. (Barbara Creed, "*Alien* and the Monstrous Feminine" 128)

From the beginning of the series, growing with each movie, is a latent equation of Ripley and her hated foe, the alien, by others around them —The Company; the people she works with to kill the alien (marines and ex-prisoners); and finally the scientists in *Alien Resurrection,* who call her a "meat by-product" of the process of reconstructing the alien queen, connecting her existence to that of the foreign species. One central image in this process of representation and resistance throughout the series is that of "mother," signifying the maternal. As Eaton points out, Ripley has been tied to maternal images throughout the series: "After saving Jones the cat in *Alien,* Ripley had been given the role of surrogate mother when she cradles Newt in *Aliens;* at the end of *Alien³* she was giving succor to the alien baby within her. . . . In *Alien Resurrection,* this surrogacy will be actualised" (9). As a product of techno-science, Ripley is as much a monster as a machine—as is the alien. Both are tied to the maternal in terms of narrative and in terms of representation, confirming Doane's suggestion that, in narratives of technology on screen, it is "not so much *production* that is at stake in these representations as *reproduction*" ("Technophilia" 164, emphasis hers).

Monstrous Mothers

Throughout the series, the alien is constructed as the ultimate abjection of male-defined subjectivity, which constitutes its main threat to the (male) viewer: "Outside the margins defined by abjection, what is human is endangered, and what is most human, according to androcentric human culture, is man" (Belling 38). The female body personifies the maternal, and within the binary logic of phallogocentric discourse aligns the monstrous with the feminine as a negative pole of the norm. As Braidotti explains, "Within this dualistic system, monsters are, just like bodily female subjects, a figure of devalued difference" (*Nomadic Subjects* 80), as are other "abnormal" bodies, such as black bodies, the disabled, or malnourished, sick ones.

"The monstrous in *Alien* [and the series] is maternal" (Belling 39), is the (m)other. Belling points out that *Alien* fails to place the feminine on either side of the horror spectrum: despite the female hero, sexual difference (the maternal) constitutes the source of terror, "which reveals the fundamental paradox of women's relationship to patriarchal culture" (Belling 40).[26] What differentiates *Alien Resurrection* from the earlier movies is its obvious acknowledgement of Ripley's kinship with the alien as other, and the conflicting identifications this produces in the viewer.

Throughout the series, the archaic maternal element is in conflict with patriarchal ideology of the mother as a nurturing member of the nuclear family. This conflict becomes especially apparent in *Aliens,* where Ripley is compared to her opponent in terms of maternal qualities: both she and the queen represent certain maternal qualities and drives. In "What's the Story, Mother?" Scobie discusses the dual construction of Ripley and the alien as "mothers." While Ripley is the

Figure 3.6. The archaic maternal is represented in the mindless reproductive drive of the queen, as well as in her destructive protection of the foreign species in *Aliens*.

"good" mother, the alien queen—the "monstrous mother-machine" (Doane, "Technophilia" 169)—symbolizes the "bad" mother, the all-encompassing, mindless, suffocating maternal principle which contrasts with the rational, symbolic realm of the father/patriarchal law and that can only be contained in specific social settings (such as the nuclear family) (Fig. 3.6).

Nevertheless, both Ripley and the queen represent one side of the same spectrum of reproduction ideology, and they are placed into kinship. Both are associated with nature—the irrational and uncontrollable, Man's evil counterpart: in *Alien³* Ripley is stigmatized as Woman the Sin, based on religious ideology (the comments on patriarchal Christian religion depicted in *Alien³* are echoed in the chapel scene in *Alien Resurrection*). This ideology equates her with mindless nature—and with the alien, which represents evil per se. This kinship is increasingly pathologized and carried to its extreme in *Alien³* with Ripley's horrid pregnancy. Ripley violently resists this blood tie when she seeks out the alien in the hope that it will kill her. Instead, the feared kinship is acknowledged when the (male) alien refuses to kill Ripley because it senses that she is carrying the queen—her potential *maternity* aligns her with the other. The scene where the male alien for the first time

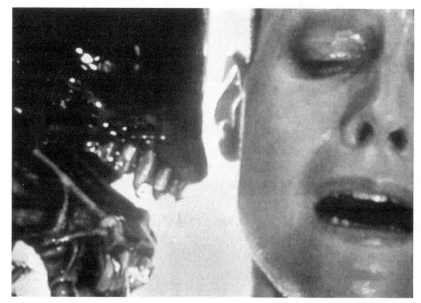

Figure 3.7. The alien senses Ripley's pregnancy with the queen in *Alien³* and does not kill her. The shared close-up of Ripley and her foe enhances a visual similarity between the two that foreshadows their kinship in *Alien Resurrection*.

senses the queen inside her also establishes a visual similarity between Ripley, with her clean-shaven head, and the alien's skull-like jaw, further emphasizing Ripley's alignment with the other (Fig. 3.7).

In *Alien Resurrection*, Ripley's connection to the alien culminates when the quasi-human woman becomes mother to a new race; she becomes "the monster's mother." With this development, Ripley's alignment with the alien as other has reached its most direct stage, and, in her merging with the monster as mother, she poses the most danger to the system. In "Becoming the Monster's Mother: Morphologies of Identity in the *Alien* Series," Catherine Constable examines through a psychoanalytic lens the maternal as nonidentity in the trilogy. This nonidentity changes, she argues, in *Alien Resurrection*, where Ripley's subjectivity is established, not through the rejection of the abject/object, but through the *intersection* with the other (her clones, the alien queen, and the alien infant). Constable's psychoanalytic treatment of the mother, not as object (to be rejected) but as subject position, which rethinks "physical matter as a site of subjectivity" (Constable 174), is helpful for understanding Ripley's connection to the alien as empowering. However, Constable's analysis does not consider the role of technoscience as a cultural practice in redefining the m(other) position, which is central to understanding her agency.

The most terrifying result of the bond between Ripley and the alien is the monster-child born in pain by the queen (not hatched—a genetic "gift" from Ripley), which among other things inherits Ripley's eyes, a horrifyingly human feature. It manifests Ripley's worst fear throughout the trilogy: giving birth to the monster, setting it alive. Born from a maternal body—which, as Kristeva argues, is already both a site of life and death—and genetically contaminated, the monster-child also represents the ultimate abjection that eternally surfaces, the fear of boundary violation that might obliterate the subject: "The monstrous or deviant is a figure of abjection in so far as it trespasses and transgresses the barriers between recognizable norms or definitions" (Braidotti, *Nomadic Subjects* 82).

Through the artificial procreation of biotechnology, the link between monsters and mothers becomes inseparable from machines/technology (concepts already connected with the feminine). In *Alien Resurrection*, patriarchal desire to control the maternal is displayed in the "unnatural" existence of both Ripley and the alien, and it finds its culmination in the birth of the monster-child, which spells both triumph and defeat for the technoscience apparatus. "Technology promises more strictly to control, supervise, regulate the maternal—to put *limits* upon it. But somehow the fear lingers—perhaps the maternal will contaminate the technological" (Doane, "Technophilia" 170, emphasis hers). The extended power of science over the maternal body, which feminists voice concern over, seems specifically applicable to Ripley—after all, she constitutes biotechnology's link between mothers and monsters, and she seems to be testimony to the process which "displaces women by making procreation a high-tech affair" (Braidotti, *Nomadic Subjects* 79). However, this power is reappropriated by Ripley's resisting actions, her refusal to be paralyzed by her sexual difference as man's abnormal other, who "carrie[s] within herself something that makes her prone to being an enemy of mankind, an outsider in her civilization" (Braidotti, *Nomadic Subjects* 80). Instead, she asserts her identity as the body that is "pregnant" with otherness; she almost relishes the danger it poses to others when she declares her kinship with the alien: "I am the Monster's Mother."

The merging of Ripley and the alien due to their shared experiences of a perverted origin/birth (both are cloned) and motherhood (both share a child) seems like an ironic comment on Ripley's construction as the "good," and the alien as the "bad," mother. This irony is also reflected in the absence of the maternal feelings that were displayed by Ripley in the trilogy (towards either the cat or Newt), which grounded her in the safe realm of the "good" maternal. In *Alien Resurrection,* the only positive emotions Ripley displays are towards the aliens, especially her alien child, and Call, another construct. Her feelings for the android are devoid of any maternal projections; they are for a fellow construct, with explicit undertones of queer desire.

The use in *Alien Resurrection* of lesbian imagery disrupts the (increasingly unstable) heterosexual representation found in the trilogy. As Jennings observes in "Desire and Design—Ripley Undressed," *Alien* "managed to blur the categories of identity long enough to open a textual gap for lesbian affinities" (205). Furthermore, Ripley's feelings for the alien species in *Alien Resurrection* are contradictory and painful: as much as she feels a certain loyalty towards them, she wastes no sentiment on them. At the same time, she does not seem to hate them; she is out for her own good only. Thus she remarks, after killing one of the alien warriors: "It was in my way." Whereas Ripley before has "signifie[d] the 'acceptable' form and shape of woman" (Creed 140), supported by reassuring images of maternal qualities,[27] she now operates without the cultural markers of acceptable motherhood: since the only maternal feelings she displays are for the monster, her construction as a conventional heroine is subverted. The conflation of the monstrous and the maternal in the *Alien* series results in an appropriation of the position of other by Ripley in the fourth movie.

Monsters and Machines

Like other science fiction movies, *Alien Resurrection* challenges notions of reproduction and definitions of humanity that have evolved around them. As Doane suggests, "[These films] contemplate the impact of drastic changes in reproductive processes on ideas of origins, narratives, and histories" ("Technophilia" 169). After the queen has been removed from her, Ripley is held by the scientists like a lab animal: confined in her movements, examined on a regular basis, and in general treated as a curiosity, she is, as she explains to Call, "the latest thing." At first she is referred to by some of the scientists as "it" until she "proves" herself human enough to have a gender. Initially Ripley, who is simply named Number 8, seems not to have any recollection of who she used to be or where she came from. She needs to learn the language and the culture around her anew. Like the film *Blade Runner*, the movie problematizes concepts of identity linked to memories and childhood experiences. Ripley's personal past does not consist of an Oedipal conflict defining her relationship to others. There are no cultural memories to shape her identity, no myths to secure her within her position. The only memories she has are passed down from alien genes; they are as much part of her memory as she has become part of the monster's. Her only history, personal and as a species, is inevitably tied to that of the alien—which she has been trying to eliminate for so long—echoing her desperate declaration in *Alien³*: "You've been in my life so long, I can't remember anything else." At the same time as this lack of memory is terrifying to the viewer,[28] it is a liberating moment: Ripley does not demonstrate the haunting internalized guilt and remorse as sole survivor that characterized her in the trilogy. Her *Erinnerung*, the internalized memory that shaped her existence in the trilogy (see Scobie 88), is obsolete; the kinship with the alien disconnects her from the cultural icons of motherhood from her past.[29]

Ripley as well as the queen have been created exclusively for scientific and military purposes, and both are accordingly objectified—the queen is the "real payoff" in this endeavor, whereas Ripley is merely a "meat by-product"; both serve reproductive services other than their own. This status is already hinted at in *Alien³*, when Ripley's pregnancy makes her valuable to The Company, reducing her to the familiar role of woman as procreator. In *Alien Resurrection*, the scientists display the typical arrogance exhibited by operators of technoscience. When Ripley says that they cannot tame the alien, that "you cannot teach it tricks," the scientist condescendingly replies: "Why not—we're teaching you." In the same conversation, Ripley inquires about her origin and learns that she has been cloned. When she hears that the queen is growing, she involuntarily smiles, displaying genuine pleasure for the first time—a troublesome feature in her character throughout the rest of the movie. Whenever she feels the aliens' presence or intentions, she is seen to be visibly torn between following them and staying with the humans. Despite her unease at being cloned from the cells of the original Ellen Ripley, who died in her battle with the alien two centuries before, Ripley seems to be rather comfortable with who she is, or what she is not—"human"—displaying self-confidence and contempt for those around her. But she exhibits insecurity and hurt when insistently challenged by Call in her humanity, her right to identify as Ripley, her right to exist.

> CALL: "Ellen Ripley died 200 years ago. You're not her."
> RIPLEY: "Who am I?"
> CALL: "You're a sting. A construct. They grew you in a fucking lab."

Even though Ripley suffers from the other construct's rejection, she refuses to feel on the terms of those who constructed her; she repudiates the repulsion she initiates in others. Like the mutant superheroes of the comic world, her strength lies in her genetic abnormalities, and this is where part of her attraction lies for the viewer. At the same time, she rejects the tragic identity of the outcast who secretly saves the world while pining away for the world's acceptance (especially cultivated in the *Batman* and *Spiderman* movies as well as in *Spawn*). She is out to save herself—and then might consider the rest of the world. So when Call offers to "end this nightmare" by killing her, Ripley harshly replies, "What makes you think I would let you do that?" and thereby claims not only her right to exist but also her refusal to hate herself for what she is. In doing so, she echoes the cyborg's rejection of cultural paradigms:

> The cyborg is resolutely committed to partiality, irony, intimacy, and perversity. It is oppositional, utopian, and completely without innocence. . . . Unlike Frankenstein's monster, the cyborg does not expect its father to save it through a restoration of the garden, that is, through the fabrication of a heterosexual mate, through its completion in a finished whole, a city and cosmos. . . . The cyborg would not recognize the Garden of Eden; it is not made of mud and cannot dream of returning to dust. (Haraway, "Manifesto" 151)

Later, when Call, full of self-loathing, asks Ripley how she can stand what she is, Ripley replies, "I don't have much of a choice," again disclosing the myth of a self-defined subject and pointing to the construction of our lives, which we do not design but only negotiate.

In *Alien Resurrection,* Ripley accepts her kinship with her archenemy in stages—first instinctively, later more reflectively. From the beginning to the end, however, her loyalty emanates from her human origin; her decision to kill the aliens never wavers. Her kinship with the aliens nevertheless is a part of her being: "It's in my head, behind

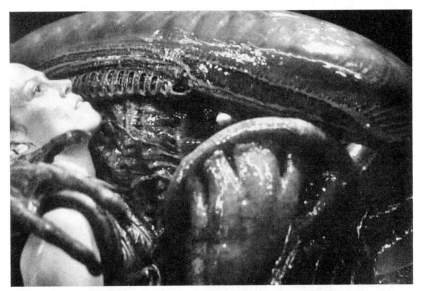

Figure 3.8. Ripley is carried to the queen's lair in *Alien Resurrection*. Her surrender to the monsters forces the spectator to acknowledge their kinship.

my eyes. I can hear it moving." So she feels the aliens' movements and hears their cries but always avoids them; if she meets them, she destroys them. When the queen is in labor, Ripley feels her pain and hears her calling her to witness the birth of their child. She is being carried to the hive by drones, whom at first she fights, then gives in to with obvious relief, with recognition. The viewer is repulsed by her being touched and protectively carried by her enemy; the dreamlike filming, with frames fading in and out, underlined by music, creates a surreal atmosphere in accord with the feelings of the overwhelmed Ripley and the stunned spectator (Fig. 3.8).

The acceptance Ripley experiences for a short period of time turns into horror when the child, after killing its birth mother, turns towards Ripley as its mother. In terror she flees the manifestation of her connection to the other. Ripley ends up killing her only child, who is the perverse answer to her dreams of family conjured in the trilogy, in order to save the other part of her heritage—humanity and its planet of origin, Earth (Fig. 3.9). Her destruction of the mutant echoes her suicide in *Alien³*, where she falls into a burning furnace while the alien queen erupts from her chest, where the "moment of birth is again the moment of death" (Scobie 91).

Figure 3.9. Prior to killing her monstrous child in *Alien Resurrection* in order to save humanity, Ripley recognizes and embraces the product of her own monstrosity.

More than merely Man's other within the structures of social power, Ripley stands *outside* of these structures. In the course of the trilogy, Ripley's refusal to form alliances with others, mainly androids, decreases the more she is considered an other herself, and vanishes completely once she *identifies* (i.e. is not only constructed) as other. The recognition of kinship with those outside the norm develops into a position first of resistance and later of power, when representatives of the system (scientists, soldiers) die in the conflict with the aliens. The "cyborg identity" at the core of this discourse on posthuman subjectivity is reflected in Ripley's growing awareness of her position and her acceptance of her origin.

In *Alien Resurrection*'s "figurations," the android Call eventually joins Ripley as a figure of resistance. Call is a Second Generation robot, constructed and programmed by androids, an illegitimate offspring of technoscience. Ironically, she is programmed by machines (who strive to be like their creators) to be more humane than humans around her. She constitutes a paradox, a mirror reflecting something nonexistent, since most humans she interacts with prove to be extremely inhumane. The paradox of Call's existence as a simulacrum, a copy without an original, made not by humans but by a technoscience commenting on the human race, is articulated in Ripley's comment once the artificial nature of Call is discovered: "I should have known. No human is so humane."[30] She is the grotesque parody of "the good, corrective human figure who signifies emotion-passion-concern," who within conventional science fiction narratives counters "reason-calculation-logic [which] is inflected as bad, or at least inhuman" (Kavanaugh 74). As an ironic product of technoscience, she imitates/represents an ideal version of the self that is far removed from reality and instead is a distorted mirror. Together with Ripley, she is a commentary on the culture's obsessive anthropocentrism and speaks to the vanishing of humans as main actors. To borrow Eaton's words, "As the series has progressed, it is the non-humans that have taken on the burden of individuated characteristics. Human beings merely panic and swear and run around a lot" (9).

The initial antagonism between Ripley and Call develops into a strong alliance. In terms of representation, their gender places them in the realms of both nature (especially the maternal) and machines —which in turn aligns them with the alien. They are two abnormal women who are horror-creations of technoscience but insist on *their* version of the story. Their friendship and coalition form the powerful and hopeful elements in *Alien Resurrection,* in extreme opposition to cultural tales of heterosexual romance as the salvation of all human interaction. Men—representative of patriarchal structure—are totally insignificant in this bond, as is sarcastically displayed in the scene where Ripley finds the room with Numbers 1 to 7, and in which Call realizes for the first time that Ripley, monster or not, is a victim of the system that created her, and she attacks the scientist. Johner, the stereotypical loud, obnoxious, sex-obsessed, drinking white man looks on and then makes a sexist remark—"What's the big deal? I don't get it. Must be a chick thing"—professing his complete ignorance of the dramatic constellations and desperate measures around him.[31]

In addition to the above-mentioned scene where Call learns to begin to accept Ripley for what she is, several other scenes convey a growing bond between the two. The first is when Call, who is programmed to pursue the elimination of the alien species, wants to kill Ripley until she discovers that the queen has already been taken out of her, and she challenges Ripley's identity. The scene concludes with Ripley leaning her face against Call's, creating a moment of sexual intimacy and closeness, and then sending her away to avoid being found out by the scien-

Figure 3.10. Ripley and Call are positioned in an erotically charged relationship in *Alien Resurrection*. Their otherness as un-human constructs heightens the queerness of their mutual attraction.

tists on the ship (Fig. 3.10). Another scene of closeness occurs when Call is discovered to be an android: Ripley is not resentful but obviously delighted to have found an ally and kin, and she protects Call against the abusive humans. The two female constructs suddenly close ranks and find strength and confidence in each other.

The scene that seals the alliance between Ripley and Call is the one in which the android is asked to access the ship's computer in order to prevent the ship from landing on Earth. Having denied her origin ("we burnt our modems"), and plunged into self-loathing when confronted with it ("look at me, I'm disgusting"), Call is unable to reconcile with what she is; she wants nothing more than to be human. Ripley makes it possible for her to acknowledge her identity: she connects her back to what she is, and why, when she forces Call to use her un-human ability to stop the aliens. Responding to Call's sentimental regret that she is not even partly human, Ripley refuses to buy into the myth of humanity as the ultimate form of being; she discloses the moral hypocrisy on which categories of humanity rest. After wondering why Call cares so much about the humans, and hearing the android confess to being programmed for it, Ripley bluntly asks: "You're programmed to be an asshole?"

All of these scenes take place in male-dominated space: the cell in Ripley's prison tower where she is held by the scientists; the laboratory, chamber of technoscience's horrors; and the chapel of the ship. It is in front of the cross—symbol of the Christian-Western cultural identity of the self as an image of God, the promise of salvation, and the justification of domination—that Ripley removes the plug of the electronic Holy Bible to insert it into Call's arm, connecting the unnatural daughter of mankind to its system of control, and thus reclaiming her from those who made her. Thus when one of the scientists—the only one who tries to act against the group of renegades fleeing the ship—tries and fails to connect to "Father" (the main computer), Call announces: "Father is dead, asshole."

Call rebels against the system because she, like Ripley, refuses to be what humans designed her to be. They are both disturbing in their existence, children of oppressive and exploitative structures, but they defy the original definitions of their function: "The main trouble with cyborgs, of course, is that they are the illegitimate offspring of militarism and patriarchal capitalism, not to mention state socialism. But illegitimate offspring often are exceedingly unfaithful to their origins. Their fathers, after all, are inessential" (Haraway, "Manifesto" 151).

Cyborg Identity or Mainstreaming of Cyborg Resistance?

In *Alien Resurrection*, Ripley is able to form an alliance that is not representative of the usual "happy ending" of mainstream cinema—she bonds and establishes a relationship, not only with another *female*, but with a scientific and technological construct, a creature as far removed from the center as she is. Her status as other is complete. In this way, the constellations in the movie resemble the ambiguous relationships between humans and technology in other science fiction movies that run against conventional dualistic patterns of representation, such as *Blade Runner*, *Videodrome*, and *eXistenZ*. *Alien Resurrection*, however, seems more affirmative in its boundary crossing than the other films are. In the end, it lacks the terror caused by the inability to differentiate between representation (the movie/screen/game) and identity in *Videodrome* and *eXistenZ*, or the despair inherent in *Blade Runner*'s characters, as reflected in its desolate urban landscape. Ripley's position in relation to the center has changed in *Alien Resurrection*. In *Alien³*, her desperation and desolation dwell in her failure to establish social relationships. The death of the girl-child Newt, whom she saved in *Aliens,* and of the other survivor, as well as the death of her lover, declare that the enriching human relations idealized and romanticized in mainstream popular culture are an illusion. This mourning is succeeded by the rearrangement of the social actors who survive the deadly encounter with the alien in *Alien Resurrection.* It is not the traditional heterosexual nuclear family found at the end of *Aliens,* but a group of outsiders and constructs: a "cripple," a female android, and a female clone/alien hybrid. The fact that the fourth survivor is an (intellectually rather limited) white male seems like an ironic comment—as if the origin of the cyborgs cannot be left behind but must be redefined in the process of transgression. These figures represent changing social configurations induced by deteriorating boundaries—they display the resisting and surviving other, not the dying or tragic one. In this focus, *Alien Resurrection* is like other contemporary science fiction films, such as *X-Men,* that do not partake in the recent backlash in terms of violent and terrifying representations of aliens as others (e.g., *Pitch Black, Battlefield Earth, Independence Day, Godzilla,* and *Supernova*) but instead concentrate on the perspective of transgressing figures.

Boundary crossing notwithstanding, in the final analysis Ripley's loyalties are with the human race. Here, the film's narrative recontains its subversive implications: Ripley ends up destroying the offspring of a new species in order to save humanity, which raises questions regarding the film's relation to posthuman subjectivities. The narrative cannot completely free itself from the cultural context of patriarchal ideology because the motivating drive is still defined by an original place—symbolized by Earth. Haraway, in "A Cyborg Manifesto," discusses this obsession with a "myth of origin" within dominant cultural texts as a patriarchal mechanism. By prioritizing mythical Earth and its inhabitants, these texts ensure that humanity—and, implicitly, humanism—remains the primary reference for identity. The boundaries between others and self have blurred, however, leaving the spectator with unease about who is out saving whom. The relieving "process of reconstitution of the self [that] is reaffirmed by the conventional horror narrative in which the monster is usually 'named' and destroyed" (Creed 137) becomes impossible. The two female monsters have no right to claim Earth as their origin, yet they inherit it. Their survival carries the potential for a new "order of difference" (Haraway, *Primate Visions* 377) that needs to come to terms with the presence of the "unrecognizables." The illegitimate offspring of technoscience, by saving humanity, claim the right to stay. The striving for sameness characteristic of modernity's "humanism"—"an ideological notion that conceals differences, contradictions, and struggles in the real under the sign of a generalized, shared essence" (Kavanaugh 73)—seems obsolete.

At the end of the movie, the alien—the ultimate other—is eliminated but at the same time is accepted as part of what remains after its confrontation with humanity, resisting "the human's reassuring defeat of the non-human" (Belling 40). The other, product and mirror of the self and its accomplishments, has become what the self never was, and it holds the potential for a much more powerful and integral way of being. This outcome opens the cultural stage for imagining a posthuman consciousness. This consciousness discloses, as Bukatman suggests, "the 'human' as a particular mythos of 'natural' individualism" (*Terminal Identity* 323). Bukatman draws on Foucault's statement in *The Order of Things* that "man is only a recent invention, a figure not yet two centuries old, a new wrinkle in our knowledge; he will disappear again as soon as that knowledge has discovered a new form" (Bukatman, *Terminal Identity* 323). The monstrous cyborg might be one of the new forms. *Alien Resurrection* draws the contradictory and disturbing underlying tendencies of the first three movies to a conclusion, offering an equally disturbing but also hopeful solution born out of the violence, corruption, and despair structuring the movies.

Still, the monstrosity of the film's prevailing figures seems its only potentially liberating aspect and makes any politically viable agency questionable.[32] Despite its at times obvious counter-imagery (such as cyberpunk elements), ultimately *Alien Resurrection* backs out of any radical subject position: in the end it is the human form and its habitat that the constructs yearn for. Most of all it is the *obvious* employment of counter-images and constellations that points to the appropriation of them by Hollywood's industry. As King and Krzywinska point out:

> [T]ransgression, of various kinds, is sometimes offered by mainstream film industry as part of its appeal, to lure viewers with the promise of elements that are usually forbidden. In most cases, however, an inherent conservatism—a desire not to offend potential

filmgoers—ensures that mainstream productions do not transgress too far from dominant and familiar constructions of gender differ-ence. (35)

The representation, then, both attracts—based on the viewer's secret longing for the other—and contains any real danger of subversion by channeling the transgression back into mainstream systems of mean-ing. Hebdige identifies two major forms of incorporation of subcultures and their styles into mainstream culture: the "conversion of subcul-tural signs . . . into mass-produced objects (i.e. the commodity form)" and the " 'labelling' and redefinition of deviant behaviour by dominant groups . . . (i.e. the ideological form)" (94). Of course cyborg feminism is not a subculture but an academic (and artistic) discourse that en-gages with representations in popular culture. Still, its affirmation of figurations that oppose the normative notion of identity constitutes a threat to dominant culture and therefore needs to be incorporated into mainstream culture.

As a Hollywood production, *Alien Resurrection* already is a commod-ity. So is the trilogy, but *Alien Resurrection*'s production is much more oriented to mass-audience formulas than, for example, *Alien³* is. It also borrows much more directly from contemporary genres in terms of style: Ripley's Xena look and Call's boyish-yet-decidedly-female ap-pearance feed into the imagery of the hip fantasy/science fiction tele-vision shows of the 1990s, in contrast to the severe and glamourless costumes of the trilogy. In this aspect, it resembles flashy superhero movies such as *Batman and Robin* and *X-Men,* whose attraction defi-nitely lies in the fashionable outfits of the characters as much as in the action.

The obvious commodification of the movie, however, does not nec-essarily remove it from every subversive appropriation. Cyborg femi-nism is approaching cultural texts *as* commodities; the awareness of the copyrights, trademarks, and merchandising that organize cultural metaphors and discourses is central to the frame of its analyses. It is what Hebdige calls the "ideological form of incorporation" that poten-tially undermines the cyborg's feminist identity (and that keeps Ripley from blowing up Earth, having alien babies, and taking Call as her lover). Hebdige draws on French philosopher Roland Barthes's theory of bourgeois mythologies, which serve to remove any ideological threat to the establishment since, as Barthes argues, the petit-bourgeois is "as a person '. . . unable to imagine the Other . . . [because] the Other is a scandal which threatens his existence'" (Hebdige 97). Mainstream/dominant culture develops two strategies to eliminate the presence of the other. In the first, it is "trivialized, naturalized, domesticated. Here, the difference is simply denied. . . ." In the second, it is "transformed into meaningless exotica"; reduced to a spectacle, "difference is consigned to a place beyond analysis" (97). Thus the dangers of romanticizing outcast existences and of eroticizing the gendered and racialized other are always immanent in mainstream's celebration of formerly counter-cultural elements, and both tendencies are present in *Alien Resurrection*. As a feminist image appropriated from the position of other, the cyborg loses its power once it is domesticated.

Recalling Hebdige's emphasis on the dialectical relationship between cultural objects (i.e. images) and the meaning production around them, *Alien Resurrection* reminds us that meaning is flexible and under constant reconstruction. Without being radical in any aspect, the film's cyborgian images nevertheless instill uneasiness in the average viewer and disrupt the pleasure of the male gaze. Ripley's assertive and decidedly queer sexuality and her pairing off with another female character remove her from being the male viewer's object of desire at the same time as the excessively displayed kinship with the alien (there are plenty of visuals of the aliens and their various body fluids) evokes repulsion for her as well as for her foe. Her "alien-ness" disrupts the conservative humanism of traditional science fiction film, where "utopia . . . lies in *being human,* and if utopia is always defined in relation to an *other,* a nonutopia, then the numberless aliens, androids, and evil computers of the science fiction film are the barbarians storming the gates of humanity" (Bukatman, *Terminal Identity* 16, emphasis his). Thus, when placed in the context of theories of alternative identities and identification processes within cultural texts, *Alien Resurrection* lends itself to a subversive feminist reading. The film provides conflicting images of boundary crossing that run against mainstream constructions of the other at the same time as it creates affirming counter-identities. It is a pleasurable narrative of survival, embracing not what we were constructed to be, but what we are—a story of despising and opposing the cause, not the product. Within this cultural representation, Ripley and Call constitute metaphors of resistance, metaphors of the system's constructs that are not complicit but defy the terms under which they are supposed to accept their existence. Representative of feminist resistance to cultural representation, they stand for the "power to survive not on the basis of original innocence, but on the basis of seizing the tools to mark the world that marked them as other" (Haraway, "Manifesto" 175).

4. Our Bodies as Our Selves

Body, Subjectivity, and (Virtual) Reality in The Matrix

As you gaze at the flickering signifiers scrolling down the computer screens, no matter what identifications you assign to the embodied entities that you cannot see, you have already become posthuman.

—N. Katherine Hayles, *How We Became Posthuman*

"Do not try and bend the spoon. That's impossible. Instead, only try to realize the truth. . . . There is no spoon."

—Spoon Boy, *The Matrix*

When *The Matrix* was released by Warner Brothers in 1999, it was an immediate blockbuster hit. Sending its message packaged in a dazzling array of special effects and a superstar cast, the film questions established notions of body, identity, and reality. At the center of the film, in terms of both narrative and form, lie experiences of reality structured by technology and the ways in which these experiences shape cultural and personal identities. The relationship between technology and identity has been widely discussed in various discourses, including those on science fiction narratives.[1] As Claudia Springer puts it in *Electronic Eros*, "When humans interface with computer technology in popular culture, the process involves transforming the self into something entirely new, combining technological with human identity" (58). The film situates its narrative within the relationship between human and technological interface, a relationship that dominates the discourse on the "posthuman."[2] The mediation of (physical) experience through technology that *The Matrix* thematizes evokes concerns voiced in feminist theories about technology's impact on gendered bodies. The body in *The Matrix* is a central factor: personal control over it defines the individual's experience of freedom, whereas the conscious mind, as it roams the constructed world of the Matrix, is the tool to free the body. Set in the future, about two hundred years from now (give or take half a century or two), the film's narrative challenges the epistemological claim that our daily experiences constitute reality. Instead, as the protagonist Neo (Keanu Reeves) learns, humankind is dominated by an artificial intelligence (the AI), and our "reality" is a computer-simulated world (the Matrix), which camouflages the enslavement of human bodies that serve as energy source for the machines. A small number of people have escaped their mental and physical enslavement and have joined the Resistance's efforts to free all humans and defeat the machines. The *conscious* experience of the material world defines the only "true" reality in the movie, represented by the subject's unified body and mind. This consciousness stands in contrast to the construction of that experience through ideology, represented by the simulations of the Matrix.

The Matrix's form reflects its narrative emphasis on technology's impact on human subjectivity; it produces a spectacle of technology that equals the narrative content in its effect on the viewer. The excessive use of special effects and innovative production technology creates, to use Brooks Landon's words in *The Aesthetics of Ambivalence,* "a sensory environment as compelling and complicated as any conventional narrative that might be set within it" (128). The technology employed in *The Matrix becomes* the story; it constitutes "an inherent narrative *of* technology, rather than the use of technology to present (tell) a conventional narrative in visual media" (Landon 129, emphasis his).[3]

The movie is rich in images and allusions that offer various approaches for interpretation. Some critics discuss the religious mythology in *The Matrix,* focusing on the belief-based elements that run through the narrative.[4] Others point to the representation of a Marxist critique of ideology in the movie, addressing power relations and personal agency.[5] My analysis argues for the ideological construction of the body as the basis for identity, and the unity of body and mind (i.e. the conscious experience of the physical world) as the definition of reality in *The Matrix.* By relating the film's constellations of these concepts to the tradition of cyberpunk from which it derives its visual aesthetics and narrative, and by placing it into the context of feminist cyberpunk critique, I argue that the film's conflicting images place it at an intersection of discourses informed by postmodern theories, such as those of Foucault and Baudrillard, and by more modernist theories, such as Marxism. Ultimately, the film abandons its potentially progressive construction of collective political agency. Instead, it reproduces a conservative individualist identity that relies on a "humanist" notion of a bodily existence unmarked by technology as it is problematized in discourses within cultural studies.[6] The intact human body that is in contact with, yet in control of, technology becomes the metaphor for an autonomous subject, ultimately rejecting the radical potential of a posthuman subjectivity.

The Matrix and Cyberpunk

The Matrix has an ambivalent relationship to cyberpunk, in both its specific visual aesthetics and its underlying philosophy. The Wachowski brothers, who directed the film, were undoubtedly inspired by cyberpunk—both film and genre share an obsession with negotiating our relationship with communication technology and its impact on subjectivity. Cyberpunk is a distinct literary form, made famous by William Gibson's *Neuromancer* (1984), which has influenced science fiction thematically and stylistically since the early 1980s.[7] Cyberpunk texts emphasize the omnipresence of communication and computer technology in Western and Asian (particularly Japanese) urban culture, and they envision a dystopian world increasingly dominated by global capitalist forces, consumerism, and multinational corporate power. Unlike in traditional science fiction, cyberpunk's heroes do not colonize distant planets but hack into computer systems and covet the abstract disembodiment of cyberspace as an alternative to the destructive forces that surround them.

Cyberpunk's stylistic influence on science fiction as a genre is substantial, even if its impact as a social or cultural movement is debated. As Nicola Nixon points out in "Cyberpunk: Preparing the Ground for Revolution or Keeping the Boys Satisfied?" cyberpunk's definition as a movement is based mainly on a small number of writers' manifestos and numerous anthologies in which they have postulated that the literary style is a movement. Cyberpunk's "roots," therefore, are understood to be either in particular science fiction ("father") texts (as Bruce Sterling writes in his introduction to the cyberpunk short fiction anthology *Mirrorshades*)[8] or in the underground culture of punk and designer drugs (as Rudy Rucker and Peter Wilson state in their introduction to *Semiotext(e) SF*). Both feminist critics and science fiction writers are suspicious of cyberpunk's self-declared political radicalism and its at times naïve celebration of technology's interventions into the subject's relationship to her/his body.

Cyberpunk's aesthetic influence is visible in *The Matrix*'s stylistic visuals, such as the sunglasses, or "mirrorshades," which are a key feature of the Resistance whenever they are in the computerized Matrix, and the distinctly urban 1990s style of attire in black leather and plastic.[9] The movie's emphasis on speed and mind-controlling computer technology, rather than muscle per se, translates into a particular notion of masculinity that links these motifs to cyberpunk's "central heroic iconography" (Nixon 197), the net-cowboys. Furthermore, the film's underground renegade band, which subverts the powers controlling the data flow, echoes the pirate bands of hackers and outlaws who roam the urban cyberpunk world of multinational corporations. The movie's aggressive soundtrack and its role in underscoring actions on screen both point to the vital role of punk music and culture in the self-definition of cyberpunk as a distinct cultural movement.

But it is especially the innovative special effects and the role technology plays as *medium* that place the film into a distinct relationship with cyberpunk. According to Landon, the relationship of cyberpunk literary narratives to media culture is reciprocal, with cyberpunk's "fantastic vision already merging with the 'fantastech' visions of cutting edge electronic technology" (Landon 120). He suggests that cyberpunk literature's emphasis on electronic media has made its own presence as cultural medium obsolete, since its prose cannot compete with the speed, imaging, and visual and acoustic special effects of media like film and video, which form a "technological displacement of narrative from print to electronic culture" (Landon 127). This displacement is reflected in the still-abundant popular *discussion* of cyberpunk in electronic media, such as the Internet (which did not exist in its present form when Gibson coined the term "cyberspace"), videos, and DVDs — most of which constitute technologies in which cyberpunk's visions are rooted. Since *The Matrix*'s representations *of* science fiction technology are defined *by* its science-fictional technology, the movie seems to be less an enactment of cyberpunk's contents than a representation of the technologies that influenced the genre, and thus it offers "the *spectacle* of technology displacing stories about the impact of technology" (Landon 141).

In terms of plot, *The Matrix* is of course placed within a computerized world, and the protagonist is a hacker—the direct descendent of the Silicon Valley hacker generation that inspired the core of cyberpunk's literary movement (see Sterling xi).[10] The film's connections to

cyberpunk are particularly interesting when considering the historical context of 1980s cyberpunk, which a late 1990s mainstream science
fiction movie redefines and appropriates.

Despite these similarities, *The Matrix* also makes some unique contributions to the discourses around cyberpunk. Take, for example, the
representation of the Matrix within the movie. As in other virtual reality (VR) movies, the computerized Matrix creates a "new space which
does not so much annihilate, as require the *refiguring* of, the subject" (Bukatman, *Terminal Identity* 225). Unlike in movies such as TRON
(1982) or *The Lawnmower Man* (1992), however, the virtual reality of
The Matrix is neither what Mike Featherstone calls the "Gibsonian
cyberspace"—technological data flow with "iconic representations" of
the operators (10)—which is reminiscent of city lights viewed from
above, nor is it a computerized VR. Instead, the Matrix is a modified version of what we think the contemporary Western world is. Our familiarity with the Matrix's representations—a simulation more than an
abstraction—is what makes the movie's special effects so effective. The
manipulation and bending of the setting beyond human capabilities
constructs this "space [that] *is* the fiction" (Bukatman, *Terminal Identity* 224). What differentiates its VR from other movies is the fact that
the people who roam the simulated world in *The Matrix* are not aware
that it is VR.[11]

Far from being iconic, the representations of the characters in the
Matrix are not constructed by the user—the key utopian and liberating
element within cyberpunk, since the manifestation of the self in cyberspace does not rely on the physical form for representation[12]—but are
the fake subjectivities of bodies enslaved and held within a state of un-
consciousness. While cyberpunk celebrates, in Featherstone's words,
the "range of ways in which one can represent one's embodied subjectivity" (12), *The Matrix*'s main concern is resistance through conscious
representation of the self, which is grounded in the unity of mind and
body in the material world. So the representations of the self within
the Matrix, "residual self images," are much closer to the physical body
than are the iconic representations in cyberpunk. They insist on the
presence of a physical shape that underlies our concept of self, even
when the body is repressed. The fact that the imprisoned mind creates
these "residual self-images"—which are, as Morpheus (Laurence Fish-
burn), the Resistance's leader, explains to Neo, "mental projections of
your digital self,"—without actually having "seen" (i.e. experienced) its

own body consciously, is congruent with the film's conservative message about an "essential" (human) body. There are no crossovers in terms of gender or race or even species (why not think of oneself as an Incredible Hulk?). Instead, the representations of selves in the Matrix are mirrors of the actual enslaved bodies (apart from their distinctly fashionable outfits). Fundamentally, then, the image that represents the identity of the person equals the normative human form.

Finally, the group that forms the center of the narrative differs from classical cyberpunk in its *political* resistance. The Resistance has the utopian/modernist revolutionary goal of destroying a system, whereas cyberpunk narratives, in postmodern fashion, are busy exploiting it. The political formation of organized resistance in *The Matrix* is crucial for understanding the conflicting representations of agency in the movie, which eventually run contrary to a feminist vision of agency within a technologized world. Despite its anarchist organization into small, independent cells and its emphasis on collective action, the Resistance is subtly hierarchical. This aspect is confirmed in the film's sequel, *The Matrix Reloaded* (2003), in which we are introduced to the highly stratified human army protecting Zion, the only remaining human city. The hierarchy within the Resistance's individual units is reflected in the members' self-chosen usernames, which they understand as their only names and as reflecting their true identities. In the cell Neo becomes a part of in *The Matrix*, Morpheus, the god of dreams and sleep, "watches" over the enslaved minds and picks those that are "ready" to be "woken." Not only is his role as prophet inspirational and paternalistic (he "fathers" the members by making them part of his group), but also he is the leader, the authority of the cell. His prime goal is to find the One, the mind within the millions he meets in the Matrix that might liberate humankind. The main female character's name, Trinity (Carrie-Anne Moss), signifies the union of the holy three; she binds Morpheus and Neo together, and her love for the One positions her as the potential mother of the sacred son. Neo—an anagram of One—is the messiah, the savior, the chosen one, who needs to be initiated and taught, but who ultimately is the only one who can threaten the system on any substantial level. So protecting and enhancing the potential of his character is what becomes the priority of the Resistance.

In typical Hollywood fashion, the film's overall appearance co-opts the representations developed by a subculture.[15] However, it is also—at times ironically—self-reflective about its relationship with cyberpunk and pays homage to its roots. Neo's surprise that Trinity, the Resistance fighter who initially contacts him, is a woman exposes the macho self-image of male-defined hacker culture: "I just thought . . . um . . . you were a guy." Trinity answers: "Most guys do." Moreover, Neo, in typical cyberpunk-hacker tradition, produces and deals in illegal recreation discs. In a scene in which a customer comes to his apartment to pick up the hot merchandise, Neo retrieves a disc from its hiding place, which is in Jean Baudrillard's book *Simulacra and Simulation;* thus the movie tips its hat to one of the best-known cultural theorists, who advances the notion of a subjectivity constructed by the human/machine interface. Baudrillard is again referred to when Morpheus quotes him while showing Neo "the desert of the real" that stands in stark contrast to the pleasures inherent in the simulated world of the Matrix (see McCaffery, "Introduction" 6). And Cypher (Joe Pantoliano), the traitor of the group, sells his freedom to AI and gets rid of his "meat" (his body) while consuming a simulated steak.

The film's gender and race representations also echo its connection to cyberpunk: Morpheus, as the wise leader whose mission is to find and prepare the "real" savior, as well as the nameless Oracle (Gloria Foster) as the only major black female figure, draw on stereotypes in which prehistorical knowledge and talents are embodied by people of color who cater to the white heroes of the narrative. They represent what David Crane, in "*In Medias* Race," criticizes as strategically placed black bodies in cyberpunk that lend "authenticity" to resistance and otherness. Within cyberpunk films, the presence of the black character lends authenticity to the bodies moving within cyberspace by creating a visual "otherness" that validates the resistance to the technosystem. Race becomes a medium for a mainstream audience's identification, erasing the historical "realness" of its oppressive workings:

[T]he blackness displayed in these films, along with the sense of the real that becomes attached to it, refers less to the realities of specific peoples or cultures and more to a position of identifiable, realizable otherness—a position that reconfigures, and reinscribes, racial marginalization in order to integrate the otherness of cyberspace into the narrative structure of mainstream film. Blackness . . . is more a medium than a message. (Crane 111)[14]

Crane points out the danger of erasing historical race relations by reducing the black experience to a position of recognizable otherness that opposes the "system." In *The Matrix*, this authenticity is represented by the Resistance fighters Dozer (Anthony Ray Parker) and Tank (Marcus Chong): both have "unmarked" bodies born the "old-fashioned way" by a woman, and both are men of color. They add to the "diverse" line-up of the Resistance, whose members' mission becomes focused and guided by the white male savior. The Oracle's telling of the future, in particular, is a typical depiction of black characters within a setting defined by technology; it evokes what Crane describes as "racist stereotypes of black natural ability as innate and unlearned" (107). After speaking to Neo in her kitchen, the apron-clad Oracle sends him on his way with a cryptic message about his fate and a home-baked cookie. Her wisdom and authority thus remain firmly rooted within the nontechnological cultural space of the "Mammy" (Fig. 4.1).

In "Humanist History and the Haunting of Virtual Worlds," Kathleen Biddick traces this phenomenon within the complex and at times problematic representations of race in William Gibson's cyberpunk literature. Gibson's work defined the key elements of the genre, and his metaphors of virtual colonization, which permeate cyberpunk discourse, are reflected in *The Matrix*'s treatment of Morpheus and the Oracle. While Gibson's literature is far more complex than the mainstream science fiction film *The Matrix*, both create a "diverse" "cyberspatial Benetton" (Biddick 47), "a narrative that constructs a humanist space based on the technologies of a humanist history and ethnogra-

Figure 4.1. In *The Matrix,* the Oracle's power is domesticated within a space historically allocated to the black "Mammy": the kitchen.

Figure 4.2. Trinity's mind-bending martial arts skills in the opening scenes of *The Matrix* introduce her as a strong and capable female resistance fighter.

phy," (50) leaving power structures based on colonial relations intact. This racial representation often takes a backdrop to feminist celebrations of gender transgressions in both criticism and fiction on cyberpunk. As Thomas Foster criticizes in "'Trapped by the Body'? Telepresence Technologies and Transgendered Performance in Feminist and Lesbian Rewritings of Cyberpunk Fiction," the celebration of VR technologies' transgressive potential in terms of theories of gender performance often neglects an analysis in terms of race. He notes that in innovative and radical texts on cyberculture, "transgendered bodies and performances do in fact seem to be increasingly naturalized in computer-mediated communication and in popular narratives about it, in ways that transracial bodies as performances are not" (Foster 709). This conventional and unreflective approach to representations of race can be found in *The Matrix*'s naïve constellations of racial "diversity."[15]

The gender arrangements in *The Matrix* confirm this figuration of the white male as the center of the narrative. The movie opens with Trinity's clash with police and agents, introducing the spectator to the mind-bending strength and speed of the Matrix (Fig. 4.2). Trinity's strength, skills, and black leather attire remind us of Molly Millions,

Figure 4.3. In *The Matrix*, Switch is the only member of the Resistance to wear white instead of black—she also stands out because of her androgyny, which is echoed in her name.

Gibson's technologically enhanced female figure that roams the Sprawl of his narratives, a descendent of Joanna Russ's Jael in *The Female Man* (1975). Yet Trinity lacks Molly's dangerous rage and is locked firmly within the rather prudish framework of her heterosexual romance with the hero.

Switch (Belinda McClory), the other woman Resistance fighter, is coded as androgynous or butch. Unlike the other members of her cell, she is always dressed in white, which makes her distinct within the group (Fig. 4.3). Representations of both Trinity and Switch resist the prominent Western model of femininity, marked by dresses, flowing hair, and makeup that softens the features. This ideal, far from being abandoned by the movie, is represented by the virtual "woman in the red dress" that Mouse (Matt Doran), the youngest member in the Resistance, designs for one of the training programs (Fig. 4.4). His remarks regarding virtual sex and his nickname, "Digital Pimp," are references to the masculinized "hypersexuality" of computer technology that Springer discusses in *Electronic Eros,* and that Bukatman traces in the technophilosophy and science fiction texts in *Terminal Identity.* The visuals of the movie correspond with the conflicting images of strong women in cyberpunk that are at the same time male fantasies. Springer comments on the contradictory representations: "[These women] clearly embody a fetishized male fantasy, but they also represent feminist rebellion against a brutal patriarchal system. It is difficult to either condemn or celebrate them, since a single interpretation cannot entirely explain their appeal" (138).

In the end, the movie contains Trinity within the heterosexual ma-

Figure 4.4. The conventional gender attributes of the virtual "woman in the red dress" contrast with the more androgynously coded "real" women in *The Matrix,* Switch and Trinity.

trix of romance and love. After rescuing Morpheus with Neo, Trinity develops a telepathic bond with Neo. Independently of technology, she can reach his mind while he is in the Matrix, and she revives him when he appears lifeless in his final confrontation with the agents. Here, the movie's gender politics feed into the cultural myth that subordinates technology to the power of human emotions. It propels Neo's role as the individual who saves humanity beyond any collective revolution, while Trinity's regenerative abilities reposition her as woman and potential mother. Finally, *The Matrix* is linked to movies connected to cyberpunk discourse, such as *Blade Runner* and the *Alien* quartet. These films, like *The Matrix*, place questions of reproduction and technology at the center of the narratives yet leave them unanalyzed.[16]

Feminist Critiques of Cyberpunk

On the surface, *The Matrix* appears to oppose cyberpunk's more radical concepts in terms of the relationship between subject and technology that links the genre to postmodern theories. As Veronica Hollinger puts it in "Cybernetic Deconstructions," "In its various deconstructions of the subject—carried out in terms of a cybernetic breakdown of the classic nature/culture opposition—cyberpunk can be read as one symptom of the postmodern condition of genre SF" (204). In cyberpunk discourse, the question of abandoning "the meat" (the body)—the representation of the mind as superior to and ultimately separate from the body—is central to its posthumanist nature, a "posthumanism which, in its representation of 'monsters'—hopeful or otherwise—produced by the interface of the human and the machine, radically decenters the human body, the sacred icon of the essential self . . ." (Hollinger 207). However, the subject in cyberpunk is always aware of cyberspace as a separate realm from the physical world to which the body is bound. Cyberpunk's notion of freedom and its utopian elements include the conscious recognition of a mind that is fused with technology. In *Electronic Eros,* Springer explains cyberpunk's relationship to technology at its most radical:

When cyberpunk characters are surgically hardwired, jack into cyberspace, load software directly into their brains, create computerized virtual bodies for themselves while their physical bodies decay, or abandon their bodies to exist inside the computer matrix, the boundary between human and computer is erased and the nature of the human psyche is redefined in accordance with the computer paradigm. Computers and human minds become thoroughly compatible because the differences between them have been effaced. (131)

Classical cyberpunk's ultimate fantasy is the downloading of the mind into the computer, the fusion of the human with the interface by abandoning the flesh. But underlying these narratives in their attempt to negotiate *Man's* interfacing with technology are cultural anxieties induced by the postmodern fragmenting of the self; these anxieties convey an inherent conservatism that resists a subversive posthuman identity. As Scott Bukatman puts it in *Terminal Identity,* "The ecstatic dissolution of the body is counterbalanced by the recuperative strategies of narrative and generic structure within which the subject maintains his autonomy and power (*'her'* autonomy and power is another question)" (244, emphasis his).

Unlike original cyberpunk discourse, which is, as Hollinger points out, "written for the most part by a small number of white, middle-class men, many of whom, inexplicably, live in Texas" (207), reconceptions of the connections between body and technology within feminist discourse on technology place them not in an antagonistic or exclusive relationship to each other, but in a complementary one. This is not to say that no male-authored narrative on the body/technology interface has ever imagined this relationship as complementary in any way, or that feminist writing on human/machine relations inherently views this relationship as positive. Rather, there is a distinct discourse *within* feminist theory that regards technobodies as an integral part of a posthuman feminist subjectivity and that stands in conflict with much feminist antitechnology writing (such as ecofeminism and cultural feminism).

Much of this posthuman feminist writing is inspired by Donna Haraway's cyborg politics, which places resistance at the conflicting and imploding intersections of the cultural and the natural that she introduces in "A Cyborg Manifesto."[17] Anne Balsamo's description of an alternative cyberpunk identity in "Feminism for the Incurably Informed" comments on the relationship between body and technology as "offering a vision of post-human existence where 'technology' and the 'human' are understood in contiguous rather than oppositional terms"

(684). Instead of conceptualizing technology as a medium to erase or overwrite the body, Balsamo argues, innovative feminist texts (she refers to Pat Cadigan's work) offer "alternative vision[s] of technological embodiment that [are] consistent with a gendered history of technology: where technology isn't the means of escape from or transcendence of the body, but rather the means of communication and connection with other bodies" (703). Here it is not the riddance of the "meat" that forms the underlying (and self-denying, thus ultimately unfulfilled) desire of the narrative. Instead, the goal becomes a mediation of embodiment and technology that refuses to treat technologically based social and interpersonal interactions as abstractions.

This vision is echoed in Katherine Hayles's concept of the posthuman in *How We Became Posthuman.* Hayles rejects the erasure of embodiment as "a feature common to *both* the liberal humanist subject and the cybernetic posthuman" (*Posthuman* 4, emphasis hers)[18] and instead argues for a concept of the posthuman that neither propagates a fusion with machines nor promotes a terror of technology as antihuman. Her concept of a posthuman subjectivity (and agency) emphasizes its dependency on the environment, the fluid and changing aspect of the human/machine interface that is always troubled and often painful, yet is ultimately subversive.

The basis of this theoretical approach to technology and the body lies, as Balsamo points out above, in the gendered history of technology, on one hand, and the concept of female embodiment in Western thought, on the other. The conceptual link of the female body to the realm of the (intellectually) unanimated, which in a Cartesian worldview includes both animals and machines, places it in a troubled relationship to disembodied VR technologies as well. This conflicted placement results in an ambiguous approach to technology in feminist texts, which either emphasize the liberating potential of an ungendered technological space (cyberspace) or point to the dangers of the ideological fusion of technology and female embodiments:

> For the female subject, "the body" is no abstract notion (as the battle for reproductive rights amply demonstrates) and is more evidently bound into a system of power relations. In SF that explicitly considers the gendered subject, the threat to the woman's body is conspicuous; the promise of physical transcendence is more dizzying but always less fulfilled. (Bukatman, *Terminal Identity* 314)

As Springer explains in *Electronic Eros,* information technology is embedded within a sexualized ideology based on heterosexual male desire, in which the gendering of representations places the female body into the realm of sexualized technology. Thus the masculinized myth of the transcended body within cyberpunk is often juxtaposed with obviously feminized technobodies and technospaces, like Gibson's cyberspace, which is coded as a female-gendered space that the male cowboy jacks into, penetrates.

Feminist critics contextualize cyberpunk's romanticizing of the mind/body split within a larger historical and philosophical Western tradition, whose gendered legacies are visible in the "much-discussed modes of 'disembodiment' that the cybernetic era has engendered [and that] remain suffused with bodily 'traces,' with abstracted but tenacious features of empowerment or disempowerment" (Hicks 4). One of the most powerful fictions that deal with the problematic of female embodiment and the ideologies of technology is James Tiptree, Jr.'s "The Girl Who Was Plugged In." Published in 1973, it constitutes a precursor to cyberpunk and critically apprehends the problems technology poses for the postmodern female body.[19]

Writers like Hayles, Balsamo, and Haraway reject the notion of an autonomous individual whose agency is unrelated to power structures. This critical element is reflected in much of what Karen Cadora terms "feminist cyberpunk," which is wary of cyberpunk's failure to address issues of oppression and instead "blends the conventions of cyberpunk with the political savvy of feminist sf" (357). To quote Jenny Wolmark in *Aliens and Others,* cyberpunk's "narratives do not respond to the implicit invitations to reconsider the construction of human subjectivity, preferring instead to restate notions of the self in terms of a technology which continues to privilege the masculine" (121).[20] Cadora argues that many of the texts she classifies as feminist cyberpunk disclose that, in cyberspace or not, "the female body is not easily disposed of" (364) and instead haunts the worlds in cyberpunk. Thus the female body meets the narrative strategies of the technological future in often disempowering forms. In cyberpunk, poverty translates into prostitution and professional surrogate motherhood for women, while men hustle—either as console cowboys or pimps who deal in women, drugs, and software. Feminist cyberpunk, Cadora suggests, while disclosing the limits of a patriarchally defined technology, also resituates the female body in narratives of the future, inserting agency into women's dealings with technology. Thus "embodiedness is a central issue in feminist cyber-punk in a way that it is not in masculinist cyberpunk" (Cadora 364).

Thomas Foster's writing on cyberculture and VR technologies fore-grounds the importance of race in feminist analyses of potential re-configurations of gender in cyberspace.[21] He explains how lesbian and feminist cyberpunk explore the potential relationship of gender perfor-mance (based on Judith Butler's theory of gender performativity) to VR technology:

> I would argue that virtual reality constitutes another form of dis-ruptive repetition, with the user's physical body repeated and reiter-ated as an image or representation in cyberspace. In effect, virtual systems spatialize the repeated performance of gender norms over time and thereby reveal the gap between embodiment and the per-formance of it, which allows for subversion, intervention, and the critical rearticulation of that relationship. (Foster, " 'Trapped by the Body'?" 721)

While he detects the potential for subversion of normative gender iden-tities in much of feminist cyberpunk writing, Foster criticizes it for its failure to substantially address issues of racial transgression.[22] He ar-gues that only if we are able to extend transgressive elements from gen-der theory to race (and, I would add, class) theory can the potentially deconstructive (and thus subversive) nature of VR technologies be ex-plored. While most of these criticisms are derived from debates around literary texts, they are all embedded within the wider context of cul-tural studies and philosophy, and are therefore central in understand-ing the complexity of *The Matrix*'s representations.

In *The Matrix*, the only way to recover a conscious subjectivity is by *reactivating* the connection between mind and material body—the mind's recognition of the material conditions surrounding it. The movie advances a notion of subjectivity grounded in a concept of a "natural body" that is very different from feminist cyberpunk critiques. Criticizing the idea of a "natural body" as a cultural norm that is pre-scriptive, feminist technowriters instead view the body as "simulta-neously a historical, natural, technical, discursive, and material entity" (Haraway, *Modest Witness* 209) that cannot be analyzed separately from power relations. Unlike movies such as *eXistenZ* (1999) that ex-plore the political and sexual implications of the nature/culture binary,

The Matrix aligns itself with the humanism inherent in most cyber-punk narratives by establishing the "natural body" as the final referent. Instead of following through with a radical concept of alternative subjectivities, most cyberpunk stories ultimately resort to an individualist notion of identity.[23] So the solitary net-cowboy strides into the neon light-infused night—as an autonomous piece of "meat."

In accordance with this return to humanism, *The Matrix* reclaims the modernist concept of reason—the rational consciousness both as human and as an indicator for reality—and, in its representations, makes cyberpunk's underlying contradictions visible. Ultimately, it is control over the experience of the material presence that counts; that is, the body is presented as the basis for individual freedom. The movie twists cyberpunk's visions of a human consciousness that can be down-loaded into machines with the body left discarded, as the body becomes an energy source for the same machines for which the body is abandoned. Meanwhile, the mind, instead of freely roaming abstract space, is "shut off." The value the AI places on the human organism (as a source of energy), while completely disregarding the human mind (which has no intrinsic value to the machines), is also an ironic comment on AI discourse, which constructs the human mind as precious and valuable, as well as on science fiction's technological bodies, which are trying to become human.[24]

The movie as a whole is situated within the strand of discourse that speculates on AI: it presents a posthuman future that is less an evolutionary option—as cyberpunk often constructs it to be—than a violent takeover by AI, which is a more traditional theme within science fiction. Springer explains this vision:

> The advent of simulated life . . . could put humans in a subordinate role or perhaps even establish a future devoid of human beings. . . . The world will be populated by artificial intelligence, artificial electronic life, genetically engineered organisms, cybernetic organisms, or human consciousness preserved on computer software and stored in mobile robots. (*Electronic Eros* 20)

In Gibson's and Pat Cadigan's literature, AI takes over cyberspace to then influence humankind. In contrast, in *The Matrix*, as in other films (e.g. *The Terminator* movies), machines take over the physical world and threaten the extinction of or control over humankind. Nevertheless, the fact that the film integrates and celebrates the pleasures of a technologically enhanced knowledge (who doesn't want to learn Kung Fu overnight?) posits it within the cultural context of the cyberpunk genre.[25] These conflicting representations in *The Matrix,* enhanced by its breathtaking special effects, create an ambivalent relationship to technology that shapes the notions of identity, body, and reality that run through the film. The pleasure depicted in the characters' relationship to technology cannot be separated from the production technology that creates the visual spectacle. *The Matrix*'s special effects create complex relationships to technology that begin before the narrative develops and exist apart from it, congruent with Landon's observation that in science fiction cinema "the depiction of science fiction narratives is being displaced by science fictional modes of depiction" (134).[26]

"Like a Splinter in Your Mind": Identity and the Body

The complex representations of body and identity in *The Matrix* are based on the contested experiences of what constitutes reality. They are conceptualized on one hand in relation to VR, and on the other in regard to the role of the body in controlling one's identity. The movie builds up to the moment of enlightenment—when Neo is shown the simulated nature of his existence—with dreamlike sequences that challenge his perception of the world and, ultimately, his sanity. Instructions that appear on his computer screen without a recognizable source tell him to "follow the white rabbit," in one of the film's frequent allusions to *Alice in Wonderland,* a narrative of destabilized reality and loss of control over one's perceptions. The unsettling realization that Morpheus knows of every step Neo is taking confuses and frightens him. Neo remembers as a dream the horrifying experience in the interrogation room with the AI's agents when his mouth grows shut. Later, when Trinity removes the "bug" they had planted within Neo's body, he learns that instead of being a dream, this experience actually occurred—it occurred within the virtual reality of the Matrix, not in "real" reality.

When Neo meets Morpheus, the leader of the Resistance, he foreshadows the deceptive nature of "reality" when he comments that Neo has "the look of a man who accepts what he sees because he is expecting to wake up." Right before Neo is to be reconnected with his body, Cypher comments: "Buckle your seatbelt, Dorothy, 'cause Kansas is going bye-bye," referring to *The Wizard of Oz*, a myth in North American culture of an identity crisis resolved after a confusing and threatening journey through unknown surroundings where reality is diffused with illusion. Until the "truth" is revealed to Neo, his world is crumbling around him—because subconsciously he refuses to accept the simulation of the Matrix and the separation of his body and mind that comes with it. This knowledge is latently present in his thoughts—as Morpheus tells him, "like a splinter in your mind."

The film intersects with VR discourse and the way that VR, as Springer puts it, "undermines certainty over the term reality, ultimately abandoning it altogether" (*Electronic Eros* 81). The movie's definition of reality as the unity of body (material conditions) and conscious mind (individual spirit) challenges the sensory reality in the discourse surrounding VR technology and its potential effects on our way of perceiving things. The film exposes experiences within VR as illusions and posits, in relationship to the Matrix, personal control over one's body as the basis for identity. Only those who control their material presences can consciously move within the Matrix and be aware of its unsubstantial existence.

The film thus challenges definitions of reality within VR discourse. Michael Heim, in "The Design of Virtual Reality," points out how VR usually works: "When a virtual world immerses a user, the entities encountered in the virtual world are real to the user—within the backdrop of cyberspace" (70). The reference point "cyberspace" is absent in *The Matrix*. The "user" is not given a choice about what s/he perceives as her/his reality; it is constructed as the only one available. In this, the film reflects the dilemma of the postmodern subject of living in the *delusion* of an autonomous subjectivity.

At the same time, the movie suggests that this subjectivity is attainable by controlling one's own destiny with a mind that transcends the power relations that surround it. The body is the contested ground, and only when the individual's mind is connected with it can one be free. Therefore, the goal in *The Matrix* is to reestablish clear boundaries between humans and machines, to recover the human body not violated by technological enhancements. The film establishes this goal by constructing a unified entity of body and mind that depends on both components for its identity—an identity formed in opposition to technology and the bodies marked by it. The body cannot live without the mind, so a death in the Matrix automatically terminates the physical body. The body perishes from injuries inflicted by a constructed experience, as Morpheus explains, because the "mind makes it real."

The same outcome occurs when the physical body is disconnected from the mind while it roams the Matrix; both mind and body die. Thus Cypher, in an act of treason, kills two Resistance fighters by "pulling the plug" on their physical bodies on the ship, forcing Trinity and Neo to watch their comrades die in front of them while they are "stuck" in the Matrix with them, unable to prevent it. This mutual dependency of mind and body makes cyberpunk's bodiless visions obsolete—the two entities are firmly attached at the proverbial hip in *The Matrix*. Control over the body becomes a metaphor for the triumph of the (Cartesian) mind, the transcendental subject.

Neo's search for an answer to the question that nags the remote corner of his (unknowingly) controlled mind—"What is the Matrix?"—is ultimately a challenge to the world that surrounds us and is perceived as normal, and an invitation to explore the ways in which power relations (that are often hidden) construct and control it. Such an exploration is consonant with a Marxist critique of the ideology that keeps consciousness imprisoned within a mode of production and commodity fetishism. It is also consonant with Foucault's concept of power as infusing every area of social relations, most potently in its construction of "normal" and "abnormal" categories.

This "splinter" in Neo's mind, as Morpheus calls Neo's nagging doubt, works against the notion that the human mind is merely a surface for the technology with which it interacts. The inner desire to question, the voice of the rational individual, places the subject within a humanist discourse that insists on the superiority of the human mind-soul, which in the end will supersede AI (see Springer, *Electronic Eros* 127). In contrast, when approached from a feminist perspective, the "splinter in his mind" is less a humanist belief in an essential self than an insistence that resistance begins with the awareness of one's position within social relations, a raising of consciousness reflected in Neo's arduous initiation into the Resistance.

Feminist critiques of cyberpunk problematize the Cartesian mind versus body dualism that subordinates materialist conditions of power structures. This tendency is also found in literary texts that inform the debate, where feminist science fiction, in Bukatman's words, "has proved more capable of recognizing the significance of the body as a site of ongoing struggle" (*Terminal Identity* 324). This insistence on material presence is what Vivian Sobchack, in "Beating the Meat/ Surviving the Text," calls the "lived-body" (206). The rejection of the body's repression challenges the celebration of a subject exclusively grounded in its relationship to technology. "At once decentered and completely extroverted, alienated in a phenomenological structure of *sensual thought* and merely *psychic experience*, it was *re-signed* to being a *no-body*" (Sobchack 206, emphasis hers). The lived-body as "*material premises* and therefore, the *logical grounds* for the intelligibility of those moral categories that emerge from a bodily sense of gravity and finitude" (Sobchack 210, emphasis hers) is reinstated in *The Matrix* through Neo's horror at the thought of "fields of humans" held in unconscious stupor by machines; thus the enslavement of the body is reflected in, not separated from, the enslavement of the mind. Approached from this vantage point, the film constitutes an ironic warning about the disconnection of cyberbody from material body. Sobchack states:

> This alienated and highly fetishized fascination with the body-object (the body that we *have*) and the devaluation of the lived-body (the body that we *are*) is a consequence of a dangerous confusion between the agency that is our bodies/our selves and the power of our incredible new technologies of perception and expression. (211, emphasis hers)

The feminist skepticism of a subjectivity based exclusively on interaction with technology is present in Sobchack's warning that such a subjectivity presents a "'false' consciousness—for it has 'lost touch' with the very material and mortal body that grounds its imagination and imagery of transcendence" (Sobchack 211).

This feminist defense of materiality is related to Marxism's insistence on materiality as the basis for any revolutionary consciousness. The moral claim of the movie—which posits the Resistance as "good," and Cypher and the people whose minds are still enslaved, if not as "bad," then as ignorant and delusional—is grounded in material existence. The AI lacks this experience and is therefore rendered completely inhuman. *The Matrix* comments on this grounding of human-

ness in the ability to suffer physical pain when one of the agents tells
Morpheus that the initial version of the Matrix failed to control human
minds. Its utopian setting and the absence of suffering were incompre-
hensible to the human minds, which kept rebelling against it. Sobchack
emphasizes the importance of the body in the construction of human
agency:

> Both significant affection and a moral stance . . . are based on the
> lived sense and feeling of the human body not merely as a material
> object one possesses and analyzes among others, but as a material
> subject that experiences its own objectivity, that has the capacity to
> bleed and suffer and hurt for others because it can sense its own pos-
> sibilities for suffering and pain. (213)

At times the film seems to align itself with a feminist theory that
insists on the presence of the body as part of a posthuman existence
(see Hayles xiv). At the end it becomes clear that the movie ultimately
rejects a posthuman existence as a whole, including the concept of
"marked bodies" that Haraway highlights in "A Cyborg Manifesto" and
that is at the heart of feminist critique of cyberpunk. Neo's horror at
his marked body, where tubes were connecting him to machines, and
at the plug in the back of his neck that is necessary to "jack into" the
Matrix, establishes a nostalgia for a pure human form, rejecting the
notion of a cyborg identity that affirms the technological invasions of
the postmodern body as part of its subjectivity (Fig. 4.5).

The bodies in the film are lean and mean when in the Matrix (i.e.
reflect the ideal, unmarked self) but utterly vulnerable in their material manifestations in the Resistance's headquarters. They stand in
contrast to mainstream culture's representations of the technologically
enhanced body of "rock-solid masculinity" (Springer, *Electronic Eros*
109), such as the Terminator and RoboCop, and they move away from
the armored body in mainstream cyborg movies. Nonetheless, the relationship to technology in *The Matrix* remains ambivalent since resistance against the system (the AI) ultimately relies on the technology
that enslaved them to begin with. One of the movie's most conflicting
representations is that it constructs the Matrix as an "unreal" (false)
reality and at the same time locates resistance within it.[27] It is here,
in the film's representations of technology, that technology as *medium*
and the pleasure it evokes is more relevant in its construction of mean-

Figure 4.5. When Neo wakes from his technology-induced unconscious state and recognizes humanity's enslavement in *The Matrix,* he is repulsed and horrified by his body's violent connections to technology.

ing than is the narrative content. The film ends with the dependency of resistance on technology intact, yet the ultimate goal is the return to the unmarked human state and the myth of an essential identity that comes with it—the final humanist statement of the movie.

"There Is No Spoon": Mind, Reality, and Agency

In the end, reality in *The Matrix,* unlike in a constructed VR, is inseparable from the material world. This unity firmly grounds the mind's experiences in its relationship to the body. As Morpheus explains, "Unfortunately no one can be *told* what the Matrix is. You have to see it for yourself." The movie thus establishes an epistemological claim based on materialism that links experience with the physical world and, in a distinctly Marxist fashion, discusses false consciousness as constructed through ideology. Thus Morpheus tells Neo, "You've felt it your entire life, that there is something wrong with the world. You don't know what it is but it is there—like a splinter in your mind—driving you mad." He continues: "The Matrix is everywhere, it is all around us, even now."

However, the reference to an individual consciousness that needs to be awakened is central to the movie's subtheme, the ability to control one's own destiny, which is ultimately valued over the collective revolution. *The Matrix*'s construction of individual freedom thus echoes the promise of liberation through awareness underlying the humanist concept of Enlightenment. Heim, referring to Immanuel Kant's definition of "apperception," places this promise within VR—distinguishing it from a concept of reality based exclusively on the experiences of the senses, which are simply, as Morpheus puts it, "electrical signals interpreted by your brain." The *awareness* of a sensation becomes as important as the sensation itself. "With perception we see something. With apperception we notice *that* we are seeing something" (Heim 72).

This belief in an independent human consciousness that somehow transcends its environment, as it is reflected in *The Matrix*, conflicts with a simultaneously displayed materialism that discloses the danger of ideology.[28] The only way for Neo to become a member of the Resistance is to become aware of the Matrix, to see it. This seeing is impossible if he cannot experience the physical world through the unity of his mind and body—inexorably linking the human mind's conceptual ability to the material body. The dreamlike sequence in which Neo's body is located through a tracing program that follows his thought's unconscious connection to his body in the vast "fields" where humans are being "grown" is reminiscent of a drug trip gone bad: the dissolution of body boundaries into the simulated world around him; the journey to his body that is weak and marked by tubes through which his life energy fuses him with the machines; and the nightmarish visuals of millions of human bodies encapsulated, imprisoned. The descent of his body through a canal into water, to be retrieved by the Resistance's ship, is composed of a series of images of rebirth, of the vulnerability of an exposed and weak body welcomed after a rite of initiation, which ultimately results in a whole and complete identity (Fig. 4.6).

The unity of mind and body is one of the basic principles of the movie, opposing the unstable identity politics in a discourse hooked on fluid subjectivities.[29] To quote Springer, "Minds and bodies change like chameleons in cyberpunk, going beyond the merely fragmented subjectivity found in other postmodern texts to display complete instability" (35). The Matrix exists because the AI, which produces energy from the human body, needs to control the minds of humans in order to forestall resistance to their enslavement. In a scene infused with references to a Marxist ideology critique—suggesting that the commodity

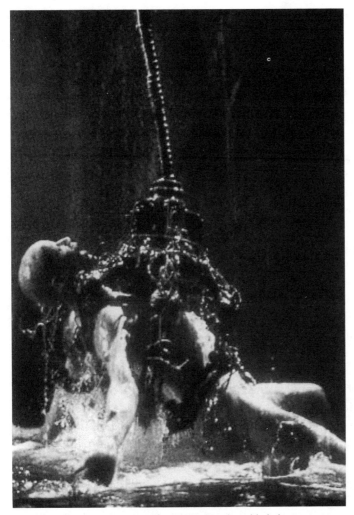

Figure 4.6. The human body appears utterly vulnerable in its encounter with technology when, after his release from his capsule in *The Matrix,* Neo's body is retrieved by the Resistance.

form mediates our relationship to "reality"—Morpheus explains to Neo the nature of the Matrix: "It is the world that has been pulled over your eyes to blind you from the truth . . . that you are a slave, Neo. Like everyone else you were born into bondage, born into a prison that you cannot smell or taste or touch. A prison for your mind." The human mind is represented as a threat to enslavement, as a powerful weapon. Thus agency lies in the realization that "there is no spoon"—the exposure of ideologically constructed experiences that prevent us from rebelling—and in "freeing our mind" to enable us to manipulate and resist the system that makes up our reality, that keeps us locked in oppression.

The human mind is the Resistance's strongest asset: congruent with most cyberpunk narratives, the battle for freedom takes place within the computerized space. The Resistance needs to find and release potential freedom fighters in the Matrix, whereas the last human city, Zion, needs to be protected from the AI. At the same time, the Matrix is also where the human mind is initially weak, compared with the AI's most formidable villains, the agents—sentinel programs that manipulate the Matrix with breathtaking speed. The search for a human mind so powerful that it can beat the agents is what brings Morpheus to select Neo (the "One"), who shows potential to be the liberator of humankind—again establishing a strong humanist concept of social change as being rooted in the individual's personal agency and contradicting the concept of a Marxist ideology critique and the need for collective revolution.

While the metaphorical constellations in *The Matrix* posit machines as "the system" and humans as "the oppressed," the film fails to acknowledge power structures among humans and relies on conservative relations in its portrayal of gender and race. *The Matrix* abandons one of cyberpunk's most radical and strongest political elements: the identification of capitalism as the force behind oppressive structures, which is such a strong presence in the visual and narrative makeup of the urban environment in movies like *Blade Runner.* The "show-down" between humans and machines denies the existence of blurred boundaries and ignores the interface between humans and machines conceptualized in postmodern discourse. It places the film firmly into the Hollywood tradition of appropriating subversive cultural elements and absorbing them into the liberal, profit-oriented industry. *The Matrix* emphasizes the terror that the notion of a posthuman existence initiates with its implications of the eradication of "humanness" (see Hayles, *How We Became Posthuman* 283).[30] The movie highlights the inherent conservatism in regard to alternative subjectivities that emerges once the radical narrative and aesthetic innovations in cyberpunk literature pull the body back from cyberspace and concentrate on the rather solid, if soured, identity of the net-cowboy.[31]

This insistence on individualism ignores the progressive visions offered by feminist cyberpunk critics, in which the body and technology are synthesized into a new posthuman subjectivity that does not call for them to annihilate each other, and therefore does not have to be rejected in favor of a humanist identity model that ultimately depends on the exclusion and containment of everything "other" for its existence. As Hayles argues in *How We Became Posthuman,*

> But the posthuman does not really mean the end of humanity. It signals instead the end of a certain conception of the human, a conception that may have been applied, at best, to that fraction of humanity who had the wealth, power, and leisure to conceptualize themselves as autonomous beings exercising their will through individual agency and choice. What is lethal is not the posthuman as such, but the grafting of the posthuman onto a liberal humanist view of the self. (286)

The Matrix, with its materialist outlook in the beginning that relates a Marxist ideology critique and collective resistance to Foucaultian power relations, fails to follow through with a progressive cyborg politics and instead reproduces one of the most prominent ideologies in our own Hollywood-entrenched society: the myth of the individual (white male) messiah/agent. This cultural myth opposes the *collective* as agent of resistance, which is an inherent part of posthuman networks and relations. This leaves *The Matrix*'s adaptation of cyberpunk's radical elements as strangely congruent with the argument that cyberpunk's celebration of its own narrative techniques as countercultural propels it into mainstream culture's apolitical stance. As Nixon comments: "For all its stylish allusions to popular culture—to punk rock, to designer drugs, to cult cinema, to street slang and computer-hacker (counter?) culture—cyberpunk fiction is, in the end, not radical at all" (204). Instead, "its slickness and apparent subversiveness conceal a complicity with '80s conservatism" (Nixon 204), a trivializing of positions appropriated by "others" as sites of resistance that is reflected in *The Matrix*'s stylish and hip late 1990s representations. John Fekete's critique of cyberpunk summarizes Neo's role in *The Matrix:* "What remains is the *figure* of the rebel, outsider, social inferior, victim, punk, monster, Other. A narrative strategy. Strike a pose" (398).

[T]he human has been reduced to a moment, but not an evolutionary moment: it is a moment of flesh that interrupts a more intimate relation between body and machine.

—Judith Halberstam and Ira Livingston, *Posthuman Bodies*

For it is a production, usually in response to a request, to come out or write in the name of an identity which, once produced, sometimes functions as a politically efficacious phantasm. . . . [I]dentity categories tend to be instruments of regulatory regimes, whether as the normalizing categories of oppressive structures or as the rallying points for a liberatory contestation of that very oppression.

—Judith Butler, "Imitation and Gender Subordination"

Bodies are produced at the intersections of technology, race, class, and gender. Within science fiction, social power is often sexualized, while the narrative drive focuses on other aspects that do not thematize gender hierarchies. The texts I examine here—Richard Calder's *Dead Girls,* Octavia E. Butler's *Imago* and *Wild Seed,* and Melissa Scott's *Shadow Man* —emphasize sexual difference and the process of regulating desires for "unfamiliar" bodies by declaring them as perverse. The different regimes depicted share an obsession with defining the "normative" versus the "deviant," which Foucault has defined as crucial for sexual regulation in Western history. If we consider sexuality and desire as parts of posthuman existence, how do we understand desire within changing technologies of the gendered body? How do feminist (gender) politics translate into fiction, and what part does desire play? Can desire and the sexual subjects it creates be separated from politics of representation? If feminists understand representations to be irrevocably connected to realities, and fantasy is that which we imagine, how do feminists read the projection of desire onto (female) future bodies?

Cyborg feminism takes into account the effects of technology and capitalism on the reconstruction of bodies and identities. It focuses on technological interventions that give us bodies whose "natural" gender/sex is modified and redefined. This is a tendency that Richard Calder also explores in his fiction. Aside from debating technology's denaturalization of bodies, how do we conceptualize alternative classifications of gender and sexuality not modified by technology? Octavia Butler and Melissa Scott speculate on our response to the materiality of the alien body, which challenges our naturalized binary sex/gender system. The body as the basis for experience is reinserted into the discussion of the correlation of sex/gender/sexuality and identities, but with at times unsettling and destabilizing phenomenological representations.

Technologies of Dystopia

Technology has always been controversial in feminist theory and politics. In 1970, radical feminist author Shulamith Firestone, in her book *The Dialectic of Sex,* called for the complete embrace of technology (especially in terms of reproduction) in order to achieve women's liberation. Later, ecofeminists and cultural feminists rejected any form of modern technology as an instrument of patriarchal control. Therefore, technology and its implications for feminist politics are at the core of the discourse on imaginary utopian futures. Feminist writers explore different positions in their utopian/dystopian texts. The antitechnology cultural feminist stand was strong in the 1970s in works such as Sally Miller Gearheart's *The Wanderground* (1979) and Dorothy Bryant's *The Kin of Ata Are Waiting for You* (1971). A feminist skepticism towards any totalizing concept of gender emerged in the 1980s in novels such as Margaret Atwood's *The Handmaid's Tale* (1986) and Ursula Le Guin's *Always Coming Home* (1987). Joanna Russ's *The Female Man* (1975) and Marge Piercy's *Woman on the Edge of Time* (1978) both anticipated the complex workings of technology in later feminist science fiction by exploring the advantages of feminist technologies. Cyberpunk's explorations of technology during the 1980s were the forerunners for writers in the 1990s, who created complex feminist future visions that integrate technology.

While cyberpunk is understood to have revolutionized science fiction, today's feminist science fiction has a much broader approach to technoscience than the original cyberpunk narratives do. It seems more appropriate to speak of a trend in feminist science fiction, which (like other science fiction) has incorporated cyberpunk's emphasis on technology. Instead of trying to make cyberpunk "more feminist," these writers place cybertechnology into the context of other technologies, such as reproductive technology, cloning, bio-ecological technology, and medicine. They create explicit political narratives that do not just center on an individual's subjectivity but address *systems* that shape our world: social, technological, economic, and political systems. While cyberpunk's vision is limited in its view of these systems (corporate capitalism seems reduced to "popular culture" icons—entertainment, leisure, etc.), feminist technoscience fiction is much wider in scope and places the cyber-savvy protagonist's tale into a political and social context.

Feminist technoscience fiction of the 1990s addresses issues such as environmental developments in works such as Nicola Griffith's *Slow River* (1995), Rebecca Ore's *Gaia's Toys* (1997) and Anne Harris's *Accidental Creatures* (1998). Questions of human/machine and workers' rights are treated in novels such as Melissa Scott's *Trouble and Her Friends* (1994) and *Dreaming Metal* (1997), Laura Mixon's *Glass Houses* (1992) and *Proxies* (1998), and Edith Forbes's *Exit to Reality* (1997). These writers explore the political implications of different technologies for women and their bodies. They share with feminist cyberpunk critics a concern about embodied subjectivity and its gendered manifestations, and they create empowering visions of feminist cyborg subjectivity that include the human/machine interface.

Even though cyberpunk's main output has passed, it has profoundly influenced the outlook of science fiction as a genre on issues of the technological body and the futuristic design of social environments. Nanotechnology—also called molecular engineering—is a new system of technology inspiring another wave of science fiction narratives. Its nature and manifestations are very different from cyberpunk's hacker subculture, peopled by cowboys with mirrorshades. Nanotechnology comes straight from the labs of bioengineers and holds the promising/threatening potential for exploding existing paradigms, not only within the sciences, but also in our understanding of social orders. Whereas cyberpunk envisions a technological future mainly in terms of computer technology, consumerism, urban sprawls, and the interface of humans and machines, nanotechnology revolutionizes the notion of machine beyond boundary crossings. Molecular engineering's technology does not blur boundaries so much as it redefines the categories of boundaries. It recreates the very structure of matter—the body—and thus our understanding of the interface of body and machine: the body (the organic) *becomes* the machine (the artificial).

I place Richard Calder's *Dead Girls* within this context of an increasing feminist appropriation of cyberpunk motifs and the use of nanotechnology for imagining radically different worlds. The first book of his *Dead* trilogy creates a dystopian vision of female posthuman embodiment that stands in opposition to the empowering narratives created by feminist writers. At the core of Calder's conceptualizations lies male heterosexual desire. He explicitly sexualizes patriarchal power, paired with capitalist consumption, in relation to a fetishized female embodiment. Calder's fin de siècle style and narrative allusions to that period of *décadence* reinsert the postmodern female body into masculinist modern tensions. In this dilemma, desire is defined through simultaneous attraction and repulsion of the Freudian fetish. Calder's female posthuman bodies clash with a feminist cyborg politics; the author explores some of the ambivalence produced by a technology that both naturalizes and denaturalizes gender.

Feminist Gender Politics and the
Challenging of the Sex/Gender Binary

Relationships of bodies and desire are explored in Octavia Butler's *Wild Seed* (1980) and *Imago* (1989) and Melissa Scott's *Shadow Man* (1995). Both authors investigate the correlation between sex, gender, and sexuality that is also the subject of feminist and queer theories that analyze power in terms of gender oppression and the regulation of sexualities. The definitions of a normative body are at the center of this debate, which is regulated by discursive technologies and their institutions. Instead of calling for a "natural" relation between body and desire, these two authors explore how the relationship can be redefined, and in their works the body becomes part of transgressive and changing gender identities. Butler explores the relationship of gender identity and desire to changing bodies, and the ways these bodies are linked to other categories of identity, such as race; intersexed bodies, queer desires, and their regulation are at the center of Scott's narrative. Unlike Calder, Scott is less interested in the technologized fetishization of heterosexual desire than in exploring the ramifications of regulated, pathologized desire in the context of gender oppression and criticism of the construction of bodies and the desires they evoke as deviant versus normative.

I view these texts in the context of transgender theories as well as feminist queer thought. Transgender theories not only challenge the naturalized correlation between sex and desire (as heterosexual), as queer discourse does, but also challenge the correlation between sex and gender identity (the body as determining gender identity). The proposition is to think of gender identities as variant beyond the binary of male/female—for the individual and within our categorical system. This expanded view includes various identities, such as transsexual, transgender, and genderqueer. Transsexual identities view body modifications as a possible way to adjust the body to a gender identity and embrace the body as home. Transgender identities negotiate masculinity and femininity "in-between" the binary categories and are often used as an umbrella term to describe any gender-variant identities. Finally, genderqueer identities place gender *outside* the binary system. For people with gender-variant identities, the body's relationship to gender identity is conceptualized in diverse (and at times contradictory) ways. However, all challenge the "original" body as the only referent for a gender identity.

The stakes are high in negotiating the New Gender Politics, as Judith Butler states in *Undoing Gender*. These stakes include the livability of lives and absence of violence—as well as self-determination and sexual autonomy—of gender existences outside the binary. Thus when feminist and queer theories challenge norms regulating gender and sexuality, trans and intersexed bodies and identities need to be central in this process of "remaking the human" (4). Visibility and the acknowledgment of nonnormatively gendered and sexed subjects are the starting point here: "If there are norms of recognition by which the 'human' is constituted, and these norms encode operations of power, then it follows that the contest over the future of the 'human' will be a contest over the power that works in and through such norms" (J. Butler, *Undoing Gender* 13). I understand the futuristic constellations imagined in science fiction as part of the process of "remaking the human."

Gender is treated in feminist theories as socially constructed and therefore as fluid. The science fiction of Octavia Butler and Melissa Scott challenges the naturalization of male and female bodies as the basis for gender identities and destabilizes biology through shifting physics that escape binary classifications. While both authors complicate the relationship of gender identity and body, neither envisions gender identity as disconnected from material experiences. Instead, they question our categories and their regulation as *natural* and thus engage with an emerging feminist discourse on variant gender identities.

5. The Anatomy of Dystopia

Female Technobodies and the Death of Desire in Richard Calder's Dead Girls

[A]n apparatus of gender organizes the power relations manifest in the various engagements between bodies and technologies. . . . Gender . . . is both a determining cultural condition and a social consequence of technological deployment.

—Anne Balsamo, *Technologies of the Gendered Body*

"L'Eve Future, and their descendents, the Lilim, retain in themselves a model of the quantum field, a model of creation, a bridge, if you like, between this world and the mind of God."

—Toxicophilous, *Dead Girls*

The beginning of the new millennium is defined by globalization —in all its diverse and conflicting manifestations. While Western superpowers reinforce their dominant position politically and economically, one aspect of leftist discourse is concerned with the ramifications of a technologized globalization that reinscribes power relations into racialized and gendered bodies. Feminist voices point to the invasion of the female body and its social environment by technology and call for the examination of what Anne Balsamo terms "technologies of the gendered body."

Since globalization is driven by technology, late capitalism is defined by the commodification of biotechnologies and research. Therefore, a feminist debate without a critical examination of technoscience is incomplete. As a genre defined by its relationship to technology as well as by its futuristic framework, science fiction is understood as a cultural arena that explores the anxieties of the human/machine interface. The subgenre of feminist science fiction creates representations of the female body within technoscientific relations and explores possible subversive political identities that might develop within those representations. The ambivalent and diverse portrayals of female bodies within feminist science fiction point to the contradictory effects technology has on women's lives and to the continual necessity to explore conflicting positions within this debate.

A good example of ambivalent representations of female bodies modified by technology can be found in Richard Calder's science fiction novel *Dead Girls* (1992),[1] the first of his *Dead* trilogy.[2] While the British author usually is not considered to be a feminist writer, his consistent focus on denaturalized female bodies and desires within a technologized future poses questions of possible female posthuman subjectivities. Calder creates a dystopian vision of posthuman embodiment with his life-size "dolls": young girls infected with a nanovirus who transform into mechanical automata that seduce and infest men, dooming humankind to gradual extinction. The story is organized around Enlightenment ideology's conflicting binaries of modern/postmodern culture, West/East, and colonialism/postcolonialism, which pervade every aspect of the narrative. Strategically set in Great Britain and Thailand, *Dead Girls* depicts a posthuman, consumer-driven world that is dominated by wars over contested social and political boundaries (most notably between human and machine) that are structured by sexual and racial difference. The racialized female body is commodified through the mass production of "gynoids," lifelike dolls designed for male sexual pleasure. Through the story of Primavera, a girl-turned-machine, and her human-boy lover, Iggy, we learn of the second-generation dolls' transformation from humans into machines and of the attempts of fascist humanists to eradicate anything not human.

Cyborg feminism contends that technoscience destabilizes the essential dualism of reason versus nature. The denaturalization of bodies and thus of identities, though dangerous and harmful in many ways, offers moments of disruption with potentially liberating new constellations based in partiality. When we read science fiction texts from this vantage point, the question that becomes paramount is whether feminist subjectivity is facilitated by technology. Does gendered power disappear between nonessential bodies? Can desire and sexual relations be transformed by technology? The body's (gendered) affiliation with technology is at the center of much of cyberpunk fiction although most of these texts create a normative *male* subject. Cyberpunk's decentered subject is the (usually male) console cowboy navigating both the material realities of the urban "Sprawl" and, more significantly, the abstract realm of infinite cyberspace.[3]

These two spaces mirror an inherent tension within cyberpunk around the body's role in constituting a postmodern subjectivity: an "oscillation . . . between a biological-determinist view of the body and a turn to technological and cybernetic means in order to escape such determination" (Foster, "Meat Puppets" 11). This oscillation is "gender-coded in the paradigm texts of cyberpunk" (Foster, "Meat Puppets" 11), where the female body seems inescapably essential, through both its materiality and its historical significations. In contrast, the ultimate goal of the masculine hero is to escape the confinement of the "meat" (the body), which he does by using technology. This theme of transcendence, Veronica Hollinger cautions, "point[s] cyberpunk back to the romantic trappings of the genre" ("Cybernetic Deconstructions" 206) that mark it as different from other "posthumanist" fiction, such as feminist science fiction texts, which offer very different approaches to the "construction/deconstruction of the subject" (207). As Nicola Nixon points out in "Cyberpunk: Preparing the Ground for Revolution or Keeping the Boys Satisfied?" much feminist science fiction published during the peak of cyberpunk's impact challenges the straight, white, male subject of humanism by employing gender relations as a main analytical framework.[4]

While most of typical cyberpunk fiction reiterates conventional anxieties around the formation of a masculine subjectivity—albeit mediated by technology[5]—feminist critics appreciate the more fundamental "*reinsertion* of the human into the new reality which its technology is in the process of shaping" (Hollinger, "Cybernetic Deconstructions" 218, emphasis hers), which one can find in feminist texts on posthuman subjectivity.[6] Feminist technoscience fiction writers reconfigure the masculine console cowboy by insisting on an *embodied* posthuman subjectivity that accounts for the "constitution of the informed body" (Balsamo, "Incurably Informed" 688).[7] Instead of surrendering the material to cyberspace, these writers envision subjectivity as developing from a symbiotic relationship between technology and the material body.

I place Richard Calder's *Dead Girls* within the context of this increasing appropriation of cyberpunk themes by feminist writers. *Dead Girls* is particularly rich in its conflicting dealings with gender and technology and is thus useful for an analysis of how "[t]he process of technological development is socially structured and culturally patterned by various social interests that lie outside the immediate context of technological innovation" (Wajcman 24). How is the female body defined by technology, and how is its technological existence determined or shaped by sexual politics? How are historical significations mapped onto female technobodies? The exploration of Calder's female cyborgs and of the ways in which his narratives are critical comments on, or reinscriptions of, patriarchal technoscience contributes to the ongoing feminist debate surrounding women's relationship to global technologies and their potential appropriation for resistance.

I begin this chapter with an overview of feminist discourse on posthuman subjects (in particular the feminist cyborg), which serves as context for the analysis of *Dead Girls*, followed by an introduction to the novel and its narrative technologies. The textual analysis consists of three major parts that examine how the novel engages with issues relevant to the feminist debate on posthuman subjectivities. In the first section, I examine Calder's depiction of a dominant humanism advocating the preservation of the human form, and the sexualized, classed, and racialized bodies that defy the definition of human within neocolonial, capitalist relations. Next, I discuss the prevalence of perverse desire in *Dead Girls* and its promise of transgressive sexualities—and subjectivities. In the final section, I explore notions of feminist subjectivity and resistance in the figure of the doll and how it is kin to the feminist cyborg.

It appears that, at best, Calder's *Dead Girls* offers ambivalent representations of the gendered effects of technology. On one hand, technology in Calder's text subverts fixed patriarchal notions of the female body by offering alternative ideals that disassociate gender identity from biology and that seemingly destabilize a traditionally male-defined, humanist subjectivity. On the other hand, his nanoengineered life relies heavily on gender differences, especially in relation to heterosexual male desire, which remains the primary paradigm of sexuality throughout the novel. Calder's literary creations of female posthuman existence therefore highlight both the fixed and the fluid aspects of technological representations of the gendered body. They remain ambivalent because they simultaneously challenge existing gender categories even as they lock women into a sexual framework of patriarchal heterosexual desire.

The seemingly most "progressive" aspect of *Dead Girls'* representation of femininity—its technological denaturalization—turns out to be quite "conservative": the removal of the natural body as stable ground for a feminine/female identity, which is viewed by cyborg feminists as potentially liberating from naturalized identities and power relations, fails to produce significant changes in the status of women. They remain fetishized sexual objects within a male-dominated economy. Instead of removing the restrictive definition of the natural (maternal) female body, technology allows male subjectivity to reinsert itself into posthumanism through techno-fetishization of the female body. The technobodied dolls do not uphold the promise of partial subjectivity and genderless identities of the feminist cyborg but instead are the embodiment of the other that engenders humanist subjectivity. This becomes clear in the novel's "main" doll, Primavera, whose promising disruptive presence is negated in the end: she has no subjectivity separate from the technology that created her—and its inventor.

In Calder's imagined future, the female body becomes—again—the site onto which a patriarchy in crisis projects its fears and desires. At the same time as the novel serves as a warning against the denaturalization of gender through technology, it poses a challenge to feminist critics trying to define agency within the representations of female cyborgs. Calder's representational strategies refuse a clear "either/or" demarcation of agency and instead mark an ambivalence between pleasure and danger that is a hallmark of a techno-fetishized global capitalism.

Technobodies and the Feminist Debate on Posthuman Subjectivity

Within humanism's meta-narratives of the constitution of the subject, such as psychoanalysis and its Oedipal separation from the (m)other, and Marxism's alienation through class relations, technology can only be seen as a fundamental threat to human subjectivity. Feminist counter-discourses, especially cultural feminism and ecofeminism, in their rejection of technology, have also relied on the notion of natural female embodiment as the foundation for a feminist subjectivity—that of Woman. In contrast, posthumanist thought rejects and/or problematizes a humanism based on the idea of an original unity that the subject can and needs to recapture, and instead embraces the collapse of the Cartesian dualism of mind/body, which is propelled by high technology: "In the posthuman, there are no essential differences or absolute demarcations between bodily existence and computer simulations, cybernetic mechanism and biological organism, robot teleology and human goals" (Hayles, *Posthuman* 3).

The subject's relation to embodiment, however, historically has been gendered and racialized within exploitative economic relations. Women and people of color have always been defined by their bodies. As Haraway argues in "A Cyborg Manifesto," persons who have always been conscious of the partiality of knowledge and experience that shape their identities—such as women of color—are more equipped to envision a decentered posthuman existence not based in dominance and oppression.[8] Feminist theories of posthuman bodies are thus concerned with female technological embodiment, growing out of their concern with the complexities and dangers posed by postmodern, global capitalist relations. How can a feminist agency and politics be conceptualized if the absolute category of Woman is not available, and instead women's partial identities are recognized?

The posthuman body has no "natural" corporeality on which to base its identity; thus it denaturalizes power relations. As Judith Halberstam and Ira Livingston put it in their introduction to *Posthuman Bodies,* "Posthuman bodies are the causes and effects of postmodern relations of power and pleasure, virtuality and reality, sex and its consequences. The posthuman body is a technology, a screen, a projected image; it is a body under the sign of AIDS, a contaminated body, a deadly body, a techno-body; . . . a queer body" (3). Cyborg imagery represents competing cultural understandings of how technology reshapes embodiment and the role it has in defining a postmodern subjectivity. In " 'The Sex Appeal of the Inorganic,' " Thomas Foster puts forward the concept that cyborg imagery reflects two major narratives of technology's relationship to embodiment. The first conceptualizes the disappearance of the body, the downloading of consciousness into an abstract, computerized realm—subjectivity is based on disembodiment, and consciousness itself is viewed as separate from the body. As Hayles points out, this vision of posthuman subjectivity actually shares the separation of mind and body with the liberal subject: "Identified with the rational mind the liberal subject *possessed* a body, but was not usually represented as *being* a body" (*How We Became Posthuman* 4, emphasis hers). Posthuman existence here clings to the Cartesian dualism of mind/body and rejects material relations as formative. In the second narrative,

Foster argues, it is not the material body that disappears "but an abstract notion of *the* body as the naturalizing ground of a unitary and universalizing notion of the self" (Foster, "Sex Appeal" 281, emphasis his). The latter allows for a "reconstruction of embodiment" (281) in its inclusion of the body into the posthuman.

As semiotic tools, the cyborg and other posthuman metaphors foreground issues of representation and the construction of cultural meaning, drawing both scientific and economic theories and their representations in cultural texts into the analysis of power relations. The cyborg and related metaphors emphasize that posthuman subjectivity grows from embodiment, destabilizing continual efforts to reinstate a mind/body dualism:

> In this regard, the literary texts do more than explore the cultural implications of scientific theories and technological artifacts. Embedding ideas and artifacts in the situated specificities of narrative, the literary texts give these ideas and artifacts a local habitation and a name through discursive formulations whose effects are specific to that textual body. (Hayles, *How We Became Posthuman* 22)

As one form of posthuman embodiment, the feminist cyborg retains the body's materiality within a posthuman discourse. Representations of posthuman embodiment are therefore comments on both the future and the present; they emerge from political discourse at the same time as they inform it. As Jennifer Gonzalez puts it in "Envisioning Cyborg Bodies,"

> Visual representations of cyborgs are . . . not only utopian or dystopian prophecies, but are rather reflections of a contemporary state of being. The image of the cyborg body functions as a site of condensation and displacement. It contains on its surface and in its fundamental structure the multiple fears and desires of a culture caught in the process of transformation. (267)

The negotiations that determine the makeup of posthuman bodies such as the cyborg are always troubled and never purely empowering. Feminist technoscience fiction writers often insist on the value of technology in de- and reconstructing the female body in relation to subjectivity at the same time as they point to the patriarchal system in which this technology is embedded. They create utopian moments within the dangerous and apocalyptic settings their protagonists find themselves in by placing resistance and agency into the intersections of human and machine. Thus the problematic historical relationship of women and technology is redefined and appropriated in its current moment, welcoming the concept of posthuman embodiments that succeed the gendered, humanist ideal of the unmarked body. But how are we to understand the cyborg that "goes bad" and remains entrenched in its technological and ideological origins in militarism and capitalist patriarchy instead of transcending them, as Calder's cyborg seems to?

The issue here is not to divide posthuman bodies into "good" and "bad" cyborgs (a practice that forgets, as Carol Mason points out in "Terminating Bodies," quoting Andrew Ross, that "the cyborg itself is a contested location" [226]). A feminist cyborg cannot be defined on moral grounds or on its (her?) ability to form an identity on the "right" side of sexual difference—there is no one "correct" position to inhabit, only multiple positions. To borrow Carol Mason's words, "The practice of identifying good and bad cyborgs often reifies political identities and social relations as individual bodies" (226). Instead, a feminist cyborg identity is based on the potential for resistance that can develop from a contested and oppressed existence without reproducing identities based on exclusion. As Haraway explains, "[The cyborg] is a polychromatic girl. . . . She is a girl who's trying not to become Woman, but remain responsible to women of many colors and positions" (in Penley and Ross 20).

It is cyborg imagery's representation of posthuman *embodiment* that is central to my analysis of Calder's female technobodies. Cyborgs cannot be conflated with posthuman bodies; they are *one* cultural metaphor through which to read the effects of modern technology on posthuman subjectivities. As the feminist political metaphor of the cyborg addresses issues of female agency, it serves as the main posthuman actor in my analysis of Calder's representations of mechanized not-women. In his technological dystopia, the female technobody becomes both the mirror and the receptacle for the misogyny and hatred that seemingly inevitably accompanies male heterosexual desire and that defines gender relations. Even as they are produced by patriarchal science and Man's social order, the technobodies in *Dead Girls* and his other work constitute a threat to both aspects of patriarchy and echo the resistance of the feminist cyborg.

Calder depicts the female body's relationship to technology as beyond merely problematic; it is *defined* through technology. "The 'women' are either gynoids, cyborgs, downloaded 'ghosts' or else homo sapiens so radically modified that they have been re-categorized as a completely different species" (Calder in VanderMeer). His vision cannot reconcile a male (patriarchal) (hetero)sexual desire with the potential to shape the female body through technology into a site of empowerment and resistance. Instead, this futuristic narrative is obsessed with the female body's morbid reconstruction through patriarchal technology, and it ultimately creates a nightmarish vision of the destruction and control of female sexuality. Calder's representations stand in stark contrast to feminist writers' appropriation of technologies and their transgressions of the binary of self/other (human/machine), which enables a feminist (techno) consciousness. These conflicting elements reflect much of feminist criticism's ambivalence towards technology's role in gendering the body and address the difficult question of agency in a posthuman world.

Dead Girls' Technologies

Dead Girls is about dolls. Life-size, animated dolls—some fully artificial, others half-human; some with no consciousness, others with a machine consciousness. All of them female, all sexualized. It is in the figures of the dolls that the underlying theme of *Dead Girls* manifests itself, the obsession with imitations of the "real": counterfeit versus original, mechanical versus human, machine consciousness versus human consciousness, and the resulting dissolution of the category "real" in the wake of a terrifying, quantum-based nanotechnology.

The tension arising from these ambivalent relations is embodied in *Dead Girls*' "main" doll, Primavera. She is a Lilim, the second generation of the "doll plague" that results when young girls infected with a nanovirus turn into mechanized dolls. The nanovirus originated in one of the *L'Eve Future*, fully artificial dolls beautifully crafted by designer houses such as Dior and Cartier prior to the doll plague.[9] The virus recombines the infected girls' DNA into mechanical dimensions and turns them into a new species set on reproducing: the virus in their saliva infects the blood of men, who in turn infect human women with the virus through sexual intercourse. The girls thus conceived then transform into dolls once they reach puberty. Named after the Judaic folklore of Lilith's daughters, the Lilim are characterized by jet-black hair, porcelain-colored skin, and green eyes. Their short life span as dolls ranges from two to three years, after which they die in madness.[10]

The year is 2071, and Primavera, unlike her fellow Lilim, chooses to resist England's murderous persecution of dolls by fleeing to Bangkok with her lover, Iggy. While nanotechnology is banned in the Western world, it flourishes in the East, where it is common to find animated mechanical female bodies (gynoids)[11] for the sexual pleasure of men. Here, Primavera becomes the prime assassin under Kito, a powerful doll. After escaping imprisonment by the CIA, Primavera and Iggy ask Kito for help with a nanovirus that is destroying Primavera's matrix. Through flashbacks, Iggy tells Kito (and the reader) of Titania, one of the original Cartier dolls, and her mission to help the Lilim destroy mankind. Eventually Primavera and Iggy learn that Titania is working with the CIA, ultimately sacrificing large numbers of Lilim so the Americans can claim control over the doll plague. Devastated by Titania's betrayal, Primavera loses the will to live and dies of her infection, leaving a grieving Iggy behind. Significantly, the narrative is never told from a doll's perspective: Iggy is the main narrator, and the only other major narrative strands are in the voices of the nanoengineer Toxicophilous and his son, Peter. The dolls have no voice in how the story is related, and thus no subject position.[12]

Calder's ambivalent portrayal of posthuman female embodiment is reflected in Primavera's difference from the other dolls. There are four different kinds of dolls: original dolls like Titania, who developed the nanovirus from repressed desires subconsciously programmed into her matrix by her inventor; the gynoids, cheap imitations of the original; illegal imitation designer dolls, such as Kito; and finally the second-generation Lilim, human girls turned into dolls. Primavera, in contrast to all the other dolls, destabilizes patriarchal categories of human/machine and original/imitation by challenging the terms of her existence.

With a stylistic combination of elements from gothic and cyberpunk traditions, Calder introduces a fin de siècle aesthetic (especially in his equation of sex with death) into postmodern science fiction. As Thomas Foster points out in " 'The Sex Appeal of the Inorganic,' " Calder's narratives "presuppose the emergence of a literary movement called the Second Decadence in the 1990s, which includes the dandy as a cultural type and a preference for the artificial over the natural" (295). *Dead Girls* replays many of the major tensions evoked in modern European

literature at the turn of the twentieth century. The fundamental conflict of the age was between the Enlightenment's promise of progress
and its rational, autonomous (masculine) subject, on one hand, and
on the other the fear of technology, a growing consumerism, and the
newly discovered Freudian unconscious (i.e. natural instincts), which
threatened the coherence of a modern subjectivity.

In *The Gender of Modernity,* Rita Felski examines how this tension
found expression in a decadent symbolism "where invocation of decadence and malaise were regularly interspersed with the rhetoric of
progress and the exhilarating birth of a new age" (30). Consequently,
the dual figure of the New Woman—an independent thinker in search
of political and intellectual equality—and the chronic hysteric—the
symptomatic embodiment of repressed desires and irrationality—"*pervades* the culture of the fin de siècle as a powerful symbol of both the
dangers and the promise of the modern age" (Felski 3, emphasis hers).
Calder directly evokes the sentiments of the fin de siècle in his contrast
of British Enlightenment ideology with excessive (global) consumerism and the trap of technological development. Sexual difference, one
of the central organizing elements of the tensions of modernity, is also
the main vehicle of Calder's meditations and is embodied in the dolls.

The modern machine-woman inhabits this ambiguous symbolic
function of both danger and promise to Man. On one hand, she symbolizes a denaturalization of the essential feminine. On the other hand,
she can be read "as the reaffirmation of a patriarchal desire for technological mastery over woman, expressed in the fantasy of a compliant female automaton and in the dream of creation without the mother
through processes of artificial reproduction" (Felski 20). We find her
most recent reincarnation in Haraway's cyborg manifesto, which is
marked by the same ambiguity.

Calder's dolls, as products of a (post)modern age, encompass the
"paradigmatic symbol of a culture increasingly structured around the
erotics and aesthetics of the commodity" (Felski 4). The Lilim's murderous inclinations and insatiable sexual desires exemplify the fin de
siècle's "association of femininity with nature and the primal forces
of the unconscious," while her technological origin and her obsession
with clothes and accessories simultaneously make her "surface without substance, a creature of style and artifice whose identity is created
through the various costumes and masks that she assumes" (Felski
4). Thus within a cyberpunk reenactment of the modern dilemma, the

enlightened masculine subject is (again) replaced by "a fetishized, libidinized, and commodified femininity produced through the textually generated logics of modern desires" (Felski 4).

Calder works with metaphors of both the surreal and the baroque, and he also draws on the cyberpunk tradition of fusing the technological with the sensual. His writing at times seems a parody of fin de siècle literature's excessive psychological searching, and his portrayal of masculinity and femininity satirizes sexual anxieties of that period. As a result, Calder's work freezes sexual difference into hyberbolic figures of excessive masculinity and femininity, especially in *Dead Boys* and *Dead Things*. If we understand parody as "a comical or satirical imitation of a piece of writing, exaggerating its style and content, and playing especially on any weakness in structure or meaning of the original" (*Benet's* 778), and satire as an application of parody to institutions or persons, Calder's representation of anxieties around sexual difference are satirical. At the same time, Calder's writing often loses the necessary distance from the object of parody/satire for it to be effective, that is, revealing its weaknesses and contradictions. In the end, he seems a little too much in love with the exaggerated poles of sexual difference he creates, and they become static yet oddly personal sexual fetishes. The effect is similar with Calder's representations of postcolonial relations: his figures of British gentlemen and the Thai mania for imitation of European merchandise are satirical only until they seem to *reproduce* the structures they set out to satirize.

Dead Girls is dominated by imagery of sexual perversion infused with violence and drug abuse. The dolls are vampires; their sucking the blood of their lovers recalls the gothic imagery of Victorian horror tales of the undead. The organic quality of the dolls' sexuality accompanies the literal "deadness" of their mechanical existence. In *Consuming Youth*, Rob Latham traces the unique development of the vampire-cyborg theme in Calder's "refractory teen-rebel creatures [that] move through a hallucinatory cybernetic wasteland dominated by the kitschy detritus of rampant consumerism" (Latham 24). Viruses dominate the technological in Calder, echoing biotechnology's impotence in dealing with the AIDS virus, which transforms and destroys the human body. The mixed origins of the metaphors that Calder employs create a fusion of the Victorian gothic, obsessed with repressed sexuality, with the technological language of science fiction. Mechanical technology, in its marriage with nanotechnology, loses its "hard science" stability and becomes a threatening, unpredictably mutating technology that eludes any control.

Calder bases his dolls' existence in nanotechnology, or molecular engineering, which allows us to imagine the restructuring and building of matter on the subatomic level. Nanoengineers will supposedly be able to manipulate and create matter with the help of molecular machines, or "assemblers" (Drexler 21), at the scale of nanometers (a micrometer is a millionth of a meter; a nanometer is a thousand times smaller). Developing from combined research in biotechnology, genetics, chemistry, and computer sciences, molecular engineering is viewed as potentially enabling us to "build almost anything that the laws of nature allow to exist. In particular . . . almost anything we can design" (Drexler 14). The dangerous but tempting potential of nanotechnology is explored in contemporary science fiction.[13] The influence that the concept of molecular engineering has on our perception of futuristic communication technologies is (almost ironically) worked into Calder's *Dead Girls*, in which information technology's reign is superseded by nanotechnology. Just as cyberpunk's world, dominated by computer technology, has shaped the way we think about bodies, subjectivity, and agency, we must ask how nanotechnology, as a concept that allows us to reimagine matter and even time and space, changes our very conception of who we are. How we conceptualize nanotechnology, therefore, provides insight into how we conceptualize posthuman subjectivity.

Perhaps the most important aspect of nanotechnology is that it is a technology that is hard to control. Like a virus, a nanomachine can develop its own agenda that is part of, or becomes part of, its program. Quantum uncertainty (the fact that the exact location of particles is based on probability, not certainty) and/or quantum indeterminacy (the inability to isolate and immobilize—and thus manipulate—individual particles), two overlapping, prevailing major physical concepts in quantum mechanics, dominate science fiction's fearful approach to nanotechnology. The unpredictability of nanomachines threatens to end modern notions of science and technology, emphasizing instead chaos and an organic-like technology that carries the danger of emergence and self-organization from below. These unpredictabilities are at the heart of the dolls' threat to rational order in Calder's *Dead Girls* (81).

In the novel, the tension between a prevailing colonial, Victorian sentiment of an ideal femininity (representing Enlightenment ideology) and a postcolonial, global capitalism (representing postmodern disruption) is reflected within the new technology's principles. Nano-technology's underlying principles are *mechanical* rather than digital; they are based on atomic assembling, not electrical impulses. The me-chanical basis of molecular engineering links it to the precomputer age of automata, or the mechanical sciences. The conceptual fluidity of the reality of surfaces in computer technology and the cybernetic empha-sis on information are both absorbed by nanotech's premise that reality *is* real, but not unique—that it can be re-created. This is a much more frightening concept than virtual reality, which merely questions the *conceptions* of reality, not its *materiality*. Nanotechnology makes vir-tual reality appear as a minor glitch in our ontology of the real—with molecular engineering, we not only simulate our world; we re-create it.

In Calder's novel humans are doomed to die as the Lilim spread the techno-viral plague. Yet the "real" space of humanism, represented by the Human Front (a political party dedicated to establishing human supremacy, based on the historical and ideological referent of patriar-chal colonial oppression), results in a fascist humanism that is exploit-ative of everything other. Between the realities of "doll space" and fas-cism, there seems no space for a feminist subjectivity to develop from Calder's doll-cyborg. Instead, those in the novel who are eager to resur-rect clear boundaries declare posthuman biology a "biology of master and slave" (*Girls* 23), favoring the human above all else, while the dolls' fate is inscribed in their program's innate death wish.

Hierarchies of Consuming Desire: Racial, Sexual, and Class Difference

Calder's representations of women's relationship to technology and the controlling impact it has on the female body are conflicted. On one hand, they echo the concerns of cultural feminists and ecofeminists who demonize any technology as inherently patriarchal; on the other, they point to the role that social, political, and economic structures play in technology's impact on people's lives. The social-sexual impli-cations of technology are dependent on the political and social climate in which they are produced: in *Dead Girls*, dolls are locked into a posi-tion in which both patriarchal ideology and an uncontrolled techno-philia define them. As Fran Mason states, "[The dolls] inhabit a metaphorical domain between patriarchal histories of women (and their exploitation in masculine power structures) and utopian fantasies of liberating technologies" (112).

In *Dead Girls*, suppressed patriarchal desire infuses *all* technology; it is embedded in its very structure, and thus technology can never be "neutral." "The world . . . will be a little boy's fantasy. The dream of a morbid child" (*Girls* 111). Not only are power and the will to control inherent in the subconscious makeup of the dolls, but sexual confusion and repressed desire cannot find room in the enlightened, ordered patriarchal space: "Sexless, he wanted us, your priceless Papa. Not like those cheap imports from the Far East! But his subconscious desires made us whores. Virgin whores, forever enflowered!" (*Girls* 124).

The Lilim destabilize the definition of what is human: "The dolls are both living and dead, organic and inorganic, human and non-human, thus raising the question: are they machines that look and act like humans or humans that look and act like machines?" (F. Mason 111–12). Their organic/unorganic nature, the basis for their un-humanness, is signified by racial and sexual difference within a capitalist economy in which male heterosexual desire drives consumption.

Racialized Difference

The most fervent fighters for the human cause in *Dead Girls* are members of the "Human Front," whose emblem is the human DNA helix. Their goal is to ensure the purity of the human race by systematically eradicating every doll. They subject infected girls to arduous medical experimentation and then kill them through impalement with a metal rod, mimicking the "staking" of vampires. Modeled after fascist parties like the Nazis, the Human Front works with propaganda (especially through education and mass media), intimidation through police presence, and public executions of the dolls. Their rhetoric is one of salvation: they murder "[t]o save souls!" (*Girls* 21), echoing the United States Religious Right's polemic in debates around reproductive rights and their habit of bombing abortion clinics. Their ideology is a form of racist and ethnic fascism, and their perception of the dolls echoes European anti-Semitism. A teen follower of the Human Front tells Iggy: "It's them that's murdering *us*. They're parasites, Ig. They use us to propagate themselves. For them, we're just *vectors*. If we let them carry on they'll take over the world" (*Girls* 21). Dolls are forced to wear green stars, reminiscent of the yellow Star of David that Jews were forced to wear in Nazi Germany, and they are subject to constant medical surveillance until their mutation has reached a stage when they are executed.

The Human Front's crusade for human purity is a racial discourse displaced onto the demarcations between human and machine. It is a common mechanism in science fiction to explore (or reproduce) racial and national discourses in narratives of wars between humans and aliens or robots. Calder makes the reader consciously aware of this displacement when his male narrator reflects on the grouping of children on his school's playground:

> The old nationalist hatreds . . . had been submerged in a new chauvinism in which speciesism supplanted ethnicity. In the playground, human children, who before the plague, would have segregated into warring tribes, celebrated their inverted cosmopolitanism in the sun, confining the recombinant [the dolls] to the shadows of the bike sheds. (*Girls* 19)

Although Calder's text declares the conflict to be transferred onto new, denaturalized territory, representations of elements that fuel this new war are problematic and all too familiar. It is not the "old" England where the plague results in (human) fascism. (In France, the reader learns, the plague is controlled, not through the violent execution of girls, but by managing the situation through reproductive strategies such as contraceptives, abortion, and sterilization.) Instead, a flood of Eastern European immigrants has given England a new ethnic face and new cultural impulses, destabilizing traditional systems. Thus the masses behind the Human Front are not Anglo-British; the leader of the Human Front party is a Slovak. Calder criticizes British sentiment based on unrealistic ideals of gentility dependent on the exploitation of the colonies, a paradox discernible in the figure of the impotent and failed nanoengineers, who designed the original dolls after the Victorian notion of ideal femininity, causing a world crisis with their sentiment. However, it seems as if this particularly violent way of dealing with the plague is grounded in the cultural heritage of Eastern European folktales, nationalism, anti-Semitism, and superstition, and it is this cultural heritage that infiltrates the British mind of the nanoengineer:

I myself was infected. Those first *émigrés* who came to Britain after the dissolution of the Pax Sovietica were intellectuals, former dissidents, underground writers, poets without a cause. They sought new themes, a new purpose. The worst of them glorified the old demons that were again racking their homelands: nationalism, populism, the paranoia of the non-existing foe: madnesses they embodied in a revival of folk tales and images. "The Second Decadence" the critics called their movement. I was a boy and their stories of witches and golems, vampires and the eternal Jew riddled my mind. (*Girls* 111)

Primavera and Iggy are both Serbo-Croatian, a culturally displaced ethnic identity in the all-encompassing postcolonial ideological arrangement between East and West, represented by Thailand and Great Britain.[14] The dark otherness of their haunted culture unleashes the repressed sexual desires of the West; it corrupts the enlightened British gentleman, the lover of purity and beauty. The plague originated in the ultimate other—the un-human, the machine—but the otherness of the Lilim mirrors racial and cultural differences as well as those of sexuality and species.[15]

Calder, who lived in Thailand while writing the *Dead* trilogy, creates critical representations of global capitalism's subjugation of Third World countries, with arrogant Europeans pining for the glorious colonial past, and power-hungry capitalist Americans fighting over Asia's consumer market. However, his critical representations of these relations at times reproduce existing stereotypes. So even his most direct criticism of the West's exploitations of the East and the homogeneous cultural effects of capitalism has a condescending overtone, conveying a belief in the East's inability to control its own destiny. The colonized are criticized for adopting cultural patterns introduced by the colonizer; the colonizer's decadence and greed is damnable, but so is the failure of the colonized to preserve their (idealized) cultural and social integrity during the colonial process. These attitudes are revealed when the reader learns through the self-reproaching monologue of a Thai character of Thailand's history of growing consumerism, which is destroying traditional farming and sustainable local economies: "But we came to look down on ourselves, our culture. We measured our self-worth against the consumerism of the West. Our gods were brand names" (*Girls* 132).

In his representations, Calder criticizes the extreme racism that is manifested in the design of artificial bodies. The only male un-humans in the narrative are seven identical black androids that Kito has created as her bodyguards and slaves. Calder's depiction of a racial stereotype (the hypersexual but emasculated black man) is satirical in its extreme hyperbole:

> . . . [B]ut here a seven-foot Negro, wearing nothing but the heavy electromusculature of a primitive walking, talking AI, was prissily attending to the evening meal. His fire hose of a member was like a third leg amputated just above the knee. 'Lordy,' cried Mr. Bones, his nigger-minstrel programme seemingly a leftover from Nana's patriotic S-M revue (pirated from Broadway and premiered before the country's top brass) *The Birth of a Nation,* 'it de white lady Miss Kito bin tellin' us about!' (*Girls* 49–50)

Despite the exaggeration and satire of the depictions of these figures, they are never countered or challenged in the course of the novel (either through alternative representations or active resistance to racism) and thus remain within a racist meta-narrative.

Postcolonial relations in *Dead Girls* are also embedded in various cultural and political dealings with sexuality. While England tries to control the doll plague through a violent repression of female sexuality, Thailand continues to produce gynoids—female dolls without consciousness—as sexual toys for men to torture and rape. The target group of this particular sex industry are the *farangs,* white men who travel from Europe, the United States, and Australia to indulge in the forbidden inhuman sexual pleasures generated by nanotechnology. The "pornocracies" that rule Thailand in the novel seem to be direct descendents of the sex-tourism economy developed throughout Southeast Asia in the 1990s. The Human Front's crusade against impure female sexuality stands in contrast to the East's continuing profiteering from white men's perverse desire; this creates the ideological illusion of England as the keeper of virtue and Thailand as the corrupter of innocence. Calder undermines this binary by disclosing the fascism that is at the heart of any crusade for "purity" and makes clear that it is the colonizer's repressed desire that is the most dangerous, the darkest in its desperate manifestations (both in the sexual behavior of *farangs* and in the existence of the doll plague itself).

The construction of the West as "original" culture and the East as "imitation" takes place on various levels. *Dead Girls* reflects a Thailand with an economic system of counterfeit European merchandise that is based on today's counterfeit industry in Asia. Calder's emphasis on the Thai obsession with anything European, with its looting and reusing of products outlawed in Europe, associates the East with an illegitimate pursuit of wealth, devoid of any true intention or originality:

> Then the capitalists of narcissism would emerge, the warrior merchants who had raped Europe's empire *de luxe* and carried off her ideas, her names, her designs, to sell them in the thieves' market that was Nana . . . : A pornocracy of copyright ponces and technopimps; an island shimmering with the bootlegged flotsam of Europe's shipwrecked past; an apotheosis of all that was fake. (*Girls* 6–7)

As the quintessential imitation, a human-turned-machine—not an artificial human, but a human artifact—the Lilim undermines the ideological origin of colonial relations, the idea of the original and the counterfeit (see *Girls* 93–96, 100).

Racial difference constructs sexual difference, and vice versa. In *Dead Girls,* this interdependency is reflected in the modeling of the original doll after the "original" ideal of Enlightenment: the Western European woman.[16] Even though it is never explicitly mentioned, it appears that all dolls are white; Latham describes them as "Euroasian" (251). Thus the (uncommented on) absence of black female dolls maintains the border war regarding what is human within a racialized context. All the dolls' physiques are similar; their uniform appearance is created by the designer—seemingly creating a "bloodline" that is independent from nationality. Yet the new hierarchy falls between original and imitation, between "true" beauty and "fake" beauty that strives to represent the original commodity, where the purity of "bloodline" is superseded by the authenticity of the logo.

Sexual Difference

While Calder superimposes racial discourse onto a conflict between species, his story is fundamentally a war of the sexes, and its site of battle is the female body.[17] Patriarchal technology affects the female body differently from the male body. In *Dead Girls,* the female body is produced for consumption (both the original dolls and gynoids) while the male body consumes; the Lilim (mutated dolls) disrupt this sexualized exchange system—consuming *their* bodies is life-threatening. Categories that constitute what is "human" are defined along the lines of gender and heterosexuality: the dolls, in all variations (Lilim, gynoids, illegal imitations, original automata) are female, simulacra of a feminine *ideal*.[18] There are male robots, such as the black androids and artificial beggar children that collect money for Kito, but only female dolls and replicas (gynoids) are (mass-)produced as sexual objects or pose a threat to male sexuality and potency. Sexuality and perverse desire are at the core of Man's relation to the doll.

Western culture has a tradition of envisioning Man creating the "perfect" woman, from the Greek myth of Pygmalion, to the robot woman Maria in Fritz Lang's film *Metropolis,* to the female cyborg in *Eve of Destruction.*[19] In *Dead Girls,* the female body is transformed from a "natural" form (which the Human Front attempts to re-create) into a surface onto which male fantasies are projected. Created by men and their patriarchal technology, the doll incorporates conflicting male heterosexual desires: there is the ideal of an asexual feminine beauty that is tied to the Western ideal of womanhood (woman as "angel"), and there is the tradition of a secret love of men for violent, humiliating sexual relations typically found in hardcore pornography, which is based both on the objectification of women and s/M fantasies (woman as "monster"). These extreme poles of difference in patriarchal desires are embodied in the dolls: the feminine innocence of the original automata, such as Titania before she turned, stands in stark contrast to the exclusively sexual definition of the nameless gynoids that represent woman as sex object—as fetish—in its purest form. This binary construction reflects the historical conflict within patriarchal desire that finds new manifestations in a technological postmodernity.[20]

The doll's deadly sexuality clearly falls within the realm of the "monster" and mirrors the patriarchal origins of this view of female sexuality. This monstrosity can only be resolved in the death of the desired object, a common theme in fin de siècle literature. The Human Front's perception of the Lilim is based on pre-Enlightenment Europe's ancient images of the fear of the other—in this case women and their sexuality—and its connection to the supernatural. Encounters with Lilim are infused with images of the witch, the vampire, Lilith's succubi, and the mythical golem. The implications often are as racist as they are sexist. When schoolchildren corner Primavera during her transformation, the confrontation echoes gang-rape, lynching mobs, and pogroms (*Girls* 23–24). The doll as demoness/witch/whore (*Girls* 58) is an ancient classification of female sexuality as other, whose abjection is fundamental to the humanist subject formation of the Western literary imagination.

While (Eastern) European anti-Semitic folklore feeds the fear of the Lilim, the repressed sexual desire of the British (also linked to these fears) produces her through technology. Her fragile-seeming beauty is paired with vampiric, bloodsucking deadliness that recalls Victorian gothic seductresses, such as the vampire women in Bram Stoker's *Dracula*. These pretechnological monsters—witches, vampires, sexual seductresses—are deviant female bodies that haunt the Empire's imagination. Their means of reproduction is counter to Man's "natural" order, and this supernatural origin links them to the technobodies of contemporary imagination: "Posthuman monstrosity and its bodily forms are recognizable because they occupy the overlap between the now and the then, the here and the always: the annunciation of posthumanity is always both premature and old news" (Halberstam and Livingston 3). It is in the dolls' bodies that the two major principles that oppose Man's rational subjectivity merge: the artificial/technological and the (super)natural—the fundamental sexual economy that underlies the vampire-cyborg figure.

The Lilim's deadly female bodies reflect the threat the female body poses to male rationality and ego formation: they are based on the principle of a "dirty" female sexuality, the dangerous (other) body. A doll's body is infectious, seductive, powerful (the Lilim possess superhuman strength), and magic (the quantum powers of her nanotechnology allow her to bend the laws of physics). Her reproductive function is perverted: her womb, no longer an incubator for male children, is the center of her power; she cannot reproduce herself directly but only infect men, who carry the virus to fertile human women. Not only does she suck men dry, but she also possesses the most horrific sexual organ Man can imagine (which lies at the heart of his castration fear of the phallic mother), a *vagina dentata* (*Girls* 32).

The Lilim's infectious nature is a threat to the normative heterosexual body and is reminiscent of the AIDS body today in that both "not only disintegrate, [but] produce . . . disintegration at large" (Halberstam and Livingston 15). Conventional measures do not curb the danger of a doll's perversity, as Primavera gleefully states: "Well a piece of rubber never protected a guy from *me*" (*Girls* 120). The doll is threat-

ening not only because of the danger she embodies for human reproduction but also because of her addictive effect on men. She cannot
be discarded. The doll's dangerous sexuality is paired with a fundamentally hysteric personality and is congruent with the female sexuality reproduced in fin de siècle literature: Primavera's unruly behavior is contained within the discourse on irrational femininity. Calder
taps into the "taxonomy of the irrational" (*Girls* 177) when he describes
the Lilim.

The principle of the doll plague is based on an impure female sexuality, and the only remedy seems to be a phallic disciplining of the
female body—a rape-murder. The sentence, initially directed at sexually active girls-turned-dolls, is then broadened to all dolls: "Just the
bad girls, Vlad [the leader of the Human Front] had said. The thirsty
ones. The teases. The flirts. The *provocateurs*" (*Girls* 60). The Lilim's
body is a perversion of the ideal female body, after whose basic form
the doll is modeled. Turning into a Lilim at about age twelve, the doll
is a Lolita. "In her white nightdress Primavera seemed the incarnation
of those bubble-gum cards we swapped in school: No. 52, *Carmilla.* An
underage Carmilla. Carmilla's kid sister, perhaps" (*Girls* 56).

Significantly, a girl mutates into a doll when she reaches puberty,
when her reproductive ability aligns her with her role in patriarchal
ideology as the potential mother of Man's children. Thus the female reproductive system defines a doll and her world. Her womb (where her
matrix sits!) is sacred to her, and she is killed through impalement of
her abdomen. It is here that the maternal is reinscribed onto the doll's
body. The quantum technology of her womb holds everything; it is the
site for the laws of the universe—and carries the potential to destroy
the world as we know it. It is both the ultimate promise and the ultimate threat; it re-creates reality foreign to Man.[21]

Instead of reproducing Man in his image, the doll has a reproductive
desire that is geared towards humans' extinction—and, therefore, ultimately her own. Since the doll cannot carry a child, she needs "to find
a womb that she herself does not possess" (*Girls* 129). She needs another body to infect in order to reproduce. Therefore, her basic sexual
drive is to be promiscuous.[22] Promiscuity in patriarchy is a male privilege; to ensure certainty of paternity, a woman must be monogamous
in her sexual relations. The doll's reproductive role threatens this dic-
tum, further separating her from the "natural" female body at the same
time as it places her in firm relationship to it. Since men serve as car-

riers of the virus and infect human women with doll software clones, and the Lilim's drive is to reproduce, Man becomes a mere means to reach the goal. (As Titania puts it, "Boys have their use, of course." [75]). Men's role in this process instills the fear that they will become through technology what women are within a patriarchal order: not subjects in their own right, but vessels for reproduction. For Calder, the doll plague is conceptualized exclusively within a heterosexual framework. The possibility that a doll could *directly* infect a human woman by having sex with her is never considered.

Consuming Class Relations

Global capitalism is a major part of Calder's dark vision. The contested boundary between human/machine is always informed by class and obsessive consumerism—what Latham characterizes as "hypercapitalism" (252). Calder's focus on copyright violations and illegal trade in fake designer merchandise mirrors fin de siècle concern with newfound mass consumerism. The dolls are assigned both gender and class status the moment they are created: female, and either servants (Titania) or sexual objects (gynoids). This assigned status reveals the supposedly "universal" human subject as *constructed*—constructed as male, white, and in opposition to the other, the servant/machine.

A man's relation to any doll is defined by her dual status as both the object of male heterosexual desire and a commodity of capitalist consumption.[23] Capitalism creates a hierarchy of desire that places each form of doll in a particular relation to men. The original dolls, such as Titania, were designed as luxury items in Europe; in their construction, nanotechnology made an embodiment of patriarchal ideology possible: "Europe['s] investment was in superminiaturization . . . the empire *de luxe* became a magic toyshop, a creator of adult fantasies. And among its *bimbeloterie,* nothing was so fabulous, so desired, as the *automata*" (*Girls* 12). These purely mechanical automata were created by and for "innocent" men to enjoy feminine beauty, the European ideal of the sexually pure woman. They functioned as servants as well as playmates for children. As servants in private households, their technology was not mass-produced, and only the privileged could afford them. These "Big Sisters" were considered "all-precious *joaillerie*" (French for "jewelry," *Girls* 4). In them contradictory male desires are most transparent once the virus develops: they are created as asexual beauties, but programmed into the substructure of their matrix are the repressed violent desires and longings from which the doll plague originates.

The original automata are the most desirable; their technology is the "purest" because they are the furthest removed from humans. They are entirely artificial. In contrast, the gynoids' technology is cheap and aimed at mass production, not exclusivity:

> In the vat's bubbling, aerated liquid, a half-formed gynoid stared back at me with the mindless eyes of mindless creation. No su-perscience attended her nativity. Above her, a neural network pro-grammed with pirated software instructed the vat's microrobots to duplicate a doll, Cartier, Seiko, Rolex, whatever, not by engineering base elements, but by reorganizing the atomic structure of a human foetus, aborted (so ran the rumours) by force. Illegal, of course. . . . But this dream bar belonged to the Weird [part of Thailand], and the Weird was moneytown, its forbidden technologies commanding huge amounts of foreign profit. A gynoid was cheap; it turned a quick profit; and a profit made you a patriot. (*Girls* 105–6)

Unlike the original dolls, which had exclusive status, the illegal (sex-ual) gynoids serve postmodern mass consumption. They have no con-sciousness and no value beyond pleasing men's violent sexual desires — they are the "new proletariat" (Latham 252). Aside from the gynoids, in contrast to the original Cartier dolls, most other dolls are *bijouterie,* "hybrid jewels" (*Girls* 4), with both human and mechanical elements. The main difference between the different kinds of *bijouterie* dolls is that the Lilim *become* dolls after being human, whereas the others are *designed* as dolls from birth. Products of both human and gynoid com-ponents, the *bijouterie* are imitations of designer dolls like Kito. Unlike the Lilim, these dolls are not vampires and, despite their machine con-sciousness, do not posses quantum powers.

The dolls' irreversible link to heterosexual desires locks each doll's identity into existing gendered and racialized power. Oppressive re-lationships to the system that made them are reinscribed into their bodies.[24] Yet the polarizing effect of a technologically mechanized femi-ninity is destabilized by the unpredictable aspects of the Lilim — par-ticularly Primavera. While the original dolls, the imitation designer dolls, and the gynoids are all commodities within particular value sys-tems, the Lilim, a fusion of the extremes of "original" and "fake," resist commodification. They pose a threat to their consumers, cannot be profitable or bestow status, and therefore have no place in patriarchal capitalism.[25] This is one moment in *Dead Girls* where a potentially liberating disruption takes place and some form of agency within a female techno-subjectivity is discernable. This disruptive moment seems furthered by perverse sexual desire, which pervades the narrative and highlights the connection between subjectivity and sexuality within a rampant consumerism. Calder's sexual world of violence, pornography, and s/m desire at first glance challenges normative notions of heterosexual relations and offers provocative speculations about posthuman sex.

Ambivalent Posthuman Desire

Dead Girls' organizing element is sexual difference, and its main narrative drive is desire. Calder's consciously postmodern, sensuality-driven language seems conducive to a re-envisioning of gender and sexual relations within a techno-defined future, and to queer explorations of consumerism's seductive liaison with illicit desires, especially if we understand sexuality as being formative to subjectivities. This intention seems confirmed in "A Catgirl Manifesto," published eleven years after *Dead Girls*. In this purported piece of critical writing, Calder —writing as Christina X—inserts his fiction into feminist and queer explorations of the pleasure of excessive, unrestricted desire. A reader familiar with both feminist and science fiction studies will notice that the title is a play on Haraway's "Cyborg Manifesto." The text reads as an introduction to a manifesto—which the reader never actually gets to see—in the tradition of "the calls-to-arms of the Futurists, Dadaists, and Surrealists, and (*in light of the fact that it is signed by a woman and has such a transgressive agenda*) other so-called, if less celebrated, manifestos" (158, emphasis mine). Calder then lists historical radical feminist documents—Valerie Solanas's SCUM manifesto and the CLIT statements—as examples of other "acts of *poetic terrorism*" (158, emphasis his).

The "Catgirl Manifesto," which Calder presents as a document addressing those "who found themselves abandoned to an already unstable universe" (162), has as its topic a (fictitious) mysterious disease that turns women into sex-hungry, catlike creatures, defined by "a desire—as instinctive as the murderousness of a cat's—to drive human males insane with lust" (160). This condition, named after the fictitious scientist Reinhardt, is then placed into the context of writings on desire by Sigmund Freud, Michel Foucault, and Herbert Marcuse, setting the stage for the declaration of the "Reinhardt female"—dehumanized, animal-like, irrational, hysterical, infantile—as the epitome of transgressive femininity.[26] This claim, however, clashes with the feminist/queer themes that Calder invokes by referring to Susan Sontag and Julia Kristeva on the construction of (perverse) sexuality and gender. The manifesto's combination of polarized sexual difference and "perverse" sexual practices (mainly s/m themes), which is also present in *Dead Girls,* prompts the question of how Calder understands feminist/queer sexualities, "in light of the fact that [the manifesto] is signed by a woman and has such a transgressive agenda."

Like the "Catgirl Manifesto," *Dead Girls* displays a "glamorization of perversion" (Felski 174) that we find in much fin de siècle writing. The violent persecution of the dolls, which culminates in their ritualized and sexualized murder by the medical establishment, echoes the role medical discourse has played in the censoring and pathologizing of perverse sexualities. However, in *Dead Girls* Calder does not engage the discourse on "perverse" and normative sexualities that he later raises in "The Catgirl Manifesto"; instead, he reproduces repressed traditional male heterosexual fantasies.[27] Instead of speculating on possible refigurations of desire, Calder creates dolls that remain fetishized *objects:* the gynoids are publicly reduced to objects of perverse and illegal male desire, while the Lilim are executed because they are not human. Primavera and Titania are the only dolls who are also *subjects* of desire (Titania, especially, lusts after power). However, both are still bound by the hysteric nature of their sexuality, which in sexology has not been defined as a perversion, unlike male (s/m) sexuality. Hysteria was historically defined as a feminine erotic disorder, while perversion was a primarily masculine pathology (Felski 183–84).

That sexual perversion is inherently transgressive is not uncontested but definitely worth exploring. In "The Utopia of the Perverse: An Exercise in 'Transgressive Reinscription,'" Veronica Hollinger examines how concepts of perversity intersect with concepts of utopia. She argues that while utopian narratives most often write perverse desire out of their visions of perfect communities, perversion might have much to offer in terms of transgressive subjectivities. Perverse desires produce alternative subjectivities, which, according to Foucault, come into being through their sexual practices and censoring discourses. Both Freudian psychoanalytic and poststructuralist constructivisms "posit perversion as a turning away from a normatively regulated and deeply ingrained set of psycho-social behaviours" (Hollinger, "Utopia of the Perverse" 34), offering potential disruptions that destabilize normative heterosexuality and its relations of power. Accordingly, what is of interest here is less a psychoanalytic understanding of Calder's female and male perversions than their cultural meaning—"aesthetics and sexuality as markers of resistive identity" (Felski 174). Understood in this context, perversion in Calder's narrative is not transgressive, since it is not based in an "aesthetic logic structured around the viewpoint and sexual and social positioning of the female subject" (Felski 189). Instead, sexual desires—and their perverse creatures—are based exclusively on the conventional male fetish of simultaneous repulsion by and attraction to the female object, and the inevitable reinstating of male domination/subjectivity through the death of the desired object.

Calder does not utilize the most destabilizing aspect of perverse sexuality: queer sex. Instead, the concept of the doll is built exclusively around (white) heterosexual fetishism.[28] I understand "queer" as a "slippery" term to describe sexual constellations and desires that cannot be contained within the "*nonce* taxonomy" of sexual categories reliant on a stable sex/gender/sexuality correlation (Sedgwick, *Epistemologies* 23–27). I also understand "queer" as undermining or challenging what Judith Butler calls "the heterosexual matrix," "that grid of cultural intelligibility through which bodies, genders, and desires are naturalized" (*Gender Trouble*, 151n6). "Queer" does not necessarily designate same-sex or trans desire, but it does connote sexual practices and desires that destabilize heteronormativity. Thus queer thought resists the dichotomy of heterosexual/homosexual and recognizes that "sexuality extends along so many dimensions that aren't well described in terms of the gender of object-choice at all" (Sedgwick, *Epistemologies* 35). Calder seems to acknowledge the decentering of gender as the defining category for desire—his dolls are fetishized because of their mechanized existence as well as their gender. However, he locks desire into a binary of sexual difference that in the end operates as statically as the categories of man and woman.

The only character that destabilizes the omnipresent heterosexual desire in *Dead Girls* is Mosquito, the man-turned-doll. The protagonist of a short story by Calder, Mosquito appears only briefly in *Dead Girls*. His/her presence has the most subversive effect in the text in that it discloses the construction of both desire and sexuality. As the "fake of fakes" (*Girls* 131), Mosquito is not only transgender but also transspecies. Emulating not a woman but the essence of idealized femininity —a doll—s/he is attempting to achieve the ultimate gender identity. To be a doll is to be desired—and hated—by men: "Dolls aren't women; they're man's dream of women. Made in Man's image, they're an extension of his sex, female impersonators built to confirm his prejudices. Sexual illusionists . . ." (*Girls* 131). Echoing Judith Butler's work on the performativity and imitation of gender, Mosquito's desire for dollhood reveals gender to be an imitation based on ideals, not corporeal truths, and destabilizes the technobody's relation to gender. As Thomas Foster notes, Mosquito "identifies with the position of the fetish"—as both the feminine and the "orientalized other of Europe" ("Sex Appeal" 298). Thus Mosquito can be understood as part of a "counternarrative of claiming the position of fetish as a strategy of subversive mimicry" (Foster, "Sex Appeal" 299). However, in *Dead Girls* this position is limited to Mosquito. Her/his (voluntary) construction as fetish is based on his/her pleasure and desire, while the dolls are constructed purely by desires not their own. Instead of countering pervasive (patriarchal) heterosexual relations with queer/other sexualities within the narrative, Calder freezes Mosquito into a position of freakish otherness.

The most frightening aspect of Calder's representations is the seemingly inevitable death wish as the basis for female sexuality, since the dolls represent embodied projections of male heterosexual desires. Not only does Calder's version of heterosexual male fetishism contain necrophilic elements and a passion for violence against women—that is not aimed at the masochistic pleasure of the bottom, only at the sadistic desire of the top—but it also represents the wish to die as part of female sexuality; self-annihilation is the ultimate turn-on. Thomas Foster, in " 'The Sex Appeal of the Inorganic,' " gives a psychoanalytic reading of fetishized sexual female cyborgs, arguing that the combination of technological and feminine fetish actually reconfigures desire into one that "accommodates libidinal investments in male lack, rather than a phallic ideal" (295). The fetishized female cyborg, once it identifies with the position of the fetish, contributes to this reconfiguration. Foster's analysis, even though it destabilizes the masculine subject's relation to the feminine, still relies on the feminine as *object*, not subject, in the reconfiguration of desire. It is questionable whether this is the only way to comment critically on the romantic notion of a "pure," gentle hetero-patriarchal love that prevents the development of a feminist subjectivity that is independent of patriarchal desire.

In the end, Calder's potentially radical insertion of sex(uality) as one defining element in a technologized futuristic world fails to subvert existing sexual relations. A *deconstruction* of normative sexuality (not simply an expression of the "flip side" of it) is much more promising for imagining transgressive, queer sexual relations. The theme of perverse desire Calder employs strictly reproduces heterosexual male fantasies: Calder plays into mainstream notions of the "naughtiness" of straight, perverse sex. Representations of sexuality in *Dead Girls* validate the existing discourse of straight male desire as the norm, and its unwillingness to explore alternative sexualities denies transgressive sexualities. Considering the limited transgression that Calder's sexual constellations offer, which are contrasted with Primavera's disruptive self-determination, how are we to understand the Lilim's posthuman, denaturalized existence in relation to feminist notions of resistance?

Doll Identity, Agency, and Resistance

In the Lilim, the feminine ideal is subsumed within the darker side of Man's fantasies; his own repressed desires induce a perversion of his ideology. The mutated girls are a secret sexual fantasy gone bad — gone bad because it actually comes true. "Primavera was a little dream of feminine evil: hateful because desired; desired because hateful. She was the dream of the age" (*Girls* 11). Lilim are descendents of the commercial original (Cartier's) and the biological/ontological original (human) and therefore the most frightening manifestation in both their *loss* of humanity through their transformation and their independence of man in their existence (the virus, not man, created them). It is their role as *agents* — even though limited — that makes them a threat to their creators.

The ideological division of the angel versus monster of Western patriarchal cultural imagination, which divides dolls into "good" creations (the asexual, aesthetically pleasing and technologically complex "Big Sisters") and "bad" objects (the sexually defined gynoids), implodes when combined in the Lilim. Her sexual desirability — her deadly "allure," which makes her irresistible to men — is paired with violent sexual practices and ultimately the death of patriarchal order and mankind as we know it. The misogyny that meets the Lilim (the Human Front's fear is sexually charged) is also what created her—she embodies man's simultaneous and conflicting love (desire) and hatred (fear) of both women and machines.

Considering the ambivalent representations in *Dead Girls*, the question remains whether it is possible to extract a feminist potential from Calder's dystopian vision. On one hand, the Lilim's existence seems to disrupt the norm of the human body, and their intelligence challenges the superior status of the human mind. In this way, the Lilim pose a postmodern threat to a male-defined humanism. On the other hand, they do not display resistance in general, despite the power their quantum technology gives them; they do not possess any agency beyond their man-made programming. Iggy reflects on the uncanny willingness with which the Lilim comply with their tormentors: "Why didn't they run? They were Lilim. Nutcrackers. Why didn't they fight? Death's chorus line moonlighted in pornographic movies, bit-part actresses passively colluding in their own obscene deaths. . . . Sisters, poor sisters, sisters, why weren't you all like Primavera?" (*Girls* 57) In their agency both Primavera and Titania seem to differ from other dolls: Titania controls and disposes of dolls as she needs, and Primavera resists her implanted impulse towards self-destruction. In these two characters, Calder creates creatures that precariously balance the ambivalence between domination through technology and female resistance through technology.

Dead Girls is concerned with the fear of humans' becoming machines. The artificial intelligence discourse on how and whether machines will be able to gain human consciousness is displaced onto the question of how and whether humans will develop *machine* consciousness. Dolls are called "dead girls" because their humanness is transformed into a mechanical substance. Dollhood is perceived as a mere imitation of life, which turns the girls into "A nexus of formal rules. Non-reflective" (*Girls* 88). Their bodies become alien,[29] un-human, and thus are declared dead. The Lilim represent the culmination of centuries-old fears of the "possibility that people's identities and emotional lives would take on the properties of machines" (Julie Wosk, quoted in Gonzalez 269). Their intelligence/consciousness develops from the attempt to emulate the neuroelectrical activity of the human brain through "fractal programming" (*Girls* 13), yet the dolls' consciousness is not that of a human adapting to its embodied state as a cyborg, nor is it that of an android developing a human consciousness. The dolls have a distinct machine consciousness that does not grow from a *fusion* of human and machine but is derived directly from technology, in Titania's case, and from the *transformation* from human to machine in Primavera's case. This transformation results "not so much in a human intelligence, but in a mind, a robot consciousness, which act[s] as a bridge between classical and microphysical worlds" (*Girls* 13). Instead of copying the human brain and becoming human, the dolls' consciousness is distinct and enables them to manipulate matter.

Her machine consciousness does not provide each of the Lilim with a "soul," a spiritual essence. Her personality is composed merely of images without substance, which are reflected onto a surface. As a simulacrum of the ideal feminine woman, she has no subjectivity beyond gestures and signs; she is the ultimate representation of woman as machine. Iggy, her male lover, defines Primavera's subjectivity:

Was she beautiful? No; . . . Beauty has soul. Beauty has resonance. But a doll is a thing of surface and plane. Clothes, make-up, behavioural characteristics, resolve, for her, into an identity that is all gesture, nuance, signs. She has no psychology, no inner self, no metaphysical depths. She is the glory, the sheen of her exterior, the hard brittle sum of her parts. She is the ghost in the looking glass, the mirage that, reaching out to touch, we find nothing but rippling air. She is image without substance, a fractal receding into infinity, a reflection without source and without end. (*Girls* 36–37)

Lilim are without reason or emotions beyond their needs, which usually focus around sexual recreation necessary to spread the plague. In accordance with the Enlightenment's perception of women, irrationality (hysteria and chaos), which stands in contrast to men's self-proclaimed rationality (control and order), characterizes the Lilim. A doll's consciousness is located in the womb, not in the head/brain, where patriarchal ideology situates rationality and enlightenment. Apparently, the ideological fusion of woman as nature/machine has found embodiment in the doll. At the same time, she transcends the Cartesian dualism of mind and matter since she *creates* matter with her mind. This materiality of thought constitutes a threat to patriarchal science, which relies on the separation of subject and object, and it makes the dolls' technology terrifying. For her, "reality isn't consensual": "For all Lilim—thought is denser, more material, than for you and I [Iggy and Toxicophilous]. *Her* dreams have substance" (*Girls* 95). Machine consciousness incorporates matter into thought and senses into embodiment, making boundaries impossible to sustain.

The machine consciousness of the dolls does not enable them to *feel*, a classical (often unclear) distinction between machines and humans in science fiction.[30] The Lilim can desire, however, since desire is a physical experience as well as an emotional one, and this fact blurs the distinction between "pure" emotions and desire as well as between human and machine: "But if my programme won't allow me to love you, Iggy, at least I can love your blood" (*Girls* 39). Calder's writing conveys an underlying nostalgia for human emotions, a mourning of the human touch of "love" that each Lilim loses on her entry into dollhood. Here the evocation of "authentic" heterosexual romance revokes any liberating potential of a technological denaturalization of sexual difference. Calder seems caught between the two extreme poles of imagining a female cyborg-body with the potential for a radical new subjectivity and the insistence that "love" (i.e. human emotion) needs to prevail in any posthuman future. This insistence pulls the narrative back into the familiar liberal sentiment of a humanist subjectivity. So the novel ends with Primavera dying in Iggy's arms, and we are given a flashback to the time when they fled England and were on their way to Bangkok:

"[T]hank you, Iggy."
"Me?"
"For being my friend. I'm a doll, I can't say it but I, I—"
"Yes, Primavera?"
"I do. I, I—"
"I love you too, Primavera."
"Yes, Iggy." (*Girls* 147)

However, it is also in Primavera's character that the feminist cyborg potential finds some resonance. As a creature who moves between human and mechanical realms, she violates boundaries. At the same time, she also rejects her role as a disempowered boundary creature by breaking the "rules" of dollhood: she kills, unlike other dolls, and she is monogamous in her relationship with Iggy. Most of all, she seems immune to the death wish lying dormant in her program, which Titania tries to activate: "Of course some dolls don't surrender that easily, Primavera being a case in point. I understand Titania's being [sic] calling *her* for years . . ." (*Girls* 114). Primavera's strength is to resist her designated position as victim, which both the Human Front and Titania want her to inhabit.

Nevertheless, despite Primavera's disruptive identity, Calder's dystopia does not offer an alternative to the posthuman female embodiment he creates—after all, Primavera, the only doll who resists, dies. Her identity as resisting cyborg does not prevail; instead, her consciousness is haunted by her lost humanness. Through flashbacks, the reader learns of her fear of becoming Lilim, which stands in stark contrast to her defiant identity as doll throughout the novel. As a girl, her fear was not only the loss of her human identity but, perhaps more importantly, the loss of a self that would not be defined by male desire alone: "She knows that she is becoming that other, that vertigo of desire, that dead girl who shares her name" (*Girls* 26). Thus dollhood means a loss of subjectivity, of identity. Initially Primavera seems to have accepted her existence as doll; in fact, her response to Toxicophilous's remorse at having taken her "humanity" is defiant: "So who wants to be human?" (*Girls* 111). However, in the end, when her death seems inevitable, she confesses to Iggy her wish to be human. Evoking the fairy tale of the wooden boy Pinocchio, whose dream it is to become a "real" boy, she states: "None of us wants to be dolls, Iggy. We all want to be real girls, no matter what we say" (*Girls* 134). With this longing for the human form (and its status as "real" embodiment), Primavera rejects the cyborg identity that requires an acceptance of the constructed self while rejecting the oppression—that is, the fetishism—that comes with the package. It is in the human boy Iggy that the myth of the clean, pure *human* origin is disclosed as part of an oppressive patriarchal ideology, such as in this dialogue between Iggy and Primavera:

> "It would have been nice," she said, "to have been normal, wouldn't it?"
>
> "Like the medicine heads?" I said. "Like the Hospitals? Like the Human Front? . . . I'm the guilty one. And all those like me. We made you what you are."
>
> "It's not your fault," she said. "England made us both. We've been programmed by her perversities. Sometimes you seem as much a machine as me." (*Girls* 135)

At the end of *Dead Girls,* the inventor of the simulacrum of the patriarchal ideal woman appears to be merely a victim of a cruel accident played by his unconscious, shaped by ideology and history, while the "true" evil is embodied in his creation, Titania. It is she, and not the Human Front, who eventually kills Primavera, thereby dismantling any concept of an alliance between the oppressed or collective resistance. The only subjectivity available to the mechanical dolls is a victim subjectivity that leads to their collective and individual deaths, "with the fatalism of the abandoned—the self-abandoned who regard themselves as neither martyrs nor criminals, but as things" (*Girls* 58). Calder's representations reinscribe the dichotomy of the rational masculine and the irrational/nature-bound feminine produced by the discourse of modern culture.[31] Even if understood as a critical exploration of a continuously patriarchal ideology, *Dead Girls'* depiction of the feminine "does not allow for any independent conception of female identity, agency, or desire. Woman is reduced to the libidinal, inexpressible, or aesthetic, the repressed Other of patriarchal reason" (Felski 7). The dolls remain within the logic of the crisis of masculine subjectivity and do not engage with a possible resolution of that crisis through an alternative feminine subjectivity.

In his narratives, Calder reworks much of the classic modern dilemma while placing it into the context of postmodern cyberpunk literature. In *Dead Girls,* the original conflicts that gestate both modern and postmodern anxieties (reason/desire, progress/destruction, and human/technology) are reformulated in a futuristic scenario, echoing the formulations of a previous fin de siècle: "simulation, pastiche, consumption, nostalgia, cyborgs, cross-dressing" (Felski 15). Calder's depiction of the turn of the twenty-first century—the Second Decadence—which lets loose the destructive doll plague comments on the anxieties of the historical moment in which the author writes the novel while it draws on the symbolism of many late-nineteenth-century literary texts. Disappointingly, Calder replicates the dilemma; he does not reinvent it. Instead, his writing seems to join other cyberpunk fictions in their reinscription of Western narratives of "capitalist imperialism and phallic projection" onto a technologized future that Sharon Stockton criticizes in " 'The Self Regained': Cyberpunk's Retreat to the Imperium" (590).

The dilemma of dissolving boundaries between human and machines, real and counterfeit, woman and doll, seems irresolvable in

Dead Girls. Even though the constructed existences Calder creates at times contest prevailing patriarchal ideology, they do not succeed in undermining it. Primavera, potentially the most disruptive figure in *Dead Girls,* ultimately does not possess a subjectivity separate from that of her creator. Unlike Haraway's feminist cyborg, who turns against her patriarchal military origins and develops her own agency, Primavera is unable to transcend the origins of her creation. Since the cyborg's main characteristic is to contest categories of identity, and a domestication of its metaphor into a comfortable and unambiguous (even when feminist) pattern of identity endangers its subversive potential, it is difficult to view Calder's vision as *either* a critical comment on existing power structures *or* a tale that reinforces patriarchal oppression.

What can be stated without ambiguity is that, in Calder's future, "masculine power systems will be there to contain the transgressive desires of the female cyborg" (Fran Mason 124); in Calder's text, patriarchal technology creates disempowering, death-seeking female cyborgs who are denied agency in their role as mirror for male heterosexual desire. The author opts for representing capitalist patriarchy as totalizing, with no potential for disruption. The evolution of the virus is predictable and inevitable; Calder does not imagine the emergence of elements that might destabilize his newly imagined order—such as a mutated "queer" strain of the nanovirus that would upset heterosexuality. This observation is even more troubling when one considers that Calder's narratives are never told from the perspective of the female cyborg. She is always the object of the desire that throws the male antihero into crisis in his attempts to position himself within posthuman relations.[32] Never is her own sexuality the center of the events. The novel highlights the historical as well as imaginative complexities of patriarchal power and desire (Calder is quite clear on how much higher women's stake is in the renegotiations around posthuman embodiment).

While feminist readers may appreciate the critical eye Calder casts on technologies of power and desire, the absence of any female (and/or feminist) agency—or desire—in his dystopia casts doubt on its subversive potential. His posthuman fantasy is void of women (but not of men!): "As for the women characters in my novels—there aren't any" (Calder in VanderMeer). While feminist theories on posthuman existence conceptualize subjectivity outside the categories "man" and "woman," it is startling that Calder describes a society whose high technology only amplifies gender polarities even though it carries the potential to undermine them. There is an odd lack of ambivalence in Calder's (seemingly ambivalent) representations of women's relationship to technology: in the end, they collapse into the familiar ideological alignment of women with machines, and the transgression of boundaries affirms domination by patriarchal needs and desires. The dolls' lack of voice and substance evokes Samuel Delany's observation, in a conversation about cyberpunk, that "the simple truth has been that the test of the novel is always in the crafting of its female characters" ("Some *Real* Mothers" 178). In terms of this criterion, Calder's novel fails.

Maybe the question we need to ask is what use feminists can hope for from a science fiction narrative beyond representations of transgressive agency. Calder's dystopia evokes disturbing constellations of patriarchal desire and speculates on its manifestations within a global capitalism. The ambivalence of the posthuman female bodies present in his text reproduces not only systems of oppression but also moments of disruption. Instead of simply rejecting projections like Calder's, feminist resistance may need to consider within its bright future visions the threatening aspects of posthuman embodiments—and their darker pleasures—in order not to reproduce the oppressive humanism that gave birth to them. Even though Calder refuses his female cyborgs a subject position other than one based exclusively in patriarchal fear and desire, his representations mark the ambivalence inherent in cyborg resistance, and feminist politics need to pay attention to this ambivalence.[33] That may be the lesson of the dolls.

6. Beyond Binary Gender

Genderqueer Identities and Intersexed Bodies in Octavia E. Butler's Wild Seed and Imago and Melissa Scott's Shadow Man

It might seem natural to regard intersexuals and transgendered people as living midway between the poles of male and female. But male and female, masculine and feminine, cannot be parsed as some kind of continuum. Rather, sex and gender are best conceptualized as points in a multidimensional space.

—Anne Fausto-Sterling, "Five Sexes Revisited"

As I stood in line to pick up my ticket at a movie theater in South Philadelphia on a Saturday night in 2003, I got caught up in the fever of anticipation that had the crowd around me buzzing— the *Matrix Reloaded* obsession had me firmly in its grip. Afterwards I could not shake the nagging sense of disappointment that dominated my reaction to the movie. It was the same reaction I had had to *The Matrix*—disappointment in the unimaginative ways in which the film represents how individuals envision themselves while in the Matrix. The concept that we project our self-image into a digital matrix potentially offers mind-bending physical constellations, yet this potential is never fully realized in the films. Just as people re-envision their identities in the online virtual reality games known as multi-user dimensions (MUDS),[1] the Matrix should be crawling with fantastic creatures such as dragons, goblins, aliens, comic heroes, fairies, and an array of human variants of multiple races, ages, abilities, and a variety of gender expressions. Instead, we encounter the same two-gender/sex system our cultural world is organized around, which the Matrix reflects as our reality. Why is it that we are so invested in maintaining (and reproducing) the naturalized sex/gender/sexuality correlation that orders heteronormativity, even in cultural texts that gesture towards alternatives?

In its criticism of social power, feminist research historically has relied on a stable relationship between sex (biology, anatomy), gender (social roles and their expression), and sexuality (sexual preference, desire). Sex and sexuality are frequently collapsed into the category of gender, and although the social construction of gender has been broadly criticized by feminists, the normative correlation of the three concepts has received much less criticism. Genderqueer and other transgender identities pose a challenge to feminist treatments of gender and sexuality that either perpetuate dominant systems of sexual repression (a heterosexual concept of gender and sexuality) or maintain exclusive mechanisms in their criticism of patriarchy and heterosexism (lesbian feminist essentialism). Queer interventions into feminists' analyses of power destabilize the "natural" correlation between gender and sexuality and examine the material reality of the body in relation to discursive power. They assume a stable sexed body neither for the subject nor for the object of desire, and they therefore disconnect identity from a stable sex/gender/sexuality correlation. Transgender and transsexual theory thematizes the unstable relationship between assigned genders, sexualities, and identities and reconceptualizes feminist strategies against gender oppression (Fig. 6.1).[2]

Science fiction *literature* as a medium offers more complex ways of envisioning future worlds than does mainstream science fiction cinema; the reader looking for alternative sexual and gender politics may encounter radical and subversive assortments of sexual identities (such as in Samuel Delany's work).[3] In particular, feminist science fiction of the past thirty-five years has challenged existing gender relations and has explored lesbian and increasingly queer sexual identities as well as new gender roles. Always current, feminist science fiction mirrors and/or anticipates theoretical and political debates.[4]

Much of classic feminist science fiction literature relies on the binary of man/woman in its reimagining of social orders.[5] While some of the texts challenge heteronormative assumptions of opposite-sex desire, the naturalized correlation between sex (male or female) and gender (man or woman) remains intact. In their envisioning of worlds in which women are not oppressed within a patriarchal system, some of these texts create separatist societies modeled after lesbian cultural feminism, such as the feminist utopias in Joanna Russ's *The Female Man* (1975), Suzy McKee Charnas's *Motherlines* (1978), Sally Miller Gearhart's *The Wanderground* (1979), and Katherine V. Forrest's

	Stable correlation			↔	Destabilized correlation (queer)			
		normative/ straight	**gay, lesbian**	**bisexual**	**transsexual**	**transgender, genderqueer**	**intersexed**	
identity political and personal = coherent								**identity** political and personal = diverse
sex biology = natural, coherent		female/male	female/male	female/male	female/male	female/male	intersexed/ variable	**sex** biology = unstable, constructed, real, not factual
gender expression is social = constructed roles		woman/man	woman/man	woman/man	opposite to sex	close to opposite woman/man feminine/ masculine fluid: either/between/ neither	either/none	**gender** expression is social = con-structed roles
sexuality desire = biological or social? once "discovered" = fixed, unchanging		opposite sex/gender = heterosexual	same sex/gender = homosexual	either sex/gender = bisexual	various sexualities: either sex/gender or both = homosexual, heterosexual, or bisexual	various sexualities: heterosexual, homosexual, bisexual, across/between genders/sexes	either sex/gender: no classified sexualities unless explicit identity	**sexuality** desire = biological or social? changing, unstable

Figure 6.1. The Correlation between Sex, Gender, and Sexuality: a queer position asserts that the way the body relates to gender and desire is highly variable and unstable. This claim allows for a destabilization of any "natural" correlation between sex/gender/sexuality, and thus of heterosexuality and the gender binary as normative.

Daughters of a Coral Dawn (1984). They envision reproduction independent of heterosexual relations and see a separation of the sexes as the only viable way to end women's oppression. Other feminist texts redefine traditional gender roles to create an equality of men and women or reverse power relations, often re-creating tension between radical and liberal feminist approaches, such as in Dorothy Bryant's *The Kin of Ata Are Waiting for You* (1971), Marion Zimmer Bradley's *The Shattered Chain* (1976), and Pamela Sargent's *The Shore of Women* (1986). Where a transcendence of gender binaries is envisioned, often sex, gender, and sexuality collapse into an androgyny modeled after masculine identities, such as in Ursula Le Guin's *The Left Hand of Darkness* (1969), or explore the biological basis of sexual difference in terms of modern biotechnology, resulting in a separation of the sexes, as in Nicola Griffith's *Ammonite* (1992).

Few of these works challenge the opposition of man and woman as a social system by changing the binary gender system.[6] Samuel Delany destabilizes the naturalized correlation between sex, gender, and sexuality in *Triton* (1976) by adding a number of genders and also through the trope of socially accepted transsexuality, and Marge Piercy, in *Woman on the Edge of Time* (1976), does so by abandoning gendered pronouns along with gender roles.[7] In the past 10 years, a growing number of science fiction novels focusing on gay and lesbian subject positions have been published, and awards such as the Spectrum Award and the annual LAMBDA Literary Award honor gay and lesbian science fiction. Works such as Severna Park's *Speaking Dreams* (1992) and *Hand of Prophecy* (1998), Edith Forbes's *Exit to Reality* (1997), Anne Harris's *Accidental Creatures* (2000), Kelley Eskridge's *Solitaire* (2002), and Melissa Scott's novels have contributed to an increasing representation of lesbian voices in science fiction. The establishment of gay and lesbian science fiction is also reflected in publications such as the anthology *Bending the Landscape: Science Fiction* (1997), edited by Nicola Griffith and Stephan Pagel.

Within science fiction criticism and narratives, transgender identities have been explored mainly in relation to cyberspace and bodiless identification.[8] Both in theory and in the science fiction texts in question, the body's insistent presence asks for a debate that includes the materiality of existence outside the gender binary of "male" and "female." When categories of male and female are destabilized, the narratives often rely on the solitary, transgressive transsexual/

transgendered character, who is caught between genders. Examples include the crazy, spiritual-prophetic, castrated trans figure in Suzy McKee Charnas's *The Furies* (1994) and the transgendered protagonist in Maureen F. McHugh's *Mission Child* (1998), who acts as cultural and spiritual healer/translator/ambassador. Even though these figures disrupt and destabilize the gender system in which they live (fulfilling a narrative function similar to that of the cyborg and the alien),[9] the gender/sex system *itself* is not alternatively envisioned.

Exceptions to this phenomenon are narratives that in their reconceptualization of gender relations envision worlds not organized by the gender binary. In her *Xenogenesis* trilogy and *Patternist* series, science fiction writer Octavia Butler creates alternative gender identities and explores how they are linked to desire through her characters Anyanwu and Doro—immortal shapeshifters who appear in *Wild Seed* (1980) and *Mind of My Mind* (1977)—and the Oankali, an alien race that consists of three rather than two sexes. The Oankali travel across space in search of other species to crossbreed with—to "trade" genes with—in *Dawn* (1987), *Adulthood Rites* (1988), and *Imago* (1989). In *Shadow Man* (1995), Melissa Scott creates a five-sex system and explores how acknowledgment of the existence of bodies other than male and female can undermine power relations between men and women. These narratives not only reimagine gender roles and normative heterosexuality but also question stable gender identities as well as the binary underlying the contemporary concept of biological sexes. This analysis focuses on two main aspects of the narratives' treatment of gender and sexuality: how the authors' narratives destabilize the sex/gender/sexuality correlation and how they revisit the debate between the extreme poles of constructed versus essentialist identities. Finally, I discuss how Melissa Scott's *Shadow Man* makes a case for including transgender rights in any progressive (and feminist) political agenda by pointing to the limits of exclusive oppositional politics.

Shapeshifting as Transgressive Gender Performativity in Octavia E. Butler's *Wild Seed* and *Imago*

If a sexuality is to be disclosed, what will be taken as the true determinant of its meaning: the phantasy structure, the act, the orifice, the gender, the anatomy? And if the practice engages a complex interplay of all of those, which one of these erotic dimensions will come to stand for the sexuality that requires them all? (Judith Butler, "Imitation and Gender Insubordination" 17)

Octavia Butler's narratives confront the reader with trans-morphing human and alien bodies that trouble our notions of sexuality and gender. Her representations undermine stable sexual identities through their unstable bodies, while at times insisting on identities that exist outside of social construction. The tension between social construction and inexplicable desire in her stories mirrors contemporary debates in queer theory on how the body and gender presentation relate to sexual identity.[10]

In her influential 1984 essay "Thinking Sex," queer activist and theorist Gayle Rubin criticizes lesbian feminism's tendency to collapse sex and sexuality with gender and insists on the specificity of sexual regulatory regimes: "Gender affects the operation of the sexual system, and the sexual system has had gender-specific manifestations. But although sex and gender are related, they are not the same thing, and they form the basis for two distinct arenas of social practice" (33).[11] Queer theory and activism ultimately challenge the (hetero)normative alignment of sex/gender/sexuality and the naturalization of specific forms of desire. Feminist queer theory proposes a complicated and unstable relationship of the body to gender identity and desire. The body is not a material given that predates discourse; instead, as Judith Butler states in *Gender Trouble*, "sex is itself a gendered category" (7). The goal is to resist dualisms and the construction of otherness on any level, including the split between heterosexual and homosexual identity. In terms of subjectivity, queer theory undermines the notion of a collective, gender-based identity (and politics) in its method of deconstructing hierarchies by rejecting their implicit categories.

Judith Butler argues that gender identity is not a true inner "self" but is produced discursively, through political and social powers that privilege heterosexuality. She cautions against assuming a correlation of sex/gender/desire, which is obviously unable to integrate various nonheterosexual desires. Disregarding queer desires, psychoanalytic discourse constructs sex as producing desire—making (hetero)sexual orientation seem a given instead of understanding the body as discursively gendered. Judith Butler insists that "gender is an identity tenuously constituted in time, instituted in an exterior space through a *stylized repetition of acts*" (*Gender Trouble* 140, emphasis hers). The idea of "gender as performative" conceptualizes it as a parody of an ideal gender identity, which is itself an illusion and therefore unattainable. This concept explicitly deconstructs the notion of a core gender identity based on a "natural" (i.e. pre-discursive) sex and radically destabilizes normative sexual behavior.

Judith Butler recognizes the powerful effects of our discursively constructed identities: the gender *identification* is real, even though it takes place within a constructed fantasy; as she puts it, "coherence is desired" ("Gender Trouble, Feminist Theory" 336). The performative act is not, as many critics misread it, a voluntary, liberating act of defiance. Instead, it constantly strives for a normative gender ideal that is inscribed in our bodies by discourse and that we alternatively negotiate, re-create, and challenge in our gender presentations. Gender presentations that do not adhere to this ideal (e.g., the masculine woman or the feminine man) disrupt the illusion that *any* gender identity and presentation is "natural." Gender performativity is ultimately melancholic since the ideal can never be attained. It is within this *failure* that Judith Butler situates agency—that is, in the displacement of desire for gender identity. The failure of gender performativity discloses gender identity as an imitation of a nonexistent original.[12]

Classical psychoanalysis generally assumes sexual desire to be derived from the bodies of both the subject and its object of desire, and it insists on causally linking sexuality with gender. "Normal" sexuality is heterosexual: a man desires a woman with whom to have intercourse, based on the physicality of their bodies. Yet Sigmund Freud early on destabilized this causality with his distinction between "sexual object" ("the person from whom sexual attraction proceeds") and "sexual aim" ("the act towards which the instinct tends")(*On Sexuality: Three Essays on the Theory of Sexuality* 45-46). Despite Freud's classification of certain variations of object choice and sexual practices as "aberrations" and "perversions," the separation of sexual object from sexual aim helps to move away from the established view of object choice as the defining element of sexuality (as either heterosexual or homosexual) toward a queer concept of sexuality as an array of pleasurable sexual acts. This queer concept of sexuality understands "perversions" (acts not aimed at heterosexual intercourse) to be liberating from regulated identities. A queer understanding of the unstable correlation between sex, gender, and sexuality frees us from categories of "normal" and "deviant" sexualities—heterosexual versus homosexual—since it is not the sex/gender of the object that defines the subject's identity but the aim of sexual pleasure. This understanding questions stable sexual categories, as Judith Butler does in "Imitation and Gender Insubordination" when she states that

> it is necessary to consider that sexuality always exceeds any given performance, . . . which is why it is not possible to derive or read off a sexuality from any given gender presentation. . . . There are no direct expressive or causal lines between sex, gender, gender presentation, sexual practice, fantasy and sexuality. None of those terms captures or determines the rest. Part of what constitutes sexuality is precisely that which does not appear and that which, to some degree, can never appear. (25)

This suspicion of stable sexualities based on categories of the sex/ gender of the subject and its object choice is echoed in "More Gender, More of the Time" by transgender activist Dean Spade. His insights explicate queer theory's attempt at disconnecting gender performance from a naturalized correlation with sexuality. Instead of defining human sexuality in terms of heterosexual (normal/oppressive) versus homosexual (deviant/oppressed), a definition on which both straight and gay/lesbian identities rely, Spade points out the complexities of desire and advocates a genderqueer understanding of sexuality:

> What I love is specific, detailed, stimulating, inventive uses of language to constantly re-inscribe and re-identify body and sex experiences, rather than simplistic terms that shut down conversations about how hot we all really are. If I'm chasing a scrawny, new-wave, eyeliner wearing faggotbutchswitch lesbian, and a jocky-but-sensitive preppy trannyfag, and a tough-but-gentle punk activist translady top, how can that be made to fit me into one of 4 categories?

Categories of sexual orientation and their relationships to gender identity are insufficient to describe desire and irrelevant to social identity—and, more importantly, impotent to regulate desire. The correlation between sex, gender, and sexuality—and thus that between sexual subject, sexual object, and sexual aim—is destabilized.

Queer theory thus challenges the notion of a stable gender and sexual identity based on the body of the self and its sexual object. Gender *identities*, like gender *roles*, are performative. Therefore, the distinction collapses, destabilizing the correlation between a body, the gender produced by that body, and the socially prescribed role produced by that gender. This collapse of distinction does not mean that the body is necessarily separate from identity—for example, a transsexual body is modified, and its somatic experiences are central in shaping the subject's gender identity.[13] However, the sex/gender/sexuality correlation and its regulatory norms are destabilized.

Many transgender identities are "in between" the binary or a refiguration of it; they can be understood as a queered form of androgyny, a "blend" of both masculine and feminine gender attributes that makes a clear assignment as either impossible. However, "genderqueer" as an identity conceptualizes gender, not as a blend of masculine and feminine into a "neutral" gender position, but as placing masculine and feminine into contradictory relationships with each other, or else it perceives gender as outside the binary. Therefore, genderqueer cannot be contained in the androgynous model of a combination of masculine and feminine characteristics, and it evades categorization as either heterosexual or homosexual.[14] Genderqueer as an identity poses a challenge to the gender binary without necessarily erasing sexual difference as a source of erotic pleasure.

Science fiction enables us to experiment with language and imagery to think about objects of desire and identities/subjects that desire them in new and innovative ways. Certain tropes and themes that recur in science fiction serve a symbolic function as possible androgynous identities *outside* of the gender binary, such as the shapeshifter. Not bound to any stable form, the shapeshifter moves between bodies and is without an essence that defines the self as either woman or man. This ability to move between bodies—and ultimately between identities—lends the shapeshifter a distinctly transgender quality. The transgendered person, too, resists an "either/or" identity and often moves in and out of gendered categories. The unstable relationship of body to (gender) identity is threatening to the status quo, which relies on a dual gender concept; it enables transgressive forms of rethinking gender relations and challenges the structure of power between them.

In her science fiction, Octavia Butler employs three different types of shapeshifters. In *Wild Seed*, Anyanwu is a human shapeshifter who is able to take on any living form, including those of animals, yet has an "original" human female body. Anyanwu's counterpart is Doro, a vampiric shapeshifter without any physical form of his own—he is a parasite who relies on the bodies of others. Finally, in *Imago*, Butler creates alien/human hybrids that are shapeshifters. Constituting a third sex/gender, these shapeshifters take on specific forms only in the context of intense personal relationships, and they are able to change their bodies according to the desires of those with whom they interact.

In Anyanwu and Doro, Butler explores possible androgynous identities *within* the gender binary: both characters have a gendered sense of self as either man or woman that is independent from the sex/gender of the body they inhabit. Each one's gender identity is stable but is not defined by any specific sexual desire, which varies. In the end, Butler's insistence on these "core" gender identities cancels out the shapeshifters' symbolic value as androgynous characters. In contrast, in *Imago* the shapeshifting hybrids complicate binary gender—here, Butler introduces a decidedly "queer" aspect of gender and sexuality. She explores the notion of the body as constructed by desire, which translates into a variety of constantly changing sexual desires and, ultimately, genders. She creates bodies that transform based on sexual desires and needs, thereby recognizing various *sexual objects* as essential for our sexual desires, but not specific bodies or any stable, prescribed sexual identity. Unlike in heteronormative discourse, the sex/gender of the object of desire does not define our sexuality since the *subject's* sexed/gendered form is unstable.

The Human Shapeshifter and the Parasite: Limited Gender Transgression

In Octavia Butler's narratives, the subject positions of her characters' complex genders and sexualities form the center of her stories. Butler generally avoids the construction of her female characters as "feminine"; she rejects both a disempowered sexual identity and a racially charged ideal that defines "true" womanhood based on qualities desired in white, middle-class women (e.g., chastity, frailty, helplessness, weakness, etc.).[15] Instead, Butler creates female figures who often are "genderless" in their appearance, such as Lauren in *Parable of the Sower* (195–96) and Amber in *Patternmaster* (132), or possess "atypical" bodily attributes, such as Alanna's extreme height in *Survivor* (5). In *Wild Seed*, Butler explores gender in the androgynous characters of the immortal, physically changing Anyanwu and the immortal, bodiless existence of Doro, who both embody a particular "genderlessness" in that they don't have a constant, gendered material body. Both characters define their own gender based on their sex at birth, yet they form identities that go beyond conventional biological (i.e. anatomical) definitions of "sex" as the basis for gender. This approach echoes experiences of transsexual people who find themselves trapped in the "wrong" body (e.g., a woman confined in a man's body and vice versa). The inconsistency of bodies, and therefore the unstable embodiment of sexual differences, is reminiscent of queer theory's denaturalized gender identities. At the same time, Butler's characters often retain gender identities that *are* stable, but the characters don't rely on a physical form to produce these identities. Their stable gender identification complicates queer theory's assertion that gender identity is unstable, just as the body is discursive and thus unstable. This assertion is challenged by transgender people's experience of a *stable* gender identity that does not correspond with the body's assigned gender (e.g., that of a male-identified, female-bodied person), which is echoed in the shapeshifters' unchanging gender identities.

The two major characters in *Wild Seed*, Anyanwu and Doro, seemingly embody versions of Judith Butler's gender performativity in that their physical makeup is often a parody of the gender they temporarily need to represent, not the "original." Simultaneously, they undermine the concept of gender performativity in that each claims a "core" identity that exists independently of a discursively constructed body. Doro is a four-thousand-year-old Nubian who transformed from human to become a parasitical mental-energetic form of being. Without a physical body, he inhabits the bodies of humans he kills. He is a parasite—a form of vampire—in that the "soul" (life-energy) of his victims is what sustains him, forcing him to continually take human life. His mission is to create a unique human breed of "talented" humans (capable of telepathy), whom he will rule and who will give him access to absolute power. He force-breeds humans he selects; most are his descendents. During his millennia-long breeding program, he searches for "potentials" and produces interbred offspring all over the world—who, because of their latent telepathic abilities, are mentally unstable and socially marginalized.

Anyanwu (who takes on the human name Emma in *Mind of My Mind*) is an Igbo immortal shapeshifter who is three hundred years old when Doro "finds" her while purchasing slaves in Africa to bring to seventeenth-century America. He considers her "wild seed," a previously undetected product of his breeding program. He coerces her into coming to the United States, where she becomes a central figure for Doro's people. As a healer and a protector of Doro's afflicted children, she forms an opposition to his heartless dealings with the humans he encounters. Their relationship is tense and conflicted. She feels drawn to him, despite his cruelty, because they are both immortal, and he remains the only constant presence in her existence. Beyond her value to him as a "breeder," she becomes his anchor; she is also the only person who has any influence over him and who can negotiate—and set limits on—his power over her. When Doro is terminated in *Mind of My Mind*, Anyanwu/Emma kills herself. The fundamentally heterosexual relationship between the two characters keeps their androgynous quality firmly rooted within the binary and forecloses a genderqueer conceptualization of their gender and sexuality.

In these two figures, Butler negotiates two extreme approaches to gender identity: constructivism (the idea that there does not exist an identity outside of discourse) and biological essentialism (the idea that identity is located prior to discourse). Both positions rely on the body as referent. A constructed gender identity is fundamentally unstable over time since the body is read and understood differently through history. Even though identity can develop in opposition to social assignment, it does so only through what Foucault termed "reverse discourse," which comes into existence through opposition to dominant discourse. The gendered body as discursively constructed remains a central reference for identity as it is socially and geographically monitored, based on its gendered status as well as on categories such as race, ability, nationality, age, and class. Biological essentialism, on the other hand, relies on the natural body and its functions as the primary basis for identity. Physical abilities and experiences based within them, such as reproductive functions, determine one's gender identity. Gender identity is a given, depending on one's natural body physique, and the only variance is gender *expression*, which is controlled by social powers.

In *Wild Seed*, both Anyanwu and Doro maintain a stable *gender* identity while constantly changing *bodies*, thus destabilizing both a constructivist claim that the discursive body determines one's identity and an essentialist insistence on the physical experience of a naturally gendered body as fundamental to gender identity. In either case, a changing body would produce a changing gender identity. Instead, Butler refers to each character consistently as either male or female in her use of pronouns, and in Anyanwu's case she describes an original female body to which the character ultimately reverts. Anyanwu identifies as a black woman, no matter what form she takes on. As a shapeshifter, she accumulates various experiences and forms of knowledge through taking on the physical form of animals and of men, yet her sense of self is always female, and the original form she takes on whenever circumstances allow her is that of a black woman. Her gender identity— as well as her racial identity—is based on an essential idea of an original body yet transcends any social understanding and control of that identity since it is retained no matter what body it inhabits. Her identity is linked to the material existence of the bodies she becomes; it is adaptive and contextual.

In contrast, Doro's original form is irrelevant to his sense of self. His identity appears to be independent from bodies—in terms of both gender and race. Doro's disembodied self echoes the Cartesian split of mind/body and is reminiscent of cyberpunk's valorization of the abstract mind as existing separate from the body. His inhuman nature places him outside the realm of discourse; his lack of a physical presence discloses the body as a site of difference he claims to be free of. In a conversation with Mary, one of his descendents, he discloses his African origin and declares it irrelevant to his being:

> "God! You're white so much of the time, I never thought you might have been born black."
>
> "It doesn't matter."
>
> "What do you mean, 'It doesn't matter'? It matters to me."
>
> "It doesn't matter because I haven't been any color at all for about four thousand years. Or you could say I've been every color. But either way, I don't have anything more in common with black people —Nubian or otherwise—than I do with whites or Asians."
>
> "You mean you don't want to admit you have anything in common with us. But if you were born black, you *are* black. Still black, no matter what color you take on."
>
> . . . "I'm not black or white or yellow, because I'm not human." (*Mind* 87)

Doro changes bodies on a regular basis by killing a person and moving into her or his skin, regardless of gender: "I've been a woman I-don't-know-how-many times" (*Mind* 157). Doro takes over bodies with all their biological consequences. Accordingly, he has given birth with a pregnant woman's appropriated body and has become pregnant by a man (*Wild Seed* 88). While he inhabits differently gendered bodies and experiences their various functions, his gender identity remains male and is not affected by the materiality of the bodies. He is clearly coded and referred to as a masculine person, and he remains male in interactions with humans who know him, even when appearing in female form. His identity is nonmaterial; it does not adapt or change and thus remains static.

As a shapeshifter, Anyanwu can also take on the body of a man. Since she, contrary to Doro, actually *has* her own body, she needs time to develop new biological features, such as reproductive functions, which never completely cease to refer to her "original" sex.

> She was becoming a small, well-muscled man as she spoke. . . .
> "Could you father a child?" he asked.
> "In time. Not now."
> "Have you?"
> "Yes. But only girl children." (*Seed* 16)

While Anyanwu is able to change her appearance and to inhabit various social positions, Butler sets limits on the flexibility of identity—in this case, the limits of the body's biological makeup (Anyanwu's chromosomal sex). Nevertheless, Anyanwu is, in contrast to Doro, an adaptive figure—she changes her own body and studies and observes that of the "other," to then become it. Doro never changes his core identity; he merely appropriates the body of the human he kills. Anyanwu's identity includes the experiences of other socially located bodies; she actually inhabits the various positions she chooses to become—echoing the experience of the transsexual, who lives positions s/he does not identify with. Anyanwu *is* what she becomes, while Doro never identifies with the person he kills. His physical transformation thus is located apart from his identity, while Anyanwu's seemingly essential identity *incorporates* the "other." In both characters, gender *identity* itself is not destabilized—just its relationship to the body. But Anyanwu's androgynous nature is more transgressive than Doro's since it acknowledges the material basis of identity and physical experience by having the self adapt to new forms of expression, while his denies any sense of identity rooted in physical experiences of the assumed body.

Throughout her work, Butler depicts most of her figures as transcending gendered appearances—that is, the expression of either "feminine" or "masculine" characteristics. For example, Lauren, the main female character in *Parable of the Sower* and *Parable of the Talents,* at times "passes" as male during her travels. Despite their gender transgressions, most of Butler's characters are heterosexual. Only Amber, the main female character in Butler's early novel *Patternmaster,* is a bisexual heroine—a rather "conventional" way of questioning existing gender structures. " 'When I meet a woman who attracts me, I prefer women,' she said. 'And when I meet a man who attracts me, I prefer men' " (*Patternmaster* 133). This bisexuality is later echoed in Lauren's temporary desire for a woman in *Parable of the Talents,* Butler's most recent novel. In contrast, the androgynous gender quality of Anyanwu and Doro is queered through the instability of their bodies, which makes the classification of a sexual act as either homosexual or heterosexual impossible.

The shapeshifter Anyanwu in *Wild Seed* has relationships with both men and women. Hers, though, represents a more radical form of bisexuality, one that is constructed within a context of *racialized* power and desire: in a time period when slavery existed in the United States, she, in the form of a white man, is married to a white woman and possesses a plantation in the South. Protected by her appearance and the social status it brings, she is safe to gather her "family," her people— other blacks and the misshapen products of Doro's breeding attempts— on her property. She has sexual relations in the body of a man, and even produces children with her wife, yet both women love each other as *women,* the gender with which both characters identify.

The extent to which Butler destabilizes power structures based on both race and gender is extraordinary. On one hand, gender is prescribed in discourses of power (Anyanwu takes on the body of a white man in order to be able to protect her people in the antebellum South). At the same time, desire binds two women across heterosexual and racist prescriptions (a white and black woman fall in love). Anyanwu explains to Doro:

"Why did she marry you?"

"Because I believed her . . . And because after a while, we started to want each other."

"Even though she knew you were a woman and black?"

> "Even so." Anyanwu stared up at [the portrait of] the solemn young woman, remembering that lovely, fearful courting. (*Seed* 218)

The desire of Anyanwu's lover transcends conventional forms of sexuality. Initially, Butler's insistence on a core gender identity might appear conservative in that it does not promote gender variance and/or genderqueerness. Yet its simultaneous independence from a body that represents it (Anyanwu identifies as a woman while inhabiting a male body) is significant when considering transgender people's identities, which are denied by the social assignment of their gender based on physical bodies.

The symbolic value of the shapeshifter as androgynous does not lie in a male-defined synthesis of "masculine" traits combined with a few "positive" feminine ones.[16] Instead, it represents the ability to attain identity—a coherent sense of self—not through socially defined gender assignments, but through a subjectivity that transcends biology and in turn adapts to desire. Thus Doro's nonmaterial interior identity is apart from external appearance; it is not contextual and is thus static. In contrast, Anyanwu's identity is linked to the material; it is mediated both by external appearance/material makeup and social standing. This identity can be understood as evading the extremes of identity as either socially constructed or essential. Anyanwu's fluid body enables her adaptive identity, which challenges the stable sex/gender/ sexuality correlation without erasing the materiality of the body. Ultimately, however, Butler's insistence on Anyanwu's female identity and Doro's male identity contradicts their symbolic function as gender-transgressive or "genderless." This insistence keeps their relationship within a heterosexual context, confirmed by the narrative's underlying emphasis on reproduction—Doro's breeding program. Butler's depiction of the alien race of the Oankali, however, further complicates sexualities, genders, and reproduction and enables a genderqueer understanding of not just desire but the social order.

Queer Essences: The Body's Transgressive Desires

In Octavia Butler's *Xenogenesis* trilogy, the alien ooloi—like the shapeshifter Anyanwu and the parasite Doro in *Wild Seed*—are symbolically androgynous. Unlike Anyanwu and Doro, however, the ooloi are a third sex/gender and thus reconfigure gender and sexual identities beyond the gender/sex binary. Butler explores the effect of desire on the body as a foundational element, particularly in *Imago,* the third book of the series. In the figure of the ooloi, Butler conceptualizes the notion of a sexuality based not on a fixed gender identity but on the pleasure of transgressive sensual exchange—even across species.

The Oankali are an alien species who travel through galaxies, interbreeding with foreign species. After a nuclear holocaust on Earth, the Oankali save the surviving humans from certain death and regenerate the planet. Their goal, the "gene trade"—interspecies breeding with humans—is met with fear and at times violent resistance. The Oankali, in their present form, are humanoid but with additional tentacle-like limbs and organs. They are able to communicate nonverbally by linking with their extra limbs and physically accessing each other's neurotransmitters, and they live in symbiotic relationship with their surroundings. They have three sexes/genders: male, female, and ooloi. As a species, they do not have a normative form; instead, each generation, after having completed a gene trade with another species, appears different from the previous one. Their constantly changing physique is not a source of anxiety to the Oankali. Their defining characteristic is not an exterior marker but the "organelle," the organ that facilitates the gene trade. The ooloi offspring of the alien/human xenogenesis are called construct ooloi. They have no stable individual shape; instead, they are shapeshifters who can remodel the physical makeup of their bodies.

Unlike Anyanwu's sense of self, which is rooted in the materiality of both her original body and those she becomes, the queer sensibility of the Oankali emphasizes the interdependence of subjectivity with surroundings. Moreover, the shape that desire gives their "play of differences" (White 403) places the space-traveling nomads within a framework of queer theory. Therefore, the ooloi play a particular role in Butler's construction of sexuality, introducing a third gender to her otherworldly constellations and thus undermining our understanding of gender by troubling the dichotomy of sexual difference.

An ooloi is not an androgynous synthesis of woman and man (or, more specifically, of female and male Oankali); instead, it constitutes its own sex (and gender), with "sensory arms" (*Dawn* 81) that contain sensitive sexual organs. It forms the core of the Oankali/human reproductive unit once the gene trade begins. With its sensory arms, the ooloi links all five members of the reproductive unit: two humans (female and male), two Oankali (female and male), and the ooloi itself. These sensory arms enable the ooloi to inseminate the mothers by fusing the respective parents' reproductive cells, thereby performing the gene trade. With the cells, the ooloi "construct" the offspring from the parents' genetic material, heal other Oankali or humans, and—with biochemical reactions—produce sensual joy for the others. The central theme in the *Xenogenesis* series is reproduction; the trilogy's main narrative conflict is human resistance to the aliens' breeding plans, and Butler critically depicts women's agency in relation to this conflict. Because of the aliens' third sex/gender and the number of members necessary to form a reproductive unit, the Oankali "queer" the process of reproduction and challenge the gendered relations of power within a heterosexual context.

Sexual pleasure within a family unit of Oankali and humans is derived, not through penetration or sensual touch, but exclusively through a neurochemical reaction facilitated by the ooloi, whose sensory arms form the "link" between the otherwise physically separated partners. The lack of any physical genitals as indicators of this sexual practice renders Oankali-human sex impossible to classify in terms of sexual identities. It is even impossible to separate the "act" from "fantasy" since the partners never actually touch, yet they share intense sexual experiences though the parallel stimulation of their brains. Unlike sex in virtual reality, sexual contact here is not facilitated through external technology; the exchange *is* physical but mediated through a designated participant, and it can result in reproduction. Once humans become accustomed to sexual pleasure mediated through the ooloi, it is impossible for them to engage in human sex—their bodies become repulsive to each other. Desire, then, is not a psychologically based phenomenon originating in a gendered body and aimed at a gendered sexual object, but one rooted in the body's amorphous craving for physical pleasure. The genitals of both subject and object are secondary, rendering any relation between object choice and sexual aim obsolete.

"Ooloi" means several things in Oankali language: "'Treasured stranger.' 'Bridge.' 'Life Trader.' 'Weaver.' 'Magnet'" (*Imago* 6). The ooloi inhabit a special position that is decidedly queer—a phenomenon that is hard to comprehend in our dichotomous way of conceptualizing gender and sexuality. As Eric White states in "The Erotics of Becoming," "They thus trouble what is arguably the source of all dualistic thought: the (apparent) sexual dimorphism that serves as the basis for every hierarchized binarism" (404). Butler uses the neutral form of address for the ooloi, thereby rejecting the universalizing use of the "generic" male pronoun and forcing the reader to acknowledge a denaturalization of the gender binary.[17]

In general, the Oankali define themselves mainly through their bodily connections with others and their surroundings, and any social hierarchy is alien to them. Arts and literature are unknown to them, symbolizing an aesthetic derived from the beauty of the concrete sensual body, not abstract thought. Accordingly, Oankali gender identity develops through physical affirmation with a same-gendered/sexed parent, not psychologically through rivalries and the rejection of the other. Thus the gender of a child is not decided until "metamorphosis" (*Dawn* 80) at the end of puberty (which begins between the twentieth and thirtieth year since the Oankali life span ranges to up to three hundred years), marking the transition to adulthood. Until then the young Oankali enjoys a "long, easy childhood" (*Rites* 206) without learned gender roles or distinctions. Bodily changes begin for the child once it begins to "develop . . . an affinity for one of the [two human or three alien] sexes. Beginning to know what it would become" (*Rites* 178). So gender identification is a process of individual (if unconscious) choice and sexual pleasure—not one of forced assignment, as in the dualistic thinking of Western cultures. This process undermines any possible (biological) essentializing of gender identity, echoing Judith Butler's gender performativity.

Unlike much psychoanalytic theory, Judith Butler's gender performativity conceptualizes identification ("wanting to be," for example, like the mother) and desire ("wanting to have," for example, the mother) as not mutually exclusive. "It is important to consider that identification and desire can coexist, and that their formulation in terms of mutually exclusive oppositions serves a heterosexual matrix" ("Imitation and Gender Insubordination" 26). When placed in a context of queer desire, "identificatory mimetism *precedes* 'identity' and constitutes identity as that which is fundamentally 'other to itself' . . . the self is from the start radically implicated in the 'Other'" ("Imitation and Gender Insubordination" 26, emphasis hers). There is no self without desire for, and affirmation with, the other. This concept is mirrored in the Oankali's subjectivity: desire is the aliens' main drive for self-recognition—to exchange genes, to know the other, to become the other. Thus the Oankali's queerness lacks the melancholy of human gender performativity, the yearning to "be" the ideal gender. Their desire (and gender identification) is not shaped after an illusion of unity or an imagined original, or based on a loss, but is formed by the goal of fusion with the other. Neither the object of desire nor their own sex is constant. They illustrate the observation that "the psychic subject is . . . constituted internally by differentially gendered Others and is, therefore, never, as a gender, self-identical" (J. Butler, "Imitation and Gender Insubordination" 27).

In the first book of the *Xenogenesis* trilogy, *Dawn*, the story is told by a human woman who encounters the Oankali and their breeding plans. The second book is narrated from the perspective of a construct (human/alien) male child; there are no ooloi born from both human and Oankali genes in *Adulthood Rites*. In the third book, *Imago*, the narrative voice is that of the first construct ooloi, Jodahs. Unlike all other Oankali and hybrids, construct ooloi are shapeshifters. They are able to reconfigure not only future generations (through gene trades), as other Oankali ooloi can, but their own bodies as well. Consequently, there is a distinct performative quality to construct ooloi's gender identity in *Imago:* they have the ability to adapt their individual bodies to desire, and their desire precedes any physical form. Their bodies have no stable, original form. Their skill as genetic engineers is inextricably tied to their bodies, which are equipped to manipulate genes without the interference of external technology. Their biology *is* their technology.

In the figure of the shapeshifting aliens, Octavia Butler creates a "queer essence," the inevitable drive to adapt one's appearance to the needs of the desired object, which is compulsive and at times threatening to the self. The sexual object, therefore, is crucial but irrelevant in its function of defining the subject's sexuality (as either homosexual or heterosexual) since the material sex/gender of the subject is unstable. The sexual object is chosen based on the need to reproduce—to do the gene trade—and the subject adapts to the needs of the desired one to fulfill its sexual aim. Thus Butler complicates the notion of what constitutes desire (what Freud calls the "sexual instinct"). Where does desire originate when the body in which it resides is completely constructed by the desire the body produces? The centering element of the ooloi's sexuality is the aim to reproduce—a fundamentally queer aim since the Oankali/human reproductive unit consists not of a heterosexual couple but of five members of two species with three sexes/genders. The primary goal of reproducing outside a heterosexual context is the foundation of the "queer essence" of the construct ooloi. This "queer essence" not only challenges notions of sex/gender/sexuality and th : dichotomy of sexual difference but questions the very social order the heterosexual matrix relies on—the nuclear family—and demands queered concepts of family.

Once a potential partner is identified, construct ooloi can change their physicality to correspond to what the partner needs. Their shifting appearance echoes the attempt to reproduce the gendered norm and exposes it as discursively constructed, like drag's efforts to represent the ideal "feminine" or "masculine." Gender does not reflect an inner "truth" but is aimed at pleasing the object of desire and therefore can never be stable or static.

> [S]o gender parody reveals that the original identity after which gender fashions itself is itself an imitation without an origin. . . . [I]t is a production which, in effect, that is, in its effects, postures as an imitation. This perpetual displacement constitutes a fluidity of identities that suggests an openness to resignification and recontextualization, and it deprives hegemonic culture and its critics of the claim to essentialist accounts of gender identity. (J. Butler, "Gender Trouble" 338)

At times, a shapeshifter cannot control its instinctive response to an object's needs, and the power of the desire for the other becomes undeniable. The construct ooloi Jodahs, without noticing, takes on the shape of a young woman when taking care of a frightened, resentful human male: "I wasn't surprised this time. My body wanted him. My body sought to please him. What would happen to me when I had two or more mates? Would I be like the sky, constantly changing, clouded, clear, clouded, clear? Would I have to be hateful to one partner to please the other?" (*Imago* 76). The construct ooloi's embodiment does not take form apart from its desire, and its lack of a coherent self outside of relations with others is threatening to our notion of identity.

The construct ooloi has no longing for an ideal or original gender that it performs. Instead, it is the desire for its mates that compels its body to transform—perform—depending on its mates' needs. Outside of its relation to others, there is no self. When asked by young constructs "When can you be yourself?" Jodahs reflects: "I thought about that. I understood it because I remembered being their age [before metamorphosis] and having a strong awareness of the way my face and body looked, and of that look being *me*. It never had been, really" (*Imago* 90). While its gender remains stable based on its sex (ooloi), this category of gender is empty and devoid of meaning when it comes to external presentation. At the same time as the disconnection from (re)presentation frees gender from social and physical power, its collapse with sex links it to biological (reproductive) functions: a construct ooloi's sensory arms, and thus its role within the reproductive unit, never change and are its essence. The body is paramount, yet it is disconnected from any determined presentations; gender disappears, and only sex and highly volatile sexualities remain.

Contact with others, both pleasurable and social, is a prerequisite for any sense of self within the infinite transformations of the Oankali as a species. In the case of the construct ooloi, once the object of desire is removed, the individual ooloi's shape is without direction and purpose, and the ooloi has no control over its physical dissolution. Its referential self extends to the body: when construct ooloi are without a family structure, they regress to a primordial, indistinct form. The other's role in forming a (temporary) identity is paramount, especially for construct ooloi; the exercise of impurity becomes a necessity, as Jodahs explains: "It's easier to do as water does: allow myself to be contained, and take on the shape of my containers" (*Imago* 89). Constant change and adaptation to the object of desire becomes the self-defining act: "Structural complexity, and the consequent possibility of further differentiation and metamorphosis, depends on their being situated in a social matrix less chaotically mutable than themselves" (White 406). Jodahs worries about its sibling, Aaor, also a construct ooloi, who wanders off into the wilderness only to revert to "a kind of mollusk, something that had no bones left. Its sensory tentacles were intact, but it no longer had eyes or other human sensory organs. Its skin, very smooth, was protected by a coating of slime. It could not speak or breathe air or make any sound at all" (*Imago* 151).

Only through close contact with others, physical and social, can Aaor achieve a form that enables it to be recognized by and communicate with others, and ultimately no one but its mates—human and Oankali —can retain it within that form. This absolutely relational self, which literally comes undone when the object is lost, speaks to the power of desire:

We're undone by each other. And if we're not, we're missing something. If this seems so clearly the case with grief, it is only because it was already the case with desire. One does not always stay intact. It may be that one wants to, or does, but it may also be that despite one's best efforts, one is undone, in the face of the other, by the touch, by the scent, by the feel, by the prospect of the touch, by the memory of the feel. (J. Butler, *Undoing Gender* 19)

Desire transcends pleasure and becomes the basis, not only for social interactions, but for life itself. "We called our need for contact with others and our need for mates *hunger.* The word had not been chosen frivolously. One who could hunger, could starve" (*Imago* 158).[18]

The Oankali's queer nature is strangely biological: the body's need to reproduce—the genetically anchored drive to mate with others, to *become* other—is the foundation for the aliens' shifting genders and sexualities. Octavia Butler's concepts here are positioned neither in a biological essentialism that insists on gender identity (woman) as derivative of a body's sex (female), nor in a social and/or psychological constructivism that understands the body's materiality as dominated by (social) discourse. Instead, desire and sexuality are based in the body's need for others. Identity is based in difference and pleasurable experience of the other without trying to retain a certain form; the self is relational and contextual. The body follows desire, not vice versa, disrupting the naturalized correlation between sex, gender, and sexuality; identity *is* that indeterminate state that is resolved only through the object of desire.

The alien shapeshifters' contextual sexualities share with the human Anyanwu's adaptive identity a recognition of fluidity, but—unlike Anyanwu—construct ooloi enable us to think about sexuality outside the dimorphous gender model. Their third sex not only queers sexual desire but also enables us to conceptualize reproduction—and family—outside a heterosexual context and within genderqueer constellations. Thus Butler's ambiguous representations of the sex/gender/sexuality relationship destabilize power that relies on a naturalized heteronormativity. They represent a feminist criticism of heterosexism as a system of oppression, without abandoning the categories of gender or race as components of the analysis.

Intersexed Bodies and Gender Politics
in Melissa Scott's *Shadow Man*

> For a long time hermaphrodites were criminals, or crime's offspring, since their anatomical disposition, their very being confounded the law that distinguished the sexes and prescribed their union. (Foucault, *History of Sexuality* 38)

Like Octavia Butler's representations of transgender identities in the human female shapeshifter and the third alien sex/gender of the Oankali, Melissa Scott's *Shadow Man* engages contemporary feminist debates around the binary gender/sex system. Scott employs intersexuality—historically referred to as hermaphroditism—to question the naturalization of the prevailing dimorphous concept of gender. The world in *Shadow Man* is populated by societies with five sexes, not two, with various new genders and sexualities that demand a revision of our naturalized assumptions about sex/gender/sexuality.

In *The Battle of the Sexes in Science Fiction*, Justine Larbalestier discusses hermaphroditism as a form of biological androgyny—the combination of male and female sexual characteristics. In science fiction, she observes, hermaphroditism is usually depicted as the collapse of the two sexes into one "neutral" sex, which results in a genderless society. Often this concept is simply an incorporation or masculinization of women into the male norm. Thus hermaphroditism—intersexuality—functions as a symbol for sexual sameness, not variety.[19] By envisioning *five* sexes, not one, Scott potentially avoids this conceptual trap. Instead of one "neutral" sex, she creates a variety of sexes—the result is not the creation of a new ideal norm but the acknowledgment of biological and sexual variability.

In my reading of *Shadow Man*, I make two main arguments. The first is that Scott is challenging the naturalization of binary categories of both gender and sexuality. She complicates the normative correlation between sex, gender, and sexuality within our binary sex system of heteronormativity by juxtaposing an alternative system that challenges a dichotomous sexual difference. Through the interactions of her characters and the political alliances they forge, Scott advocates for all people's right to live in the gender(s) they choose. Ultimately, Scott views any form of systematic categorization of bodies and sexualities as regulatory, even if it accounts for a greater biological and social variety. The second argument I make is that Scott is advocating for organized resistance—that is, social movements—as the only true catalyst of social change, and for the importance of forming alliances between progressive causes. Instead of relegating one individual figure to the symbolic task of challenging and overcoming a discriminatory system, Scott places her protagonist in the context of collective resistance and challenges the necessity for agency outside a social context. She also criticizes the ineffectiveness of progressive groups when they insist on exclusionary political agendas. She thus supports Judith Butler's contention that "changing the institutions by which humanly viable choice is established and maintained is a prerequisite for the exercise of self-determination. In this sense, individual agency is bound up with social critique and social transformation" (J. Butler, *Undoing Gender* 7).

Sexed Bodies and the Links between Biology, Ideology, and Desire in Shadow Man

In order to appreciate Melissa Scott's approach to radically reconceptualizing gender identities, it is necessary to place her book into the context of a growing body of feminist work that questions the common understanding of "gender" as socially constructed but "sex" as biologically essential. Recent works by feminists within the field of science studies have questioned the "naturalness" not only of gender but also of sex (i.e. the body/biology). Work in this field includes Suzanne Kessler's *Lessons from the Intersexed* (1998), Alice Domurat Dreger's *Hermaphrodites and the Medical Invention of Sex* (1998), and Anne Fausto-Sterling's *Sexing the Body* (2001), as well as her earlier, controversial article "The Five Sexes: Why Male and Female Are Not Enough" (1992). Connecting scientific findings with Foucault's theory of discursive power, these feminists question the "natural" existence of two sexes/genders/sexual identities and instead understand it as an exclusive model applied to natural sexual variability.

These critiques draw on Foucault's work on the historical construction of sex (bodies) and sexualities. Foucault criticizes modern Western societies' insistence on identifying every person's *"true"* sex (Foucault, "Introduction" to *Herculine Barbin* vii, emphasis his) as a means of knowing the core of that person's being.[20] The establishment of the medical profession as the major authority for determining a person's "true" sex eliminated any pleasurable experience of the ambiguously sexed body—the body was understood as "hiding" the one sex a person was to have, so that only medical practitioners could "discover" it.

> Biological theories of sexuality, juridical conceptions of the individual, forms of administrative control in modern nations, led little by little to rejecting the idea of a mixture of the two sexes in a single body, and consequently to limiting the free choice of indeterminate individuals. Henceforth, everybody was to have one and only one sex. Everybody was to have his or her primary, profound, determined and determining sexual identity; as for the elements of the other sex that might appear, they could only be accidental, superficial, or even quite simply illusionary. (Foucault, "Introduction" viii)[21]

The study of intersexuality and how it is perceived by medical and legal discourse provides a basis for queer theory's claim that the body and sexualities are discursive. Instead of designating the intersexed body as an example of regulated bodies, we need to understand it as representative of the regulation of *all* bodies and the construction of *all* sexualities/genders. Intersexuality teaches us to be critical of our understanding of any "genitals as evidence of gender" (Kessler 7).

The major claim of feminists critical of a naturalized binary sex/ gender system is that biology is real but not factual (i.e. that we categorize, elevate, and ignore material realities so that they fit our social model, not vice versa). This claim becomes apparent when examining debates in biology and behavioral sciences about hormones, chromosomes, and primary and secondary sexual characteristics, as well as when considering the medical treatment of intersexed infants— "babies born with genitals that are neither clearly male nor clearly female" (Kessler 12)—and intersexed adults through history. In the case of intersexuality, children are born with a sexual anatomy that cannot be clearly classified as either male or female but instead consists of a variety of sexual characteristics—genetic and hormonal traits and external and internal genitals—that contradict a clear, dimorphic understanding of the sexes.[22] The insistence on a dimorphous sex system as the only natural form of human bodies results in the marginalization and demonization of nonnormative bodies, which are declared "unnatural" and are conceived of very differently through history and within disparate cultural contexts.[23] The main argument is that the existence of intersexuality complicates concepts of sex/biology and points to the fact that the two-sex system is socially constructed, not biologically determined.

At the heart of Melissa Scott's differently conceived notions of gender and alternative ways of categorizing sexes in *Shadow Man* lies the recognized existence of intersexuality, not as an aberration of the two "natural" sexes, but as evidence for the complexity of natural human sexuality beyond a socially constructed, two-sex system. Nonnormatively sexed bodies are considered a "variability," not an aberration of the norm or "ambiguous" (Kessler 8). Scott's narrative traces the controversies around intersexuality by imagining two cultures that deal with the reality of intersexuality in profoundly different ways. In doing so, Scott not only criticizes the limits of our two-sex system but also discloses the regulatory nature of *any* gender regime. The often ironically complicated re-constellations in *Shadow Man* remind us of the shared imperative of trans and queer theories not to deny identities but to resist any form of unwanted legislation of identity: "What is most important is to cease legislating for all lives what is livable only for some, and similarly, to refrain from proscribing for all lives what is unlivable for some" (J. Butler, *Undoing Gender* 8).

Melissa Scott's *Shadow Man* creates a five-sex system similar to that offered by Anne Fausto-Sterling's 1993 essay "The Five Sexes: Why Male and Female Are Not Enough." Fausto-Sterling discloses the randomness of the declaration of human sexuality as dimorphous by pointing to the existence of a variety of differently sexed bodies. Why ignore the existence of intersexed bodies of various kinds and insist on either male or female as the "natural" sexes? Scott uses a model of five, not two, sexes to play out the progressive as well as problematic implications of a variable sex system for gender relations and for the relationship of the body to gender attribution.

Shadow Man is set on Hara, a planet colonized by humans that was immediately abandoned by its colonizing forces, the Concord World Federation, during the ensuing chaos triggered by a genetic mutation that began transforming humankind, both on the planet and off it. The recurrent mutation resulted in an increased number of intersexed births (children with variable genitals), which in turn produced a growing prevalence of three sexes in addition to the existing male and female (called "fem," "herm," and "mem"). Haran culture subsequently developed for four hundred years isolated from the rest of humankind (a typical science fiction device when depicting conflict between human cultures). The mutation, which was caused by hyperlumi-A, a drug to prevent the side effects of space travel, affected the humans on Concord as well as those who had settled Hara. Unlike Concordians, however, Harans never officially acknowledged the existence of any sex other than male and female. After centuries, Hara is "rediscovered" by Concord society, which has embraced the five-sex/gender system and has adapted to its variety by acknowledging all five sexes legally, instituting nine official sexual preferences, and eventually discharging gender from any social power. At the time the narrative begins, Harans have accepted the off-worlders' presence based on business with Concordian pharmaceutical companies, who profit from Hara's botanical variety and provide Harans with access to desired off-world metal and technology. Despite the commercial relations with Concordians, Harans do not officially recognize what they term the "odd-bodied," even though these people make up 25 percent of the population.

The story is organized around the tensions between the two societies resulting from their different sex/gender systems (Fig. 6.2) and is told from two alternating perspectives: by Mhyre Tatian, an off-world man to whom the two-sex system of Hara seems alien and fundamentally wrong, and by Warreven Stiller (Raven), an indigene herm to whom the off-world five-sex system seems intriguing, and whose political struggles for the rights of the odd-bodied on Hara form the center of the plot. Raven's resistance against the persecution of Haran fems/herms/mems who refuse to be forced into the two-sexed system highlights the threat that nonnormatively gendered people pose to a system whose power dynamics rely on oppressive gender categories.

The five-sex system Scott envisions in Concordian culture consists of "woman," "fem," "herm," "mem," and "man," and includes nine official sexual preferences that undermine the heterosexual/homosexual polarity. The "additional" three sexes possess variable combinations of female and male sex characteristics—as do "men" and "women." A fem's chromosomes are XY, and the body possesses testes and some aspects of female genitalia (such as breasts and some form of vagina) but no ovaries. A mem's chromosomes are XX, and the body possesses ovaries and some aspects of male genitalia (such as some form of penis). A herm can have any combination of chromosomes and possesses both testes and ovaries as well as other aspects of male and female genitalia.[24] Although gender is not tied to roles or particular

Haran culture	Concordian culture	
two officially recognized sexes/genders:	**five officially recognized sexes/genders:**	
woman / man	woman	fem
	herm	
(People whose bodies do not fit the assigned sex characteristics choose and declare an official gender and live their lives according to it.)	mem	man
one officially recognized sexual preference	**nine officially recognized sexual preferences**	
opposite gender (to the official sex)	bi / demi / di / gay / hemi / omi / straight / tri / uni	

Figure 6.2. The sexual orders that regulate desire in Haran and Concordian cultures in *Shadow Man* destabilize any naturalized sex/gender system.

visual expressions, gender identity is not truly flexible: one's body *is* one's gender. In this way, Concordian culture resembles Western society's insistence on "genitals as evidence of gender." At the same time, the body's diverse realities are recognized and named (including pronouns for each of the sexes) and are thus made visible. Unlike contemporary medical management of intersexed infants, no person in Concordia is subjected to surgical interventions or hormonal treatment based on their sexual anatomy.

Because of rampant HIV mutations, the nine official sexual preferences are rigidly regulated, and it is not assumed that adults can or should change their "declared" preferences. Sexuality is thus not fluid but varied. The abolishment of roles tied to traditional genders and the detailed definition of what each sexual preference entails marginalize people with "perverse" sexual tendencies within Concord World (i.e. those who are associated with gender roles from the two-sex system but have bodies that do not correspond to those roles). These marginalized sexualities are pushed into an illegal system of prostitution referred to as "trade," in which odd-bodied Harans play out their legal gender of either male or female in girl/boy roles during sex. On Hara, trade has developed into a complex economic market that includes the selling of documents that permit entrance into the city. Trade involves privileges and economic advantages for both Concordian and Haran officials who control the access and conditions under which trade takes place (like prostitution in Western cultures). Thus "abnormal" sexualities that find themselves outside of either system are tolerated but not integrated into dominant culture.

However, within the context of the novel, reading about Hara's two-sex system is like reading an anthropological report on the existing gender regime of the United States. Another typical device in science fiction is the alienation produced by the futuristic, alien setting, which allows an "outsider's" perspective on one's own culture. Scott's depiction of the consequences that the Haran repressive system has on the odd-bodied almost exactly describes the criticisms of transgender rights activists and scholars concerned with the destructive effects our social norms have on nonnormatively gendered people.

Hara's social fabric—as well as its political and economic system—is structured around heterosexual relations, such as those coded into marriage and inheritance laws. Because the odd-bodied threaten the heterosexual economy and its gendered power—the ultimate threat of the intersexed body—their existence must be denied. As in Western cultures, within Haran culture everyone knows that more than two sexes exist, but since law and custom admit only two, male and female, others are rendered invisible. As Raven puts it, "I remain a man. . . . Legally, at any rate, which is what matters" (*Shadow Man* 14). Gender laws on Hara deny the biological reality of intersexed bodies; every body has to fit into a binary system. In remote parts of the planet, the intersexed are surgically altered to fit the "natural" sex system. Gender, declared to be based on a natural body, in actuality has to be constructed by altering the body to adhere to the dual-sex system.

> Thus, the medical management of intersexuality, instead of illustrating nature's failure to ordain gender in these isolated, "unfortunate" instances, illustrates physicians' and Western society's failure of imagination—the failure to imagine that each of their management decisions is a moment when a specific instance of biological "sex" is transformed into a culturally constructed gender. (Kessler 32)

The result of this practice is invisibility—or rather, "unrealness." Failing to imagine bodies outside the binary denies recognition to their existence and thus renders them outside culture.

To be oppressed you must first become intelligible. To find that you are fundamentally unintelligible (indeed, that the laws of culture and of language find you to be an impossibility) is to find that you have not yet achieved access to the human, to find yourself speaking only and always *as if you were* human, but with the sense that you are not. (J. Butler, *Undoing Gender* 30, emphasis hers)

Once an official gender is taken on by the odd-bodied, one's gender is signified, not by the body, but by the clothing and social activities designated for one's legal gender. There is enormous pressure to appear as either one of the legal genders, so "the odd-bodied had to pass" (*Shadow Man* 208).[25] Even though on Hara gender seems more fluid since people can choose their gender (one's legal gender trumps one's "true" gender identity), the odd body—one that is neither female nor male—stands outside of the social norm and is condemned to invisibility. Because official sexual preferences are so limited (heterosexuality is the only legal choice) and do not account for the complex physique of the odd-bodied, a broad subcultural scene develops that caters to queer sexualities—they are not regulated, because they are outside the system, and Harans are immune to any HIV mutations. The queer sexualities' invisibility ensures the existence of the official gender system.

The effects of this gender regime on the Haran odd-bodied are oppressive in multiple ways. The odd-bodied are economically oppressed (often illegal trade is the only way to exist) and lack adequate health care (there is no knowledge of medical treatment of sexes other than male or female). They are also forced to wear traditional clothing that designates assigned gender, and if they do not pass adequately, they face harassment. There is no legal recognition of their difference and hence no protection. In rural provinces, the odd-bodied are often surgically altered. There is also no language to represent them; therefore, their legal and cultural invisibility makes them vulnerable in a system of power that relies on their nonexistence.

One of the startling differences between Haran and Concordian culture is the link between gender roles and power. Haran society is patriarchal and relies on traditional gender divisions in its distribution of power (in terms of lineage, roles of husband and wife, and male authority and political power). Therefore, undermining the gender system represents a direct threat to existing power structures. When

Raven, a herm, is asked to change "his" legal gender from man to woman in order to enter a favorable marriage, ʒe[26] declines. This is based partly on ʒer reluctance to become someone's wife, which would mean a loss of control and of social status: "[I]f he had not been the one to become the wife, Warreven admitted, it would have been a tempting offer" (12). Those who refuse to choose a legal gender (either man or woman), such as the herm Haliday, are degraded to the less powerful and "less rational" gender "woman." In contrast, Concordian society does not have old gendered hierarchies, and power works mainly through economics. Assigned gender roles/identities do not structure relationship affiliations, such as those of husband and wife, or the division of labor. Race as an organizing factor in *Shadow Man* is not thematized beyond the generally darker skin of the indigenes of Hara, but nationality/planetary affiliation is crucial. Access to both technology and mobility (the ability to leave Hara) are extremely regulated, which results in a black market for papers and the semi-illegal profession of trade.

The differences between the two cultures are processed in the relationship of the two main figures. The reader's gendered reading habits are disrupted every time the Concordian Tatian narrates the story, and we encounter not two but five sets of pronouns. Tatian's continuous use of herm pronouns for Raven gains symbolic significance at the end when Raven, rejecting ʒer chosen male gender, uses them for ʒimself and embraces them as a token of political struggle: "we need names of our own" (203).[27] The interactions between Tatian and Raven, infused with desire, form the glue of the narrative and also lay out the limits of both systems. Tatian is conflicted about how much to get involved in local politics and how to handle his sexuality (he is attracted to Raven even though he is "straight"), while the queer Raven unabashedly desires Tatian during their growing friendship. After Raven gets beaten up by a group of ghost *rana*[28] hunting any odd-bodied in the streets, Tatian assists Raven with ʒer bath and is confronted with his growing attraction for the herm:

> Not that ʒe was particular feminine, anymore than ʒe was masculine—ʒer body beneath the water drew his eyes, long legs, long, clearly defined muscles, cock and the swell of the cleft scrotum behind it. ʒe had forgotten to hunch ʒer shoulder, and ʒer breasts, herm's breasts, small and definite against the bony ribs, were fully exposed. . . . The [drug] broom sang in his blood, [Raven] lay passive

in his hands, and he made himself look away, feeling depressingly adolescent, concentrated on rinsing the last of the soap from 3er hair until his erection subsided. (253)

Struggling with his culture's understanding of sexual orientation/desire as stable and unchanging, Tatian attempts to contain his desire for Raven within the parameters of his identity as "straight" by evoking his off-planet female ex-lover: "A perfect herm's body, Tatian thought, and felt himself flushing, embarrassment as much as desire, well aware that he was responding as much to the memories of Kaysa as to Warreven's presence" (253). Throughout the novel, Tatian's reluctant desire for Warreven undermines Concordian regulation of the sexualities that grow from the complex bodies it legally acknowledges.[29]

Probably the most disturbing aspect of the narrative is the familiarity of the arguments of those opposed to any change (to acceptance of the five sexes). In order to reinstate the "natural" state of humanity, they argue, one should "stop coddling these people and force them to make up their minds what they really were" (174). Raven is told by Tendlathe, 3er former almost-fiancée and the second most powerful man on Hara, who later murders his own father to gain full control over Hara's governance: "We, what we are, is too important, we're all that's left of what people, humans beings, are supposed to be. . . . And I refuse to believe that they are human" (227). Being denied human status, the odd-bodied are declared "unnatural." Passing as one of the recognized sexes becomes synonymous with passing as human, since being odd-bodied is outside the category of human and within an "order of unlivable life" (J. Butler, *Undoing Gender* 2). The five-sex system, even though it is limited, has evolved into a social order in which sex and gender do not function as categories of power. Ultimately, however, Scott criticizes our reliance on the biology of the body to define our desire.

Organized Resistance: The Gender Law
Reform Movement in Shadow Man

If I can't dance I don't want to be part of your revolution. (attributed to Emma Goldman)[30]

In some ways, *Shadow Man* reads as a political manifesto for the rights of nonnormatively gendered people. Just as the novel's model of the five sexes echoes feminist science studies, Raven's political work (first as a lawyer, then as a political officeholder, and finally as a political exile) parallels the struggle of the international gender rights movement. The transgender rights movement consists of those organizing from their intersexed, transsexual, transgendered, or genderqueer positions against the oppressive forces of our gender regime. Members of this movement demand the right to chose one's gender as either man or woman independently from the biological categories in which one's body is classified, the right to safely modify one's body to correspond with one's gender identity, the right to *not* have one's intersexed body mutilated in order to conform to the two-sex system, and the right to express an ambiguous gender identity. The political work of local and national activists such as Cheryl Chase, founder of the Intersex Society of North America, and Dean Spade, founder of the Sylvia Rivera Law Project, has been accompanied by publications such as Martine Rothblatt's *The Apartheid of Sex* (1995); Kate Bornstein's *Gender Outlaw* (1994); Riki Wilchins's *Read My Lips* (1997); Joan Nestle, Clare Howell, and Riki Wilchins's edited volume *GenderQueer* (2002); and works by Leslie Feinberg, such as *Stone Butch Blues* (1993) and *TransLiberation: Beyond Pink or Blue* (1998). While the gender rights movement is slowly gaining (often distorted) visibility in dominant culture, mainstream feminist and gay and lesbian organizations, as well as feminist academic theorists, often exclude transgender issues from their agenda. Raven's experiences in *Shadow Man* echo the invisibility of the intersexed and transgender rights movement on most dissidents' political radar.[31]

Scott's work in general is noted for its exploration of social movements.[32] Examples include her portraits of queer hackers roaming the net and evading government control in *Trouble and Her Friends* (1994) and of workers' rights movements clashing with machine-AI-rights activists in *Dreaming Metal* (1997). Resistance takes place either against governments or against gigantic economic cartels that regulate social and political interactions. Rarely do Scott's main characters act outside a context of political dissent. In *Shadow Man*, she places her protagonist's resistance to an oppressive gender system in relation to a wider social movement around labor rights and the modernization of old social hierarchies. The conservatives who resist change in gender law and the influence of off-worlders identify as "Traditionalists," while "Modernists" advocate for reforming government structures and off-world alliances. In the narrative, Raven is not an individual hero whose struggle is defined in terms of "his" individual happiness. Instead, ʒe becomes a symbol for a political movement. In representing Raven's struggle as a political rather than a personal issue, Scott resists the exploitation of the lone trans figure as transgressive and instead discloses the complete sex/gender system as repressive.

Like many conservative groups, the Traditionalists on Hara are dominated by their fear of the other and of changing the standard of "normal." In their denial of experiences outside their own, they oppress those affected by their imposed "truth." Thus the Haran traditionalists say that the Concordian explanation for the existence of the five sexes "might tell facts, but they [aren't] true" (28). This denial echoes Foucault's observation that our culture's obsession with one of two "true" sexes does not allow for the reality of variability. Scott's depiction of the Traditionalist position confirms the argument that biological findings are turned into "truths" with which our social order is comfortable.

The Traditionalists' refusal to adapt to changes introduced by the offworlders' treatment of the five sexes one hundred years earlier, when Hara was "rediscovered" by the Federation, is represented by the reactionary Tendlathe. As the heir to the position of Most Important Man on Hara (a title his father retains until Tendlathe kills him), Ten has the authority and influence to violently repress any dissenting political expression. Raven learns of the extent of his power when Ten makes it impossible for a dissident to ever find work again on Hara (152–53). Using both legal and illegal measures, Ten orders Hara's militia, the *mostaas*, to repress and prevent resistance. In addition to making organizing difficult, the terror against the Modernist odd-bodied includes psychological intimidation, often accompanied by severe physical violence. A political leader of the Modernist movement is assassinated; his murder is tolerated, if not instigated, by the government. The indigene odd-bodied face constant police harassment as well as economic repression of their independent crafts when they don't adhere to the codes of their culture's two-sex model, and the trade bars, a main source of income for the odd-bodied, are burnt down by government-backed terror groups. The odd-bodied are subject to Klan-like terror by sets of ghost *ranas* who harass and beat up nonnormatively gendered people; the *ranas* make them strip and then humiliate and ridicule their bodies. On Hara, fems, herms, and mems do not receive protection from police against random and organized violence. The scene in which Raven and Haliday are attacked by ghost *ranas* because they are herms eerily mirrors hate crimes committed against trans and queer people. While beating them up, the *ranas* taunt the two and force them to expose their bodies:

> "You got a pretty face, but the body's a mess. What the hell are you?" The circle moved closer, closing in. . . .
> "What've you got under there?" the leader asked. "Show us, War-reven. Show us what a man you are." . . . He couldn't fight them, not unarmed . . . and [removing his clothes] might get them out of this alive. He'd done worse, he told himself, and didn't believe it. . . . He pulled the torn cloth apart, baring his breasts to the fog and the cold. The house-lights left no hope of concealment; he stood half naked and fought to seem unashamed. . . . (234–35)

They are reminded by their tormentors: "We don't have herms on Hara, just titicocks who can't make up their minds" (236). The group then proceeds to beat up Raven and Haliday; Haliday almost dies, due to the lack of adequate healthcare, and is saved only through the presence of an off-world doctor.

Scott contrasts Traditionalists with Modernists, social reformers who attempt to organize politically within a system that severely restricts political opposition. The Modernists' "New Agenda" (120, 202) demands reforms in trade issues and contracts with pharmaceutical off-world companies, and it advocates for Hara's acceptance into the federation of Concord Worlds. The movement's agenda implicitly includes gender laws since issues of trade affect mainly the odd-bodied. In the end, however, the Modernists sacrifice the reform of gender laws in their negotiations with those in power.

In her depiction of the Modernists' political strategizing, Scott points to the structural obstacles that any political system poses to those who challenge the status quo. Modernists use the legal system to fight existing trade laws (Raven is a partner in a group of Modernist legal advocates), and they (unsuccessfully) attempt to challenge the two-sex/gender system through the courts. The failure of existing structures of political decision making to change gender laws channels the energies of political activists into other forms of resistance. Scott creates mechanisms of subversive resistance in *Shadow Man* that are symbolic of contemporary progressive movements' political work—such as direct action and staged cultural events that function as political movements.

Aside from legal measures, the Modernist movement relies on subversive modes of public protest, since Haran society allows political dissent outside its rigid traditional clan system only within the contained context of cultural events. *Ranas* are traditional drum dances wherein the dancers express political opinions by representing one of the "spirits," entities who are believed to be mediators between humans and God. Public protest takes part mainly though *presances,* political versions of *ranas* employed by radical political groups. "Not that the *ranas* had ever really been apolitical, of course, but the Modernists had honed and focused the protests, trying to say new things in an old voice" (75). At times this use of *ranas* is reminiscent of the strategies of religious leaders who employ the spiritual framework of their communities to rally around political issues. *Ranas* are tolerated by the system as long as they adhere to a certain protocol of protest (as our system tolerates direct action and organized demonstrations within the parameters it dictates). *Rana* dancers are considered "sanctioned protesters," as Raven explains to Tatian:

> ". . . [U]nder Genevoe's—the Trickster's—protection, they can say anything as long as they stay within the form." (189)

> ". . . The ways things have always been done, political gatherings can be suppressed—that's supposed to be reserved to the *mesnies* [units of households within the clan system]—but political gets defined as 'getting together to talk about issues.' If you dance and sing . . . it can't be politics." (197)

Scott insists on the importance of creating moments of political opposition within systemic restrictions that prohibit dissent. The use of cultural and social customs to express politics becomes a necessary act of resistance.

The evocation of the planet's ancient belief in "spirits" turns Raven into the symbolic figure of odd-bodied resistance. In the book's final chapters, Raven's attempts to address the right to have one's sex/gender/sexual identity recognized are rejected, not only by those in power, but also by the majority of those organizing for social justice. The Modernist leaders practice exclusionary liberatory politics when they "shelve" gender law issues because those issues might jeopardize the general political agenda. Their argument that "we need to present a unified front" (271) is an ironic comment not only about New

Left politics but also about trans people's experiences with the gay and lesbian Human Rights Campaign's assimilationist agenda (and the earlier experiences of lesbians in the Women's Liberation movement). In ʒer final stand against both officials and resisters, Raven takes on the persona of "Agede the Doorkeeper, the spirit of death and birth and change" (261), which is symbolically an identity that subverts power structures. Raven is unsure how to relate to ʒer newfound identity as herm, which ʒer culture has not prepared ʒim for: "I've been a man all my life—yesterday, I was still a man. Now I'm a herm, and I don't know what that means, except that half of my people say it's not really human. How in all the hells can I lead anybody to anything when I don't know what I am asking them to become? I have to be able to offer something in place of what we've got" (304). The power of a naturalized sex/gender model cannot be defeated simply by the revelation of individuals who insist on a place within the system. Instead of reducing one trans character to a lonely transgressive figure, Scott transforms her protagonist into a symbol for a *movement*. There is no tradition of revolution on Hara—"we don't even have a word for it" (304)—so Raven goes into exile to learn it. The artistic murals that spring up overnight and depict his face as that of the Doorkeeper predict the political inspiration his resistance has ignited in those who share his oppression. The reader is left with the sense that, even though the narrative ends with Raven's departure, it signals the beginning of a gender rights movement on Hara.

The two main points that emerge from *Shadow Man* are, first, the fundamental right of all persons to determine their own gender identity; and, second and more troubling, the limitedness of either of the two cultural systems depicted. The juxtaposition of Haran and Concordian cultures discloses that, in the end, neither of the two systems truly destabilizes the sex/gender/sexuality correlation: as long as we insist on categories to classify our bodies and our desire within, we will give others the power to regulate us. In Raven's resistance as herm, the reader gets a glimpse of the potentials of a society where neither sex nor gender nor desire is regulated by naturalized categories that define what it should be. In addition to pointing to the limits of any sex/gender system, Scott points to the significance of organized resistance. Change is achieved, not by simply envisioning it, but through active political engagement, which thrives on theoretical and creative alternatives to the system. Scott's narrative reminds us of the importance of fusing theory with activism when pursuing social change, and the danger of marginalizing those whose oppression by the system does not make the larger movement's limited agenda.

Science fiction narratives like the work of Octavia Butler and Melissa Scott make clear that no form of social organizing into a gender system is inherently liberating. Instead, it is the fluidity of categories and the acknowledgment of the repressive effect of what Foucault termed "biopower" which can potentially lead to subversive ways of understanding the correlation between sex, gender, and sexuality.

WHEN PEOPLE ASK me what my book is about, the answer "intergalactic feminism" usually evokes a puzzled look and a polite "How interesting?" The explanation "I look at science fiction's relationship to feminist theories" earns me an "Ahh—how interesting!" usually followed by the question "But why?" The theoretical and textual explorations presented here make a case that feminist theorists should pay closer attention to science fiction's alien constructions and understand that science fiction offers valuable tools for feminist theorizing.

The science fiction texts discussed in this study are diverse in their representations, in terms of both content and medium. The issues that continually surface in these texts' explorations of power relations are the same as those discussed in much contemporary feminist thought: the complicated relationship of subjectivity/identity and difference; the epistemological and ontological shifts that take place in the wake of a global technoscience; and the New Gender Politics of queer desires and transgender and intersexed bodies and identities. Post- and neo-colonization and current social and economic politics are the historical contexts that find entry into fantastic new worlds, both here on Earth and in galaxies far, far away. The alien constructions that take shape in science fiction—cyborgs, aliens, hybrids, and monstrous bodies—all contribute to the denaturalization of norms and of identities based in dualisms. They allow new constellations in feminist debates on difference, globalization, and technoscience. In science fiction, the category "human"—the main signifier of our declared commonality—is destabilized to make visible its exclusive and violent workings in our world. Thus these alien constructions pose a challenge to an exclusive humanism, and their promise is that of new posthuman subjectivities based on partiality and recognition of difference.

The three major areas of feminist thought discussed here in relation to science fiction—identity/difference, technoscience, and sex/gender/sexuality—contain a variety of approaches, including cyborg feminism, theories on the subjectivities of women of color, and queer theory. Even though these diverging theories arrive at different conclusions, it is in their attention to the *material*, or the *body*, and how it exists in the world, that they all come together. There is an urgency present in the current debates on how to conceptualize (and organize around) the (female) body. The stakes are high within a global culture dominated by capitalism, militarism, and Western imperialism. The issue of denaturalizing identities and bodies is at the center of these debates: how can we conceptualize the violence that bodies experience externally in relationship to the pleasure and potential resistance that lies in the impurity of the denaturalized body?

Alien Constructions traces two tensions that are recurrent in attempts at formulating agency and self-determination for posthuman existences in science fiction narratives. The first is the tension between standpoint knowledge—based on shared material experience—and subjectivity and desire. The second is between essentialism and constructivism. Standpoint theory is an important tool enabling feminists to challenge power structures. Standpoint theory understands particular knowledge systems as based on shared social experiences. "Epistemic privilege"—to be in the position to know—is linked to social location. This way of conceptualizing knowledge decentralizes the cultural and political authority that historically has rested with a small group, and instead insists on situational knowledge, which creates the need to negotiate claims of truth. Standpoint theory denaturalizes categories—and thus identity—by grounding them in the specificities of daily experience, not in an eternal ontological truth about the human self. This shift enables alliances between diverse bodies of knowledge, grounded not in an essential notion of the body and desire as pre-givens but in social formations. We find this position taken by Octavia Butler's female figures, who negotiate identity and power from a partial position that is always informed by their standpoint as women of color, and in Ripley's cyborg subjectivity, which creates partial vantage points from which to understand the world.

But standpoint theory also seems to return to notions of *shared* identities (within social groups), which can result in the trap of having identities be defined by normative categories. How can standpoint epistemologies accommodate the location of those identities and differences located *outside* the binary gender system—such as transgender identities, which seemingly contradict the social positions/groups/

identities they have been assigned? Melissa Scott's character Raven demands the creation of new categories that make visible the experiences of those who remain unnamed—agency is developed in the face of a recognized and legitimized standpoint. Octavia Butler explores the tension between materiality and subjectivity in the shapeshifter Anyanwu, whose identity is contextual and adaptive (i.e., relational to the material) even as it is stable at its core (i.e., essential). Butler investigates this tension more radically in the construct ooloi, whose standpoint is grounded exclusively in the other, and whose material reality is preceded and mediated by desire.

Despite their limitations in terms of subjectivity and desire, standpoint theories are compelling in that they provide us with a concept that insists on social power as distributed through economic power, and that recognizes the central role that community—those who know "me"—plays in our applications of agency. This concept has to be understood as what Michelle Renee Matisons terms "*mediated* standpoint"—one that is learned and acquired and can be challenged and modified. Most importantly, our standpoint can never be the limit of our ability to understand others' oppressions. The cyborg's partiality—the recognition that our subjectivity is comprised of the intersections of standpoints—is a useful metaphor here.

Queer and trans theories problematize and complicate notions of standpoint. Desire and subjectivity counter material experiences: for example, in a heterosexist society, people treat you as if you desire boys (assigned standpoint as a girl), but you really like girls (queer desire develops despite the social position as girl). Transgender identities challenge the absolute authority of material experiences: just because people treat me like a boy (assigned standpoint as boy based on the body) does not mean I *am* a boy (nonnormative gender identity develops despite the social position as boy). Both queer and trans subjects end up experiencing the world from nonnormative positions, which in return shape their knowledge—that is, their standpoints as either queer or transgender subjects. In our understanding of subjectivity, what was there first—the nonnormative gender identity or the social position as that which is read as normative? Here, it is central to recognize that the relationship between identity and material experiences is never static but constantly in negotiation. This element of constant negotiation is reflected in the construct ooloi in Octavia Butler's *Xenogenesis* series and the intersexed bodies we encounter in Melissa Scott's

Shadow Man. These bodies and subjectivities complicate the relationship between body and assigned social position, and how both relate to knowledge (such as in Raven's unstable standpoint as hermaphrodite in a society that denies his physical consistency). They also introduce desire as *formative* for the body (not as determined by the body), thus not just preceding but *discounting* standpoint knowledge/the material, as in the shapeshifting construct ooloi.

The second tension within feminist thought that informs *Alien Constructions* is that between essentialism and constructivism. Essentialism assumes that gender identity is derived from the (biological) body, and social behavior and categories are developed from these (biological) differences. Constructivism understands the body's materiality as dominated/constructed by (social) discourse, from which categories of identity are created. Different forms of resistance evolve from the two positions, some of which are in conflict with each other. In Octavia Butler's work, we encounter the fear inherent in abandoning the essential (i.e. pure) definition of "human" when aliens breed with resisting humans, and the naming of hybrid offspring—*constructs*—reflects the investment in stable notions of self and identity that are challenged by posthuman configurations. Ripley's cloned, impure genes in the *Alien* series also reinsert the body into concepts of the self; her body's monstrosity is as real as it is socially constructed, and the biological (essential) makeup of the self is mirrored in mutants that share her genes, even though their monstrous forms deny their kinship. Recognition of the self in the other—the other *as* the self—becomes a self-defining act. The question of how technology mediates these different positions is also explored in cyberpunk writing, such as in Richard Calder's ambivalent female technobodies: does technology destabilize or reinforce sexual difference? In *Dead Girls*, Calder problematizes cyborg feminism's notion that denaturalized bodies necessarily destabilize heterosexuality and existing gender polarities, and he instead creates a dystopian vision of extreme binary sexual difference. Technology here facilitates patriarchal capitalism, and cyborgian resistance seems foreclosed. In *The Matrix*, technology's role in constructing subjectivity is more ambivalent: subjectivity is defined as based on the experience of the body, but *agency* is facilitated by technology.

Octavia Butler's and Melissa Scott's creatures with nonnormatively gendered bodies and desires, as well as those in *The Matrix*'s technologized (virtual) world, explore the poles of essentialism and constructivism: how does gender identity relate to the body, and how do we define desire outside a sexual binary? In Richard Calder's writing, technology's impact on bodies recreates a male-dominated, violent heterosexuality; desire finds new expression in his female technobodies but remains unchanged in its underlying heterosexual structure. In contrast to this essential heterosexuality, in *Imago* Octavia Butler introduces the concept of what I term "queer essence," seemingly a contradiction in terms. It is the inevitable drive to adapt one's body to the sexual desire of the other, which threatens any coherent sense of self outside of intimate relations. Here, the body is not essential in its makeup and therefore does not determine desire based on anatomy; instead, it is *absolute* in its malleability, dependent on where desire takes it. This existence, in which desire for the other supersedes materiality because the body is exclusively shaped by social relations, nevertheless has an essential quality. Desire is aimed at reproduction (the gene trade) and is rooted in one organ (the organelle); thus (sexual) drive becomes the only source of the self's identity.

Queer essence is compelling because it insists on pleasure and desire as fundamental categories of existence outside of a heterosexual economy, and it integrates the materiality of bodies into the debate without essentializing them. At the same time, queer essence is so complete in its projection of the self through others—the self's dependence on the other is absolute—that it poses the question of whether the concept of self is not obsolete. Either sex/gender system discussed in *Alien Constructions* is limited and results in some kind of regulation. It appears that as long as we insist on categorizing our bodies and desires—which, when we engage in political work, may be unavoidable—others will have the power to regulate us.

While some science fiction relies on feminism for its conceptualizations, feminist theorists tend to ignore the genre as either fantastic or unsophisticated and "nerdy." They miss the often crucial insights science fiction offers in its dialogue with feminist theories. Most importantly, feminist theorists do not utilize the genre as a forum to broaden the debate and to bring it outside academic and activist circles. It could help make an impact by drawing in consumers of popular culture who otherwise are not considered participants in feminist debates. An active exchange between cultural texts and theory can only enrich feminist discourse. Science fiction can contribute to feminist debates by disclosing the limits and strengths of theoretical concepts and by offering an imaginative way of exploring the issues at hand. Its fantastic constellations challenge social power and point to the danger of reproducing it within feminist theories.

Science fiction critics, who have established science fiction criticism within academic discourse, too often dismiss feminist or queer theories as one of many side discourses that inform the genre, instead of recognizing the pervasive presence of gender as an organizing principle within *any* narrative. Gender need not be prioritized in analyses focusing on systemic reflections in cultural texts, but no analysis is complete without acknowledging the mutual construction of categories that creates a subject (or its absence).

Bodies and the ways in which they are positioned and read in our social order form the basis for our lives. Posthuman narratives denaturalize the body without removing its claim to self-determination. Their liberating potential lies in the instability of categories that assign places in our order and in the deregulation of desire and reproduction/family. Technology has become a major factor in history that mediates the presence of our bodies and, with that, our sense of being in the world. Cyborg feminism explores the potential of (often violently induced) partiality that grows from denaturalization, and the danger of discarding those posthuman bodies that do not align with a persistently exclusive definition of "human." Science fiction's alien constructions provide unfamiliar images for familiar identities and concepts and explore the implications of theories within a (pleasurable) narrative framework. When encountering these metaphors—and while creating them—cyborg feminism, augmented consistently in dialogue with related discourses such as queer and critical race theory, is a useful mode of reading cultural texts for making visible the negotiations of power people experience in a global capitalist world. Cyborgs and other unworldly creatures make it possible for us to reimagine our potentials and goals as well as our concepts of agency and resistance. They force us to take another look, to question our assumptions by creating new perspectives and positions. It is from their alien perspectives that we are able to realize that, in terms of explaining our world, we are very much like *Alien Resurrection*'s Ripley when she contemplates her position on Earth: "I'm a stranger here myself."

Introduction: Science Fiction's
Alien Constructions

1. My use of "feminist" not only
spans articulations of the "Second
Wave," as its historical use in United
States discourse suggests, but refers
to concepts embraced in Ann Brooks's
definition of "postfeminism"—a "conceptual frame of reference encompass-
ing the intersection of feminism with
a number of other anti-foundationalist
movements including postmodernism, post-structuralism and postcolonialism" (Brooks 1)—as well as
transgenderism. The term "feminist" thus describes a diverse set of
thoughts that stand in relation to other
progressive theoretical and political
movements and are concerned with
the manifestation and perpetuation
of power structures based on various
social, political, cultural, and economic
factors, including those structured by
gender.

2. The following titles offer dis-
cussions of various aspects of these
genre-specific issues: Marc Angenot,
"The Absent Paradigm"; Marleen
Barr, *Lost in Space;* Scott Bukatman,
Terminal Identity and *Blade Runner;*
Samuel R. Delany, "Some Reflections
on sf Criticism" and "About Five Thou-
sand One Hundred and Seventy-Five
Words"; Theresa de Lauretis, "Signs of
Wo/ander"; Vivian Sobchack, "Cities on
the Edge of Time: The Urban Science
Fiction Film" and *Screening Space;*
Claudia Springer, *Electronic Eros;* and
Darko Suvin, *Metamorphosis of Science*

Fiction, "On the Poetics of Science Fiction," and "The River-Side Trees, or sf
and Utopia: Degrees of Kinship."

3. A recent example of how science fiction provides a cultural point
of reference is the antiwar movement's distribution of flyers during
the week when *The Matrix Reloaded*
was released in 2003. The flyers drew
an analogy between *The Matrix* and
the Bush administration's representation of the political situation in
Iraq. The authors of the flyers relied on the reader's knowledge about
the film's concept of a manipulated
version of reality. The flyer can be
reviewed on the website of the antiwar organization *Not in Our Name:*
[http://www.notinourname.net/war/
redpill.html].

4. As Camille Bacon-Smith explains
in *Science Fiction Culture,* "it's the science fiction community that creates
and popularizes the language with
which we name the future" (1). One
example of science fiction's influence
on general culture is Gibson's term
"cyberspace," which remains a popular
way of referring to the Internet despite
the United States government's efforts
to implement the term "Information
Superhighway."

5. Suvin borrows the concept of estrangement *(Verfremdungseffekt)* from
German playwright Bertolt Brecht, who
introduced it to the theater in the first
half of the twentieth century. Suvin
quotes Brecht as follows: "A representation which estranges is one which

allows us to recognize its subject, but at the same time makes it seem unfamiliar" ("Poetics" 374).

6. In his influential study *Postmodernism, or, the Cultural Logic of Late Capitalism,* Frederic Jameson discusses the implications of cultural and economic relations within the historical period of postmodernism for political subjectivity. In *Aliens and Others,* Jenny Wolmark gives a comprehensive analysis of science fiction's role in Jameson's theories of postmodern culture (6–16).

7. I use the term *feminist science fiction* as inclusive of both feminist science fiction narratives *and* feminist critical readings of science fiction texts. Feminist fiction and critical texts together form the feminist debate around science fiction and influence each other.

8. I use the term *postmodern science fiction* within a literary/cultural studies context to designate the disruption and boundary crossing of genre markers and the break with stylistic conventions and narrative structures that emerged in the 1960s. This literary development took place within the context of a cultural and media re- and devaluation of the Western world and a consequential crisis of Western subjectivity.

9. Here I discuss mainly aspects of the debate on the relationship of science fiction *literature* to feminist thought, since much of feminist science fiction criticism relates to literature more than film. Part II discusses the particularities of science fiction film as a medium in relation to feminist thought.

10. However, the increased concern with race relations in contemporary science fiction is visible in the popularity of books such as Nalo Hopkinson's *Brown Girl in the Ring* (1998) and *Midnight Robber* (2000), which have narratives that are embedded in black Caribbean culture. This increased concern is also reflected in two critical publications on science fiction of the past: *Into Darkness Peering: Race and Color in the Fantastic* (1997), edited by Elisabeth Anne Leonard—a collection of critical essays on race and fantastic literature—and *Dark Matter: A Century of Speculative Fiction from the African Diaspora* (2000), edited by Sheree R. Thomas—an anthology of black speculative fiction including critical essays.

11. Also see the following titles for an examination of feminist science fiction and its relationship to the traditions of the genre: Lucie Armitt, ed., *Where No Man Has Gone Before;* Marleen Barr, *Future Females* and *Lost in Space;* Justine Larbalestier, *The Battle of the Sexes in Science Fiction;* Robin Roberts, *A New Species;* and Jenny Wolmark, *Aliens and Others.*

12. Between 1953 (the year the award was created) and 1967 no woman won the *Hugo Award,* but in the years between 1968 and 1984, eleven did. This fact points to the influence of women science fiction writers and the growing acknowledgment of their contributions.

13. Veronica Hollinger in "Feminist Science Fiction: Breaking Up the Subject" points to a tension within feminist science fiction between the construction of a strong feminist subject in humanist-oriented feminist science fiction and the deconstruction of subjectivity (and of the subject) in postmodern feminist science fiction.

14. See Jane Donawerth, *Frankenstein's Daughters: Women Writing Science Fiction,* and Robin Roberts, *A New Species: Gender and Science in Science Fiction,* for a discussion of alternative sciences in feminist science fiction.

15. A direct link between theories and narratives is visible in some feminist science fiction authors who also are feminist activists/writers—such as Sally Miller Gearheart, who wrote *The Wanderground* (1979) in the context of 1970s lesbian/cultural feminism, and

Marge Piercy, whose science fiction novels *Woman on the Edge of Time* (1978) and *He, She, and It* (1991) respond to specific feminist discourses at the time of their publication.

16. The idea that science and literature inform each other indirectly through a shared culture is not limited to science fiction. In *The Cosmic Web* (1984), N. Katherine Hayles lays out connections between scientific theories and literary strategies by exploring first scientific field models (in diverse fields such as quantum physics and linguistics) and then tracing similar concerns within texts of the twentieth century, showing how literature has been shaped by changes in paradigms. Her argument is not that certain literature is "caused" by scientific field models, but that both areas are connected in their common interests, and that literature "is an imaginative response to complexities and ambiguities that are implicit in the models but that are often not explicitly recognized. Thus a comprehensive picture of the field concept is more likely to emerge from the literature and from science viewed together than from either alone" (10).

17. Throughout this book I use *identity* and *subjectivity* as terms that shape our notion of self, our sense of being. Instead of prioritizing either concept as a separate component of the subject (identity as the social and cultural position and experiences that construct an individual, and subjectivity as the conscious agent, the rational subject), I view each as constructing the other, together in a constant process of re-creating the subject.

18. Works published in the 1980s that introduced aspects of difference other than sexual into feminist discourse include bell hooks, *Ain't I a Woman: Black Women and Feminism;* Cherríe Moraga and Gloria Anzaldúa, eds., *This Bridge Called My Back;* and Barbara Smith, Patricia Bell Scott, and Gloria Tull, eds.,

All the Women Are White, All the Blacks Are Men, But Some of Us Are Brave; as well as Angela Davis's groundbreaking historical study *Women, Race, and Class.*

19. Higginbotham quotes Elizabeth Spelman's *Inessential Woman:* "In other words, the womanness underneath the black woman's skin is a white woman's and deep down inside the Latina woman is an Anglo woman waiting to burst through" (95). Instead, in *White Women, Race Matters,* Ruth Frankenberg discloses the cultural norm "white" to be as much materially and discursively constructed as the "ethnicities" of people of color.

20. Braidotti continues by stating that she views this tension as a historical contradiction: "[T]hat the signifier *woman* is both the concept around which feminists have gathered, in a movement where the politics of identity are central, and that it is also the very concept that needs to be analyzed critically—is a perfect description of our historical situation in late capitalism" (*Nomadic Subjects* 200; emphasis hers).

21. See Linda Nicholson, ed., *Feminism/Postmodernism;* Judith Butler and Joan Scott, eds., *Feminists Theorize the Political;* Rosi Braidotti, *Nomadic Subjects* and *Patterns of Dissonance;* Susan Hekman, *Gender and Knowledge;* Ann Brooks, *Postfeminisms: Feminism, Cultural Theory and Cultural Forms;* and the introduction to Inderpal Grewal and Caren Kaplan, eds., *Scattered Hegemonies,* for insights into the debate on the relationship of feminist thought to postmodernism.

22. See Braidotti, Chapter 8 in *Nomadic Subjects* for a discussion of the concept "gender vs. sexual difference" that shaped Western-based feminist discourse; Judith Butler's Chapter 9 in *Undoing Gender* problematizes feminist theory's insistence on binary sexual difference.

23. See Judith Butler, *Gender Trouble,*

Bodies that Matter, and *Undoing Gender,* and Eve Sedgwick, *Epistemologies of the Closet,* for theoretical approaches that complicate the binaries male/female and heterosexual/homosexual; and Judith Halberstam, *Female Masculinity,* for an application of alternative categories of identities in readings of cultural texts.

24. Examples are Judith Butler and Joan W. Scott, eds., *Feminists Theorize the Political;* Gayatri Chakravorty Spivak, *A Critique of Postcolonial Reason;* and Trinh T. Minh-ha, *Woman, Native, Other.*

25. For insights into the feminist debate on epistemologies and the critique of science, see Linda Alcoff and Elizabeth Potter, eds., *Feminist Epistemologies;* Ruth Bleier, ed., *Feminist Approaches to Science* and *Science and Gender: A Critique of Biology and Its Theories on Women;* Susan Bordo and Alison Jaggar, eds., *Gender/Body/Knowledge: Feminist Reconstructions of Being and Knowing;* Anne Fausto-Sterling, *Myths of Gender: Biological Theories about Women and Men;* Donna Haraway, *Simians, Cyborgs, and Women: The Reinvention of Nature* and *Modest Witness@Second Millennium. FemaleMan©Meets OncoMouse™: Feminism and Technoscience* and *Primate Visions: Gender, Race, and Nature in the World of Modern Science;* Sandra Harding, *The Science Question in Feminism;* Evelyn Fox Keller, *Reflections on Gender and Science;* Marian Lowe and Ruth Hubbard, eds., *Woman's Nature: Rationalization of Inequality;* Carolyn Merchant, *The Death of Nature: Women, Ecology, and the Scientific Revolution;* Linda Nicholson, ed., *Feminism/Postmodernism;* Val Plumwood, *Feminism and the Mastery of Nature;* and Londa Schiebinger, *Nature's Body: Gender in the Making of Modern Science.*

26. In *Woman on the Edge of Time,* Marge Piercy explores two different extremes of future employment of technology and its impact on social orders: the utopian, egalitarian future of Mattapoisett, which uses technology to enhance social justice, and a dystopian, destructive future in which patriarchal technology has furthered social injustices based on class, race, and gender. Piercy establishes ways in which technology has the potential to be developed and employed in a nonpatriarchal fashion, but her narrative makes clear that a feminist concept of social structure that defines and shapes the goal of technological development is crucial in order for this outcome to be realized.

27. For a discussion of feminist concepts of science in feminist science fiction, also see Robin Roberts, *A New Species: Gender and Science in Science Fiction,* and Sarah Lefanu, *In the Chinks of the World Machine: Feminism and Science Fiction.*

28. It was Norbert Weiner who elaborated on the idea of cybernetics as "a technoscience that explained both organic and machine processes as part of informational systems" (Gray, Figueroa-Sarriera, and Mentor, "Introduction" 5). See Haraway, *Primate Visions* 102–8, for a discussion of the growing impact of cybernetics on communication and systems theory in the 1950s and 1960s.

29. Haraway discusses the implication of an invisible technology that infuses our lives in "A Cyborg Manifesto." This aspect forms a major component in the works of scholars like Bukatman, Hayles, and Springer, who furthermore place their analyses in relation to postmodern theories of media and communication such as those of Jean Baudrillard, Paul Virilio, and Marshall McLuhan.

30. The page references here are from the reprinted version of Haraway's article from *Simians, Cyborgs, and Women* in 1991: "A Cyborg Manifesto:

Science, Technology, and Socialist-Feminism in the Late Twentieth Century."

31. Donna Haraway's work reflects interdisciplinary approaches that form the basis for cyborg discourse: *Primate Visions* examines primatology as an ideological discourse rooted in race, gender, and class; *Simians, Cyborgs, and Women* includes a collection of articles dealing with semiotics and material manifestations of power relations in knowledge, science, technology, and feminist theories; and *Modest Witness* further examines the implications of technoscience, and its semiotic and material monsters, for women's lives.

32. See Valerie Plumwood, *Feminism and the Mastery of Nature,* for a critical examination of dualistic thinking. Also see Carolyn Merchant, *The Death of Nature: Women, Ecology and the Scientific Revolution;* Vandana Shiva, *Staying Alive: Women, Ecology, and Development;* and Karen Warren, ed., *Ecological Feminist Philosophies* for examples of ecofeminism, a school of feminist thought that developed from the criticism of patriarchal science and technology and its exploitation of both women and nature.

33. Additional books on cyborg discourse include cross-disciplinary anthologies such as *The Cyborg Handbook,* edited by Chris Hables Gray, Heidi J. Figueroa-Sarriera and Steven Mentor, which incorporates texts from the natural sciences, social sciences, and humanities. The essay collection *Cyberspace/Cyberbodies/Cyberpunk,* edited by Mike Featherstone and Roger Burrows, focuses on both representation and realities of technological environments. Scott Bukatman's *Terminal Identity* places poststructuralist and media theories of subjectivity in relation to postmodern science fiction literature and film. All of these texts are concerned with articulations of a posthuman subjectivity and

understandings of power relations in a postmodern world.

34. For example, Judith Squires, in "Fabulous Feminist Futures and the Lure of Cyberculture," criticizes the tendency in some feminist "cyberdrool" writing to neglect the material basis that created the cyborg metaphor in the first place. Yet Squires herself does not emphasize that the theoretical and material basis of "nitty-gritty . . . lived social relations" (Squires 367) is shaped by race as well as class, and that Haraway developed her cyborg myth from within the context of work by women of color.

35. Standpoint theory makes the claim that the experiences of a social group shape and produce knowledge that is specific to that group. Feminist standpoint theory at its most sophisticated does not biologically essentialize women as a group but bases women's commonalities in shared social experiences that are also structured by race and class.

36. In commentaries responding to the "Cyborg Manifesto" collected in Elizabeth Weed's *Coming to Terms,* Haraway's cyborg identity is criticized for both its lack of a theory of subjectivity and its reliance on terms and positions of socialist feminism in its claim to transcend them. See especially Mary Ann Doane, "Cyborgs, Origins, and Subjectivity," and Joan W. Scott, "Commentary: Cyborgian Socialists?" Donna Haraway revisits some of these questions in "Cyborgs at Large," an interview with Constance Penley and Andrew Ross in *Technoculture,* and in "The Actors Are Cyborgs, Nature Is Coyote, and the Geography Is Elsewhere: Postscript to 'Cyborgs at Large.'"

Introduction to Part I

1. See Ruth Salvaggio, "Octavia Butler"; Randall Kenan, "An Interview with Octavia E. Butler"; and Frances M. Beal, "Interview with Octavia Butler:

Black Women and the Science Fiction Genre," for further biographical information on Octavia E. Butler.

2. Her work includes, in order of publication: *Patternmaster* (1976); *Mind of my Mind* (1977); *Survivor* (1978); *Kindred* (1979); *Wild Seed* (1980); *Clay's Ark* (1984); the *Xenogenesis* trilogy *Dawn* (1987), *Adulthood Rites* (1988), and *Imago* (1989); *Parable of the Sower* (1993); *Bloodchild and Other Stories* (1995); and *Parable of the Talents* (1998).

3. In her exploration of issues of race and gender, Butler joins other feminist science fiction writers, such as Gwyneth Jones. In *Aliens and Others,* Jenny Wolmark reads both Octavia Butler's and Gwyneth Jones's work in relation to their critical constellations of human/alien relations that question the stable relationship of self/other and identity/difference. Wolmark discusses how both writers "use the science fiction metaphor of the alien to explore the way in which the deeply divisive dichotomies of race and gender are embedded in the repressive structures and relations of dominance and subordination" (27).

4. Michael Hanchard quotes Raymond Williams: "[T]he conventional distinction between the material and symbolic does not correspond to the social reality of 'language and signification as indissoluble elements of the material process itself.' The analytic space between 'names and appearances' and 'real problems' is socially traversed by collective and individual narratives engaged in discourse" (233).

5. I use the term "black" when referring to Butler since I agree with Hanchard's ambivalence regarding the term "African American": first, because it reduces "American" to the United States, and second, because it isolates people of African descent living in the United States from those living, for example, in the Caribbean (see Hanchard 231). I also use it here in the U.S.

tradition as distinct from "people of color." At the same time I respect the (academic) tradition of referring to the African American imagination within the context of U.S. culture. Butler uses African cultural elements throughout her fiction, and even though her characters come from a wide range of multicultural backgrounds, her protagonists often explicitly identify with their African origin. For a detailed discussion of the importance of terminology in critical race discourse, see Davies, *Black Women* 5-15.

6. The contradiction within the contrast of the idioms "popular culture" and "mainstream" (which Doerksen uses to describe literature by Toni Morrison, Alice Walker, etc.) as two opposite phenomena is obvious. The unpopular phrasing of "high" versus "popular" literature more clearly expresses the separation of texts common in literary and cultural studies.

7. Butler's narratives are often closely linked to United States culture in their critiques of it. Nevertheless, I place her into Davies's theory of transnational black female subjectivity since the constructions of black experience in the United States are tied to those of black women elsewhere. Furthermore, Butler's writing contains strong thematic critiques of United States imperialism (e.g., the *Parable* novels problematize global capitalism and its production of a cheap labor force as well as the war aspirations of the United States) and link her characters' experiences to the Black Diaspora. Finally, Butler in general undermines categories of United States race discourse.

8. Davies's concern with canonizing "Black Women's Writing" is that the privileging of U.S. black women's writing produces a hegemonic understanding of "black identity" that excludes all black women not from the United States and obscures the complexities of African American identity itself

(Davies, "Introduction: Black Women Writing Worlds" 2–3). I would add that the focus on "high" literature in this process excludes constructions of identities that take place in the category of "popular culture," rendering important critical texts on black female writers in the United States—like Barbara Christian's "Trajectories of Self-Definition"—incomplete through their exclusion of texts of popular culture. Christian's significant examination of black women's struggles to define themselves in their literary texts should also place writers like Butler into this literary tradition: "The extent to which Afro-American women writers in the seventies and eighties have been able to make a commitment to an exploration of self, as central rather than marginal, is a tribute to the insights they have culled in a century or so of literary activity" (317).

9. I appreciate the term *intersectionality* of systems of oppression for its moments of connection without having to establish a shared identity. Yet I believe it falls short in that it does not account for the mutual *construction* of categories. Intersectionality tempts one to envision otherwise *independent* factors that intersect at certain moments in time and space. See Evelyn Nakano Glenn's criticism of an "additive" model of oppression that privileges gender and "adds" on race, class, and so on, in "From Servitude to Service Work." Also see Evelyn Brooks Higginbotham's "African-American Women's History and the Metalanguage of Race," where she describes how race also constructs gender identity and discloses how an exclusive focus on gender renders a feminist analysis incomplete.

10. In science fiction, the encounters between human space travelers and "un-human" creatures often are metaphors for existing social relations based on differences such as race and class and on colonial histories. I use the term "un-human" instead of "non-human" to designate a particular theoretical posi-

tion. "Non-human" defines a category separate from that which it describes, and denies any boundary blurring within its classification. The term "un-human" acknowledges differences, but recognizes the ideological investment in the exclusive category "human" and denaturalizes it.

11. Butler was awarded the MacArthur "genius" Award in 1995 and the PEN Center West Lifetime Achievement Award in 2000.

12. See Sandra Govan, "Homage to Tradition: Octavia Butler Renovates the Historical Novel."

13. I extensively examine utopia as the main narrative force in my reading of the two *Parable* novels in "'All That You Touch You Change': Utopian Desire and the Concept of Change in Octavia E. Butler's *Parable of the Sower* and *Parable of the Talents.*"

14. In "New Sciences: Cyborg Feminism and the Methodology of the Oppressed," Chela Sandoval traces the origin of Haraway's cyborg political identity to the transgressive elements in women of color's resistance to colonization, reiterating the direct influence of anticolonial feminist theory on cyborg feminism, which often is ignored.

15. For further critical readings of Delany's work and his role as a public intellectual, also see Ross Posnock, *Color and Culture: Black Writers and the Making of the Modern Intellectual;* and James Sallis, editor, *Ash of Stars: On the Writing of Samuel R. Delany.*

1. Cultural Chameleons

1. It is significant that the discourse on race representation in science fiction *film* has yet to produce a complete book dedicated to this subject. There are, of course, individual articles on race in science fiction film (and television), such as "Creole Identity Politics, Race, and *Star Trek: Voyager*" by Neal Baker in *Into Darkness Peering* (the volume's only article on science

fiction film), edited by Elisabeth Anne Leonard; and "Race, Space, and Class: The Politics of Cityscapes in Science-Fiction Films" by David Desser in *Alien Zone II*, edited by Annette Kuhn, a collection dedicated to science fiction film (the only article in the collection that specifically addresses issues of race).

2. One example is the work of Heinlein, one of the "classic" science fiction writers, whose work inspires controversial reactions. Some argue his work is not foundationalist; others (such as Delany) point to social and political activities that place his narratives within a racist framework of thinking.

3. In *Colonialism/Postcolonialism*, Loomba points out that even though different forms of colonial encounters between various countries have existed in history, modern European colonialism was "distinctive and by far the most extensive" (xiii), and its ideological and economic/political aftermath is an irreversible element of international relations as well as national identities.

4. See Inderpal Grewal and Caren Kaplan, Introduction to *Scattered Hegemonies*, for a discussion of the problematic model of "center vs. periphery" (especially 9–12).

5. One example of this sort of narrative that is wedded to liberal ways of dealing with difference would be Amy Thomson's novels *The Color of Distance* (1995) and *Through Alien Eyes* (1999). The narratives start out as progressive deconstructions of the self/other binary, only to reestablish it in the end.

6. See Frances Bonner, "Difference and Desire, Slavery and Seduction: Octavia Butler's Xenogenesis"; Teri Ann Doerksen, "Octavia E. Butler: Parables of Race and Difference"; Maghu Dubey, "Folk and Urban Communities in African-American Women's Fiction: Octavia Butler's *Parable of the Sower*"; Frances Smith Foster, "Octavia Butler's Black Female Future Fiction"; Sandra Y. Govan, "Connection, Links, and Extended Networks:

Patterns in Octavia Butler's Science Fiction"; Michelle Erica Green, "There Goes the Neighborhood. Octavia Butler's Demand for Diversity in Utopias;" Ruth Salvaggio, "Octavia Butler and the Black Science-Fiction Heroine" and "Octavia Butler"; and Thelma J. Shinn, "The Wise Witches: Black Women Mentors in the Fiction of Octavia E. Butler."

7. "Embedded in the tale of the diaspora is a symbolic revolt against the nation-state, and for this reason the diaspora holds a considerable significance. It suggests a transnational dimension to black identity: the African diaspora was a human necklace strung together by a thread known as the slave trade, a thread thrown across America with little regards to national boundaries" (Hanchard 238).

8. In "Subaltern Studies in a U.S. Frame," Eva Cherniavsky discusses Butler's *Dawn* in the context of subaltern studies, which she believes to be a useful theoretical framework in the attempt to theorize United States imperialism.

9. I use the term "anticolonial" since it links the academic "postcolonial debate" that takes part in both the First and the Third World with political and activist anti-globalization work. Loomba references Ella Shohat, who points out in "Notes on the 'Post-Colonial'" that the term "postcolonial" is widely accepted in academic discourses partly because it is not as political as "imperialism" or "geopolitics." The danger, argue critics like Grewal and Kaplan, lies in a debate in which the "circulation of the term 'postcolonial' has transformed a complex, historically specific concept into a literary and disciplinary signal for what comes after colonialism," instead of recognizing it "as a term that positions cultural production in the fields of transnational economic relations and diasporic identity constructions" (*Scattered Hegemonies* 15), an argument

which Gayatri Chakravorty Spivak also makes in *Post-Colonial Reason.* "Anticolonial" describes a political as much as a theoretical position, and includes the texts of a "feminism of women of color in the United States" whose links to postcolonial studies are rarely considered.

10. For a discussion of postcolonial feminist thought and Third World Feminism critiques, see M. Jacqui Alexander and Chandra Talpade Mohanty, eds., *Feminist Genealogies, Colonial Legacies, Democratic Futures;* Angelika Bammer, ed., *Displacements: Cultural Identities in Question;* Inderpal Grewal and Caren Kaplan, eds., *Scattered Hegemonies;* Mary E. John, *Discrepant Dislocations: Feminism, Theory, and Postcolonial Histories;* Caren Kaplan, *Questions of Travel: Postmodern Discourses of Displacement;* Anne McClintock, Aamir Mufti and Ella Shohat, eds., *Dangerous Liaisons: Gender, Nation, and Postcolonial Perspectives;* Chandra Talpade Mohanty and Biddy Martin, "Feminist Politics: What's Home Got to Do with It?"; Chandra Talpade Mohanty, Ann Russo, and Lourdes Torres, eds., *Third World Women and the Politics of Feminism,* especially Mohanty's "Cartographies of Struggle: Third World Women and the Politics of Feminism" and "Under Western Eyes: Feminist Scholarship and Colonial Discourse"; Uma Narayan, *Dislocating Cultures: Identities, Traditions, and Third World Feminism;* Rajeswari Sunder Rajan, *Real and Imagined Women: Gender, Culture and Postcolonialism;* Chela Sandoval, *Methodology of the Oppressed;* Trinh T. Minh-ha, *Woman, Native, Other.*

11. One could argue that since the colonial discourse is hegemonic, everyone must participate in it. However, Spivak argues that the subaltern— the colonized woman in particular— is explicitly *silent,* even though she is the subject of colonial conflict. Bhabha's concept evokes the *active* participation—the immediate contact with and response to—the colonizer, which Spivak argues excludes large groups of people affected by colonial negotiations.

12. See John Flodstrom's excellent analysis of colonialism in Robert Silverberg's novels that displays a critical awareness of representations of colonialism in science fiction that differs from other popular texts by authors such as Heinlein, "Enlightening the Alien Savages: Colonialism in the Novels of Robert Silverberg."

13. In "Race and Subjectivity in Science Fiction," Ellen Bishop argues that the destruction of Earth represents a geographical manifestation of history destroyed. The displacement is based on the fact that existing power structures are destroyed with it (Bishop 92). In Butler's work, the constant physical transformation/destruction of Earth represents the (often painful) restructuring of social power relations.

14. This redeeming aspect of the Oankali—their embracing of difference and the transcendence of hierarchies— sets them apart from the classical colonizer, such as the Missionaries, and is extensively discussed in Chapter 2.

15. A closer examination of the Kohns' different strategies of resistance would be interesting, but I want to concentrate on the figure of Alanna. Another author who cleverly problematizes issues of power within colonizing processes is Nalo Hopkinson. In *Midnight Robber* (2000), she creates complex figurations between exiled humans on a prison planet and its native species, the douens. The relationship of the descendents of black Caribbean people who colonized a planet to the species they colonized is complex and at times disturbing in its reproduction of power relations by a people formerly disempowered themselves.

16. See Grewal and Kaplan 7–8 and Loomba 173–83 for discussions of the

concept of *hybridity* in postcolonial discourse.

17. See Loomba for a discussion of the problems involved with ideologies of exclusion in much of anticolonial discourse, such as nationalism and pan-nationalism (184-215).

18. This discourse dominated, for example, Great Britain's dealings with Indian women, who had to be "saved" by the Raj from patriarchal customs such as widow burning. Spivak in "Can the Subaltern Speak?" criticizes both colonial power and anticolonial resistance for silencing the woman as subject in the debate surrounding *sati*. She views the colonized woman as positioned between patriarchal oppression by her culture and oppression by the colonizer. This strategy of using women as symbols in conflicts between patriarchal opponents is reflected in the way the United States government co-opted Afghan women's oppression by the Taliban as a justification for the war on Afghanistan in 2002. See the speech of Laura Bush, then First Lady, at the United Nations Commission on the Status of Women on International Women's Day in 2002 at [http://www.whitehouse.gov/news/releases/2002/03/20020308-2.html] or at [http://www.un.int/usa/02_030.htm].

19. In her *Parable* novels, Butler extensively criticizes Christian traditional values and mythology. She creates an elaborate new belief system, Earthseed, as an alternative spiritual system and the basis for a new society. These utopian concepts counteract patriarchal mythology: "God *is* Change, and in the end, God *does* prevail. But we have something to say about the whens and the whys of that end" (*Sower* 269). See my article "'All that you touch you change': Utopian Desire and the Concept of Change in Octavia Butler's *Parable of the Sower* and *Parable of the Talents*"; and Teri Ann Doerksen, "Octavia E. Butler: Parables of Race and Difference." Next to motifs from

the Christian belief system, Butler alludes to Western fairy tales, such as in "Bloodchild," which includes elements of the German folk tales of "Rumpelstielzchen" and "Rapunzel" and the French "Beauty and the Beast," where parents lose their children to shady creatures after making a deal with them: ". . . my mother promised T'Gatoi one of her children. [. . . S]he came back to my mother to collect what she probably saw as her just reward for her hard work" ("Bloodchild" 8).

20. In Jewish folklore, Lilith was Adam's first wife, who was, like him, created from dust. Her refusal to submit to Adam (symbolized in her refusal to lie beneath him during sexual intercourse) ignited God's fury, and she was banned from Paradise. She fled to the Red Sea, where she lived with demons. God punished her with the daily death of one hundred of her children. Lilith and her demon-children in traditional folklore are responsible for men's erotic dreams, as well as for the death of male infants—her revenge for her dead children. The story of Lilith was removed from the Bible, but can be found in the Talmud (see B. Walker 541-42).

21. Butler appropriates Christian imagery throughout her work. In her portrayal of Anyanwu as the founding mother of the Patternist society in *Wild Seed,* Butler directly quotes the figure of the Madonna, and the conventional racism that it implies: "The portrait was a black madonna and child right down to Anyanwu's too-clear, innocent-seeming eyes. Strangers were moved to comment on the likeness. . . . [Some] were deeply offended, believing that someone actually had tried to portray the Virgin and Child as 'black savages'" (*Seed* 142). Anyanwu and Doro, a bodiless immortal spirit, at the same time are the "Black Adam and Eve" (Govan 84), the founders of a new people. Anyanwu is not made of his rib, though—she is fatherless, "wild seed." In her, the shapeshifter, the myth

of the Mother-Goddess with her infinite forms, finds an origin, whereas the masculine divine principle that Doro represents fails. With Anyanwu and Doro, Butler also introduces elements of African mythology. Doro, in Nubian, means "the direction from which the sun comes, East," whereas in the language of the Igbo Anyanwu means "sun;" the figure of Anyanwu is modeled after an Onitsha-priestess in Igbo mythology. According to the myth, Atagbusi was a shapeshifter, who aided her people with her medical healing powers (see Butler in Kenan, 499–500).

22. This epistemic privileging of the slave perspective is also the basis for feminist standpoint theory, such as Patricia Hill Collins's concept of black women's standpoint, which she introduces in *Black Feminist Thought* and further develops in *Fighting Words.* See also Donna Haraway's theory of situated knowledges in "Situated Knowledges."

23. Even though the Missionaries' reverence for the "One" also corresponds with Judaic and Islamic monotheism, they are distinctly "coded" as Christian, so their name reflects the Christian tradition of systematically converting "heathens."

24. Teri Ann Doerksen's "Octavia E. Butler: Parables of Race and Difference" discusses in detail the colonial oppression suffered by the humans at the hands of the alien natives of the destination planet in "Bloodchild." She convincingly argues that in the short story, "Butler has highlighted the racial problems evident in contemporary culture by creating a close allegorical parallel, a parable, of Western culture, replacing our dominant racial paradigm with another in order to create an awareness of oppression in a reader blinded by familiarity" (26). However, Doerksen does not credit Butler for the subtle complications of the narrative. She observes that "the human colony has tried to escape its 'otherness' as

defined by Terran prejudice and has instead stepped into a closely parallel situation of domination by an alien race" (25), yet she fails to mention the hostility the humans bring with them, their refusal to engage in negotiations with the native alien race. Thus the alien tells the human child: "We saw them as people and gave them the Preserve when they still tried to kill us as worms" (25). The containment of the humans on Preserves, of course, echoes the genocide of Native American tribes and the banishment of the few survivors onto reservations. The complication (and historical irony) added by Butler is that it is the *arriving* people who are colonized—the image of British royal subjects or American "Patriots" on reservations is quite powerful. The oscillating slave-master-slave positions in "Bloodchild" are mirrored in the colonizing aspirations of the Missionaries in *Survivor,* who flee persecution by the Patternists and end up trying to oppress others—ultimately failing in their attempt to do so.

2. The Alien in Us

1. See Val Plumwood, *Feminism and the Mastery of Nature,* in which she discusses the dominating character of Western dualisms. Dualisms construct identities similar to those in Hegel's model of master and slave, in which the master denies his dependence on the slave's existence and bases his worldview on his own experiences (Plumwood 42–68).

2. One narrative element in which both of these contradictory themes are manifested is in the ambivalent role of the Oankali, the alien species in the *Xenogenesis* series. While I examine their oppressive presence as colonizers in Chapter 1, in Chapter 2, I focus on their alternative, anti-essentialist logic of identity, which allows for a progressive rethinking of difference and identity. Butler resolves these contra-

dictions less on a theoretical level—it is precisely the ambivalence of these relations that she emphasizes—than through narrative closure: through plot developments and the characters' relationships with each other.

3. The fundamental conflict of the human as creator of independently acting creatures was introduced into English-speaking literature with Mary Shelley's *Frankenstein*, first published in 1818. The ethical question of the "becoming human" of machines did not begin to be frequently discussed in science fiction literature until the 1950s (see Scholes and Rabkin 168, 180–83). In film, this issue was problematized as early as 1926, in Fritz Lang's *Metropolis*.

4. In her early work, Butler anticipates the current revived debate on humanness and the definition of human rights. For example, Judith Butler, in her explorations in *Undoing Gender* of "livable lives" and "unlivable lives," which are governed by norms, returns to the fundamental question of what constitutes the category "human" in the face of global violence, terrorism, and racial, sexual, and gender oppression.

5. Examples include Robin Roberts, *A New Species: Gender and Science in Science Fiction;* Sarah Lefanu, *In the Chinks of the World Machine;* and Marleen Barr, *Future Females: A Critical Anthology, Lost in Space: Probing Feminist Science Fiction and Beyond,* and *Alien to Femininity.*

6. This juxtaposition is discernible in the violence that Lilith encounters from humans she "wakes," and is staggering in *Clay's Ark*, where the animal-like mutants are contrasted with the extreme violence of the "car families," who in a mind-numbing scene rape one of the girl protagonists to death. As I discuss elsewhere, in *Parable of the Sower* Butler portrays human violence uncurbed by social control, and in *Parable of the Talents* she presents

social control based on hatred of difference (see Melzer, "'All that you touch you change': Utopian Desire and the Concept of Change in Octavia Butler's *Parable of the Sower* and *Parable of the Talents*").

7. In "Identity, Meaning, and the African American," Michael Hanchard quotes Ellen Rooney as defining "liberal pluralism in its critical form as a 'heterogeneous yet hegemonic discourse'" and adds: "It masks struggle for voice inherent in symbolic encounters with a myth of egalitarian representation" (232).

8. Only since the New Wave of the 1960s and 1970s has a more complex approach to un-humans appeared in science fiction literature (and, in the 1970s, in film), in which the perspective of the other becomes part of the narrative's structure. It is interesting that in the late 1990s a backlash has taken place, especially in mainstream Hollywood films, that returns to the tradition of constructing the other as evil and a threat to humankind. This backlash can be seen in films such as *Independence Day, Starship Troopers,* and *Pitch Black*, some of which stand in the tradition of the *Alien* series, which links horror with science fiction. But even science fiction movies that tap into the adventure-tale marketing pool, such as the *Star Wars* film *The Phantom Menace* (1999), are surprisingly racist in their depiction of aliens. In the *Star Wars* film, Jar Jar, the gentle but rather stupid alien with a Caribbean-English accent, is a racist representation.

9. The typical science fiction themes of colonization and war, which—despite *Star Trek*'s prime directive— are still prevalent in popular science fiction, are heavily criticized by Butler.

10. See Wolmark's *Aliens and Others* for a discussion of this scene in regard to Butler's use of gendered language: the alien immediately is referred to as "he" since power is associated with a patriarchal order (Wolmark 31).

11. This problem of being forced into the position of "collaborator" echoes conflicts within colonized/occupied peoples' identities and their relationship to the colonizers.

12. Multiplicity is also the main component of the subjectivity developed in Jane Flax's *Disputed Subjects*. According to Flax, a person perceives herself, not as one constant personality, who gradually develops with a basic core as an ultimate reference point, but as *being* more than one, echoing Trinh Minh-ha's "infinite layers that form 'I'" (Trinh, *Woman, Native, Other* 94). In correlation with Trinh, Flax locates political agency within this structure of identity: "I believe a unitary self is unnecessary, impossible, and a dangerous illusion. Only multiple subjects can invent ways to struggle against domination that will not merely recreate it" (93).

13. The Western subject's fear of being absorbed by some consciousness with no separate identity (and thus no difference) is prevalent in science fiction film as well. This fear is manifested in the Borg in *Star Trek—Next Generation*, who attempt to assimilate humanity into their collective in the film *Star Trek—First Contact*.

14. The "essence" of the Oankali is not based on a homeland/place or on an original form, but transcends geographical and genetic boundaries. This fact gives the term "essence" a new meaning that is derived, not from stagnation and stability, but rather from transformation and flexibility.

15. Concerns with the simultaneous ideological construction and appropriation of difference by dominant culture are also part of feminist postcolonial theory. Anne McClintock, Aamir Mufti, and Ella Shohat warn of the depoliticizing effect of the new hype around "multiculturalism" in their introduction to *Dangerous Liaisons:* "The ever present danger in the formulation of multicultural agendas has been the risk of sliding into forms of liberal pluralism to which existing cultural regimes can easily prove hospitable" because those forms are not threatening (5).

16. In *Clay's Ark* and the two *Parable* novels, she also emphasizes class and its connections to race.

17. Teri Ann Doerksen analyzes some of the analogies between science fiction metaphors and race relations in "Octavia E. Butler: Parables of Race and Difference."

18. Butler destabilizes behavior based on gender ideologies that we perceive as "natural" when she constructs Kohns' behavior in *Survivor* as guided by the color of their fur, rather than their gender. While male humans try to protect the "weaker sex" (i.e. women), Kohns try to protect their "nonfighters," who are Kohns with little or no blue in their fur (see *Survivor* 125). Both categories are disclosed as constructed.

19. Even though telepathic abilities are not externally visible markers of difference, their categorization is mirrored in external consequences. Also, the ability of the telepaths to communicate mentally with each other makes the "passing" of mutes as telepathic nearly impossible, just as passing for a person of a different race is made difficult by the visibility of skin color as an external marker.

20. The traditional reception of science fiction is apparent in Robert Scholes and Eric Rabkin's history of the genre. In a discussion of the hero's relationship to the father of the heroine, they refer to her as the "sexual object" (184) that makes possible within the world of science fiction a reconstitution of order "that the father figure and the hero share" (184). The authors then conclude: "Hence, the imaginary being reminds *us* of *our* ambivalences toward *our* father figures, those who stand for the rules of society which, as *we* are growing up, *we* question" (185, emphasis mine). The "we" is obviously aimed at a male audience.

21. Only Amber in *Patternmaster* is openly bisexual; the shape-shifter Anyanwu in *Wild Seed* partners with women when she takes on a male form, and Lauren in *Talents* admits a sexual attraction to a woman but does not act on it.

22. See Chapter 6 for a queer reading of Butler's narratives.

23. Butler criticizes gendered anti-colonial, nationalist rhetoric, as well as colonial ideologies, that treat colonialism as a struggle between colonizing *men* and colonized *men,* and in which native women become objects/symbols of the contested territory.

24. In Butler's work, aggression, and the potential for violence, is a male-defined characteristic. Lilith's son, Akin, who is the first male construct child, is a threat to the genetic exchange between humans and Oankali. He carries the (male human) potential to be aggressive, which, together with his Oankali abilities, could be lethal (see *Rites* 9-10). The Oankali make biology responsible for men's higher level of aggression, whereas, as Green observes, "the women attribute [the higher level of the human contradiction in males] to conditioning that trains women to demonstrate their skills through nurture rather than force" (186). This provocative and unresolved contradiction within her narratives is typical for Butler.

25. Tension between formal marriage, representative of social order, on the one hand, and personal independence, on the other, is often an issue in Butler's narratives. Anyanwu in *Wild Seed* and Mary in *Mind of My Mind* are being forced into marriage by Doro; Amber decides against marriage in *Patternmaster;* and in *Parable of the Sower* and *Parable of the Talents,* marriage is depicted as an outdated social custom that is modeled after the (white) upper middle class and is especially restrictive for women (*Sower* 79-80). In the *Xenogenesis* series, mar-

riage becomes obsolete—bonds are defined through family relations and reproduction. In *Survivor,* reproduction is primary: Alanna becomes "automatically" the wife of Diut, a Tehkohn, once she expects their child; only after conception do partners enter a monogamous relationship. The ceremony to welcome the child into the community is simultaneously the parents' wedding ritual (*Survivor* 179-80).

26. Butler further destabilizes binary categories of gender/sexuality through Anyanwu's androgyny in *Wild Seed* and a three-gender/sex system in the *Xenogenesis* series, as well as through the concept of shape-shifting in both.

27. See Elyce Helford's analysis of "Bloodchild," " 'Would you really rather die than bear my young?' " for a detailed discussion of Butler's treatment of differences based on gender, race, and species.

28. See Wolmark for an elaboration of the lack of portraits of homosexuality in *Xenogenesis* (*Aliens and Others* 37).

29. The only boundary established by Oankali is through smell: kinship groups differ in their smell. Within the kinship group, individual families possess their own distinct smell, developed during the time the family is founded, which finds its origin with the ooloi. These differences function less as exclusion than as a connection; the effects of the smells are mainly affirmative.

30. The crossing of sensual boundaries that enables (or rather forces) an inclusive dealing with difference is echoed in the symptom of "sharing" in the *Parable* novels. A neurological disorder, induced by drug abuse by the parents, transmits any physical condition (pain or pleasure) that the sharer witnesses, no matter what her/his relationship is to the person experiencing the pain/pleasure.

31. See Wolmark for a discussion of the gender-specific violence the enforced insemination of Lilith represents (*Aliens and Others* 35).

32. See Angela Davis's *Women, Race, and Class* for a discussion of the construction of sexual violence between the white man (slave owner) and the black woman (slave) as racial power over black people.

33. Ana Castillo points out the complexity of the identity commonly described as Chicana or Latina: "The woman in the United States who is politically self-described as Chicana, mestiza in terms of race, and Latina or Hispanic in regards to her Spanish-speaking heritage, and who numbers in the millions in the United States cannot be summarized nor neatly categorized" (1).

34. It is important to remember the different dislocations produced by different trajectories of migration, a point that sometimes recedes into the background of Davies's use of the term "migratory subjectivity," which emphasizes the experience of dislocation per se as its defining factor (Davies, *Black Women*).

35. The concept of nomadic subjectivity is not restricted to physical migration/travel, but is a metaphor that refers to a "critical consciousness that resists settling into socially coded modes of thought and behavior" (Braidotti, *Nomadic Subjects* 5).

36. As Davies puts it for the African Diaspora, "The political basis of identity formation is a central issue in all of these interrogations. . . . [T]he reconstruction of 'Africa' as homeland occurred, also for management of reality" (Davies, *Black Women* 10).

37. Two examples of cybernetic organisms are those imagined by Joanna Russ in *The Female Man* and Marge Piercy in *He, She, and It*.

38. Other writers who problematize genetic engineering include Rebecca Ore and Ann Thomson.

39. It is interesting that the protagonists in Butler's work who come the closest to the "technical" definition of the cyborg as a half-human are nonfemale: Akin, Lilith's first construct son in *Adulthood Rites*, and a later child of hers, Jodahs, the first construct ooloi—the Oankali's third gender. Both possess both human and alien gene material. In "Bloodchild" the connection between aliens and humans is established through a boy who significantly inhabits the gender role usually prescribed to "woman."

40. In "Cyborg Feminism: The Science Fiction of Octavia E. Butler and Gloria Anzaldúa," Catherine S. Ramirez gives a good overview of boundary transgressions inherent in the writings of Octavia Butler, Gloria Anzaldúa, and Donna Haraway.

41. See "The Wise Witches" by Thelma Shinn in *Conjuring* for an article that argues for elements of conjuring in Butler. In contrast, Madhu Dubey, in "Folk and Urban Communities in African-American Women's Fiction: Octavia Butler's *Parable of the Sower*," argues that Butler actually counters culturally exclusive notions of black women's subject positions, a point I also explore in "'All that you touch you change': Utopian Desire and the Concept of Change in Octavia Butler's *Parable of the Sower* and *Parable of the Talents*."

42. In *Fighting Words: Black Women and the Search for Justice*, Patricia Hill Collins develops the idea that complex demographics, based on race and class as well as gender, shape knowledge. For a detailed discussion of the relationship between gender and racial/class consciousness, see Matisons, Chapter 3, in which she further differentiates the "achieved" standpoint into "immediate" and "mediated" standpoints.

43. Classical Freudian theory, which rests on the white, bourgeois model of the nuclear family whose gender roles are based in social power, has been challenged by critical race theory. The American slave family is one case study where gender roles (father/mother)

do not correspond to classical Freudian family structures since the slave father is not legally and socially the father (and often not part of the family as such), and frequently the father is the white slave owner. Butler's narratives contribute to the debate that destabilizes traditional approaches to psychoanalysis.

44. See Scholes and Rabkin for a historical discussion of the father-son narrative in science fiction (165–83).

45. In "Posthuman Bodies and Agency in Octavia Butler's *Xenogenesis*," Naomi Jacobs discusses the un-human, alien bodies in Butler's narratives in the context of the discourse on the "posthuman" and reads them as a critique of the humanist subject.

46. The secondary female characters in Butler's writing often mirror the tense relationships/situations in which the protagonists find themselves. They complete the characters of the protagonists, produce contradictions, or serve as explanations for circumstances that are challenged by the protagonists (see F.S. Foster 40–42).

47. Examples of "actual" cyborgs in feminist science fiction may be found in Marge Piercy's *He, She, and It;* Vonda McIntyre's short stories, such as "Fireflood"; and Joanna Russ's *The Female Man.*

Introduction to Part II

1. Feminist scientists have shown how scientific theories and methodologies, instead of being neutral, construct sexual, racial, and class differences by interpreting biology in connection with existing ideologies. See Ruth Bleier, *Science and Gender: A Critique of Biology and Its Theories on Women;* Anne Fausto-Sterling, *Myths of Gender: Biological Theories about Women and Men* and *Sexing the Body;* Donna Haraway, *Primate Visions;* Sandra Harding, *The Science Question in Feminism;* and Evelyn Fox Keller, *Reflections on Gender and Science.*

2. David Bordwell and Kristin Thompson, in *Film Art: An Introduction,* list and explains different filming techniques and their role in the viewer's interaction with the film. Also see Timothy Corrigan and Patricia White, *The Film Experience: An Introduction.*

3. I am referring here to the cinematic privileging of the "male gaze" in narrative films, which psychoanalytic feminist film theories problematize. The most frequently cited article in this context is Laura Mulvey's "Visual Pleasure and Narrative Cinema," published in 1975, in which she introduces her psychoanalytical analysis of traditional narrative film. Mulvey argues that "mainstream film coded the erotic into the language of the dominant patriarchal order" (30), locking the image of woman into the fantasizing gaze of the male spectator. Mulvey's theory has been extensively criticized for its exclusive psychoanalytic framework, which does not account for identities outside of the heterosexual, white matrix, yet the idea of a privileged gaze (i.e. a privileged identity within the audience) is still a useful concept within film studies.

4. One example of positions of counter-readings is the lesbian viewer, who resists the heterosexual structure of the narrative. This point is developed in Shameem Kabir, *Daughters of Desire: Lesbian Representations in Film;* Patricia White, *unInvited: Classical Hollywood Cinema and Lesbian Representability;* and Tamsin Wilton, ed., *Immortal, Invisible: Lesbians and the Moving Image.*

5. In his study of British youth subcultures, *Subculture: The Meaning of Style,* Dick Hebdige examines how groups of young people appropriate mundane objects of mainstream culture and, by giving them specific meanings, create styles (such as the safety pin in punk culture) that reflect their subcultural affiliation and posi-

tion them in opposition to bourgeois values. Once the style of a subculture is recognized by mainstream culture, it becomes subject to incorporation and thus reassimilation into dominant values, since it represents opposition and threat to dominant culture as well as the potential to be commercially marketed for profit as the latest trend.

3. Technoscience's Stepdaughter

1. *Alien* was directed by Ridley Scott, *Aliens* by James Cameron, *Alien³* by David Fincher, and *Alien Resurrection* by the French director Jean-Pierre Jeunet. In 2003 the director's cut of *Alien* was released.

2. Other genres the movies borrow from are the action/war movie (*Aliens*) and the disaster movie (*Alien Resurrection*) (see Newman 37).

3. In "Feminism and Cultural Studies," Anne Balsamo discusses feminist strategies within cultural studies: the significance of feminist reading and writing practices that challenge existing systems of meaning, the analysis of the politics of representation (such as in relation to social gender roles) as well as the creation of new forms of representation (which include the appropriation of existing images), and an examination of technology's relationship to the body, in both its discursive quality and its material reality.

4. A feminist account of the history of Western scientific thought conveys how the Scientific Revolution and later the Enlightenment, both of which took place during the 500 years of the European colonial project, produced scientific categories based on, and confirming, power relations. Women's lack of subject status was explained by her innate "irrationality." Because of her reproductive abilities, a women's body was perceived to be closer to nature and thus separate from Man. The exploitation of people of color was also justified by their inability to be ratio-

nal subjects. While women retained human status (even though a lesser one) through their relation to the white man, people of color were classified as "animals" and thus retained un-human status. Since machines shared nature's irrationality, women and people of color were placed ideologically closer to machines than to the "human" (i.e. white man). See Valerie Plumwood, *Feminism and the Mastery of Nature,* and Londa Schiebinger, *Nature's Body.*

5. The alien figure in science fiction film takes on the form either of invading masses of horrific, strange creatures (reminiscent of the immigrant alien, the descendent of the colonized, who evades industrialized societies) or of an individual messiah character who enlightens the humans it encounters (similar to the noble savage). The threat of the alien can lie both in its visibility, in its extreme difference from "Us," and in the opposite, "its invisibility, its outward resemblance to Us, or its capacity to mimic the human form. . . . [T]hese undesirable aliens are invading our territory and undermining our culture and way of life" (Kuhn, "Border Crossing" 17). Also see Geoff King and Tanya Krzywinska, *Science Fiction Cinema* (30-37), and Ziauddin Sardar's introduction in *Aliens R Us: The Other in Science Fiction Cinema* (6, 12).

6. The release of the director's cut of *Alien,* twenty-four years after its original release, speaks to its status as "classic."

7. The approach to feminism in the *Alien* movies has from the beginning dominated discussion of the series, with a shared interest in how feminist issues are represented in popular culture. Analysis has focused mainly on Ripley's role as the "hero" and on the recurrent imagery of the maternal in the representations of the alien (see Scobie 81-82). Also see Catherine Belling, "'Where Meaning Collapses': *Alien* and the Outlawing

of the Female Hero"; Rebecca Bell-Metereau, "Woman: The Other Alien in *Alien*"; Ilsa Bick, "'Well I Guess I Must Make You Nervous': Woman and the Space of *Alien³*"; Barbara Creed, "*Alien* and the Monstrous-Feminine"; Ros Jennings, "Desire and Design—Ripley Undressed"; James H. Kavanaugh, "Feminism, Humanism, and Science in *Alien*"; Judith Newton, "Feminism and Anxiety in *Alien*"; Janice Hocker Rushing, "Evolution of the 'New Frontier' in *Alien* and *Aliens*: Patriarchal Co-optation of the Feminine Archetype"; Mark Schemanske, "Working for the Company. Patriarchal Legislation of the Maternal in *Alien³*"; Vivian Sobchack, "The Virginity of Astronauts: Sex and the Science Fiction Film"; and Robert Torry, "Awakening to the Other: Feminism and the Ego-Ideal in *Alien*." The one book published that is devoted exclusively to Ripley in the four *Alien* films, *Alien Woman: The Making of Lt. Ellen Ripley* by Ximena C. Gallardo and C. Jason Smith, also works within a feminist framework.

8. *Alien Resurrection* is distinct from the other films in its borrowing of cyberpunk features. Ripley finds (at times unwilling) allies in the space pirates who come aboard the military craft, carrying illegal human freight for the scientists' experimentation. The renegades' position is outside the official relations of technoscience (United Military Systems, which is reminiscent of cyberpunk's capitalist companies). Like the console cowboys of cyberpunk, they rob and profit from United Military Systems but are not politically organizing against them. (Call, the android, has a personal mission—having been programmed to be an "asshole," that is, compliant with humanism—to destroy the system's deadly project, and initially she rejects Ripley.) The film's relationship to cyberpunk lies mainly in its emphasis on technology and the knowledge the outlaws have

of it. Call's talent with computer technology is central to the narrative, and Ripley's inhuman strength—gained through biological enhancements produced by the cross-cloning with the alien—constructs her as a high-tech female warrior, similar to William Gibson's Molly in the cyberpunk classic *Neuromancer*. Although the film is obviously produced within the visual aesthetic legacy of cyberpunk movies such as *Blade Runner*, it also reflects the influence of other genres in both literature and film. Ripley's outfit is reminiscent of both a Klingon woman and Xena, and her deadly skills echo those of Joanna Russ's Jael in the radical feminist science fiction novel *The Female Man*. Her genetic "contamination" aligns her with popular culture icons such as Spider-Man and Spawn, as Michael Eaton points out: "This is the film's structural equivalent of a radioactive spider's bite: the origin of the Super-Hero" (9). If there is one consistency within the series, it is its constant shifting in terms of genre, which assures that it meets the expectations of a historically situated audience. "In its necessary impulse to remake itself every few years the *Alien* series must continually plunder other genres, other modes of story organisation. It must itself embark upon a process of hybridisation" (Eaton 9).

9. The primary example in science fiction is Mary Shelley's Frankenstein, whose scientific curiosity (and self-interest) leads to the creation of a monster who has no place in the social order.

10. Jennifer Gonzalez differentiates between "an organic cyborg [that] can be defined as a monster of multiple species, [and] a mechanical cyborg [that] can be considered a techno-human amalgamation" (268). In *The Cyborg Handbook*, Chris Hables Gray, Heidi Figueroa-Sarriera, and Steven Mentor mention various subcategories

within cyborg terminology, such as "neo-, proto-, multi-, ultra-, semi-, hyper-, retro-, omni-, pseudo-, mega-, and meta-cyborgs" (4).

11. *Alien Resurrection,* like the trilogy, is obsessed with birth metaphors. The tank in which Ripley is developing fits into the visual symbolism of wombs and birth chambers that runs through all four movies.

12. Sardar argues that the presentation of "monstrous races" in science fiction cinema, which is largely a Western film genre, mirrors classical and medieval tales of encounters of Western civilized cultures with other peoples, and in general retells the story of the West's superiority: ". . . the monstrous races . . . are none other than the extraordinary beings that decorate the sets of *Star Wars.* The imaginative aliens of 'a galaxy far, far away' have their inception in the anthropophagi, troglodytes, the dog-headed people and the beings with no feet but appendages so profuse they can function as sunshades when they lie on their back" ("Introduction" 8–9).

13. In the first and third movies, the enemy is an individual monster, enhanced and complicated by Ripley's monstrous pregnancy in *Alien³,* whereas in the second and fourth films, the terror derives from the immense mass and high number of aliens. *Aliens,* especially, is reminiscent of a war movie, with marines as main actors and military-style action as the main narrative drive—a feature extremely reduced in *Alien³,* in which the battle again consists of outwitting the alien and destroying it with primitive weapons.

14. The art of H. R. Giger, the designer of the alien, is known for its combination of mechanical and organic structures that create disturbing sexual images. See John Cobbs's "*Alien* as an Abortion Parable" for a discussion of misogynist depictions of sexual encounters between women and monsters and between women and machines, which, together with an obsessive repetition of birth scenes, dominate Giger's art.

15. This reference to cultural fears and anxieties related to the repressed, the unrecognizable, and the unknown, in opposition to the rational (male-identified) self, presents a moment of reflexivity usually more commonly found within science fiction literature since science fiction film is restricted by its producers' drive to find a mass audience to generate financial returns.

16. See Ros Jennings's "Desire and Design—Ripley Undressed" for a discussion of the complex, crossover gender construction of Ripley as female hero in the trilogy.

17. Both Eve VIII and the woman in *Species* are products of technoscience—either androids or genetically manipulated humans. The woman in *Species* starts out as the victim of crazy scientists who mix her genes with those of aliens. Once she is developed, however, she is pure evil, and the spectator is discouraged from identifying with her.

18. See Sheree Thomas, ed., *Dark Matter: A Century of Speculative Fiction from the African Diaspora;* Elisabeth Anne Leonard, ed., *Into Darkness Peering: Race and Color in the Fantastic;* and Ziauddin Sardar and Sean Cubitt, eds., *Aliens R Us: The Other in Science Fiction Film.*

19. The issue of the "passing" of aliens and/or machines as humans is a familiar theme in science fiction and is repeatedly taken up by mainstream science fiction films and television. Just as this analysis examines the dangers of appropriation of subcultural elements, an examination of the theme of passing in science fiction movies might reveal an appropriation of a historical and political phenomenon that is part of the lives of people of color. Thus the movie *Gattaca* is sometimes understood as creating an analogy to black

people's passing with its protagonist's attempts to "pass" as a genetically perfected human. Instead, the film fails in various ways to portray contemporary race relations. The racial analogy is deflated by the presence of black people in positions of power (and by the fact that all the janitors are white men), and in the end it is the individual perseverance of the hero that enables him to fulfill his dreams, depoliticizing the issue of racism. Thus I want to emphasize that I am opposed to a conflation of sexual and racial difference when discussing Call's "passing" as human; I merely want to point to the kinds of complex representations that inform cyborg feminism's analysis of boundary transgressions.

20. For feminist examinations of technology (and its meanings) as gendered, see Judy Wajcman, *Feminism Confronts Technology,* and Joan Rothschild, ed., *Machina ex Dea: Feminist Perspectives on Technology.*

21. It is interesting that neither in *Aliens* nor in *Alien³* is there a computer that is at the center of control, even though in the third movie the computer is the only connection to The Company.

22. Donna Haraway discusses the products of technoscience with the metaphor of Oncomouse™ in *Modest Witness.*

23. See Springer for an excellent analysis of *Eve of Destruction,* 114–17.

24. See Patricia Melzer and Shelley Price, eds., "Gender and Technology in Science Fiction Film," special issue of *Femspec,* for articles that problematize the gendered representations of technology.

25. In "Psycho-Cybernetics in Films of the 1990s," Claudia Springer points out how, in the mid-1990s, the hypermasculine cyborg's "relentlessly destructive power eventually became a predictable cliché and object of parody. Its ability to fascinate had run its course" (204). Instead, in response to science fiction literature's new hip subgenre,

cyberpunk, in films the "rampaging muscle-bound cyborgs were replaced by slim young men and women jacked into cyberspace" (204), such as in *Johnny Mnemonic* (1995), *Strange Days* (1995), and *Hackers* (1995). The cyborg returned in the third *Terminator* movie, *Terminator 3,* in 2003 to challenge a destructive female cyborg. Arnold Schwarzenegger's performance as a rather aging terminator reflects the waning influence of the protofascist male cyborgian body as a representation of posthuman embodiment. In Chapter 4, I discuss the changing representations of embodiment in *The Matrix.*

26. In "'Where Meaning Collapses': *Alien* and the Outlawing of the Female Hero," Catherine Belling takes Julia Kristeva's definition of the abject as the basis for her analysis of the movie, which firmly places the otherness in the film into the maternal, the realm of the mother. As Belling explains, according to Kristeva the subject can maintain its illusion of wholeness within the symbolic order only by rejecting the abject, which then, at the same time as it threatens the subject, defines it. As a site of primary rejection, the maternal is understood as a realm of the abject. Quoting Kristeva, Belling explains: "the 'jettisoned object' which is 'radically excluded and draws me toward the place where meaning collapses' . . . [is] the other side of the border, the place where I am not and which permits me to be. '[T]he place where meaning collapses' does not only refer forward to death. It also connects the loss of subjectivity in death with an earlier 'place,' where, preceding entry into the symbolic, the subject has not yet been formed. This place is the imaginary, or what Kristeva calls the *chora,* a fluid and yet womb-like maternal space which underlies and potentially undermines the stability of the symbolic, the paternal structure" (37).

27. Creed refers in her article to

Ripley's obsession with saving the cat. Her argument can be extended to include Ripley's role as surrogate mother to Newt in *Aliens* and *Alien³*.

28. The viewer later is consoled when Ripley appears to recover some sense of memory as she picks up her old "hobby" of killing the aliens.

29. In Joss Whedon's *Alien Resurrection Scriptbook*, Ripley makes a statement that speaks to this issue that was cut from the movie itself: "I tried to save people—didn't work out. There was a girl. She had bad dreams. I tried to help her and she died—and I can't remember her name."

30. This statement echoes the claim of the corporation in *Blade Runner*, which advertises their Replicants (genetically engineered androids) as "more human than human."

31. Johner's remark also refers to the notion that reproduction is a "chick thing," and that its violation through cloning mainly affects female bodies and subjectivities.

32. King and Krzywinska raise the point that, because of Sigourney Weaver and Winona Rider's star status, neither Ripley nor Call are ever "true" others with the audience and thus never constitute a real threat in terms of identification (35).

4. Our Bodies as Our Selves
Thanks to Michelle Renee Matisons, who, in endless phone conversations and patient review sessions, inspired and supported me in the process of writing this chapter. In the end, it seems, it all is about the "red" and the "blue" pill—glad you came along for the ride!

1. I treat *The Matrix* as a science fiction narrative based on its general narrative elements, which include a futuristic setting as well as a speculative approach to technology. Furthermore, the movie displays a strong kinship with cyberpunk, which is generally understood to be a specific manifestation or subgenre of the science fiction genre.

2. As Katherine Hayles points out, "Michel Foucault famously suggested that 'man' is a historical construction whose era is about to end in *The Order of Things*" (*How We Became Posthuman* 293n5). Influential work on the posthuman in terms of technology can be found in Donna Haraway's concept of the cyborg in "A Cyborg Manifesto" and in *Modest Witness@Second Millennium*, especially in regard to gene technology and information technology. Anne Balsamo's *Technologies of the Gendered Body* and Scott Bukatman's *Terminal Identity*, as well as N. Katherine Hayles's *How We Became Posthuman*, deal extensively with the posthuman condition as both a concept and a lived condition.

3. The public's fascination with the technology of the film is manifested in the hype prior to the release in 2003 of the two sequels, *The Matrix Reloaded* and *The Matrix Revolutions*. In the cover story of *Newsweek: The Who's Next Issue* from January 2003, the article on the two sequels focuses almost exclusively on the technology of producing the two films, the nine animated films set within the universe of the two movies (called *The Animatrix*), and the video game *Enter the Matrix*. It appears that the narrative of the films was less anticipated than were the special effects.

4. Examples of this criticism focused on religious mythology can be seen in James Ford, "Buddhism, Christianity, and The Matrix: The Dialectic of Myth-Making in Contemporary Cinema"; and Frances Flannery-Dailey and Rachel Wagner, "Wake Up! Gnosticism and Buddhism in *The Matrix*." See also Glenn Yeffeth, ed., *Taking the Red Pill: Science, Philosophy, and Religion in* The Matrix.

5. For a selection of philosophical readings of *The Matrix*, including a

Marxist analysis, see William Irwin, ed., The Matrix *and Philosophy.*

6. The term "humanist" here is used, not in the philosophical tradition of human versus nature or humanism versus historical determinism, but as distinctly related to the debate in cultural studies that is concerned with the intersections of machines and humans, and with the transformations of body and identity through technology. "Humanist," then, is opposite to "posthuman" in that it clings to a notion of an essential identity and a body that is recognizably "human" in contrast with the animal or technological body. Of course, this debate grew out of and is connected to classical humanist discourse.

7. Early manifestations of cyberpunk are found in literature, but elements of it, especially regarding the definition of identity by relationships to technology, are also present in films of the early 1980s, such as *Blade Runner* (1982). Since then, an increasing number of movies have drawn on cyberpunk for visual aesthetics as well as content, while these films simultaneously inform cyberpunk literature. Brooks Landon, in *The Aesthetics of Ambivalence,* discusses the relationship between science fiction film and literature, including cyberpunk. He argues that science fiction film needs to be analyzed not only in terms of narrative content but also in terms of its form—that is, the technology it employs to depict its science-fictional worlds. For more information on the debates around cyberpunk, see Larry McCaffery, ed., *Storming the Reality Studio: A Casebook of Cyberpunk and Postmodern Fiction;* George Slusser and Tom Shippey, eds., *Fiction 2000: Cyberpunk and the Future of Narrative;* and Mark Dery, ed., *Flame Wars: The Discourse of Cyberculture.* Doug Kellner's *Media Culture* contains a chapter on cyberpunk that places it within the wider context of popular culture.

8. In "Some *Real* Mothers . . . : The *sf Eye* Interview," Samuel Delany points out the "cyberpunk patriarchal nervousness" (177) in the obsessive search for "fathers" and the ignorance of "mother" texts—writings by feminist science fiction authors that have shaped cyberpunk in many nonlinear ways by exploding genre conventions— "without which we wouldn't be able to read it": "Cyberpunk is, at its basis, a bastard form of writing. It doesn't have a father. Or, rather, it has so many that enumerating them just doesn't mean anything. What it's got are mothers. A whole set of them—who, in literary terms, were so promiscuous that their cyberpunk offspring will simply never be able to settle down, sure of a certain daddy" (177).

9. The establishment of "Mirrorshades" as part of cyberpunk's aesthetic profile is symptomatic of the movement's self-celebration and self-construction as a subculture. Thus Bruce Sterling mentions, in his preface to the cyberpunk anthology *Mirrorshades,* "Mirrorshades—preferably in chrome and matte black, the Movement's totem colors" (Sterling xi).

10. Sterling explains how the cyberpunk understands cyberpunk culture: as "an integration of technology and the Eighties counterculture. An unholy alliance of the technical world and the world of organized dissent—the underground world of pop culture, visionary fluidity, and street level anarchy" (Sterling xii). In "Cyberpunk," Nixon questions cyberpunk's self-declared radicalism and its real impact as a *political movement.* She refers to Darko Suvin, who suggests in "On Gibson and Cyberpunk sf" that cyberpunk, rather than constituting a "movement," is the result of "a couple of expert PR-men (most prominently Sterling himself) who know full well the commercial value of an instantly recognizable label, and are sticking one onto disparate products" (50).

11. The movie *The Thirteenth Floor* (1999) is one of the few exceptions: it shares the element of conflicting realities with *The Matrix*.

12. Springer points out that "although pop culture enthusiastically explores boundary breakdowns between humans and computers, gender boundaries are treated less flexibly in the same texts" (64) in their corporeal representations, which still rely on gender difference.

13. In *Subculture: The Meaning of Style* (1979), Dick Hebdige discusses the phenomenon that every subculture is developed in opposition to the dominant culture but ultimately is appropriated by mainstream culture. While his analysis is concerned with style as a political and cultural counter-expression, cyberpunk's definition as countercultural is debated. Brooks Landon, in *The Aesthetics of Ambivalence*, argues that mainstream, technologized culture not merely appropriates cyberpunk's aesthetic but *is* cyberpunk's obsession. The impact of cyberpunk—as simultaneously a reflection and a definition of mainstream technoculture—on representations in texts of popular culture is substantial. This appropriation (or reflection?) of images is common in prime-time television in the United States and reflects a growing mainstream concern with these issues. For example, the cyberpunk author William Gibson wrote one episode of *The X-Files* that has at its narrative center a man who is in the process of downloading himself into the Internet. Another episode of the series deals with VR games and cyber-creatures who develop minds of their own.

14. In *The Matrix Reloaded*, the viewer learns that the Oracle, represented as a black woman, is part of the original computer program that created the Matrix. As the "intuitive" aspect of the program, the Oracle aims at helping the humans resist the "logical" source of the AI, represented by a white man. The representations of race relations in *The Matrix* are further complicated by the fact that Keanu Reeves, who is partly Native Hawaiian, is marketed and framed within a white American identity. The problematic representation of the black body as authentic and "earthy" accompanies the unconventional casting of actors of color as Zion's inhabitants and the Resistance's army in *The Matrix Reloaded*.

15. For additional analyses of race in cybertechnology and narratives about it, see Baruth's "The Excesses of Cyberpunk: Why No One Mentions Race in Cyberspace"; and Hayles's "The Seductions of Cyberspace." Lisa Nakamura, in "Race in the Construct and the Construction of Race: The 'Consensual Hallucination' of Multiculturalism in the Fictions of Cyberspace," Chapter 3 in her *Cybertypes*, gives a more positive reading of *The Matrix*'s racial representations, reading the matrix in the film as a metaphor for race-based slavery, and the Resistance's work as geared towards race liberation. However, at the end, Nakamura argues, the film fails to live up to its liberating potential.

16. See Mary Ann Doane, "Technophilia: Technology, Representation, and the Feminine"; Constance Penley, "Time Travel, Primal Scene, and the Critical Dystopia"; and Claudia Springer, *Electronic Eros*, for discussions of women, technology, reproduction, and representation in science fiction movies.

17. Haraway further develops her cyborg myth in her essays in *Simians, Cyborgs, and Women* and in *Modest Witness*. She discusses the conceptual implosion of the nature/culture dualism extensively in *Primate Visions*.

18. Hayles continues: "Identified with the rational mind, the liberal subject *possessed* a body but was not usually represented as *being* a body" (*Posthuman* 4, emphasis hers). As I point

out later in this chapter, Vivian Sobchack, in "Beating the Meat/Surviving
the Text," also makes this distinction
between the body that we "have" and
the body that we "are."

19. Heather Hicks examines the different forms of embodied technology
and technological embodiment in
" 'Whatever it is that she's since become': Writing Bodies of Text and
Bodies of Women in James Tiptree, Jr.'s
'The Girl Who Was Plugged In' and
William Gibson's 'The Winter Market.' "
Bukatman, in the final chapter of *Terminal Identity*, contrasts the same two
texts, criticizing the naïve, masculinized, and romanticized perspective in
Gibson's story, which lacks the finesse
and depth of Tiptree's gender-sensitive
narrative.

20. The following texts give insight
into the feminist debate on cyberpunk: Anne Balsamo, "Feminism for
the Incurably Informed"; Karen Cadora, "Feminist Cyberpunk"; Thomas
Foster, " 'Trapped by the Body'? Telepresence Technologies and Transgendered Performance in Feminist and
Lesbian Rewritings of Cyberpunk Fiction"; Heather Hicks, " 'Whatever it
is that she's since become': Writing
Bodies of Text and Bodies of Women
in James Tiptree, Jr.'s 'The Girl Who
Was Plugged In' and William Gibson's
'The Winter Market' "; Nicola Nixon,
"Cyberpunk: Preparing the Ground for
Revolution or Keeping the Boys Satisfied?"; Claudia Springer, *Electronic
Eros;* and Jenny Wolmark, "Cyberpunk,
Cyborgs, and Feminist Science Fiction" (Chapter 5 in *Aliens and Others*).
The recent anthology *cybersexualities*,
edited by Jenny Wolmark, which in-
cludes some of the texts listed above,
is an excellent source on cyberspace
and feminist theory, as is *The Gendered
Cyborg: A Reader*, edited by Gill Kir-
kup, Linda Janes, Kath Woodward, and
Fiona Hovenden.

21. Class is another aspect that often
is neglected in feminist critiques (or

celebration) of cybertechnologies, even
though it is (or rather should be) a
basic part of any materialist analysis.

22. Foster is careful not to fall into
the conceptual trap of "cyberdrool"
and instead grounds his views in the
presence of material embodiment by
emphasizing "the necessity of establishing connections between cyberspace and the world outside the Nets,
of setting up a feedback loop between
those two kinds of spaces and therefore between virtual and the physical
bodies" (Foster 724).

23. In *Electronic Eros*, Springer discusses cyberpunk's inability to imagine
the mind within cyberspace as separate
from the human form, resulting in its
insistence on a "meatless" existence
bound to the representations of the
material body.

24. Examples of technological bodies
trying to become human include, of
course, the android Data in *Star Trek—
Next Generation* and, in a more ironic
context, the female android Call in
Alien Resurrection.

25. Even though the movie appre-
ciates technology visually and in the
narrative, it resists the at times uncritical celebration of cyberspace as
liberating in "cyberdrool" writings,
and it avoids romanticizing the simulated world as a utopia with potential
for redefining human interactions.
Bukatman points out the limitations
of uncritical assumptions about VR:
"There is little understanding revealed
in these writings, just an obsolete and
naive liberalism that believes that if
we all just *thought about it like reason-
able human beings*, social inequities
and the drive for power would evapo-
rate" (Bukatman, *Terminal Identity* 190,
emphasis his).

26. The "science fictional modes
of depiction" in *The Matrix* are also
manifested in its digital (DVD) version, which includes special features
on the production of the movie (especially its special effects) and alternative

narrative developments. The general perception is that the film was "made for DVD"—that is, that its technology is at least as fascinating as its narrative.

27. The concept of resistance against a system using that system's own tools is employed in much of feminist discourse on what Haraway in *Modest Witness* coins as "technoscience"; it is most directly represented in the metaphor of the cyborg whose existence is based on the system it undermines/resists.

28. Cypher's treason undermines the definition of human consciousness as the basis for freedom. For him, ignorance is bliss; he wishes to be returned to the energy fields and reloaded into the Matrix—remembering nothing of the past, free of the burden of knowing of his enslavement. His name reflects this: meaning Zero, the ∅ component within arithmetic, it also connotes vacancy, emptiness.

29. This reliance on an unmarked body that constitutes the authentic self stands in contrast to a feminist acknowledgment of the *constructed* nature of the body that constitutes the material experience of the self. In *The War of Desire and Technology at the Close of the Mechanical Age*, Allucquere Rosanne Stone introduces the concept of "BUGS (body unit grounded in a self)" (85) as the basic principle of how we imagine individuals who enter communities, and she foregrounds our reliance on BUGS in the narration of our lives. The virtual selves we meet in cyberspace at times destabilize this concept and threaten the coherence it potentially offers. Stone discusses the many complex ways bodies relate to selves, both in terms of identities and in terms of numbers—more than one body to one self and vice versa. This complexity is not acknowledged in *The Matrix*, as the stable self is *reflected* in the "residual self-image" of people in the matrix, not *re-created*.

30. Contemporary publications on (communication and medical) tech-

nology reflect this fear of the eradication of the human life form and its implicit humanness. Thus the title page of *Wired* in April 2000 reads "Why the Future Doesn't Need Us." The main feature of the issue addresses debates around robotics, genetic engineering, and nanotechnology and speculates on a future in which humans have become superfluous.

31. As Bukatman observes, "Within the fictions of terminal identity, the subject is brought to the limits of self-definition, but the metaphorical solutions to the problems posed by a postmodern existence often recenter subject power as an untested, unchanging, and eternal phenomenon" (*Terminal Identity* 301). In general, science fiction literature is considered more radical and innovative than science fiction cinema in its contents (an analytical approach that Landon criticizes in *The Aesthetics of Ambivalence*). Nevertheless, criticism of cyberpunk literature has established that it is, apart from its quite radical stylistic elements, politically conservative in its treatment of subjectivity.

5. The Anatomy of Dystopia

1. Other fiction by Richard Calder includes the novels *Dead Boys* (1996), *Dead Things* (1996), *Cythera* (1998), *Frenzetta* (2002), *Twist* (2003), and the short stories "Toxine" (1989), "Mosquito" (1989), "The Lilim" (1990), "The Allure" (1990), and "Stabat Mater" (2003). He has also published, under the pseudonym Christina X, "The Catgirl Manifesto: An Introduction" (2003), in an attempt to place his writing into a (feminist) academic context.

2. In Chapter 6 of *Consuming Youth*, a study of the vampire-cyborg figure in popular youth culture, Rob Latham discusses Calder's *Dead* trilogy and *Cythera* in the context of a Marxist reading of popular youth culture's fascination with the undead. Latham traces Marx's metaphor of capital as

a "vampire" that "prosthetically link[s the worker] to a despotic, ravening apparatus" (3), turning the worker into a "cyborg," in youth consumer culture. He credits Calder for illuminating the vampire-cyborg figure's "ability [as a] dialectical metaphor to capture at once the transformative longings and the binding limitations of capitalist consumer culture" (251). However, as Latham's analysis of Calder's writing is grounded in a critical framework focusing on consumer culture, his comments on gender constellations are peripheral to his central argument. For example, he points out the polarization of masculine and feminine types within the sexual economy in *Dead Boys* and *Dead Things*, in which the dolls have become the archetypical " 'superfeminine' while their brothers are hypomacho berserkers [in a] fashion-driven dichotomy between a 'maquillage- and couture-subverted femininity' on the one hand (p. 176) and a 'doomed demon-lover's semiotic' of ruffled shirts and leather breeches on the other (p. 298)" (253).

3. For a historical context and information about the cyberpunk "movement," see Mark Dery, ed., *Flame Wars: The Discourse of Cyberculture;* Thomas Foster, "Meat Puppets or Robopaths? Cyberpunk and the Question of Embodiment" (12–14); Larry McCaffery, ed., *Storming the Reality Studio;* Andrew Ross, *Strange Weather;* and George Slusser and Tom Shippey, eds., *Fiction 2000: Cyberpunk and the Future of Narrative.*

4. Nixon names the following feminist science texts as "posthumanist" fiction: Margaret Atwood, *The Handmaid's Tale* (1985); Zoe Fairnairns, *Benefits* (1979); Suzette Haden Elgin, *Native Tongue* (1984) and *The Judas Rose* (1986); and Pamela Sargent, *The Shore of Women* (1986).

5. Hollinger points to Frederic Jameson's suggestion that "fragmentation of subjectivity may be the postmodern equivalent of the modernist predicament of individual alienation" ("Cybernetic Deconstructions" 211), the historical crisis of the straight, white, male subject.

6. For a feminist critique of cyberpunk as a fundamentally male-defined genre that places conventional tropes of masculine subject formation into a technologized setting (the conquest of feminized [cyber]space), see Nicola Nixon, "Cyberpunk: Preparing the Ground for Revolution or Keeping the Boys Satisfied?" and Sharon Stockton, " 'The Self Regained': Cyberpunk's Retreat to the Imperium."

7. In "Feminist Cyberpunk," Karen Cadora points to the innovations in what she calls "feminist cyberpunk," which explores the interface of human/machine in a more progressive way than does earlier "masculinist" cyberpunk. Cadora insists on feminist science fiction's potential to refigure gender roles and to show ways of survival in a technological world. In " 'Trapped by the Body'?" Thomas Foster concludes that "racial performativity may not be subversive in a way that is analogous to gender and sexual performativity" (732), the latter of which he examines in lesbian cyberpunk fiction. Feminist technowriters who reconceptualize cyberpunk fiction include Pat Cadigan (*Mindplayers,* 1989; *Synners,* 1991), Melissa Scott (*Trouble and Her Friends,* 1994; *Dreaming Metal,* 1997), and Laura Mixon (*Glass Houses,* 1992; *Proxies,* 1998).

8. In *Coming to Terms: Feminism, Theory, Politics,* edited by Elizabeth Weed, feminist theorists respond to Haraway's "Cyborg Manifesto." In the volume, Mary Ann Doane's "Commentary: Cyborgs, Origins, and Subjectivity," criticizes the lack of a theory of subjectivity in Haraway's envisioning of the cyborg outside of any psychoanalytic framework, and she points to the body of feminist work that disrupts classical psychoanalysis' account of a unitary origin.

9. The name of the dolls echoes the nineteenth-century novel by Villiers de L'Isle-Adam, *L'Eve Future*, a text that imagines the creation of a mechanical woman by a man, recalling the Greek myth of Pygmalion and Galatea (see Springer, *Electronic Eros* 148).

10. Lilith—in Judaic folklore Adam's first wife, who defies him and his creator—and her demonic brood, the Lilim, are popular symbols for "unnatural" beings. While Calder evokes the destructive force that threatens patriarchy, other writers appropriate Lilith as a feminist symbol for resistance against patriarchy, as Octavia Butler does with her protagonist in her *Xenogenesis* series, also published in one volume as *Lilith's Brood*. A more recent example is in Anne Harris's *Accidental Creatures* (2000).

11. The term "gynoid" was first introduced by the British feminist author Gwyneth Jones, who used it in *Divine Endurance*. See T. Foster, " 'Sex Appeal' " (377).

12. The absence of the female dolls' perspective continues in *Dead Boys* and *Dead Things*.

13. Nanotechnology is still in its early developmental stage, but, as Jack Dann and Garner Dozois put it in their Preface to *Nanotech*, "In science fiction, . . . nanotechnology is already here, an accepted part of the consensus vision among science fiction writers as to what the future is going to be like—to the point where, if your future society *doesn't* feature the use of nanotech, you have to explain *why* it doesn't in order to give your future world any credibility at all" (x). Greg Bear's short story "Blood Music" (1983), which he later developed into a novel with the same name, is one of the first works of fiction in English to explore the potentials and dangers of nanotechnology. Fueled by nonfiction publications on nanotechnology (most notably Eric Drexler's *Engines of Creation: The Coming Era of Nano-technology* in 1986), nanotechnology has become the most influential new technological development in science fiction. Thus nanotechnology defines the popular science fiction worlds of Neal Stephenson's *The Diamond Age* (1995) and Kathleen Ann Goonan's *Queen City Jazz* (1994) and *Mississippi Blues* (1999), and it forms the basis of the anthology *Nanotech* (1998), edited by Dann and Dozois.

14. This East/West binary is further disrupted by the role the United States plays in the narrative as it seeks new ways to reassert its world power, now that "History's finished: democracy and capitalism won" (*Girls* 114). Acquiring control of the doll plague by working with Titania would secure world power for the United States.

15. The conflict between the promise of postmodern, and potentially transgressive, posthuman existence through (nano)technology and an Enlightenment-based, modern sentiment/nostalgia that is inherently conservative is also present in Neal Stephenson's *The Diamond Age*. In it, a powerful caste of neo-Victorians with a conservative value system is in control of potentially transgressive nanotechnology. It is rather disappointing that Stephenson, after spending two-thirds of the book deconstructing the historical element of Enlightenment ideology, returns to a rather conservative affirmation of the neo-Victorians' powerful position.

16. See Lola Young, "Racialized Femininity," for a discussion of whiteness as the basic component of ideal femininity.

17. The transference from race to gender discourse is never complete, and the novel (as well as each of the two discourses) displays the mutual interdependency of the construction of gender and race.

18. In *Dead Girls* there are male automata in the past, but they do not exist in the time of the narrative itself; all

existing dolls/Lilim are female because only female chromosomes are affected by the virus. This aspect changes in *Dead Boys* and *Dead Things,* where the doll virus also infects male bodies and turns them into something un-human. These mutants are not dolls, however, and are not sexualized, but rather are driven to sexually mutilate and kill dolls/girls to control the development of the plague.

19. See Chapter 6, "Men and Machine-Women," in Claudia Springer's *Electronic Eros,* for a discussion of mechanical women in Western imagination.

20. Sandra M. Gilbert and Susan Gubar give a comprehensive study of conflicting images of women as either angel or monster in the Western English-speaking literary imagination in *The Madwoman in the Attic.*

21. Calder explores this ultimate promise/ultimate threat duality further when in *Dead Boys* and *Dead Things* it becomes apparent that the doll plague is a concrete strategy of the nanovirus Meta, an alien race that possesses its own systematic agenda—to change not just material reality but history.

22. Interestingly, Primavera seems committed to Iggy in a monogamous relationship; she never infects other men without also killing them.

23. In his introduction to *Consuming Youth,* Latham comprehensively surveys Marxist theories on consumer culture and the vampire-cyborg figure.

24. The dolls are reminiscent of the figures of the prostitute and the actress in fin de siècle literature. Both commodity and seller, they unsettle the male-dominated economy. Dolls have a fractured relationship to the image of the female performer; they echo the prostitute as "ultimate symbol of the commodification of eros, a disturbing example of the ambiguous boundaries separating economics and sexuality, the rational and irrational, the instrumental and the aesthetic" (Felski 19). Like the prostitute, they are simultaneously consumed and rejected by men.

25. The Lilim resist the patriarchal economy, not through participating in it (as Kito does in Thailand), but rather by refusing a place within it. Here they differ from other cyberpunk female technobodies. For example, William Gibson's Molly in *Neuromancer* works first as a prostitute, then as a street-samurai—in both cases hiring out her body for money, which she then uses to enhance it technologically: "Molly's self-commodification, then, may be read as a form of politically charged self-authorship" (Cherniavsky, "(En)gendering Cyberspace in *Neuromancer*" 43). See also Thomas Foster's "Meat Puppets or Robopaths?" (25).

26. The "Reinhardt females" are the same species as females in Calder's *Frenzetta,* the result of mutations with different animal genes. Frenzetta herself is a "ratgirl." In the "Catgirl Manifesto," feline women—a new "subspecies of human being" (166)—are described as possessing "extreme degrees of exhibitionism; an overriding need to be admired and pampered; infantilism; hyperaesthesia; a hatred of maternity and childbirth; and a tendency to spite, deceit, and treacherousness in direct proportion of deferred gratification" (160). For them, "life was a neurotic masquerade, in which they continuously fretted about how to maintain the delicate balance between *cuteness* and *whorishness*" (179). Thus, the catgirls display the exact same pattern of fetishization of dehumanized female bodies as is found in all of Calder's work. As in his other novels, these female mutants are hunted and killed by men, in this case by "WINDOW (Worldwide Investigation into Death, Orgasm, and Womanhood)" (162).

27. Calder explores normative sexuality and perversion more directly in *Frenzetta,* where societies defined by their sexual practices are at war with each other. The tension between per-

verse and normal is expressed through the transgression of the boundary between animal (connoting the perverse, savage) and human: "perverts" have the ability to genetically engineer, and both animal and human genes shape their sexuality. Any mechanical technology is lost—biology is everything. Female sexuality is defined by a death wish: pervert cats/rats die after having sex once and becoming impregnated since they die giving birth. Here, as in *Dead Girls*, perversion is defined exclusively through heterosexual desire and finds ultimate expression in (female) death through reproduction.

28. The emphasis in doll sex is on heterosexual reproduction. The spreading of the plague takes place through displaced reproduction (the doll does not give birth herself) through heterosexual intercourse. This uncompromising heterosexuality dominates all of Calder's work. In contrast, other perverse science fiction narratives explore the subversive relationship between technology and queer (s/m) sexuality that undermines the prescriptive and productive power of normativity. Examples of such explorations may be found in Cecilia Tan's *The Velderet: A Cybersex s/m Serial* and her edited anthology *Sexcrime*, as well as in Severna Park's *Speaking Dreams*. Unlike depictions of sexualities in these narratives, Calder's perverse sexuality simply reifies social domination by integrating male fetishization of female sexuality and racial otherness into his social order.

29. In *Dead Girls*, the dolls actually replace extraterrestrials/aliens as the ultimate other of the human imagination. Says Titania: "This can never be my world. To them, I'll always be the Thing from Outer Space" (*Girls* 83). This displacement becomes even more concrete in *Dead Boys* and *Dead Things*, where much of the story takes place on Mars.

30. In classical science fiction the figure of the "unfeeling" robot developed into the conflicted figure of the "feeling" android/robot who seeks human fulfillment. Isaac Asimov's "three laws of robots" for benign robots in the 1950s have been translated into endearing and emotional robots in science fiction film since the 1970s. See Robert Scholes and Eric S. Rabkin's *Science Fiction: History, Science, and Vision* (61) and Vivian Sobchack's *Screening Space* (37–42) for discussion of the emotional kinship between humans and robots in film.

31. The dichotomy of reason as masculine and pleasure as feminine is replicated in criticisms of modern (commodity) culture and produces narratives of history as absolute domination, such as in Theodor Adorno and Max Horkheimer's *Dialectic of Enlightenment* (see also Felski 5–7).

32. The only interjection of a voice that is not entirely male-identified is Mosquito's tale.

33. Calder's straight white male fantasies stand in stark contrast to other dystopian cyberpunk writings, whose authors succeed in working through much of this ambivalence from a feminist perspective, such as the Native American writer Misha's *Red Spider White Web*.

6. Beyond Binary Gender

1. MUDs are multi-user dimensions, or multiplayer virtual environments in which people play characters who encounter other players' characters in text-based or sometimes visual environments.

2. For discussions of transgender and transsexual identities, see Judith Halberstam and C. Jacob Hale, "Butch/FTM Border Wars"; Judith Halberstam, *Female Masculinity* and "Transgender Butch: Butch/FTM Border Wars and the Masculine Continuum"; and C. Jacob Hale, "Consuming the Living, Dis(re)membering the Dead in the Butch/FTM Borderlands."

3. For a comprehensive discussion of Delany's work in terms of non-normative sexualities and genders, see Jeffrey Allen Tucker, *A Sense of Wonder: Samuel R. Delany, Race, Identity, and Difference.*

4. For examples of feminist science fiction that mirrors and/or anticipates theoretical and political debates, see Lucie Armitt, ed., *Where No Man Has Gone Before: Women and Science Fiction;* Marleen Barr, *Alien to Femininity,* and her edited anthology *Lost in Space: Probing Feminist Science Fiction and Beyond;* Sarah Lefanu, *In the Chinks of the World Machine;* Robin Roberts, *A New Species: Gender and Science in Science Fiction;* and Jenny Wolmark, *Aliens and Others: Science Fiction, Feminism and Postmodernism.*

5. In *The Battle of the Sexes in Science Fiction,* Justine Larbalestier identifies three forms of "solutions or alternatives to the conflict between the sexes that do not involve the re-inscription of male rule" (73) in science fiction in the period 1926-1973: equality of the sexes within a heterosexual setting, lesbian separatism, and one-sex societies with hermaphroditism and/or androgyny.

6. Vonda McIntyre's novel *Dream-snake* (1979) challenges naturalized notions of male/female as the fundamental sexual difference. The protagonist is a healer who accidentally discovers the biological reproduction of the precious dreamsnake, a reptile with magical powers. For centuries, healers had been unable to breed the animal since male and female snakes refused to mate. Their binary concept of sex prevented the healers from realizing that the reproductive unit of the mythical snake was made up of three, not two, snakes.

7. More recently, queer science fiction criticism has examined many classic science fiction texts in relation to subversive sexualities, but not as frequently in terms of (trans)gender

identities. See, for example, Wendy Pearson, "Alien Cryptographies: The View from Queer" and Veronica Hollinger, "(Re)reading Queerly: Science Fiction, Feminism, and the Defamiliarization of Gender." Both articles were published in the section "On Science Fiction and Queer Theory" in *Science Fiction Studies* 26 (1999).

8. This is not to say that every discussion of gender identity in cyberspace privileges an association of transgender performance with disembodiment. In *The War of Desire and Technology,* Allucquere Rosanne Stone insists on the grounding of any virtual self's experience in the material existence of the body in "real life," which for her is never essential but contextual. For a discussion of feminist and queer depictions of transgender identities in virtual space, see Thomas Foster, " 'Trapped by the Body'? Telepresence Technologies and Transgendered Performance in Feminist and Lesbian Rewritings of Cyberpunk Fiction" and " 'The Postproduction of the Human Heart': Desire, Identification, and Virtual Embodiment in Feminist Narratives of Cyberspace."

9. In " 'I Want to Be a Real Boy': A.I. Robots, Cyborgs, and Mutants as Passing Figures in Science Fiction Film," K. Surkan examines the metaphorical relationship between the cyborg and the trans figure in science fiction film.

10. Much queer theory is based on the work of French philosopher Michel Foucault, who argues in *The Order of Things: An Archeology of the Human Sciences* (originally published in 1966) and in *The History of Sexuality* (originally published in 1976) that desire is produced and classified—that is, regulated—by discursive power. Heterosexuality, then, is normative, not natural, and queer desire and its sexual practices are declared deviant. See Henry Abelove, Michele Aina Barale, and David M. Halperin, eds., *The Lesbian and Gay Studies Reader,* and

Robert J. Corber and Stephen Valoc-cho, *Queer Studies: An Interdisciplinary Reader*, for readings on gay and lesbian and queer politics. See Merl Storr, ed., *Bisexuality: A Critical Reader*, and Sharon Rose, Cris Stevens et al., eds., *Bisexual Horizons: Politics, Histories, Lives*, for insights into discussions about bisexuality, and Susan Stryker, ed., *Transgender Reader*, for readings on transgender identities.

11. Much of contemporary feminist queer theory, which expands on sexuality as an analytical category by placing it in relation to gender oppression, draws on the work of poststructuralist psychoanalysts such as Judith Butler and literary theorists such as Eve Kosofsky Sedgwick. See Judith Butler, *Gender Trouble, Bodies that Matter*, and *Undoing Gender*, and Eve Kosofsky Sedgwick, *Epistemologies of the Closet, Between Men*, and her edited anthology *Novel Gazing*.

12. Despite its melancholy, Judith Butler views gender performativity as ultimately subversive in that it discloses gender norms as discursive and therefore as malleable. She makes clear that it is paradoxical that agency lies *within* the parameters set by discourse; identity is subverted in the various repetitions of performance of the prescribed ideal (see *Gender Trouble* 145). Often the theory of gender performativity is reduced to Judith Butler's example of *drag*, which she considers one of the most gender-subversive displays in United States culture (see *Gender Trouble* 137). In Chapter 4 of *Bodies that Matter*, she critically analyzes the movie *Paris Is Burning*, a documentary on black and Hispanic drag in northern New York City, in terms of the limits of its subversive power, problematizing simplified interpretations of her theory of gender performativity.

13. While queer theory celebrates gender performativity as liberating from legislated bodies, transsexual experiences and theory reinsert the body into debates on subjectivity. The transgendered subject has become, as Jay Prosser states in *Second Skins: The Body Narratives of Transsexuality*, "a key queer trope: the means by which not only to challenge sex, gender, and sexuality binaries but to institutionalize homosexuality as queer" (5). Thus gender performativity is troubled by the transsexual body and the physical experience of transition (with hormones and surgery) as its ontological underpinning. The queer message that gender is constructed, desire is authentic, and the body should not be the basis for our understanding of gender roles and identity runs counter to much of trans people's experiences. Vivian K. Namaste, in *Invisible Lives: The Erasure of Transsexual and Transgendered People*, also examines the implication of transsexual experiences and identities for (feminist) gender theory.

14. In *GenderQueer: Voices from Beyond the Sexual Binary*, editors Joan Nestle, Clare Howell, and Riki Wilchins and the contributors explore the meaning of the growing queer youth movement, which creates connections between gay and lesbian, feminist, and trans politics by inhabiting gender-queer identities.

15. See Angela Davis's *Women, Race, and Class* for a detailed study of the historical construction of white and black womanhood, and Alice Walker's *In Search of Our Mothers' Gardens* for analysis of images of black women in black and white literature.

16. The problematic of a "masculinized" androgyny is analogous to white "mixed-race"/"mulatta" stereotypes that are white-controlled, designer hybrid imaginaries that serve to confirm the value of the dominant identity.

17. Butler's use of the neutral pronoun stands in contrast to Ursula Le Guin's use of the male pronoun for her (masculinized) androgynous people in *The Left Hand of Darkness* (1969) "because the exclusion of the feminine

(she) and the neuter (it) from the generic/masculine (he) makes the use of either of them *more* specific, *more* unjust, as it were, than the use of 'he' " (Le Guin, *The Wind's Twelve Quarters* 85, emphasis hers). Thus Butler refuses to offer men a "safe trip into androgyny and back" (Le Guin, "Is Gender Necessary?" 16). Marge Piercy, in *Woman on the Edge of Time*, uses a generic pronoun "per" (from person), which degenders language in her egalitarian society of the future. The disruption of the reading process through the use of unfamiliar pronouns also takes place in Melissa Scott's *Shadow Man*, which uses five sets of pronouns.

18. In the opening sentence of *On Sexuality: Three Essays on the Theory of Sexuality,* Freud likens desire to the physical craving for nutrition: "The fact of the existence of sexual needs in human beings and animals is expressed in biology by the assumption of a 'sexual instinct', on the analogy of the instinct of nutrition, that is of hunger. Everyday language possesses no counterpart to the word 'hunger', but science makes use of the word 'libido' for that purpose" (45).

19. Larbalestier makes this observation about hermaphroditism in her analysis of Theodore Sturgeon's *Venus Plus X* (1960) and Ursula Le Guin's *The Left Hand of Darkness* (1969) in Chapter 3 of her book.

20. Legally and socially, Western societies have always relied on the binary of man/woman for their social order. The decision about what gender the intersexed person should adopt was made initially by the family; once adulthood was attained, the subject itself decided on a gender role. The rise of modern systems of knowledge (medicine, psychoanalysis, political enlightenment) increasingly regulated a hermaphrodite's choice of gender assignment.

21. According to Foucault, the body became the primary carrier of truth about sex and needed to be classified, regulated, and ultimately altered accordingly. Most importantly, there was no room for ambiguity, and thus hermaphrodites needed to be declared as either male or female. While contemporary medicine has a more complex understanding of the human body, it uses its knowledge mainly to "correct" nature and to alter the intersexed body so it fits the binary sex system.

22. Biological variability does not carry inherent (gendered) meaning. This point becomes obvious in light of the changing status of hermaphrodites over time and from country to country. Throughout the history of Western culture, "experts" bestowed with cultural authority to declare someone's gender (identity) were located in diverse social arenas: from religious authorities this power was eventually transferred to legal representatives of the system (e.g., judges and lawyers). Once a gender was decided upon, transgressive behavior that contradicted the assigned role was viewed as criminal. Thus the understanding and management of intersexed people was socially, not medically, based. In modern Western cultures, by "the dawn of the twentieth century, physicians were recognized as the chief regulators of intersexuality," and by mid-century they had fully developed "surgical and hormonal suppression of intersexuality" (Fausto-Sterling, *Sexing the Body* 40), rendering the intersexed person culturally invisible. Instead of accepting human sexuality as various and complex, modern medicine requires that bodies that do not adhere to the scientifically established norm must be surgically and hormonally altered—if nature is not natural enough, physicians and surgeons help out. Kessler, in her criticism of the medical management of intersexed infants, which until recently has "conceptualize[d] intersexuality . . . as a correctable birth defect" (5), points out that the "correc-

tion" of the natural body so that it fits into the gendered binary often results in unnecessary surgery and medicalization with long-term health damage and negatively affected sexualities. The aggressive medical management of intersexed infants since the beginning of the twentieth century resulted in the cultural invisibility of intersexed people until the mid-1990s, when a growing intersex activism started politicizing the issue. See Cheryl Chase's "'Hermaphrodites with Attitude': Mapping the Emergence of Intersex Political Activism" for an overview of intersex activism.

23. Consequently, sexed categories do not reflect a biological given but instead reflect an attempt to understand bodies in terms of the particular moment. For a historical overview of the social, legal, and medical treatment of intersexed people over time, see Fausto-Sterling, *Sexing the Body,* and Dreger, *Hermaphrodites and the Medical Invention of Sex.*

24. In her description of the biology of the five sexes, Melissa Scott diverges from Fausto-Sterling's hypothetical model. Fausto-Sterling bases her distinctions, not on "gendered" visuals such as breasts and penises, but on invisible sex characteristics (such as chromosomes) in her naming of the additional sexes (Fausto-Sterling, "Five Sexes" 21). Scott renames the sexes so that the reader, who relies on our gendered way of thinking about bodies, can more easily associate a visual form with the unfamiliar biology. So Fausto-Sterling's "merm" becomes a fem in *Shadow Man,* since breasts are associated with the feminine word-root "fem," and a "ferm" becomes a mem, since a penis is associated with the more masculine word-root "mem."

25. The phenomenon of passing is mainly associated with the experience of African Americans and racial passing but is increasingly thematized also in terms of gender, class, and sexual pass-

ing. Passing as a concept rests on the "logic of visibility" (Schlossberg 1); the passing subject threatens the stability of identities and the social orders based on them: "The passing subject's ability to transcend or abandon his or her 'authentic' identity calls into question the very notion of authenticity itself—a passing subject calls the 'naturalness' of the 'real' subject, who is not passing, into question" (Schlossberg 2). See Elaine K. Ginsberg, ed., *Passing and the Fictions of Identity;* and Maria Carla Sanchez and Linda Schlossberg, eds., *Passing: Identity and Interpretation in Sexuality, Race, and Religion.*

26. In referring to Raven, I use the pronouns assigned to herms in Concordian culture. Raven, until later in the narrative, refers to ʒimself with male pronouns. In order not to make Raven's identity as herm invisible, I use herm pronouns for ʒim throughout the analysis. In the Glossary of *Shadow Man,* herm pronouns are listed as "ʒe, ʒer, ʒim, ʒimself" (310), with a first letter that resembles, but is not completely identical to, "z." It should be remarked that Scott's choice of herm pronouns linguistically aligns them closer with the English male pronouns than with the female, except for the possessive "ʒer."

27. In "Destabilising Sex/Gender/ Sexuality in Melissa Scott's *Shadow Man,*" Joan Haran examines the novel's complex interrogations of gender in the context of feminist and queer theory and points out the narrative and symbolic functions of the five pronouns.

28. Scott defines "ghost *rana*" as "an offshoot of the traditional political song-and-dance groups, conceived as a mirror-image and reversal of their powers; unlike a traditional *rana,* a ghost *rana* makes no noise, but will act, and act violently, to restore its conception of order. Ghost *ranas* tend to be traditional in their beliefs" (*Shadow Man* 315-16).

29. An undercurrent to the narrative

is Tatian's mourning for his relationship with the woman Prane Am, who left him for a mem. Tatian is disturbed by the fact that she acted against her "officially" declared sexuality—straight—and is partnering with a mem, which makes her "di" ("denotes a person who prefers to be intimate with persons of exactly the same and one of the two 'like' genders" [309]): *"Adults don't change their minds,* he wanted to say, *not about something as important as this. And if they do, they* tell *people and then they apologize"* (114). Tatian's confusion about his desire for Raven, a herm, and his bitterness over his expartner's fluid sexuality discloses the limits of any system that attempts to regulate—or naturalize—certain forms of sexualities over others.

30. It appears that Emma Goldman may never have said these exact words, but they paraphrase her real sentiments. See Alix Kates Shulman, "Dances with Feminists."

31. The tension between progressive social movements and their at times conflicting agendas manifests in the conflict between lesbian feminists and transwomen, who often identify as feminists and sometimes as lesbians. Some lesbian feminists, most notoriously represented by Janice Raymond and her transphobic and trans-hostile book *The Transsexual Empire,* reject transwomen's "womanhood" and refuse to welcome them to "women-identified" events. Groups such as the "Transsexual Menace" confront lesbian feminists with their biological essentialism, and Camp Trans, an event staged annually by transgender activists at the Michigan Women's Music festival in protest of the festival's exclusion of transwomen, challenges essentialist notions of identities. Another dangerous mechanism is tokenism, which often appears in queer organizations, whose names include trans issues (e.g., with the initials "LGBT": Lesbian, Gay, Bisexual, and Transgender), but whose agendas never fundamentally address trans experiences.

32. Other novels by Melissa Scott include *Dream Ships* (1993), *Burning Bright* (1994), *Trouble and Her Friends* (1994), *Night Sky Mine* (1996), *Dreaming Metal* (1997), *The Shapes of Their Hearts* (1999), and *The Jazz* (2001). She has also coauthored books with Lisa Barnett, such as *Point of Hopes* (1997) and *Point of Dreams* (2001).

Print Sources

Abelove, Henry, Michele Aina Barale, and David M. Halperin, eds. *The Lesbian and Gay Studies Reader.* New York: Routledge, 1993.

Adorno, Theodor, and Max Horkheimer. *Dialectic of Enlightenment.* London: Verso, 1979.

Alcoff, Linda, and Elizabeth Potter, eds. *Feminist Epistemologies.* New York: Routledge, 1993.

Alexander, M. Jacqui, and Chandra Talpade Mohanty, eds. *Feminist Genealogies, Colonial Legacies, Democratic Futures.* New York and London: Routledge, 1997.

Angenot, Marc. "The Absent Paradigm." *Science Fiction Studies* 6 (1979): 9–19.

Anzaldúa, Gloria. "La conciencia de la mestiza: Towards a New Consciousness." *Making Face, Making Soul/Haciendo caras.* Ed. Gloria Anzaldúa. San Francisco: aunt lute, 1990.

Armitt, Lucie, ed. *Where No Man Has Gone Before: Women and Science Fiction.* London: Routledge, 1991.

Atwood, Margaret. *The Handmaid's Tale.* New York: Fawcett Crest, Ballantine Books, 1986.

Bacon-Smith, Camille. *Science Fiction Culture.* Philadelphia: U of Pennsylvania P, 2000.

Baker, Neal. "Creole Identity Politics, Race, and *Star Trek: Voyager.*" *Into Darkness Peering: Race and Color in the Fantastic.* Ed. Elisabeth Anne Leonard. Westport, CT: Greenwood Press, 1997. 119–29.

Balsamo, Anne. "Feminism and Cultural Studies." *Journal of the Midwest Modern Language Association/MMLA* 24:1 (1991): 50–73.

———. "Feminism for the Incurably Informed." *South Atlantic Quarterly* 92 (1993): 680–712.

———. *Technologies of the Gendered Body: Reading Cyborg Women.* Durham: Duke UP, 1996.

Bammer, Angelika, ed. *Displacements: Cultural Identities in Question.* Bloomington: Indiana UP, 1994.

Barr, Marleen S. *Alien to Femininity: Speculative Fiction and Feminist Theory.* New York: Greenwood, 1987.

———. *Lost in Space: Probing Feminist Science Fiction and Beyond.* Chapel Hill: U of North Carolina P, 1993.

———, ed. *Future Females: A Critical Anthology.* Bowling Green, OH: Bowling Green U Popular P, 1981.

Baruth, Philip E. "The Excesses of Cyberpunk: Why No One Mentions Race in

Cyberspace." *Into Darkness Peering: Race and Color in the Fantastic.* Ed. Elisabeth Anne Leonard. Westport, CT: Greenwood Press, 1997. 105-18.

Baudrillard, Jean. *Simulacra and Simulation.* Trans. Sheila Faria Glaser. U of Michigan P, 1994.

Beal, Frances M. "Interview with Octavia Butler: Black Women and the Science Fiction Genre." *The Black Scholar* 17 (1986): 14-18.

Bear, Greg. "Blood Music." 1983. *Nanotech.* Eds. Jack Dann and Gardner Dozois. New York: Ace Books, 1998. 1-31.

————. *Blood Music.* New York: Ace Books, 1985.

Beauvoir, Simone de. *The Second Sex.* 1949. New York: Vintage Books, 1989.

Belling, Catherine. " 'Where Meaning Collapses': *Alien* and the Outlawing of the Female Hero." *Liberator* 13 (November 1992): 35-49.

Bell-Metereau, Rebecca. "Woman: The Other Alien in *Alien.*" *Women Worldwalkers: New Dimensions of Science Fiction and Fantasy.* Ed. Jane B. Weedman. Lubbock, TX: Texas Tech Press, 1985.

Benet's Reader's Encyclopedia. 4th ed. Ed. Bruce Murphy. New York: HarperCollins, 1996.

Bhabha, Homi K. *The Location of Culture.* New York: Routledge, 1994.

Bick, Ilsa. " 'Well I Guess I Must Make You Nervous': Woman and the Space of *Alien³*." *Post-Script: Essays in Film and the Humanities* 14 (1994-95): 45-58.

Biddick, Kathleen. "Humanist History and the Haunting of Virtual Worlds: Problems of Memory and Rememoration." *Genders* 18 (1993): 47-66.

Bishop, Ellen. "Race and Subjectivity in Science Fiction: Deterritorializing the Self/Other Dichotomy." *Into Darkness Peering: Race and Color in the Fantastic.* Ed. Elisabeth Anne Leonard. Westport, CT: Greenwood Press, 1997. 85-103.

Bleier, Ruth. *Science and Gender: A Critique of Biology and Its Theories on Women.* New York: Pergamon Press, 1984.

————, ed. *Feminist Approaches to Science.* New York: Pergamon Press, 1984.

Bonner, Frances. "Difference and Desire, Slavery and Seduction: Octavia Butler's *Xenogenesis.*" *Foundation: The Review of Science Fiction* 48 (1990): 50-62.

Bordo, Susan, and Alison Jaggar, eds. *Gender/Body/Knowledge: Feminist Reconstructions of Being and Knowing.* New Brunswick, NJ: Rutgers UP, 1989.

Bordwell, David, and Kristin Thompson. *Film Art: An Introduction.* 5th ed. New York: McGraw-Hill, 1997.

Bornstein, Kate. *Gender Outlaw: On Men, Women, and the Rest of Us.* New York: Vintage Books, 1994.

Bradley, Marion Zimmer. *The Shattered Chain.* New York: Doubleday, 1976.

Braidotti, Rosi. *Nomadic Subjects: Embodiment and Sexual Difference in Contemporary Feminist Theory.* New York: Columbia UP, 1994.

————. *Patterns of Dissonance.* Trans. Elizabeth Guild. New York: Routledge, 1991.

Brooks, Ann. *Postfeminisms: Feminism, Cultural Theory and Cultural Forms.* New York: Routledge, 1997.

Bryant, Dorothy. *The Kin of Ata Are Waiting for You.* New York: Random House, 1971.

Bukatman, Scott. *Blade Runner.* London: British Film Institute, 1997.

————. *Terminal Identity: The Virtual Subject in Postmodern Science Fiction.* Durham: Duke UP, 1993.

Bush, Laura. "Mrs. Bush Discusses Status of Afghan Women at U.N.: Remarks by Mrs. Laura Bush, U.N. Commission on the Status of Women, International

Women's Day." *The White House, Office of the Press Secretary,* March 8, 2002 [http://www.whitehouse.gov/news/releases/2002/03/20020308-2.html].

Butler, Judith. *Bodies that Matter: On the Discursive Limits of Sex.* New York: Routledge, 1993.

———. *Gender Trouble: Feminism and the Subversion of Identity.* New York: Routledge, 1990.

———. "Gender Trouble, Feminist Theory, and Psychoanalytic Discourse." *Feminism/Postmodernism.* Ed. Linda Nicholson. New York: Routledge, 1990. 324–40.

———. "Imitation and Gender Subordination." *Inside/Out: Lesbian Theories, Gay Theories.* Ed. Diana Fuss. New York: Routledge, 1991. 13–31.

———. *Undoing Gender.* New York: Routledge, 2004.

Butler, Judith, and Joan W. Scott, eds. *Feminists Theorize the Political.* New York: Routledge, 1992.

Butler, Octavia E. *Adulthood Rites.* 1988. New York: Warner Books, 1989.

———. *Bloodchild and Other Stories.* New York: Four Walls Eight Windows, 1995.

———. *Clay's Ark.* New York: St Martin's, 1984.

———. *Dawn.* 1987. New York: Warner Books, 1988.

———. *Imago.* 1989. New York: Warner Books, 1990.

———. *Kindred.* 1979. Boston: Beacon Press, 1988.

———. *Mind of My Mind.* 1977. New York: Warner Books, 1994.

———. "The Monophobic Response." *Dark Matter: A Century of Speculative Fiction from the African Diaspora.* Ed. Sheree R. Thomas. New York: Warner Books, 2000. 415–16.

———. *Parable of the Sower.* New York: Four Walls Eight Windows, 1993.

———. *Parable of the Talents.* New York: Seven Stories Press, 1998.

———. *Patternmaster.* 1976. New York: Warner Books, 1995.

———. *Survivor.* 1978. Special Edition. London: Sidgwick and Jackson, 1981.

———. *Wild Seed.* 1980. New York: Warner Books, 1988.

Cadigan, Pat. *Mindplayers.* New York: Bantam, 1987.

———. *Synners.* New York: Bantam. 1991.

Cadora, Karen. "Feminist Cyberpunk." *Science Fiction Studies* 22.3 (1995): 357–72.

Calder, Richard. "The Allure." *Interzone* 40 (October 1990): 36–41.

———. *Cythera.* New York: St. Martin's Press, 1998.

———. *Dead Girls/Dead Boys/Dead Things: A Trilogy.* New York: St. Martin's Press, 1998.

———. *Frenzetta.* New York: Four Walls Eight Windows, 2002.

———. "The Lilim." *Interzone* 34 (March/April 1990): 5–12.

———. "Mosquito." *Interzone* 32 (December 1989): 5–11.

———. "Stabat Mater." *Lost Pages* (December 2003). [http://lostpages.net/December2003Calder.html].

———. "Toxine." *Interzone: The Fourth Anthology.* Eds. John Clute, David Pringle, and Simon Ounsley. New York: Simon and Schuster, 1989.

———. *Twist.* New York: Four Walls Eight Windows, 2003.

Castillo, Ana. *Massacre of the Dreamers: Essays on Xicanisma.* New York: Plume/Penguin Books, 1994.

Charnas, Suzy McKee. *The Furies.* New York: Tor Books, 1994.

———. *Motherlines.* New York: Berkley Books, 1978.

Chase, Cheryl. "'Hermaphrodites with Attitude': Mapping the Emergence of Intersex Political Activism." *Queer Studies: An Interdisciplinary Reader.* Eds. Robert J. Corber and Stephen Valocchi. Malden, MA: Blackwell, 2003. 31–45.

Cherniavsky, Eva. "(En)gendering Cyberspace in *Neuromancer:* Postmodern Subjectivity and Virtual Motherhood." *Genders* 18 (Winter 1993): 32–46.

———. "Subaltern Studies in a U.S. Frame." *Boundary 2* 23.2 (1996): 85–110.

Christian, Barbara. "Trajectories Of Self-Definition: Placing Contemporary Afro-American Women's Fiction." *Feminisms: An Anthology of Literary Theory and Criticism.* Eds. Robyn Warhol and Diane Price Herndl. New Brunswick, NJ: Rutgers UP, 1993. 316–28.

Cobbs, John. "*Alien* as an Abortion Parable." *Literature Film Quarterly* 18:3 (1990): 198–201.

Collins, Patricia Hill. *Black Feminist Thought: Knowledge, Consciousness, and the Politics of Empowerment.* Boston: Unwin Hyman, 1990.

———. *Fighting Words: Black Women and the Search for Justice.* Minneapolis: U of Minnesota P, 1998.

Constable, Catherine. "Becoming the Monster's Mother: Morphologies of Identity in the *Alien* Series." *Alien Zone II: The Spaces of Science Fiction Cinema.* Ed. Annette Kuhn. London and New York: Verso, 1999. 173–202.

Corber, Robert J., and Stephen Valoccho. *Queer Studies: An Interdisciplinary Reader.* Malden, MA: Blackwell, 2003.

Corrigan, Timothy, and Patricia White. *The Film Experience: An Introduction.* New York: Bedford/St. Martin's, 2004.

Crane, David. "*In Medias* Race: Filmic Representation, Networked Communication, and Racial Intermediation." *Race in Cyberspace.* Eds. Beth Kolko, Lisa Nakamura, and Gilbert Rodman. New York: Routledge, 2000. 87–115.

Cranny-Francis, Anne. "Feminist Futures: A Generic Study." *Alien Zone: Cultural Theory and Contemporary Science Fiction Cinema.* Ed. Annette Kuhn. London and New York: Verso, 1990. 219–27.

Creed, Barbara. "*Alien* and the Monstrous Feminine." *Alien Zone: Cultural Theory and Contemporary Science Fiction Cinema.* Ed. Annette Kuhn. London and New York: Verso, 1990. 128–41.

Croal, N'Gai. *Newsweek: The Who's Next Issue.* 30 Dec. 2002/6 Jan. 2003. 89.

Crosby, Christina. "Dealing with Differences." *Feminists Theorize the Political.* Eds. Judith Butler and Joan W. Scott. New York: Routledge, 1992. 130–43.

Dann, Jack, and Gardner Dozois. Preface. *Nanotech.* Eds. Jack Dann and Gardner Dozois. New York: Ace Books, 1998.

———, eds. *Nanotech.* New York: Ace Books, 1998.

Davies, Carole Boyce. *Black Women, Writing, and Identity: Migrations of the Subject.* London: Routledge, 1994.

———. Introduction. "Black Women Writing Worlds: Textual Production, Dominance, and the Critical Voice." *Moving Beyond Boundaries.* Vol. 2: *Black Women's Diaspora.* Ed. Carole Boyce Davies. New York: NYU Press, 1995. 1–15.

Davis, Angela. *Women, Race, and Class.* New York: Vintage, 1981.

Delany, Samuel R. "About Five Thousand One Hundred and Seventy-Five Words." *SF: The Other Side of Realism.* Thomas Clareson, ed. Bowling Green: Bowling Green U Popular P, 1971. 130–46.

———. "Racism and Science Fiction." 1999. *Dark Matter: A Century of Speculative*

Fiction from the African Diaspora. Ed. Sheree Thomas. New York: Warner Books, 2000. 383–97.

———. "Some *Real* Mothers . . . : The *SF Eye* Interview." *Silent Interviews: On Language, Race, Sex, Science Fiction, and Some Comics.* Ed. Samuel R. Delany. Hanover and London: Wesleyan UP, 1994. 164–85.

———. "Some Reflections on SF Criticism." *Science Fiction Studies* 8 (1981): 233–39.

———. *Triton.* New York: Bantam, 1976.

De Lauretis, Theresa. "Signs of Wo/ander." *The Technological Imagination: Theories and Fictions.* Eds. Theresa de Lauretis, Andreas Hyssen, and Kathleen Woodward. Madison: Coda Press, 1980. 159–174.

Dery, Mark. "Body Politic." *Mondo 2000* 7 (1992): 101–5.

———, ed. *Flame Wars: The Discourse of Cyberculture.* Durham: Duke UP, 1993.

Desser, David. "Race, Space, and Class: The Politics of Cityscapes in Science-Fiction Films." *Alien Zone II: The Spaces of Science Fiction Cinema.* Ed. Annette Kuhn. London and New York: Verso, 1999. 80–96.

Doane, Mary Anne. "Commentary: Cyborgs, Origins, and Subjectivity." *Coming to Terms: Feminism, Theory, Politics.* Ed. Elizabeth Weed. New York: Routledge, 1989. 209–14.

———. "Technophilia: Technology, Representation, and the Feminine." *Body/Politics: Women and the Discourse of Science.* Eds. Mary Jacobus, Evelyn Fox-Keller and Sally Shuttleworth. New York: Routledge, 1990. 163–76.

Doerksen, Teri Ann. "Octavia E. Butler: Parables of Race and Difference." *Into Darkness Peering: Race and Color in the Fantastic.* Ed. Elisabeth Anne Leonard. Westport, CT: Greenwood Press, 1997. 21–34.

Donawerth, Jane. *Frankenstein's Daughters: Women Writing Science Fiction.* Syracuse: Syracuse UP, 1997.

Dreger, Alice Domurat. *Hermaphrodites and the Medical Invention of Sex.* Cambridge, MA: Harvard UP, 1998.

Drexler, Eric K. *Engines of Creation: The Coming Era of Nanotechnology.* New York: Anchor Books/Doubleday, 1986.

Dubey, Madhu. "Folk and Urban Communities in African-American Women's Fiction: Octavia Butler's *Parable of the Sower.*" *Studies in American Fiction* 27 (Spring 1999): 103–28.

Eaton, Michael. "Born Again." *Sight and Sound* 7.12 (1997): 6–9.

Ellison, Harlan. *Again, Dangerous Visions.* Garden City, NY: Doubleday, 1972.

———. *Dangerous Visions.* Garden City, NY: Doubleday, 1967.

Eskridge, Kelley. *Solitaire.* New York: HarperCollins, 2002.

Fanon, Frantz. *Black Skin, White Masks.* Trans. Charles Lam Markmann. New York: Grove Press, 1967.

Fausto-Sterling, Anne. "The Five Sexes, Revisited." *The Sciences* (July/August 2000): 19–23.

———. "The Five Sexes: Why Male and Female Are Not Enough." *The Sciences* (March/April 1993): 20–24.

———. *Myths of Gender: Biological Theories about Women and Men.* New York: Basic Books, 1985.

———. *Sexing the Body: Gender Politics and the Construction of Sexuality.* New York: Basic Books, 2000.

Featherstone, Mike, and Roger Burrows. "Cultures of Technological Embodiment:

An Introduction." Eds. Mike Featherstone and Roger Burrows. *Cyberspace/
Cyberbodies/Cyberpunk: Cultures of Technological Embodiment*. London:
SAGE, 1995. 1–19.

———, eds. *Cyberspace/Cyberbodies/Cyberpunk: Cultures of Technological
Embodiment*. London: SAGE, 1995.

Feinberg, Leslie. *Stone Butch Blues*. Ithaca: Firebrand, 1993.

———. *TransLiberation: Beyond Pink or Blue*. Boston: Beacon, 1998.

Fekete, John. "The Post-Liberal Mind/Body, Postmodern Fiction, and the Case of
Cyberpunk SF." *Science Fiction Studies* 19 (1992): 395–403.

Felski, Rita. *The Gender of Modernity*. Cambridge, MA: Harvard UP, 1995.

Firestone, Shulamith. *The Dialectic of Sex: The Case for Feminist Revolution*. New
York: Bantam Books, 1970.

Flanagan, Mary, and Austin Booth, eds. *Reload: Rethinking Women and
Cyberculture*. Cambridge, MA: MIT Press, 2002.

Flannery-Dailey, Frances, and Rachel Wagner. "Wake Up! Gnosticism and
Buddhism in *The Matrix*." *Journal of Religion and Film* 5:2 (October 2001)
[http:www.unomaha.edu/~wwwjrf/gnostic.htm].

Flax, Jane. *Disputed Subjects. Essays on Psychoanalysis, Politics, and Philosophy*.
New York: Routledge, 1993.

Flodstrom, John. "Enlightening the Alien Savages: Colonialism in the Novels of
Robert Silverberg." *Into Darkness Peering: Race and Color in the Fantastic*. Ed.
Elisabeth Anne Leonard. Westport, CT: Greenwood Press, 1997. 159–70.

Forbes, Edith. *Exit to Reality*. Seattle: Seal Press, 1997.

Ford, James. "Buddhism, Christianity, and The Matrix: The Dialectic of Myth-
Making in Contemporary Cinema." *Journal of Religion and Film* 4:2 (October
2000) [http://www.unomaha.edu/~wwwjrf/thematrix.htm].

Forrest, Katherine V. *Daughters of a Coral Dawn*. Tallahassee: Naiad Press, 1984.

Foster, Frances Smith. "Octavia Butler's Black Female Future Fiction."
Extrapolation 23 (1982): 37–49.

Foster, Thomas. "Meat Puppets or Robopaths? Cyberpunk and the Question of
Embodiment." *Genders* 18 (Winter 1993): 11–31.

———. " 'The Postproduction of the Human Heart': Desire, Identification, and
Virtual Embodiment in Feminist Narratives of Cyberspace." *Reload:
Rethinking Women and Cyberculture*. Eds. Mary Flanagan and Austin Booth.
Cambridge, MA: MIT Press, 2002. 469–504.

———. " 'The Sex Appeal of the Inorganic': Posthuman Narratives and the
Construction of Desire." *Centuries' Ends, Narrative Means*. Ed. Robert
Newman. Stanford: Stanford UP, 1996. 276–301.

———. *The Souls of Cyberfolk: Postmodernisms as Vernacular Theory*.
Minneapolis: U of Minnesota P, 2005.

———. " 'Trapped by the Body'? Telepresence Technologies and Transgendered
Performance in Feminist and Lesbian Rewritings of Cyberpunk Fiction."
Modern Fiction Studies 43:3 (1997): 708–42.

Foucault, Michel. *The History of Sexuality. Volume 1: An Introduction*. Trans.
Robert Hurley. New York: Pantheon Books, 1978.

———. "Introduction." *Herculine Barbin: Being the Recently Discovered Memoirs of
a Nineteenth-Century French Hermaphrodite*. New York: Pantheon, 1980.
vii–xvii.

———. *The Order of Things: An Archaeology of the Human Sciences*. Trans. A. M.
Sheridan Smith. New York: Pantheon Books, 1970.

Frankenberg, Ruth. *White Women, Race Matters: The Social Construction of Whiteness.* Minneapolis: U of Minnesota P, 1993.

Freedman, Carl. *Critical Theory and Science Fiction.* Hanover and London: Wesleyan UP, 2000.

Freud, Sigmund. *On Sexuality: Three Essays on the Theory of Sexuality and Other Works.* The Pelican Freud Library, Vol. 7. Trans. James Strachey. Ed. Angela Richards. Middlesex and New York: Penguin Books, 1953.

Gabilondo, Joseba. "Postcolonial Cyborgs: Subjectivity in the Age of Cybernetic Reproduction." *The Cyborg Handbook.* Eds. Chris Hables Gray, Heidi Figueroa-Sarriera, and Steven Mentor. New York: Routledge, 1995. 423–32.

Gallardo, Ximena C., and C. Jason Smith. *Alien Woman: The Making of Lt. Ellen Ripley.* New York: Continuum, 2004.

Gearheart, Sally Miller. *The Wanderground: Stories of the Hill Women.* Waterfront, MA: Persephone Press, 1979.

Gibson, William. *Neuromancer.* New York: Ace Books, 1984.

Gilbert, Sandra M., and Susan Gubar. *The Madwoman in the Attic: The Woman Writer and the Nineteenth-Century Literary Imagination.* New Haven: Yale UP, 1979.

Gilroy, Paul. *The Black Atlantic: Modernity and Double Consciousness.* Cambridge, MA: Harvard UP, 1993.

Ginsberg, Elaine K., ed. *Passing and the Fictions of Identity.* Durham: Duke UP, 1996.

Glenn, Evelyn Nakano. "From Servitude to Service Work: Historical Communities in the Division of Paid Reproductive Labor." *Signs* 18:1 (1992). 1–43.

Gonzalez, Jennifer. "Envisioning Cyborg Bodies: Notes from Current Research." *The Cyborg Handbook.* Eds. Chris Hables Gray, Heidi Figueroa-Sarriera, and Steven Mentor. New York: Routledge, 1995. 267–79.

Goonan, Kathleen Ann. *Mississippi Blues.* New York: Tor Books, 1999.

———. *Queen City Jazz.* New York: Tor Books, 1994.

Gordon, Devin. "The Matrix Makers." *Newsweek: The Who's Next Issue.* 30 Dec. 2002/6 Jan. 2003. 81–89.

Govan, Sandra Y. "Connection, Links, and Extended Networks: Patterns in Octavia Butler's Science Fiction." *Black American Literature Forum* 18 (1984): 82–87.

———. "Homage to Tradition: Octavia Butler Renovates the Historical Novel." *MELUS: The Journal of the Society for the Study of the Multi-Ethnic Literature of the United States.* 13.1–2 (Spring/Summer 1986): 79–96.

Gramsci, Antonio. *Prison Notebooks.* Trans. Joseph A. Buttigieg. New York: Columbia UP, 1996.

Gray, Chris Hables, Heidi Figueroa-Sarriera, and Steven Mentor. "Introduction: Cyborgology: Constructing the Knowledge of Cybernetic Organisms." *The Cyborg Handbook.* Eds. Chris Hables Gray, Heidi Figueroa-Sarriera, and Steven Mentor. New York: Routledge, 1995. 1–14.

———, eds. *The Cyborg Handbook.* New York: Routledge, 1995.

Green, Michelle Erica. "There Goes the Neighborhood: Octavia Butler's Demand for Diversity in Utopias." *Utopian and Science Fiction by Women: Worlds of Difference.* Eds. Jane L. Donawerth and Carola A. Kolmerten. Liverpool: Liverpool UP, 1994. 166–89.

Greenberg, Harvey. "Reimagining the Gargoyle: Psychoanalytic Notes on *Alien.*" *Camera Obscura* 15 (1986): 87–108.

Grewal, Inderpal, and Caren Kaplan. Introduction. *Scattered Hegemonies: Postmodernity and Transnational Feminist Practices.* Eds. Inderpal Grewal and Caren Kaplan. Minneapolis: U of Minnesota P, 1994.

Griffith, Nicola. *Ammonite.* New York: Del Ray/Ballantine, 1992.

———. *Slow River.* New York: Del Ray/Ballantine, 1995.

Griffith, Nicola, and Stephan Pagel, eds. *Bending the Landscape. Vol. 2: Science Fiction.* Woodstock, NY: Overlook Press, 1998.

Halberstam, Judith. *Female Masculinity.* Durham: Duke UP, 1998.

———. "Transgender Butch: Butch/FTM Border Wars and the Masculine Continuum." *GLQ* 4.2 (1998): 287–310.

Halberstam, Judith, and C. Jacob Hale. "Butch/FTM Border Wars: A Note on Collaboration." *GLQ* 4:2 (1998): 283–85.

Halberstam, Judith, and Ira Livingston. Introduction. *Posthuman Bodies.* Eds. Judith Halberstam and Ira Livingston. Bloomington: Indiana UP, 1995. 1–20.

Hale, C. Jacob. "Consuming the Living, Dis(re)membering the Dead in the Butch/FTM Borderlands." *GLQ* 4.2 (1998): 311–48.

Hanchard, Michael. "Identity, Meaning, and the African-American." *Dangerous Liaisons: Gender, Nation, and Postcolonial Perspectives.* Eds. Anne McClintock, Aamir Mufti, and Ella Shohat. Minneapolis: U of Minnesota P, 1997. 230–39.

Haran, Joan. "Destabilising Sex/Gender/Sexuality in Melissa Scott's *Shadow Man.*" *Foundation* 82 (2001): 9–25.

Haraway, Donna. "The Actors Are Cyborgs, Nature Is Coyote, and the Geography Is Elsewhere: Postscript to 'Cyborgs at Large.'" *Technoculture.* Eds. Constance Penley and Andrew Ross. Minneapolis: U of Minnesota P, 1991. 21–26.

———. "A Cyborg Manifesto: Science, Technology, and Socialist Feminism in the Late Twentieth Century." 1985. *Simians, Cyborgs, and Women: The Reinvention of Nature.* London: Free Association, 1991. 149–81.

———. *How Like a Leaf: An Interview with Thyrza Nichols Goodeve.* New York and London: Routledge, 2000.

———. *Modest Witness@Second Millennium. FemaleMan© Meets OncoMouse™: Feminism and Technoscience.* New York: Routledge, 1997.

———. *Primate Visions: Gender, Race, and Nature in the World of Modern Science.* New York: Routledge, 1989.

———. *Simians, Cyborgs, and Women: The Reinvention of Nature.* London: Free Association Books, 1991.

———. "Situated Knowledges: The Science Question in Feminism and the Privilege of Partial Perspective." *Simians, Cyborgs, and Women: The Reinvention of Nature.* London: Free Association Books, 1991. 183–201.

Harding, Sandra. *The Science Question in Feminism.* Ithaca: Cornell UP, 1991.

Harris, Anne. *Accidental Creatures.* New York: Tor, 2000.

Hartsock, Nancy. "The Feminist Standpoint." 1980. *The Second Wave.* Ed. Linda Nicholson. New York: Routledge, 1997. 216–40.

Hayles, N. Katherine. *The Cosmic Web: Scientific Field Models and Literary Strategies in the Twentieth Century.* Ithaca: Cornell UP, 1984.

———. *How We Became Posthuman: Virtual Bodies in Cybernetics, Literature, and Informatics.* Chicago: U of Chicago P, 1999.

———. "The Seductions of Cyberspace." *Rethinking Technology.* Ed. Verena Andermatt Conley. Minneapolis: U of Minnesota P, 1993. 173–90.

Hebdige, Dick. *Subculture: The Meaning of Style.* London: Methuen, 1979.

Heim, Michael. "The Design of Virtual Reality." *Cyberspace/Cyberbodies/ Cyberpunk: Cultures of Technological Embodiment.* Eds. Mike Featherstone and Roger Burrows. London: SAGE, 1995. 65–77.

Hekman, Susan. *Gender and Knowledge: Elements of a Postmodern Feminism.* Oxford: Polity Press, 1990.

Helford, Elyce Rae. "'Would you really rather die than bear my young?': The Construction of Gender, Race, and Species in Octavia E. Butler's 'Bloodchild.'" *African American Review* 28 (1994): 259–71.

Henderson, Mae Gwendolyn. "Speaking in Tongues: Dialogics, Dialectics, and the Black Woman Writer's Literary Tradition." *Feminists Theorize the Political.* Eds. Judith Butler and Joan W. Scott. New York: Routledge, 1992. 144–66.

Hicks, Heather. "'Whatever it is that she's since become': Writing Bodies of Text and Bodies of Women in James Tiptree, Jr.'s 'The Girl Who Was Plugged In' and William Gibson's 'The Winter Market.'" *Contemporary Literature* 37:1 (1996): 62–93.

Higginbotham, Evelyn Brooks. "African-American Women's History and the Metalanguage of Race." *Signs* 17 (1992): 91–114.

Hollinger, Veronica. "Cybernetic Deconstructions: Cyberpunk and Postmodernism." *Storming the Reality Studio: A Casebook of Cyberpunk and Postmodern Fiction.* Ed. Larry McCaffery. Durham: Duke UP, 1991. 203–18.

———. "Feminist Science Fiction: Breaking Up the Subject." *Extrapolation* 31 (1990): 229–39.

———. "(Re)reading Queerly: Science Fiction, Feminism, and the Defamiliarization of Gender." *Science Fiction Studies* 26 (1999): 23–40.

———. "The Utopia of the Perverse: An Exercise in 'Transgressive Reinscription.'" *Femspec* 2:1 (2000): 30–37.

hooks, bell. *Ain't I a Woman: Black Women and Feminism.* Boston: South End Press, 1981.

Hopkinson, Nalo. *Brown Girl in the Ring.* New York: Warner Books, 1998.

———. *Midnight Robber.* New York: Warner Books, 2000.

Irwin, William, ed. The Matrix *and Philosophy.* Vol. 3 of *Popular Culture and Philosophy.* Peru, IL: Open Court Publishing Company, 2002.

Jacobs, Naomi. "Posthuman Bodies and Agency in Octavia Butler's *Xenogenesis.*" *Dark Horizons: Science Fiction and the Dystopian Imagination.* Eds. Raffaella Baccolini and Tom Moylan. Routledge, 2003. 91–111.

Jameson, Frederic. *Postmodernism, or, the Cultural Logic of Late Capitalism.* Durham: Duke UP, 1991.

Janes, Linda. "Introduction to Part Two: Alien M/others: Representing the Feminine in Science Fiction Film." *The Gendered Cyborg: A Reader.* Eds. Gill Kirkup, Linda Janes, Kathryn Woodward, and Fiona Hovenden. New York: Routledge, 2000. 91–100.

Jennings, Ros. "Desire and Design—Ripley Undressed." *Immortal, Invisible: Lesbians and the Moving Image.* Ed. Tamsin Wilton. New York: Routledge, 1995. 193–206.

John, Mary E. *Discrepant Dislocations: Feminism, Theory, and Postcolonial Histories.* Berkeley: U of California P, 1996.

Jones, Gwyneth. *Divine Endurance.* New York: Tor Books, 1984.

Joy, Bill. "Why the Future Doesn't Need Us." *Wired* (April 2000): 238–62.

Kabir, Shameem. *Daughters of Desire: Lesbian Representations in Film.* London: Cassell, 1998.

Kaplan, Caren. *Questions of Travel: Postmodern Discourses of Displacement.* Durham: Duke UP, 1996.

Kavanaugh, James H. "Feminism, Humanism, and Science in *Alien.*" *Alien Zone: Cultural Theory and Contemporary Science Fiction Cinema.* Ed. Annette Kuhn. London and New York: Verso, 1990. 73–81.

Keller, Evelyn Fox. *Reflections on Gender and Science.* New Haven: Yale UP, 1985.

Kellner, Douglas. *Media Culture: Cultural Studies, Identity, and Politics between the Modern and the Postmodern.* New York: Routledge, 1995.

Kenan, Randall. "An Interview with Octavia E. Butler." *Callaloo: A Journal of American and African Arts and Letters* 14 (Spring 1991): 495–504.

Kessler, Suzanne. *Lessons from the Intersexed.* New Brunswick, NJ: Rutgers UP, 1990.

King, Geoff, and Tanya Krzywinska. *Science Fiction Cinema: From Outerspace to Cyberspace.* London: Wallflower, 2000.

Kirkup, Gill, Linda Janes, Kath Woodward, and Fiona Hovenden. *The Gendered Cyborg: A Reader.* New York: Routledge, 2000.

Kristeva, Julia. *Powers of Horror: An Essay on Abjection.* Trans. Leon S. Roudiez. New York: Columbia UP, 1982.

Kuhn, Annette. "Border Crossing." *Sight and Sound* 7.12 (1997): 13.

———, ed. *Alien Zone: Cultural Theory and Contemporary Science Fiction Cinema.* London and New York: Verso, 1990.

———. *Alien Zone II: The Spaces of Science Fiction Cinema.* London and New York: Verso, 1999.

Landon, Brooks. *The Aesthetics of Ambivalence: Rethinking Science Fiction Film in the Age of Electronic (Re)Production.* Westport, CT: Greenwood, 1992.

Larbalestier, Justine. *The Battle of the Sexes in Science Fiction.* Middletown, CT: Wesleyan UP, 2002.

Latham, Rob. *Consuming Youth: Vampires, Cyborgs, and the Culture of Consumption.* Chicago: U of Chicago P, 2002.

Lavie, Smadar, and Ted Swedenburg. Introduction. *Displacement, Diaspora, and Geographies of Identity.* Eds. Smadar Lavie and Ted Swedenburg. Durham: Duke UP, 1996. 1–25.

Lefanu, Sarah. *In the Chinks of the World Machine: Feminism and Science Fiction.* London: The Women's Press, 1988.

Le Guin, Ursula K. *Always Coming Home.* New York: Bantam Books, 1987.

———. "American SF and the Other." *Science Fiction Studies* 2 (1975): 208–10.

———. "Is Gender Necessary?" *Dancing at the Edge of the World.* New York: Harper & Row, 1989. 7–16.

———. *The Left Hand of Darkness.* New York: Walker, 1969; rpt. New York: Ace Books, 1969.

———. *The Wind's Twelve Quarters.* New York: Bantam Books, 1975.

Leonard, Elisabeth Anne, ed. *Into Darkness Peering: Race and Color in the Fantastic.* Westport, CT: Greenwood Press, 1997.

Loomba, Ania. *Colonialism/Postcolonialism.* New York: Routledge, 1998.

Lorde, Audre. "Age, Race, Class, and Sex: Women Redefining Difference." *Sister Outsider.* Freedom, CA: The Crossing Press, 1984. 114–23.

———. *Sister Outsider.* Freedom, CA: The Crossing Press, 1984.

Lowe, Marian, and Ruth Hubbard, eds. *Woman's Nature: Rationalizations of Inequality*. New York: Pergamon Press, 1983.
Lugones, Maria. "Purity, Impurity, and Separation." *Signs* 19:2 (1994): 458–79.

Mason, Carol. "Terminating Bodies: Towards a Cyborg History of Abortion." *Posthuman Bodies*. Eds. Judith Halberstam and Ira Livingston. Bloomington: Indiana UP, 1995. 225–43.
Mason, Fran. "Loving the Technological Undead: Cyborg Sex and Necrophilia in Richard Calder's *Dead* Trilogy." *The Body's Perilous Pleasures: Dangerous Desires and Contemporary Culture*. Ed. Michele Aaron. Edinburgh: Edinburgh UP, 1999. 108–25.
Matisons, Michelle Renee. *Systems, Standpoints, and Subjects: Marxist Legacies in U.S. Feminist Theories*. Diss. Clark University, 2000.
McCaffery, Larry. "An Interview with Octavia E. Butler." *Across the Wounded Galaxies*. Ed. Larry McCaffrey. Urbana: U of Illinois P, 1990. 54–70.
———. "Introduction: The Desert of the Real." *Storming the Reality Studio: A Casebook of Cyberpunk and Postmodern Fiction*. Ed. Larry McCaffery. Durham: Duke UP, 1991. 1–16.
———, ed. *Storming the Reality Studio: A Casebook of Cyberpunk and Postmodern Fiction*. Durham: Duke UP, 1991.
McClintock, Anne, Aamir Mufti, and Ella Shohat. "Introduction." *Dangerous Liaisons: Gender, Nation, and Postcolonial Perspectives*. Eds. Anne McClintock, Aamir Mufti, and Ella Shohat. Minneapolis: U of Minnesota P, 1997. 1–12.
McHugh, Maureen F. *Mission Child*. New York: Avon Books, 1998.
McIntyre, Vonda. *Dreamsnake*. London: Pan, 1979.
———. "Fireflood." *Fireflood and Other Stories*. Boston: Houghton Mifflin, 1979. 1–28.
Melzer, Patricia. "'All that you touch you change': Utopian Desire and the Concept of Change in Octavia Butler's *Parable of the Sower* and *Parable of the Talents*." *Femspec* 3.2 (2002): 31–52.
Melzer, Patricia, and Shelley Price, eds. "Gender and Technology in Science Fiction Film." Special Issue. *Femspec* 5.1 (2004).
Merchant, Carolyn. *The Death of Nature: Women, Ecology, and the Scientific Revolution*. San Francisco: Harper and Row, 1980.
Misha. *Red Spider White Web*. 1990. Oregon: Wordcraft, 1999.
Mixon, Laura J. *Glass Houses*. New York: Tor Books, 1992.
———. *Proxies*. New York: Tor Books, 1998.
Mohanty, Chandra Talpade. "Cartographies of Struggle: Third World Women and the Politics of Feminism." *Third World Women and the Politics of Feminism*. Eds. Chandra Talpade Mohanty, Ann Russo, and Lourdes Torres. Bloomington: Indiana UP, 1991. 1–47.
———. "Under Western Eyes: Feminist Scholarship and Colonial Discourse." *Third World Women and the Politics of Feminism*. Eds. Chandra Talpade Mohanty, Ann Russo, and Lourdes Torres. Bloomington: Indiana UP, 1991. 51–80.
Mohanty, Chandra Talpade, and Biddy Martin. "Feminist Politics: What's Home Got to Do with It?" *Feminist Studies, Critical Studies*. Ed. Teresa de Lauretis. Bloomington: Indiana UP, 1986. 191–212.
Mohanty, Chandra Talpade, Ann Russo, and Lourdes Torres, eds. *Third World Women and the Politics of Feminism*. Bloomington: Indiana UP, 1991.

Moraga, Cherríe, and Gloria Anzaldúa, eds. *This Bridge Called My Back: Writings by Radical Women of Color.* Watertown, MA: Persephone Press, 1981.

Moylan, Tom. "Beyond Negation: The Critical Utopias of Ursula K. Le Guin and Samuel R. Delany." *Extrapolation* 21 (1980): 236-53.

Mulvey, Laura. "Visual Pleasure and Narrative Cinema." 1975. *Issues in Feminist Film Criticism.* Ed. Patricia Erens. Bloomington: Indiana UP, 1990.

Nakamura, Lisa. *Cybertypes: Race, Ethnicity, and Identity on the Internet.* New York: Routledge, 2002.

Namaste, Viviane K. *Invisible Lives: The Erasure of Transsexual and Transgendered People.* Chicago: U of Chicago P, 2000.

Nandy, Ashis. *The Intimate Enemy: Loss and Recovery of Self under Colonialism.* Delhi: Oxford UP, 1983.

Narayan, Uma. *Dislocating Cultures: Identities, Traditions, and Third World Feminism.* New York: Routledge, 1997.

Nestle, Joan, Clare Howell, and Riki Wilchins, eds. *GenderQueer: Voices from Beyond the Sexual Binary.* Los Angeles: Alyson Books, 2002.

Newman, Kim. "Film Review: *Alien Resurrection.*" *Sight and Sound* 7.12 (1997): 36-37.

Newson, Adele S. "Review of *Dawn* and *Adulthood Rites,* by Octavia Butler." *Black American Literature Forum* 23:2 (1989): 389-96.

Newton, Judith. "Feminism and Anxiety in *Alien.*" *Alien Zone: Cultural Theory and Contemporary Science Fiction Cinema.* Ed. Annette Kuhn. London and New York: Verso, 1990. 82-87.

Nicholson, Linda J., ed. *Feminism/Postmodernism.* New York: Routledge, 1990.

Nixon, Nicola. "Cyberpunk: Preparing the Ground for Revolution or Keeping the Boys Satisfied?" *cybersexualities: A Reader on Feminist Theory, Cyborgs, and Cyberspace.* Ed. Jenny Wolmark. Edinburgh: Edinburgh UP, 1999. 191-207.

Ore, Rebecca. *Gaia's Toys.* New York: Tor Books, 1997.

Park, Severna. *Hand of Prophecy.* New York: Avon Books, 1998.

———. *Speaking Dreams.* Ann Arbor, MI: Firebrand Books, 1992.

Parry, Benita. "Problems in Current Theories of Colonial Discourse." *The Post-Colonial Studies Reader.* Eds. Bill Ashcroft, Gareth Griffiths, and Helen Tiffin. London: Routledge, 1995. 36-44.

Pearson, Wendy. "Alien Cryptographies: The View from Queer." *Science Fiction Studies* 26 (1999): 1-22.

Penley, Constance. "Time Travel, Primal Scene, and the Critical Dystopia." *Camera Obscura* 15 (1986): 67-84.

Penley, Constance, Elisabeth Lyon, Lynn Spigel, and Janet Bergstrom, eds. *Close Encounters: Film, Feminism, and Science Fiction.* Minneapolis: U of Minnesota P, 1991.

Penley, Constance, and Andrew Ross. "Cyborgs at Large: Interview with Donna Haraway." *Technoculture.* Eds. Constance Penley and Andrew Ross. Minneapolis: U of Minnesota P, 1991. 1-20.

Piercy, Marge. *He, She and It.* New York: Fawcett Crest, 1991.

———. *Woman on the Edge of Time.* London: The Women's Press, 1978.

Plant, Sadie. *Zeroes and Ones: Digital Women and the New Technoculture.* New York: Doubleday, 1996.

Plumwood, Val. *Feminism and the Mastery of Nature.* London: Routledge, 1993.

Posnock, Ross. *Color and Culture: Black Writers and the Making of the Modern Intellectual.* Cambridge, MA: Harvard UP, 1998.

Pratt, Mary Louise. *Imperial Eyes: Travel Writing and Transculturation.* New York: Routledge, 1992.

Prosser, Jay. *Second Skins: The Body Narratives of Transsexuality.* New York: Columbia UP, 1998.

Rajan, Rajeswari Sunder. *Real and Imagined Women: Gender, Culture, and Postcolonialism.* London: Routledge, 1993.

Ramirez, Catherine S. "Cyborg Feminism: The Science Fiction of Octavia E. Butler and Gloria Anzaldúa." *Reload: Rethinking Women and Cyberculture.* Eds. Mary Flanagan and Austin Booth. Cambridge, MA: MIT Press, 2002. 374–402.

Raymond, Janice. *The Transsexual Empire: The Making of the She-Male.* New York: Teacher's College Press, 1994.

Roberts, Robin. *A New Species: Gender and Science in Science Fiction.* Urbana and Chicago: U of Illinois P, 1993.

Robertson, Robbie. "The Narrative Sources of Ridley Scott's *Alien.*" *Cinema and Fiction.* Eds. John Orr and Colin Nicholson. Edinburgh: Edinburgh UP, 1992.

Rose, Sharon, Cris Stevens, et al., eds. *Bisexual Horizons: Politics, Histories, Lives.* London: Lawrence and Wishart, 1996.

Ross, Andrew. *Strange Weather: Culture, Science and Technology in the Age of Limits.* London and New York: Verso, 1991.

Rothblatt, Martine. *The Apartheid of Sex: A Manifesto on the Freedom of Gender.* New York: Crown/Random House, 1995.

Rothschild, Joan, ed. *Machina ex Dea: Feminist Perspectives on Technology.* New York: Pergamon Press, 1983.

Rubin, Gayle. "Thinking Sex: Notes for a Radical Theory of the Politics of Sexuality." *The Lesbian and Gay Studies Reader.* Eds. Henry Abelove, Michele Aina Barale, and David M. Halperin. New York: Routledge, 1993. 3–44.

Rucker, Rudy, Peter Lamborn Wilson, and Robert Anton Wilson, eds. *Semiotext(e) SF.* New York: Autonomedia, 1989.

Rushing, Janice Hocker. "Evolution of the 'New Frontier' in *Alien* and *Aliens*: Patriarchal Co-optation of the Feminine Archetype." *Screening the Sacred: Religion., Myth, and Ideology in Popular American Film.* Eds. Joel Martin and Conrad Ostwalt. Boulder: Westview Press, 1995. 94–117.

Russ, Joanna. *The Female Man.* Beacon Press: Boston, 1975.

———. "The Image of Women in Science Fiction." *Images of Women in Fiction: Feminist Perspectives.* Ed. Susan Cornillon. Bowling Green, OH: Bowling Green University Popular Press, 1972. 79–94.

———. "Reflections on Science Fiction—An Interview with Joanna Russ." *Building Feminist Theory: Essays from QUEST.* New York and London: Longman, 1981. 243–50.

Said, Edward W. *Orientalism.* New York: Penguin, 1978.

Sallis, James, ed. *Ash of Stars: On the Writing of Samuel R. Delany.* Jackson: UP of Mississippi, 1996.

Salvaggio, Ruth. "Octavia Butler." *Suzy McKee Charnas/Octavia Butler/Joan D. Vinge.* Eds. Marleen S. Barr, Ruth Salvaggio, and Richard Law. Mercer Island, WA: Starmont, 1986.

———. "Octavia Butler and the Black Science-Fiction Heroine." *Black American Literature Forum* 8 (1984): 78–81.

Sanchez, Maria Carla, and Linda Schlossberg, eds. *Passing: Identity and Interpretation in Sexuality, Race, and Religion.* New York: NYU Press, 2001.

Sandoval, Chela. *Methodology of the Oppressed.* Minneapolis: U of Minnesota Press, 2000.

———. "New Sciences: Cyborg Feminism and the Methodology of the Oppressed." *The Cyborg Handbook.* Eds. Chris Hables Gray, Heidi Figueroa-Sarriera, and Steven Mentor. New York and London: Routledge, 1995. 407-22.

———. "U.S. Third World Feminism: The Theory and Method of Oppositional Consciousness." *Genders* 10 (1991): 1-24.

Sardar, Ziauddin. "Introduction." *Aliens R Us: The Other in Science Fiction Cinema.* Eds. Ziauddin Sardar and Sean Cubitt. London: Pluto Press, 2002. 1-17.

———, eds. *Aliens R Us: The Other in Science Fiction Cinema.* London: Pluto Press, 2002.

Sargent, Pamela. *The Shore of Women.* New York: Bantam Books, 1986.

———, ed. *More Women of Wonder: Science Fiction Novelettes by Women about Women.* New York: Vintage, 1976.

———. *The New Women of Wonder: Recent Science Fiction Stories by Women about Women.* New York: Vintage, 1978.

———. *Women of Wonder: Science Fiction Stories by Women about Women.* New York: Vintage, 1974.

Schemanske, Mark. "Working for the Company: Patriarchal Legislation of the Maternal in *Alien³*." *Authority and Transgression in Literature and Film.* Eds. Bonnie Braendlin and Hans Braendlin. Gainesville: U of Florida P, 1996. 127-35.

Schiebinger, Londa. *Nature's Body: Gender in the Making of Modern Science.* Boston: Beacon Press, 1993.

Schulman, Alix Kates. "Dances with Feminists." *Women's Review of Books* 9:3 (December 1991) [http://sunsite.berkeley.edu/Goldman/Features/dances_shulman.html].

Schlossberg, Linda. "Introduction: Rites of Passing." *Passing: Identity and Interpretation in Sexuality, Race, and Religion.* Eds. Maria Carla Sanchez and Linda Schlossberg. New York: NYU Press, 2001. 1-12.

Scholes, Robert, and Eric S. Rabkin. *Science Fiction: History, Science, Vision.* New York: Oxford UP, 1977.

Scobie, Stephen. "What's the Story, Mother? The Mourning of the Alien." *Science Fiction Studies* 20 (1993): 80-93.

Scott, Joan W. "Commentary: Cyborgian Socialists?" Ed. Elizabeth Weed. *Coming to Terms: Feminism, Theory, Politics.* New York: Routledge, 1989. 215-17.

Scott, Melissa. *Burning Bright.* 1993; rpt. New York: Tor Books, 1994.

———. *Dreaming Metal.* New York: Tor Books, 1997.

———. *Dream Ships.* New York: Tor Books, 1993.

———. *The Jazz.* New York: Tor Books, 2001.

———. *Night Sky Mine.* New York: Tor Books, 1996.

———. *Shadow Man.* New York: Tor Books, 1995.

———. *The Shapes of Their Hearts.* New York: Tor Books, 1999.

———. *Trouble and Her Friends.* New York: Tor Books, 1994.

Scott, Melissa, and Lisa Barnett. *Point of Dreams.* New York: Tor Books, 2001.

———. *Point of Hopes.* New York: Tor Books, 1997.

Sedgwick, Eve Kosofsky. *Between Men: English Literature and Male Homosocial Desire.* New York: Columbia UP, 1985.

———. *Epistemologies of the Closet.* Berkeley: U of California P, 1990.

———, ed. *Novel Gazing: Queer Readings in Fiction.* Durham: Duke UP, 1997.

Shelley, Mary. *Frankenstein or, The Modern Prometheus.* 1818. London: Penguin Books, 1985.

Shinn, Thelma J. "The Wise Witches: Black Women Mentors in the Fiction of Octavia E. Butler." *Conjuring: Black Women, Fiction, and Literary Tradition.* Eds. Marjorie Pryse and Hortense J. Spillers. Bloomington: Indiana UP, 1985. 203–15.

Shiva, Vandana. *Staying Alive: Women, Ecology, and Development.* London: Zed Books, 1989.

Shohat, Ella. "Notes on the 'Post-Colonial'." *Social Text* 31/32 (1993): 99–113.

Slusser, George, and Tom Shippey, eds. *Fiction 2000: Cyberpunk and the Future of Narrative.* Athens: U of Georgia P, 1992.

Smith, Barbara, Patricia Bell Scott, and Gloria Tull, eds. *All the Women Are White, All the Blacks Are Men, But Some of Us Are Brave.* Old Westbury, New York: Feminist Press, 1982.

Smith, Dorothy E. *Texts, Facts, and Femininity: Exploring the Relations of Ruling.* London: Routledge, 1990.

Sobchack, Vivian. "Beating the Meat/Surviving the Text, or How to Get Out of This Century Alive." *Cyberspace/Cyberbodies/Cyberpunk: Cultures of Technological Embodiment.* Eds. Mike Featherstone and Roger Burrows. London: SAGE, 1995. 205–14.

———. "Cities on the Edge of Time: The Urban Science Fiction Film." *East-West Film Journal* 3, no. 1 (1988): 4–9.

———. *Screening Space: The American Science Fiction Film.* 2nd ed. New York: Ungar, 1987.

———. "The Virginity of Astronauts: Sex and the Science Fiction Film." *Alien Zone: Cultural Theory and Contemporary Science Fiction Cinema.* Ed. Annette Kuhn. London and New York: Verso, 1990. 103–15.

Spade, Dean. "More Gender, More of the Time." *Makezine: Transmissions* [http://www.makezine.org/bibi.html].

Spivak, Gayatri Chakravorty. "Can the Subaltern Speak?" *Marxism and the Interpretation of Culture.* Eds. Cary Nelson and Lawrence Grossberg. London: Macmillan, 1988. 271–313.

———. *A Critique of Postcolonial Reason: Toward a History of the Vanishing Present.* Cambridge, MA: Harvard UP, 1999.

———. "More on Power/Knowledge." 1992. *The Spivak Reader: Selected Works of Gayatri Chakravorty Spivak.* Eds. Donna Landry and Gerald MacLean. New York: Routledge, 1996. 141–74.

———. "Subaltern Studies. Deconstructing Historiography." 1985. *The Spivak Reader: Selected Works of Gayatri Chakravorty Spivak.* Eds. Donna Landry and Gerald MacLean. New York: Routledge, 1996. 203–35.

Springer, Claudia. *Electronic Eros: Bodies and Desires in the Postindustrial Age.* Austin: U of Texas P, 1996.

———. "Psycho-Cybernetics in Films of the 1990s." *Alien Zone II: The Spaces of Science Fiction Cinema.* Ed. Annette Kuhn. London: Verso, 1999. 203–18.

Squires, Judith. "Fabulous Feminist Futures and the Lure of Cyberculture." *The Cyberculture Reader.* Eds. David Bell and Barbara M. Kennedy. London: Routledge, 2000. 360–73.

Stam, Robert. "Multiculturalism and the Neoconservatives." *Dangerous Liaisons: Gender, Nation, and Postcolonial Perspectives.* Eds. Anne McClintock, Aamir Mufti, and Ella Shohat. Minneapolis and London: U of Minnesota P, 1997. 188–203.

Stephenson, Neal. *The Diamond Age.* New York: Bantam, 1995.

Sterling, Bruce. "Preface." *Mirrorshades: The Cyberpunk Anthology.* Ed. Bruce Sterling. 1986. New York: Ace Books, 1988. ix–xvi.

Stockton, Sharon. "'The Self Regained': Cyberpunk's Retreat to the Imperium." *Contemporary Literature* 36.4 (1995): 588–612.

Stone, Allucquere Rosanne. *The War of Desire and Technology at the Close of the Mechanical Age.* Cambridge, MA: MIT Press, 1995.

Storr, Merl, ed. *Bisexuality: A Critical Reader.* New York: Routledge, 1999.

Stryker, Susan, ed. *The Transgender Reader.* New York: Routledge, forthcoming.

Suleri, Sara. "The Rhetoric of English India." *The Post-Colonial Studies Reader.* Eds. Bill Ashcroft, Gareth Griffiths, and Helen Tiffin. London: Routledge, 1995. 111–13.

Surkan, K. "'I Want to Be a Real Boy': A.I. Robots, Cyborgs, and Mutants as Passing Figures in Science Fiction Film." *Femspec* 5.1 (2004): 114–36.

Suvin, Darko. *Metamorphosis of Science Fiction: On the Poetics and History of a Literary Genre.* New Haven: Yale UP, 1979.

———. "On Gibson and Cyberpunk SF." *Foundation* 46 (1989): 40–51.

———. "On the Poetics of the Science Fiction Genre." *College English* 34 (1972): 372–83.

———. "The River-Side Trees, or SF and Utopia: Degrees of Kinship." *Minnesota Review* 2/3 (1974): 108–15.

Tan, Cecilia. *The Velderet: A Cybersex s/m Serial.* Cambridge, MA: Circlet Press, 2001.

———, ed. *Sexcrime: Tales of Underground Love and Subversive Erotica.* Cambridge, MA: Circlet Press, 2000.

Theweleit, Klaus. *Male Fantasies.* Vols. 1 and 2. Minneapolis: U of Minnesota P, 1987 and 1989.

Thomas, Sheree R., ed. *Dark Matter: A Century of Speculative Fiction from the African Diaspora.* New York: Warner Books, 2000.

Thomson, Amy. *The Color of Distance.* New York: Ace Books, 1995.

———. *Through Alien Eyes.* New York: Ace Books, 1999.

Torry, Robert. "Awakening to the Other: Feminism and the Ego-Ideal in *Alien.*" *Women's Studies* 23 (1994): 343–63.

Trinh, T. Minh-ha. *Woman, Native, Other: Writing Postcoloniality and Feminism.* Bloomington: Indiana UP, 1989.

Tucker, Jeffrey Allen. *A Sense of Wonder: Samuel R. Delany, Race, Identity, and Difference.* Middletown, CT: Wesleyan UP, 2004.

Vance, Carole S. "Toward a Politics of Sexuality." *Pleasure and Danger: Exploring Female Sexuality.* Ed. Carole S. Vance. Boston: Routledge, 1984. 1–27.

VanderMeer, Jeff. "Interview with Richard Calder." *Leviathan* 2 (1998).

Wajcman, Judy. *Feminism Confronts Technology.* University Park: The Pennsylvania State UP, 1991.

Walker, Alice. *In Search of Our Mothers' Gardens: Womanist Prose.* San Diego: Harcourt, 1983.

Walker, Barbara G. *The Woman's Encyclopedia of Myths and Secrets.* San Francisco: HarperCollins, 1983.

Warren, Karen J., ed. *Ecological Feminist Philosophies.* Bloomington: Indiana UP, 1996.

Weed, Elizabeth, ed. *Coming to Terms: Feminism, Theory, Politics*. New York: Routledge, 1989.

Whedon, Joss. *Alien Resurrection Scriptbook*. New York: HarperPrism, 1997.

White, Eric. "The Erotics of Becoming: *Xenogenesis* and *The Thing*." *Science Fiction Studies* 20 (1993): 394-408.

White, Patricia. *unInvited: Classical Hollywood Cinema and Lesbian Representability*. Bloomington: Indiana UP, 1999.

Wilchins, Riki. *Read My Lips: Sexual Subversion and the End of Gender*. Milford, CT: Firebrand Books, 1997.

Williams, Sherley Anne. "On Octavia E. Butler." *Ms.* (March 1986): 70-73.

Wilton, Tamsin, ed. *Immortal, Invisible: Lesbians and the Moving Image*. New York: Routledge, 1995.

Wittig, Monique. "One Is Not Born a Woman." *The Gay and Lesbian Studies Reader*. Eds. Henry Abelove, Michele Aina Barale, and David M. Halperin. New York: Routledge, 1993. 103-09.

Wolmark, Jenny. *Aliens and Others: Science Fiction, Feminism and Postmodernism*. Iowa City: U of Iowa P, 1994.

———. ed. *cybersexualities: A Reader on Feminist Theory, Cyborgs, and Cyberspace*. Edinburgh: Edinburgh UP, 1999.

X, Christina. "The Catgirl Manifesto: An Introduction." *Album Zutique: No. 1*. Ed. Jeff VanderMeer. Portland, OR: Ministry of Whimsy Press, 2003. 156-84.

Yeffeth, Glenn, ed. *Taking the Red Pill: Science, Philosophy and Religion in* The Matrix. Dallas, TX: BenBella Books, 2003.

Young, Lola. "Racialized Femininity." *Women's Bodies: Discipline and Transgression*. Eds. Jane Arthur and Jean Grimshaw. London: Cassell, 1999. 67-90.

Zaki, Hoda M. "Utopia, Dystopia, and Ideology in the Science Fiction of Octavia Butler." *Science Fiction Studies* 17 (1990): 239-51.

Films

Alien. Dir. Ridley Scott. Twentieth Century Fox, 1979.

Alien Resurrection. Dir. Jean-Pierre Jeunet. Twentieth Century Fox, 1997.

Alien³. Dir. David Fincher. Twentieth Century Fox, 1992.

Aliens. Dir. James Cameron. Twentieth Century Fox, 1986.

Batman. Dir. Tim Burton. Warner Brothers, 1989.

Batman and Robin. Dir. Joel Schumacher. Warner Brothers, 1997.

Batman Forever. Dir. Joel Schumacher. Warner Brothers, 1995.

Batman Returns. Dir. Tim Burton. Warner Brothers, 1992.

Battlefield Earth. Dir. Roger Christian. Warner Brothers, 2000.

Blade Runner. Dir. Ridley Scott. Warner Bros., 1982.

Born in Flames. Dir. Lizzie Borden. First Run Features, 1983.

Eve of Destruction. Dir. Duncan Gibbins. MGM, 1991.

eXistenZ. Dir. David Cronenberg. Miramax, 1999.

The Fly. Dir. David Cronenberg. Twentieth Century Fox, 1986.

Gattaca. Dir. Andrew Niccol. Columbia/Tristar, 1997.
Godzilla. Dir. Roland Emmerich. Sony Pictures Entertainment, 1998.

Independence Day. Dir. Roland Emmerich. Twentieth Century Fox, 1996.
The Invasion of the Body Snatchers. Dir. Don Siegel. Walter Warner Productions, 1956.

The Lawnmower Man. Dir. Brett Leonard. New Line Cinema, 1992.

The Matrix. Dir. Wachowski Brothers. Warner Brothers, 1999.
The Matrix Reloaded. Dir. Wachowski Brothers. Warner Brothers, 2003.
Matrix Revolutions. Dir. Wachowski Brothers. Warner Brothers, 2003.

Pitch Black. Dir. David Twohy. USA Film, 2000.

RoboCop. Dir. Paul Verhoeven. Orion Pictures Corporations, 1987.

Spawn. Dir. Mark A. Z. Dippe. Newline Cinema, 1997.
Species. Dir. Roger Donaldson. Metro-Goldwyn Mayer, 1995.
Species II. Dir. Peter Medak. Metro-Goldwyn Mayer, 1998.
Spider-Man. Dir. Sam Raimi. Columbia/Tristar, 2002.
Spider-Man 2. Dir. Sam Raimi. Columbia/Sony, 2004.
Star Trek Next Generation—First Contact. Dir. Jonathan Frakes. Paramount Pictures, 1996.
Star Wars Episode I: The Phantom Menace. Dir. George Lucas. Twentieth Century Fox, 1999.
Supernova. Dir. Thomas Lee and Walter Hill. Metro-Goldwyn Mayer, 2000.

The Terminator. Dir. James Cameron. Cinema 84/Euro Film Fund/Hemdale Film Corporation/Pacific Western, 1984.
Terminator 2: Judgment Day. Dir. James Cameron. Carolco Pictures/Pacific Western/Lightstorm Entertainment, 1991.
Terminator 3: Rise of the Machines. Dir. Jonathan Mostow. Warner Brothers, 2003.
The Thing (From Another World). Dir. Christian Nyby. Winchester, 1951.
The Thirteenth Floor. Dir. Josef Rusnak. Columbia/Tristar, 1999.
TRON. Dir. Steven Lisberger. Disney Studio, 1982.
2001: A Space Odyssey. Dir. Stanley Kubrick. Warner Studios, 1968.

Videodrome. Dir. David Cronenberg. Famous Players/Filmplan/Guardian Trust Company/Universal Pictures, 1983.

The X-Men. Dir. Bryan Singer. Twentieth Century Fox, 2000.

identities, 229; and gender performativity, 28, 164, 177; New Gender
Politics, 28–29, 181, 259; power and
pleasure, 87; and psychoanalysis, 225–226; and race, 87–88; and
science fiction, 264; and sexual
categories, 226–227; and standpoint theories, 261–262. *See also*
Butler, Judith; desire; feminist
theory/thought; Sedgwick, Eve
Kosofsky; sexuality

Rabkin, Eric, 70
race: in cyberpunk films, 155–157; in
feminist thought, 15–17; in queer
theory, 87–88; racism in science fic-
tion (*see* science fiction). See also
Alien Resurrection; Butler, Octavia;
Calder, Richard
Rajan, Rajeswari Sunder, 43, 52
Robertson, Robbie, 106, 117
RoboCop (film), 130
Ross, Andrew, 190
Rothblatt, Martine, 252
Rubin, Gayle, 224
Russ, Joanna, 2, 5, 158, 178, 220

Said, Edward, 49
Salvaggio, Ruth, 36, 43
Sandoval, Chela, 26–28, 55
Sargent, Pamela, 222
Saunders, Charles, 45
Schemanske, Mark, 121
Scholes, Robert, 70
science fiction: and colonialism/coloni-
zation, 5, 47, 49; as contribution
to feminist debates, 9, 263–264; as
cultural text, 2–5, 13; dialogic relationship with feminist thought, 4,
11, 259; and feminism, 263; literature as different from film, 11–12,
32, 104–105; and nanotechnology,
195; New Wave, 5–7; as producing
feminist theory, 10, 259; and queer
desire, 227; and queer theory, 263;
and racial discourse, 198; racialized
other in, 120; racist themes/racism
in, 43–45, 50, 80; structures and/or
narrative devices of, 1–2; technology
in, 125; themes and approaches
of, 1–2; theorizing in, 3. *See also*

cyberpunk; feminist science fiction;
science fiction film; virtual reality
science fiction film: appropriation of
feminist subjectivities in, 33; boundary transgressions/crossing in, 111;
(gendered) cyborgs in, 120, 128–131;
and gender roles, 118; and identifications, 104–107; as medium, 104–105;
representations in, 32, 104–105; and
reproduction, 110, 136, 160; technologies and gender in, 103–107, 110; and
technology, 104, 128–129, 150, 160;
woman warriors in, 119, 122, 129
science and technology: feminist critiques of. *See* feminist theory/
thought
Scobie, Stephen, 109, 132–133, 137, 139
Scott, Melissa: agency in, 243; and
correlation of sex, gender, and sexuality, 242–243; *Dreaming Metal,* 179,
252; five-sex system in, 223, 242,
245–247, 251, 256; gender identities
in, 181–182, 243, 249, 250; intersexuality in, 180, 241, 261; lesbianism in,
222; Modernists in, 254–256; odd-
bodied in, 246–249, 251, 253; and
organized resistance in, 243, 250,
252, 256; passing in, 249, 251; sexualities in, 247, 249, 250; *Shadow
Man,* 34, 177, 180, 219, 223, 242, 245,
248–256; Traditionalists in, 253–
254; transgender rights in, 223, 248;
Trouble and Her Friends, 179, 252;
two-sex system in, 247–249, 253,
256
Sedgwick, Eve Kosofsky, 87–88, 209
self/other: dualism/binary of, 14–15,
67, 77, 110; and racial/sexual difference, 15. *See also* sexual difference;
subjectivity
sex, gender, and sexuality: correlation of, 17, 30, 178, 180, 219, 221,
223–224, 227, 234, 241, 256; in feminist thought, 220, 259; and queer
theory, 220; in science fiction, 28,
220–223, 257. *See also* feminist
theory/thought; queer theory
sex/gender system: binary/dimorphous,
178, 242, 244; feminist critiques of,
242–245; five-sex system, 223, 245;
naturalized, 178, 242, 256; in science